Thomas Halyburton

Natural Religion Insufficient and Revealed Necessary, to Man's Happiness in his Present State

Or a Rational Enquiry into the Principles of the Modern Deists

Thomas Halyburton

Natural Religion Insufficient and Revealed Necessary, to Man's Happiness in his Present State
Or a Rational Enquiry into the Principles of the Modern Deists

ISBN/EAN: 9783337192259

Printed in Europe, USA, Canada, Australia, Japan

Cover: Foto ©Lupo / pixelio.de

More available books at **www.hansebooks.com**

Natural Religion infufficient, and Revealed neceffary, to Man's Happinefs in his Prefent State:

OR, A

RATIONAL ENQUIRY

INTO THE

PRINCIPLES

OF THE

MODERN DEISTS;

WHEREIN

IS LARGELY DISCOVERED THEIR UTTER INSUFFICIENCY TO ANSWER THE GREAT ENDS OF RELIGION, AND THE WEAKNESS OF THEIR PLEADINGS FOR THE SUFFICIENCY OF NATURE'S LIGHT TO ETERNAL HAPPINESS:

AND PARTICULARLY

The Writings of the late learned Lord HERBERT, the great Patron of Deifm, to wit, his Books *de Veritate, de Religione Gentilium,* and *Religio Laici,* in fo far as they affert Nature's Light able to conduct us to future Bleffednefs, are confidered, and fully anfwered.

TO WHICH IS ADDED, AN

ESSAY ON THE TRUE GROUND OF FAITH.

BY THE LATE REVEREND
MR. THOMAS HALYBURTON,
Profeffor of Divinity in the Univerfity of *St. Andrews.*

A fcorner feeketh wifdom and findeth it not: but knowledge is eafy unto him that underftandeth. PROV. xiv. 6.
If any man will do his will, he fhall know of the doctrine, whether it be of God, or whether I fpeak of myfelf. JOHN vii. 17.

Solis noffe Deos & cxli numina vobis,
Aut folis nefcire, datum. Lucan. de Druid.

PHILADELPHIA:
PRINTED BY *HOGAN & M'ELROY,* N°. 1, NORTH THIRD-STREET, And fold by A. CUNNINGHAM, Wafhington, *(Penn.)* A. M'DONALD, Northumberland; C. DAVIS, New-York; and by J. M'CULLOCH, and the Publifhers, Philadelphia.

1798.

PREFACE.

THE God of glory hath not left himself without a witness; all his works do, after their manner declare his glory. *Aſk now the beaſts, and they ſhall teach thee; and the fowls of the air, and they ſhall tell thee: or ſpeak to the earth, and it ſhalll teach thee; and the fiſhes of the ſea ſhall declare unto thee. Who knoweth not in all theſe, that the hand of the Lord hath wrought this?* Job xii. 7, 8, 9. Moreover it hath pleaſed him to inſtamp upon the conſciences of men, ſuch deep impreſſions of his being and glory, that all the powers and ſubtilty of hell, ſhall never be able to eradicate them: Though, alas! through a cuſtom of ſin, and eſpecially againſt much light and conviction, the conſciences of many are debauched in theſe dregs of time, to an obliterating of theſe impreſſions, which otherwiſe would have been ſtrong and vivid. The principles of moral equity carry ſuch an evidence in their nature, and are alſo accompanied with ſo much of binding force upon the conſcience, that their obligation on rational creatures hath a moſt reſplendent clearneſs, and fills the little world with ſuch a ſtrength, and efficacy of truth, as far ſurpaſſeth the plaineſt theoretical principles.

ciples. That one maxim, Matth. vii. 12. Luke vi. 3. *Therefore all things whatsoever ye would that men should do to you, do ye even so to them;* that one maxim, I say, (to pass others) was matter of so much wonder to some of the most polite heathens, that they knew not well how to express their sense of the truth and glory of it; they thought it worthy to be engraven with letters of gold, upon the frontispieces of their most magnificent structures; an agreeable and speaking evidence of its having been imprinted in some measure upon their hearts. Nevertheless, all these, though sweet, strong, and convincing notices of a Deity, do yet evanish as faint glimmerings, when compared to that stamp of divine authority, which our great and alone Lawgiver has deeply imprinted upon the scriptures of truth, Psal. xix. 7. *The law of the Lord is perfect, converting the soul: the testimony of the Lord is sure, making wise the simple,* &c. I enter not upon this large theme, which great men have treated to excellent purpose; I only represent very shortly, that the stupendous account we have in these scripture, of moral equity in its full compass, comprised even in ten words, that wonderful account, I say, proclaimeth its Author with so much of convincing evidence, and such strains of glory, as I cannot possibly clothe with words. The greatest men among the heathen nations, have given the highest accounts of their accomplishments by framing laws; but besides the passing weakness of their performances, when viewed in a true light, the choicest of them all have a great deal of iniquity inlaid with them: but all here shineth with the glory of a Deity. Every duty is plainly contained within these small boundaries, and all concerns thereof in heart and way, are set down so punctually, and so fully cleared in the exposition which the Lawgiver himself has given of his own laws, that nothing is wanting. Here also are all

the

the myſteries of iniquity in the heart fo clearly and fully detected, theſe evils alſo purſued to their moſt latent fources, and to the grand ſpring of them all, viz. the corruption of our nature, and in ſo very few words, with ſo much of ſhining evidence and power, that no judicious and ſober perſon can deny that the finger of God is there, unleſs he offer the moſt daring violence to his own confcience. And what ſhall I ſay of the glorious contrivance of ſalvation, through the LORD JESUS our only Redeemer? Should I touch at the ground-work thereof in the eternal counſel of the adorable Trinity, and the feveral diſplays of it, until at length the complete purchaſe was made in the fulneſs of time; and if I ſhould but glance at the feveral ſtrokes of omnipotent power, and rich mercy through Chriſt, by which the purchaſed ſalvation is effectually applied to every elect perſon, I would enter upon a field from which I could not quickly or eaſily get off. All that I adventure to ſay is, that the difcoveries of a Deity in each ſtep thereof, are ſo relucent and full of glory, that the being of the material light under a meridian ſun, without the interpoſition of a cloud, may as well be denied, as theſe great truths can be difowned. Beyond all manner of doubt, they contain matter of much higher, and more glorious evidence, upon the minds of all thoſe whoſe eyes the god of this world hath not blinded, (2 Cor. iv. 3, 4. John i. 5. Deut. xxix. 4.) Yet ah! mid-day clearneſs is midnight darkneſs to thoſe who have not eyes. But not to inſiſt: If we add to all theſe, the full hiſtory of the heart of man, in the depths of wickedneſs contained in that great abyſs, together with the feveral eruptions thereof, both open and violent, as alſo ſubtile and covered, together with all the engines of temptations for ſetting it to work, and keeping it ſtill bufy; if, I ſay, the perfect account of theſe things which is given in the word,

be

be seriously pondered, who can escape the conviction, that He, and He only who formed the Spirit within him, could have given such a display. From all this, I would bewail, were it possible, with tears of blood, the blasphemous wickedness of those, who, from the grossest darkness and ignorance, oppose, malign, and deride such great and high things. But it is enough; *wisdom is justified of all her children*, Matth. xi. 19. The worthy and now glorified author of this work, had a plentiful measure, beyond many, of the surest and sweetest knowledge of these matters: his soul, (may I so express it) was cast into the blessed mould of gospel truth. Who is a teacher like unto GOD! Sure an enlightening work, by his word and Spirit upon the soul, filleth it with evidence of a more excellent nature, and attended with a penetrancy quite of another kind, than any mathematical demonstration can amount to. In this case, the soul (2 Cor. iii 3.) is an epistle of Jesus Christ, wherein these great truths are written by himself, in characters which the united force and subtilties of hell shall be so far from deleting, that their strongest efforts shall render the impressions still deeper, and more vivid. No mathematical demonstration can vie with this: forasmuch as the authority of the God of truth, that conveys his own testimony into the heart with a strong hand, has a glory and evidence peculiar to itself. And though well known to those who enjoy it, yet of a beauty great and mysterious, such as the tongues of men and angels could not suffice to describe. The empty cavils of that execrable herd of blasphemous Atheists, or Deists, as they would be called, amount to a very small and contemptible account, seeing the most subtile of them, fall very far short of the objections which unclean spirits propose, and urge in a way of temptation, against persons exercised to godliness, which yet the Father of lights dispelleth
mercifully

PREFACE.

mercifully from time to time, and maketh thefe dark fhades to evanifh, as the Sun of righteoufnefs arifeth upon the foul with a glory and evidence ftill upon the afcendant, Mal. iv. 2. Prov. iv. 18. Hof. vi. 3. Neverthele:s, the learned and godly author hath encountered thefe filly creatures at their own weapons, both offenfively and defenfively, and to fuch excellent purpofe, as needeth not my poor teftimony. He hath fearched into the very bottom of what they allege. With great and unwearied diligence did he read their writings carefully from the very firft fprings, and hath reprefented fairly their empty cavils, in all the fhadows of ftrength they can be alleged to have, and has refuted them plainly and copioufly. On which, and the like accounts, I hope the work will be, through the divine blefling, of great ufe in the churches of Chrift.

JAMES HOG.

TO THE PUBLIC.

THOUGH the editors will not presume to offer any recommendation of the ensuing work; yet they conceive themselves justifiable, in presenting to the public the sentiments of some eminent characters respecting it. This they do chiefly with a view to obviate an objection that possibly may arise in the minds of some, viz. That it is not adapted to the present state of the controversy with the Deists. To this we would observe, that a careful perusal of the book will at once prove, to any person acquainted with the controversy, that the arguments latterly produced against divine revelation, are in substance precisely the same with those formerly advanced by Herbert and his adherents, with whom our author chiefly contends. And that he has fully succeeded in this contest, was the judgment of the celebrated Dr. WATTS. He here " proves," says the Dr. " by un- " answerable arguments, the utter insufficiency of the Deists' " religion for the salvation of men, and beats them fairly at their " weapons*." Dr. JOHN NEWTON, in one of his letters to the rev. Mr. S——, to whom he had sent Mr. HALYBURTON's book for perusal, thus expresses his sentiments respecting it : " I " set a high value upon this book of Mr. HALYBURTON's; so " that unless I could replace it with another, I know not if I " would part with it for its weight in gold. The first and long- " est treatise, (meaning that against the Deists) is in my judg- " ment a master-piece†." Dr. JAMEISON of Edinburgh, who no doubt will be allowed to be well acquainted with the *present state* of the controversy, in a late publication, having occasion to mention Mr. HALYBURTON's treatise, says, It is " a book not sur- " passed, if equalled, by any of the numerous *anti-deistical* writ- " ings that have appeared since the time of its publication ; and " which has this special excellency, that it carries the war into " camp of the adversary‡."——Eulogiums could be multiplied, and the testimonies of eminent clergymen in this country produced, were it deemed necessary. We are authorised in saying, that it has the decided approbation of Dr. NISBET, President of *Dickinson College;* to whom we are indebted for the translation of the Latin quotations, and a number of literal corrections, which much increases the value of the present edition.

Philadelphia, Feb. 1798.

* See his Recommendation prefixed to Mr. Halyburton's Memoirs, page 7, of Philadelphia edition.
† Newton's Letters, vol. 1. pag. 148, Philadelphia edition.
‡ Alarm to Britain, pag. 25.

SUBSCRIBERS' NAMES.

REV. James Abercrombie, minister of the Protestant Episcopal church, Philadelphia.
Rev. John Anderson, minister of the Associate congregations at Mill-creek and Harman's-cr. near Pittsburgh
Dr. Henry Arnot, York county
Dr. James Armstrong, Carlisle,
Thomas Allison, stud. of divinity
Col. Allison, Philadelphia
Mr. Robert Armstrong, Juniata
Abraham Anderson, Carlisle
James Anderson, do
William Alexander, do
William Aitkin, York cou.
Alexander Allison, do
Ja. Agnew, Marsh creek, do
Jno. Agnew, do do
Thos. Adams, Wash. county
Samuel Agnew, do
John Ashton, Camb. *(N.Y.)*
James Ashton, do
John Armitage, do
Archibald Armstrong

B
Rev. Thomas Beveridge, Cambridge, *(N.Y.)*
Mr. George Barber, do
Mrs. Hannah Barton, *(N. J.)*
Lewis Berry, do
Robert Boyd, do
James Buchanan, Washington county

Mr. Evert Bush, New-York
John Pennie, do
Alexander Bradley, Carlisle
James Blaine, do
Charles Bovard, do
William Bresden, student, do
John Brown, West Pennsborough township
Randel Blair, do
David Blaine, Big-spring, 2 copies
James Brown, do
John Brown, do
Andrew Branwood, Marsh-creek, York county

C
Rev. James Clarkson, York co.
Rev. William Clarkson, near Bridgetown, *(N.J.)* 12 copies
Mr. Abraham Craig, A. B. Big-spring
John Creigh, Carlisle
Thomas Craighead, do
James Chriswell, Lewis township, Mifflin county
James Conchy, Philadel.
James Creag do
Michael Cozrod, do
Alexander Castel, Wash. co.
Randel Cowden, do
Samuel Caldwell, do
Andrew Christie, N. York
Alexander Cunningham, merchant, Wash. *(Pen.)*
C

SUBSCRIBERS' NAMES.

Mr. John Cunningham, Delaware county
William Collins, York co.
Samuel Collins   do
John Collins,   do

D
Rev. John Dunlap, Camb. *(N.Y.)*
Jonathan Dorr, physician, do
Rev. Robert Davidson, D. D. minister of the Presbyterian church, Carlisle
James Duncan, preacher of the gospel
Mr. Thomas Dick, New-York
Hugh Dodd, Philadelphia
Ja. Duncan, Carlisle
Thomas Duncan, attorney at law, do
Robert Dawson, Wash. co.
John Donaldson, Northum.

E
Rev. John Ewing, D. D. pastor of the first Presbyterian church, Philadelphia
Mr. Benjamin Egbert, N. York
James Edmiston, Lewistown, Mifflin county
Peter Eisenbray, Philad.

F
Mr. Alexander Fridge, Philad.
James Furze,   do
John Frirth, Salem, *(N.J.)*
John Forsythe, Carlisle
Samuel Fullerton, York county

G
Rev. Ashbel Green, D. D. pastor of the second Presbyterian church, Philadelphia
Rev. David Goodwille, Barnet, *(Vermont)*
Mr. Samuel Gustine, Carlisle
Francis Gibson,   do

Mr. George Gosman, N. York 12 copies
Jacob Grove, York county
Thomas Grove, do
Alexander Gowens, do
Gaion Grier, Wash. county

H
Rev. Matthew Henderson, Allegany county
David Hays, stud. at law, Carlisle
Thomas Hamilton, student of divinity, Washing. co.
Mr. Jno. Hughes, Carlisle
Robert Huston, do
Peter Hattrick, New-York
Cornelius C. Hoffman, do
David Hall, Philadelphia
James Hogan, do
Samuel Harper, York co.
Hugh Henderson, do
Joseph Hamilton, do
Ebenezer Henderson, do
Alex. Henderson, Wash. co.
Ezekial Hill, Monrgom. co.
John Hays,   do
Amasa Hinchley, Cambridge *(N.Y.)*
James Hoy,   do

I
Mr. James Irwin, Cumb. county
William Innes, Philadel.
John Johnston, do.

K
William Kersey, Chief Judge of Steuben county, *(N.Y.)*
Mr. Andrew Kevan, New-York
David Kempton, Carlisle
John Kemen, Washing. co.

L
Rev. John Linn, Shearman's Valley
Mr. Wm. Liggat, sen. York co.

SUBSCRIBERS' NAMES.

Mr. Francis Linch, New-York
Samuel Longcope, Philad.
Archibald Loudon, Carlifle
William Lyon, do
James Lamberton, do
Samuel Laird, do
Philip K. Laurence, do
John Lecky, Northum. co.

M
Rev. Samuel Magaw, D. D. rector of St. Paul's church, Philadelphia
Rev. William Marfhall, A. M. minifter of the Affociate church Philadelphia
Rev. John Mafon, New-York 12 copies
James M'Cormick, profeffor of mathematicks in Dickinfon College
John Montgomery, Efq. Carlifle
Samuel Murdoch, ftud. of divinity, Wafhing. county
John M'Pherfon, Efq. Northum.
Dr. Sam. A. M'Cofky, Carlifle
James Magill, A. B. near Mifflin town
Mr. Samuel Millar, (N. Y.) 10 copies
John M'Clellan, do
Alexander M'Donald, Northumberland, 2 copies
William Macky, do
Robert M'Neal, do
John M'Allifter, Philadel.
John M'Ara, do
Andrew M'Ara, do
Andrew M'Calla, do
Robert Millikin, do
William W. Moore, do
John M'Clenechan, do
Walter Mickeljohn, do
James M'Glathery, do
Peter M'Eachan, N. York
Daniel M'Lauren, do

Mr. Andrew Mitchell, Carlifle
William M'Cluer, do
Andrew Munro, do
William Moore, do
Alex. M'Kechan, jun. do
William M'Craken, do
Hugh M'Cormick, near do
Hugh Morrifon, York co.
Andrew Martin, do
Robert M'Clellan, do
David M'Clellan, do
Frederick M'Pherfon, do
John Main, Shippenfburgh
James M'Nary, Wafh. co.
Samuel M'Bride, do
Samuel M'Gowen, do
John M'Call, do
Henry Maxwell, do
James Morrifon, do
Charles Moore, do
James M'Keman, do
James Marfhall, do
Samuel Marfhall, do

N
Rev. Charles Nifbet, D. D. Prefident of Dickinfon, Carlifle
Mr. John Noble, do

O
Mr. Jacob Orwitt, Cambridge, (N. Y.)
Robert Oliver, do
William Ouells, do

P
Rev. Samuel Porter, minifter at Congruity and Poke run, Weftmoreland, near Pitfburgh
Robert Patterfon, profeffor of mathematicks in the Univerfity of Pennfylvania
Mrs. Mary Patton, Carlifle, 2 copies
Mr. George Pattifon, Carlifle
Charles Pattifon, do
James Paxton, near do

SUBSCRIBERS' NAMES.

Mr. James Peden, York county
Archibald Purdie, do
James Philips, Philadelphia
Charles Pettit   do
Hugh Patton, Washing. co.

R
Rev. William Rogers, D. D. professor of English and Oratory, in the University of Pennsyl.
Mrs. Mary Rea, Philadelphia
Frances Reid, Carlisle
Mr. Archibald Ramsey, do
James Robertson, N. York
Thomas Robertson, do
Simon Ross, Hopewell township, Cumb. county
Isaac Ralston, Philadelphia
Samuel Roseburgh, York co.
David Reed,   do
James Ralston, Wash. co.
Andrew Russel,   do
James Russel,   do
John Reznor, Northumb.

S
Rev. Thomas Smith
John Steele, A. B. Carlisle
Snowden & M'Corkle, printers, Philadelphia
Mr. John Scotland, New-York
    2 copies
James Small, Camb. *(N.Y.)*
Alexander Skelly, do
William Story
Henry Scheetz, Montg. co.
Justus Scheetz,   do
Woolry Slaughter, do
Jeremiah Simpson, Wash. co.
John Struthers, sen. do.
John Struthers, jun. do
Robert Simpson,   do
William Smiley, Philadel.
John Smith, Big-spring near Carlisle

Mr. James Stirling, store-keeper Burlington
Elisha Steele, Carlisle

T
William Thompson, teacher of languages in Dickinson College, Carlisle
Samuel Tate, teacher of Eng. do.
Mr. Archibald Tompson, Franklin county
Andrew Thomson, do
John Thompson,   do
Joseph Thompson, York co.
Samuel Tagart, Wash. co.
John Tagart,   do
James Thompson, Philad.

U
Rev. Thomas Ustick, minister of the Baptist church, Philadel.

W
Rev. Samuel Waugh, Silver-Spring
William Wilson, preacher of the gospel
David Watts, attorney at law, Carlisle
Jonathan Walker, Esq. Northum.
Mr. William Wilson,   do
David Walker, Cumb. co.
John Wright, Carlisle
John Walker,   do
Andrew Wright, New-York
Charles Whyte, Philadel.
William Wear,   do
David Wallace, York coun.
Alexander Wallace, do
John Wilson, jun. do
John White, Washing. co.
Andrew White, Cambridge *(N. Y.)*

Y
Mr. Joseph Young, Carlisle
Stephen Young, Philadel.

☞ The following names came too late for insertion in their proper place.

From Camb. and Argyle, (N. Y.)
Dr. Andrew Proudfit
William Reid, Esq.
Mr. John Reid
  James Beatie
  John Gilchrist
  Peter M'Euchron
  John Hersha
  John Millar
  Finley M'Naughton
  John White
  Archibald M'Neal
  John M'Neal
  William Robertson
  Roger Campbell
  Duncan M'Arthur
  Casperus Baine
  Daniel Mothieson
  Thomas Walson

From Northumberland, (Penn.)
William P. Brady, Esq.
Mr. John Cowden
  John Wilson
  Daniel Rees
  Peter Jones
  Mordecai M'Kay
  William Reynolds
  James Shaddon
  Jared Irwin
  William Murray
  James Armstrong
  Isaac Hannah
  John Jones
  Andrew Kennedy
  David Steel

* The binder is directed to place these immediately after the last page of the Subscribers' Names.

TO THE READER.

READER,

WHOEVER thou art, the queſtion agitated in the enſuing diſcourſe is that wherein thou haſt a conſiderable concernment. If thou art a Chriſtian, the enſuing diſcourſe is deſigned to juſtify thy refuſal of that religion which has now got a great vogue amongſt thoſe gentlemen, who ſet up for the only wits, and aim at monopolizing reaſon, as if they alone were the *people*, and *wiſdom was to die with them.* They cry up their religion as the only reaſonable religion, and traduce all who will not join with them, as credulous and unreaſonable men. Whereas, on the contrary, no man that uſes his reaſon, can cloſe with that which they would obtrude on us as rational religion: nor can any man, without being guilty of the fondeſt credulity, venture his ſalvation upon this modern Paganiſm, that ſtruts abroad under the modiſh name of *Deiſm*, which I hope the enſuing diſcourſe will evince; wherein it is made appear, that the *light of nature is utterly inſuf-ficient to anſwer the great ends of religion*, and that conſequently we had the juſteſt reaſon in the world, if there were none, to wiſh for a revelation from God, as what is of abſolute neceſſity to our happineſs; and ſince

there

there is one, with the greatest thankfulness to embrace it, cleave to it, and comply with it.

Reader, if thou hast thy religion yet to choose, which I am afraid is too common a case in this unstable age, then it is high time thou wert bethinking thyself of religion in earnest.

>To-morrow thou wilt live, thou still dost say;
>To-day's too late, the wise liv'd yesterday.

And if after too long a delay thou mean to avoid an unhappy choice, reason advises thee to consider well, that when the choice is made, care be taken to make it so, as to prevent the necessity either of a second choice, or a too late repentance for choosing amiss. There is a set of men, who cry up at this day natural religion, and especially commend it to such as have no religion. It is such as thou art that they desire to deal with, and among such it is that they are most successful. But if thou hast a mind not to be deceived in a matter of such moment, it imports thee not a little to consider what may be said against that, which it is likely may be offered thee, as a fine, modish, reasonable religion, meet for a *gentleman*, a man of *wit* and *reason*. I have here offered to prove this all to be said without, yea against *reason* and *experience*. Well, first hear and then judge, and after that choose or refuse as thou seest cause.

As for the management of this useful inquiry, it is wholly suited to that which at first was only designed, viz. the satisfaction of the writer's own mind about the question that is here proposed. I entered not upon this inquiry with a view to oppose any man, or triumph over adversaries, and so did industriously wave those catches, subtilties, and other nicities, used frequently by writers of controversy. My only design was to find the truth, and therefore I chose clearly to state

state the question, which I found the Deists always avoided, and plainly propose my reasons for that side of it I took, after trial, to be the truth. As to the opposite opinion, I made it my business to make a diligent inquiry into the strongest arguments advanced for it, candidly to propose them in their utmost force, and closely to answer them; avoiding, as much as might be, such reproaches as are unworthy of a Christian, or an inquirer after truth, though I met with frequent provocation, and found sometimes how true that is, *Difficile est non scribere satyram contra satyrum* *.

It was not amusement I aimed at, or to please my own fancy, or tickle the reader's ears with a gingle of words, or divert and bias the judgment by a flood of rhetorick. I never designed to set up for an orator. My business lies quite another way, it is what I lay no claim to, and what I think is to be avoided in discourses of this kind. All I aimed at as to language, was to clothe my thoughts in plain and intelligible expressions. The reader is to expect no more, and if he miss this I hope it will be but rarely.

It is not to be expected, that a discourse which was begun in an inverted order, the middle part being first writ; and that was composed in the intervals of business of a very different nature, at spare hours, by one of no great experience, and an utter stranger to writings of this sort, shall be free of blemishes that may offend nicer palates. Some few repetitions could not, at least without more pains in transcribing than I had either leisure or inclination for, well be avoided. Nor could a discourse so often interrupted by other business, and upon so very different subjects, be carried on with that equality of stile that were to be wished, especially by one who was never over much an affecter of elegan-

cy

---

* " It is difficult not to write a satyr against satyr."

cy of language. In a word, the work is long, much longer than I defigned; and yet without wronging the fubject, at leaft as I am otherwife fituated and engaged, I could not eafily fhorten it. If he pleafes to infpect the book, he may poffibly find, that I had reafon for infifting at the length I have done. However, every one has not his art, who could enclofe Homer's Iliads in a nut's fhell.

I am fenfible, that what I have difcourfed in the firft chapter of the enfuing treatife, concerning the *Occafions of Deifm*, will grate hard upon a fet of men, who have for many years bygone carried all before them, and fo took it ill to have any cenfures beftowed on them, though they did feverely animadvert upon the real or fuppofed faults of others. As to this I have not much to fay by way of apology. That Deifm has fprung up and grows apace amongft us, is on all hands confeffed. Others have offered their conjectures concerning the occafions of its increafe. Why I might not offer my opinion alfo, I know no reafon. The principal fubject of the enfuing treatife fuffers not, though I fhould herein be miftaken. In propofing my conjecture I did not purfue the intereft of any party; but have freely blamed all parties. If the fticklers for the Arminian or Socinian divinity are touched, it was becaufe I thought they were to be blamed, and therefore I have withftood them to their face. As to the tendency of their principles I have been fparing, becaufe that debate has been fufficiently agitated in the Low Countries betwixt the contending parties. The reader who would be fatisfied as to this, may perufe thofe who have directly managed this charge, and the anfwers that have been made, and judge upon the whole matter as he finds caufe[*]. But whatever

---

[*] See Arcana Arminianifmi, by Videlius, and Videlius Ropfodus, with Videlius's Rejoinders, &c.

whatever may be as to this, the manner of their management may perhaps be found lefs capable of a colourable defence. And it is upon this that I have principally infifted. To oppofe, efpecially from the pulpit, with contempt, buffoonry, banter and fatyr, principles, that fober perfons of the fame perfuafion do own to have at leaft a very plaufible like foundation in the word of God, and which have been, for near fixty or feventy years after the reformation, the conftant doctrine of the fathers, and fons of the church of England, and have by them been inferted into her articles, and fo become a part of her doctrine*, is a practice that I do not well underftand how to excufe, or free from the imputation of profanity, and which hath too manifeft a tendency to Atheifm, to admit of any tolerable defence. The fcriptures, and truths, that have any countenance in them, or opinions which they feem really to perfons otherwife fober, pious and judicious, not only to teach, but to inculcate as of the higheft importance, are not a meet fubject for raillery; nor is the pulpit a meet place for it. This is that for which principally I have blamed them, and this I cannot retract. If they take this ill, I afk them, Have not others as much reafon to take it ill, that the doctrines of the church of England taught in her articles and homilies, and profeffed by her learned bifhops, who compofed them, and by her fons for fo long a tract of time, as confonant to, found in, and grounded on the word of God, fhould be fo petulantly traduced by wit, raillery, and declamatory invectives from prefs and pulpit; and that too by thofe who have fubfcribed to thefe articles and homilies? This management has been complained of by fober perfons of all parties, churchmen and diffenters, contra-remonftrants and remonftrants too, as I could make appear, if there were occafion for it: And why

* See Bifhop of Sarum on the Articles, Preface, pag. 7, 8.

TO THE READER.

why I might not alſo complain, I want yet to be informed. None is charged ſave the guilty. Others who are free have no reaſon to be angry. And, perhaps, they who will be offended at this, would ſcarce have been pleaſed if I had let it alone.

In the tenth chapter of this treatiſe, I have oppoſed the opinion that aſſerts the Heathen world to be under a government of grace. I know it is maintained by many learned men both at home and abroad, from whoſe memory, if dead, or juſt reſpect, if alive, I deſigned not to detract. Nor did I deſign to liſt them with the Deiſts, whom I know to have been ſolidly oppoſed by ſeverals that were of this opinion. But yet I do think the opinion itſelf deſtitute of any ſolid foundation, with all deference to them, who think otherwiſe, either in ſcripture, reaſon or experience. And I am further of the mind, that the learned abettors of it, had never embraced an aſſertion, that expoſes them to ſo many perplexing difficulties, and puts them upon a neceſſity of uſing ſo many, I had almoſt ſaid, unintelligible diſtinctions for its ſupport, if they had not been driven to it by ſome peculiar hypotheſis in divinity which they have ſeen meet to embrace. If any intend to prove what I have denied, I wiſh it may be done by proper arguments, directly proving it, and not by advancing an hypotheſis that remotely infers it, and which, in itſelf, or, at leaſt as propoſed by thoſe whom I have met with, is ſo darkened by a huge multitude of ſubtile, myſterious and uncouth diſtinctions, that I can ſcarce ever project ſo much time as to underſtand them. However this much I muſt ſay, that ſo croſs does this opinion ſeem to ſcripture, reaſon and experience, that it will go a very great way to weaken the credit of any hypotheſis on which it inevitably follows. However, I hope this may be ſaid, and different opinions about this point without any breach of charity may be retained. *Diverſum ſentire*

TO THE READER.

tire duos de rebus iifdem incolumi licuit femper amicitia*. I know the abettors of this opinion are hearty friends in the main to the caufe I here maintain.

The fcheme I have in the clofe of that chapter offered by way of digreffion, of God's government of the Heathen world, is not defigned as a full account of that matter, which as to many of its concernments, is of thofe things that are not revealed, and fo belong not to us; much lefs is it defigned to be the ground of a peremptory judgment as to the eternal ftate of them, who are without the church: But only to fhew, that any thing we certainly know as to God's dealings with them, in the common courfe of his providence, may, upon other fuppofitions and principles, befide that rejected, be accounted for. The judicious and fober reader may judge of it as he fees caufe. I hope I have, in a matter of fuch difficulty, avoided any unbecoming curiofity, or affecting to be wife above what is written.

If any blame me for the multitude of quotations, I anfwer, the fubject I undertook rendered this unavoidable. I have ufed the utmoft candor in them. Sometimes out of a regard to brevity I have avoided the tranflation of teftimonies quoted from authors who writ in a different language. The learned will not complain of this: And if any perfon of tolerable judgment, who is not learned, will be at pains to perufe the enfuing difcourfe, he will find as much faid, without regarding thofe quotations, as may fatisfy his mind upon this fubject.

As to what I have, in the enfuing papers afcribed, to Mr. Gildon publifher of the Oracles of Reafon, I had written it before I underftood his recovery from Deifm. But yet I thought it not meet to alter it, becaufe there are

† " It was always allowed, that two perfons might think differently " of the fame things, without breach of friendfhip."

are, no doubt, many others who entertain the same notions he then did maintain, and my opposition is to the principles and not the persons. As for his recovery, I congratulate it, and wish it may be such as may secure him from after-reckoning for the hurt he has done.

If any Deists shall see meet to undertake this debate, I decline it not. If they treat my book as they have done those of others, every way my superiors, and as rats are wont to do,—gnaw only the outside, divert to incident things that are not to the purpose, and single out rather what seems exceptionable than what is of moment, following him who did so,

————————— & quæ
Desperat tractata nitescere posse relinquit*,

I have somewhat else to do, than to take any notice of such impertinency. If any shall offer a solid and rational confutation, which yet I am not much afraid of, and convince me, not by jest, buffoonry and raillery, but by solid arguments, of my being in a mistake,

Cuncta recantabo maledicta, priora rependam
Laudibus, & vestrum nomen in astra feram †.

---

* " And leaves out whatever he despairs of being able to shine in
" if they were touched on."

† " I will recant all my reproaches, I will make amends for my for-
" mer slanders by praises, and will exalt your name to the stars."

INDEX.

INDEX.

INTRODUCTION, - - Page 41
[*Wherein it is proved a matter of the highest import and necessity to make a right choice of religion; and wherein it is further evinced, that no man without the most manifest violence to reason, can turn Heathen, Mahometan, or acquiesce in Atheism or Septicism, and that consequently every man must acquiesce in the Scriptures, or turn Deist. This latter undertaken to be demonstrated false and ruining.—The author's inducements to this undertaking.*]

CHAP. I.
Giving a short account of the rise, occasions, and progress of Deism, especially in England; the opinions of the Deists; the different sorts of Deists, mortal and immortal, 61

CHAP. II.
Mortal Deists who, and what judgment to be made of them and their sentiments, - - 76

CHAP. III.
Wherein the controversy betwixt us and the Immortal Deists is stated and cleared, - - 80

CHAP. IV.
Wherein the insufficiency of natural religion is proved from the insufficiency of its discoveries of a Deity, - 88

CHAP. V.
Proving the insufficiency of natural religion from its defectiveness as to the worship of God, - - 106

CHAP. VI.

Proving the insufficiency of natural religion from its defectiveness as to the discovery wherein man's happiness lies, 112

CHAP. VII.

Nature's light affords not a sufficient rule of duty. Its insufficiency hence inferred, - - 127

CHAP. VIII.

Proving the insufficiency of natural religion from its defects as to sufficient motives for enforcing obedience, 138

CHAP. IX.

Shewing the importance of knowing the origin of sin to the world, and the defectiveness of nature's light as to this, 147

CHAP. X.

Proving nature's light unable to discover the means of obtaining pardon of sin, or to shew that it is attainable, 161

   SECT. I. *The importance of this difficulty stated,* 162

   SECT. II. *Shewing the darkness of nature's light as to pardon,* - - 171

   SECT. III. *Wherein it is inquired whether repentance is sufficient to atone for sin? How far nature's light enables to it? What assurance nature's light gives of pardon upon repentance?* 178

   OBJECTIONS *considered,* - - 209

   DIGRESSION *concerning God's government of the Heathen world, shewing that there is nothing in it whence any design of God to pardon them may be certainly inferred,* 238

CHAP. XI.

Proving the insufficiency of natural religion to eradicate our inclinations to sin, or subdue its power, 248

CHAP. XII.

Wherein the proof of the insufficiency of natural religion is concluded from a general view of the experience of the world, 260

CHAP. XIII.

Wherein we make a tranſition to the Deiſts' pleas for their opinion, and take particular notice of the Articles to which they reduce their catholick religion; give ſome account of Baron Herbert, the firſt inventer of this catholick religion, his Books, and particularly of that which is inſcribed De Religione Gentilium, *as to the matter and ſcope of it, and the importance of what is therein attempted to the Deiſts' cauſe,* 266

CHAP. XIV.

Wherein it is inquired, Whether Herbert has proved that his Five Articles did univerſally obtain, - 278

CHAP. XV.

Wherein it is made appear that Herbert's Five Articles did not univerſally obtain, - - 306

CHAP. XVI.

Wherein ſome general conſiderations are laid down for proving that many of the beſt things, which are to be met with in the Heathens, were not the diſcoveries of nature's light, but came from tradition, - - 327

CHAP. XVII.

Wherein we conſider what Herbert's opinion was as to the ſufficiency of his Articles, and offer ſome reflections, ſhewing how fooliſh, abſurd and ridiculous the Deiſts' pretences to their ſufficiency are, - - 333

CHAP. XVIII.

Containing an anſwer to ſome of the Deiſts' principal arguments for the ſufficiency of natural religion, - 345

CHAP. XIX.

Wherein Herbert's reaſons for publiſhing his books in defence of Deiſm are examined and found weak, 361

CHAP. XX.

Wherein the Queries offered by Herbert and Blount, for proving the ſufficiency of their Five Articles are examined, 370

ESSAY ON FAITH.

CHAP. I.

Containing some general remarks concerning knowledge, faith, and particularly divine faith, and that both as to the faculty and actings thereof, - - 401

CHAP. II.

Wherein the nature of that faith, which in duty we are obliged to give to the word of God, our obligation to, and our ability for answering our duty, are inquired into, · 404

CHAP. III.

The ground, or the formal reason, whereon faith assents to the scriptures is inquired after; the Rationalist's opinion about it, and particularly as stated by Mr. Locke in his book on Human Understanding, is proposed and considered, 409

INTRODUCTION.

IN this fceptical age, which queftions almoft every thing, it is ftill owned as certain, that *all men muſt die*. If there were any place for difputing this, there are not a few, who would fpare no pains to bring themfelves into the difbelief of a truth, that gives them fo much difturbance, in the courfes they love and feem refolved to follow: But the cafe is fo clear, and the evidence of this principle fo pregnant, which is every day confirmed by new experiments, that the moft refolved infidel is forced, when it comes in his way, though unwilling, to give his affent, and moan out an *Amen*. The *grave is the houſe appointed for all the living*. Some arrive fooner, fome later; but all come there at length. The obfcurity of the meaneft cannot hide him, nor the power of the greateft fcreen him from the impartial hand of death, the executioner of fate, if I may be allowed the ufe of a word fo much abufed. As its coming is placed beyond doubt, fo its afpect is hideous beyond the reach of thought, the force of expreffion, or the utmoft efforts of the fineft pencil in the moft artful hand. It, in a moment, dafhes down a fabric, which has more of curious contrivance than all the celebrated pieces put together, which the moft refined human wits have invented, even when carried to the greateft height, which the improvements of fo many fubfequent generations, after the utmoft of application and diligence, could bring them to. It puts a ftop to many thoufand motions, which, though ftrangely diverfified, did all concur, with wonderful exactnefs, to maintain, and carry on the defign and intendment of the glorious and divine Artificer. How this divine and wonderful machine was firſt erected, ſet a going, and has, for ſo long a tract of time, regularly performed all its motions, could never yet be underſtood by the moſt elevated underſtandings. *Canſt thou tell how the bones grow in the womb of her that is with child,* is a challenge to all the ſons of art, to unfold the myſtery? Many have accepted it, but all have been foiled. Something they could ſay: but, in ſpite of it all, the thing they found a myſtery, they left ſo ſtill. How can one then look on the diſſolution of ſo admirable a contrivance, a machine ſo curious, and ſo far ſurpaſſing human art, without the deepeſt and moſt ſenſible regret. It untwiſts that myſterious tie, whereby ſoul and body were ſo faſt linked together; breaks up that intimate and cloſe correſpondence, that entire ſympathy which was founded thereon; diſlodges an old inhabitant; and while it lingers, being unwilling to remove, *death* pulls that curious fabric, wherein it dwelt, down about its ears, and ſo forces it thence, to take up its lodgings, it can ſcarce tell where. And upon its removal, that curious fabric, that a little before was full of life, activity, vigour, order, warmth, and every thing elſe that is pleaſant, is now left a dead, unactive, cold lump, or diſordered maſs of loathſome matter, full of ſtench and corruption. Now the body is a ſpectacle ſo hideous, that they who loved, and who embraced it before, cannot abide the ſight or ſmell of it; but ſhut it up in a coffin, and not content with that, away they carry it and lodge it amongſt worms, and the vileſt inſects in the bowels of the earth, to be conſumed, devoured, torn and rent by the moſt abominable vermin that lodge in the grave.

Quantum mutatus ab illo *.

We have all heard of the afflictions of Job. Two or three meſſengers arrive, each after another, and ſtill the laſt is worſt. Every one tells a ſtory. The firſt is ſad; but its ſtill more melancholy that follows. The diſaſter is ſo terrible, that it fills the world with juſt aſtoniſhment. And yet after all, what is this to *death*, which alone is able to furniſh ſubject, more than enough, for ſome thouſands of ſuch melancholy meſſages! One might bring the dying man the melancholy tidings, that he is diveſted of all his beneficial, pleaſant, and honourable employments: While he is yet ſpeaking, another might be ready to bid him denude himſelf of all his poſſeſſions: A third, to

continue

---

* "How greatly changed from what it once was."

continue the tragedy, might aſſure him that there is a commiſſion iſſued out to an impartial hand, to tear him from the embraces of his dear relations, without regarding the hideous outcries of a loving wife, the meltings of tender infants, the interceſſions of dear friends : While others continuing ſtill the mournful ſcene, might aſſure him that he was no more to reliſh the fragrancy of the ſpring, or taſte the delights of the ſons of men, or ſee the pleaſant light of the ſun, or hear the charming airs of muſic, or the yet more uſeful converſe of friends. And to make the matter ſadder ſtill, if it can well be ſo, the ſtory might be ſhut up with a rueful account of the parting of ſoul and body, with all the horrible diſaſters that follow upon this parting.

Thus the caſe evidently ſtands. Not a title of all this admits of debate. To every man it may be ſaid, *De te fabula narratur* *. What a wonder is it, that ſo grave and important a ſubject is ſo little in the thoughts of men? What apology can be made for the folly of mankind, who are at ſo much pains to ſhelter themſelves againſt leſſer inconveniences, quite overlooking this, that is of infinitely greater conſequence?

Here is the *light-ſide* of death, which every body may ſee. What a rueful and aſtoniſhing proſpect doth it give us? Where ſhall we find comfort againſt that diſmal day, whereon all this ſhall be verified in us? He is ſomething worſe than a fool or madman, that will not look to this. And he is yet more mad that thinks, that rational comfort in ſuch a caſe can be maintained upon dark, ſlender and conjectural grounds.

It is certain, that which muſt ſupport, muſt be ſomething on the *other ſide of time*. The one ſide of death affords nothing but matter of terror; if we are not enabled to look forward, and get ſuch a ſight of the other as may balance it, we may reaſonably ſay, that *it had been better for us never to have been*.

Undoubtedly, therefore, no queſtion is ſo uſeful, ſo neceſſary, ſo noble, and truly worthy the mind of man as this—What ſhall become of me after death? What have I to look for on the other ſide of that awful change?

Thoſe arts and ſciences which exerciſe the induſtry and conſideration of the greater part of the thinking world, are calculated for time, and aim at the pleaſure or advantage of a preſent life. It is *religion* alone that directly concerns itſelf in the

important

---

* "It is of you that the ſtory is told."

important queſtion laſt mentioned, and pretends to offer comforts againſt the melancholy aſpect of death, by ſecuring us in an up-making for our loſſes on the other ſide of time. Men, who are not blind to their own intereſt, had need therefore to take care of the choice of their *religion*. If they neglect it altogether, as many now do, they forfeit all proſpect of relief. If they chooſe a wrong one, that is not able to reach the end, they are no leſs unhappy. The world may call them *wits*, or what elſe they pleaſe, who either wholly neglect and laugh over all inquiries after *religion*, or who ſuperficially look into matters of this nature, and paſs a haſty judgment: But ſober reaſon will look on them as *ſomewhat below the condition of the beaſts that periſh.*

It is much to be regretted, that the bulk of mankind found their principles, as well as practice and hopes, on no better bottom than *education*, which gives but too juſt occaſion for the ſmart reflection of the witty, though profane poet—

> By education moſt have been miſled;
> So they believe, becauſe they were ſo bred.
> The prieſt continues what the nurſe began:
> And thus the child impoſes on the man*.

Moſt part ſeek no better reaſon for their belief and practice than cuſtom and education. Whatever thoſe offer in principle, they greedily ſwallow down, and venture all on ſo weak a bottom. And this ſure is one of the great reaſons why ſo many miſcarry in this important matter. It is true, in this inquiring age, many, eſpecially of the better quality, ſcorn this way. But it is to be feared that the greater part of them, flying on extremes, as is common in ſuch caſes, have fallen into another and a worſe one, if not to themſelves, yet certainly of more pernicious conſequence to the public. They ſet up for *wits* and *men of ſenſe*. They pretend to have found out great miſtakes in the principles of their education, the religion of their country; and thereon, without more ado, reject it in bulk, and turn *ſceptics* in religion. And yet after all this noiſe, moſt of them neither underſtand the religion they reject, nor know they what to ſubſtitute in its room, which is certainly an error of the worſt conſequence imaginable to the public; ſince men once arrived at this paſs, can never be depended on. Men may

* *Hind* and *Panther.*

may talk what they pleafe. A man of no religion is a man not to be bound, and therefore is abfolutely unmeet for any fhare in a fociety, which cannot fubfift, if the facred ties of religion hold it not together.

But whatever courfe fuch perfons, on the one hand or other, fteer, the more confiderate and better part of mankind, in matters of fo high importance, will, with the nicest care, try all, that they may *hold faft what is good*. If a man once underftands the importance of the cafe, he will find reafon to look fome deeper, and think more ferioufly of this matter, than either the *unthinking generality*, who receive all in bulk, without trial, as it is given them, or, the forward *would-be-wits*, that oftentimes are guilty of as great, and much more pernicious credulity in rejecting all, as the other in receiving all.

But whereas there is fo many different *religions* in the world, and all of them pretend to conduct us in this important inquiry; which of them fhall we choofe? The *deifts*, to drive us into their religion, which confifts only of five articles, agreed to, as they pretend, by all the world, would bear us in hand, that a choice is impoffible to be made of any particular religion, till we have gone through, with fuch a particular examination of every pretender, and all things that can be faid for or againft it, as no man is able to make. *Blount* tells us, as *Herbert* before had done, That " unlefs a man read all authors, " fpeak with all learned men, and know all languages, it is " impoffible to come to a clear folution of all doubts*." And fo in effect, it is pretended impoffible to be fatisfied about the truth of any particular religion. If this reafoning did hold, I fhould not doubt to make it appear, that no truth whatfoever is to be received; and in particular, that their, fo much boafted of, *catholic religion*, cannot rationally be entertained by any man. If we can be fatisfied upon rational grounds about no truth, till we have heard and confidered all, that not only has been faid, but may be alleged againft it; what truth can we believe? Here it is eafy to obferve that fome cannot do, unlefs they overdo. The intendment of fuch reafoning is obvious: Some men would caft us loofe as to all religion, that we may be brought under a neceffity to take up with any fancy they fhall be pleafed to offer us; a man that is finking will take hold of the moft tender twig. The Papifts have vigoroufly purfued this

* Blount's *Religio Laici*, page 91. Herbert's *Religio Laici*, page 12.

this courfe in oppofition to the Proteftants, to drive them into the arms of their *infallible guide.* And indeed the learned Herbert's reafonings on this point, after whom the modern deifts do but copy, feem to be borrowed from the Romanifts, and are urged upon a defign not unfavourable to the church of Rome, of which perhaps more afterwards.

But to wave this thin fophiftry; any one that will, with a fuitable application, engage in the confideration of what religion he is to choofe, will quickly find himfelf eafed of this unmanageable tafk, which the deifts would fet him. His inquiry will foon be brought to a narrow compafs, and the pretenders, that will require any nice confideration, will be found very few.

For, a very overly confideration of the *religion in the heathen world*, will give any confiderate mind ground enough to reft fully affured, that the defired fatisfaction as to *future happinefs*, and the means of attaining it, are not thence to be expected. Here he will not find what may have the leaft appearance of fatisfying. The wifeft of the heathens fcarce ever pretended to fatisfy themfelves, much lefs others, upon thefe heads. All things here are dark, vain, incoherent, inconfiftent, wild, and plainly ridiculous for moft part; as will further appear in our progrefs. Their religions were, generally fpeaking, calculated for other purpofes, and looked not fo far as eternity.

Nor will it be more difficult to get over any ftop that the religion of Mahomet may lay in our *inquirer's* way. Let a man ferioufly perufe the Alcoran, and if he has his fenfes about him, he cannot but there fee the moft pregnant evidences of the groffeft, moft fcandalous and impudent impofture, that ever was obtruded upon the world. Here he muft expect no other evidence for what he is to believe, but the bare affertion of one, who was fcandaloufly impious to that degree, that his own followers know not how to apologize for him. If you inquire for any other evidence, you are doomed by the Alcoran to everlafting ruin, and his flaves are ordered to deftroy you *. He forbids any inquiry into his religion, or the grounds of it, and therefore you muft either admit in bulk the entire bundle of fopperies, inconfiftencies, and fhocking abfurdities, that are caft together in the Alcoran, without any trial, or reject all;
And

* Alcoran, chap. 4.

INTRODUCTION.

And in this cafe, no wife man will find it hard to make a choice.

After one has proceeded thus far, he may eafily fee, that he is now inevitably caft upon one of four conclufions: Either 1ft, He muft conclude it certain that *all religion is vain*, that there is nothing to be expected after this life, and fo commence *atheift*. Or 2dly, He muft conclude, that *certainty is not attainable in thefe things*; and fo prove *fceptic*. Or 3dly, He muft pretend, that every one's *reafon unaffifted is able to conduct him in matters of religion*, afcertain him of future happinefs, and direct as to the means of attaining it; and fo fet up for *natural religion*, and turn *deift*. Or 4thly, He muft acquiefce in the *revealed religion* contained in the fcriptures, and fo turn *Chriftian*, or at leaft *Jew*.

As to the firft of thefe courfes, no man will go into it, till he has abandoned reafon. An atheift is a monfter in nature. That there is nothing to be expected after this life, and that man's foul dies with his body, is a defperate conclufion, *which ruins the foundation of all human happinefs*; even in the judgment of the deifts themfelves*. There are two material exceptions which are fufficient to deter any thinking man from clofing with it.

The one is, the *hideoufnefs of its afpect*. Annihilation is fo horrible to human nature, and has fo frightful a vifage to men who have a defire of perpetuity, inlaid in their very frame, that none can look at it ferioufly without the utmoft dread. It is true, guilty atheifts would fain take fanctuary here; yet, were they brought to think ferioufly of the cafe, they would not find that relief in it which they project. I have been credibly informed, that a gentleman of no contemptible parts, who had lived as if indeed he were to fear or hope nothing after time, being in prifon, and fearing death, (though he efcaped it and yet lives) fell a thinking ferioufly, when alone, of *annihilation:* And the fears of it had fo deep and horrible impreffion on his mind, that he profeffed to a gentleman, who made him a vifit in prifon, and found him in a grievous damp, that the thoughts of annihilation were fo dreadful to him, that he had rather think of a thoufand years in hell. Guilty finners, to eafe their confciences, and fcreen them from the difquiet'ng apprehenfions of an *after-reckoning*, retreat to this, as a refuge;

but

---

* Letter to a Deift, page 125.

but they think no more about it, save only this and that in an overly way, that it will free them from the punishment they dread and deserve. But if they would sedately view it, and take under their consideration all the horror of the case, their natures would recoil and shrink: It would create uneasiness instead of quiet, and increase the strait rather than relieve them from it.

Besides, which is the other exception against it, were there never so much comfort in it, as there is none, *yet it is impossible to prove that there is nothing after this life.* There is nothing that is tolerable can be said for it. None shall ever evince the certainty of the soul's dying with the body, till he has overthrown the *being of a God*, which can never be done so long as there is any thing certain among men. Further, as there is little or nothing to be said for it, so there is much to be said against it. Reason affords violent presumptions, at least, for a future state. And all the arguments, which conclude for the truth of Christianity, join their united force to support the certainty of a state after this life. Till these are removed out of the way, there is no access for any to enjoy the imaginary comfort of this supposition. But who will undertake solidly to overturn so many arguments, which have stood the test of ages? They who are likely to be most forward, and favour this cause most, dare scarce allow these reasonings *a fair hearing*, which plead for a future state, for fear of rivetting the impression of the truth deeper on their minds, which they desire to shake themselves loose of. And how then will they overthrow them? In fine, he is a madman, who will go into a conclusion, whereof he can never be certain, and wherein, were it sure, he can have no satisfaction. The first forbids the *judgment*, the last dissuades the *will* and *affections* from resting in it.

As to the second conclusion above-mentioned, that sets up for *scepticism* in matters of religion, and bids us live at peradventures as to what is to be feared or hoped after time; it is a course that nothing can justify save absolute necessity. It lies open to the worst of inconveniences. Nothing can be imagined more melancholy than its consequences, and the pretences to it are vain and frivolous.

If it is really thus, that man can arrive at no certainty in matters of religion, and about his state after time, how deplorable is man's condition? His case is comfortless beyond what can be well conceived. Nor can his enjoyments afford him
any

INTRODUCTION.   49

any folid fatisfaction, while ghoftly death looks him in the face, and the fword hangs over his head, fupported by a hair. Will not the profpect of this rueful change (of whofe difmal attendants we have given fome account) imbitter his fweeteft enjoyments? And will not the horror of the cafe be much increafed by refolving upon a perplexing uncertainty as to what may come after? In how difmal a plight is the poor man, who on the one hand is certain of the fpeedy arrival of death with all its frightful attendants; and on the other, is told that he muft rove in uncertainty, till the event clear him, whether he fhall be entirely annihilated, and fo plunge into that horrible gulf where atheifts feek fanctuary! or if he fhall not be hurried headlong into thefe endlefs torments, which the confciences of guilty finners, when awakened, prefage; or, if he fhall foar aloft into regions of endlefs blifs, which finful mortals have but little reafon to expect; or, finally, whether he is not to launch out into fome ftate reducible to none of thefe. If here we behoove to fix, one would not to know how to evite two conclufions that are horrible to think of : " That our reafon, " whereby we are capable of forefeeing, and are affected with " things at a diftance, is a heavy curfe ; and that the profligate " atheift, who endeavours to mend this fault, in his conftitu- " tion, by a *continual debauch*, that never allows him to think " any more of what is certainly to come, than if he were a " a brute incapable of forethought, is the wifeft man."

Befide, as was above infinuated, the pretences for this courfe are vain. It is true, moft of thofe who fet up for *wits* in this unhappy age, are mere fceptics in religion, who admit nothing as certain, but boldly queftion every thing, and live at peradventures. Yet we are not obliged to think that this fcepticifm is the refult of a ferious inquiry, and the want of certainty thereon; but thofe gentlemen's way of living is inconfiftent with ferious religion ; they are therefore defirous to have fuch a fet of principles as may, if not favour them in the practices they have a mind to follow, yet not incommode them fore. This principle gives not abfolute fecurity of impunity ; but it *feems*, and *but feems*, to juftify them in a prefent neglect of religion, and gives them a *may be* for an efcape from feared and deferved punifhments ; and favours that lazinefs that cannot fearch for truth, where it lies not open to the eye, even of thofe who care not to fee it. Their practice and courfe of life fhew them fo impatient of reftraints, that they

F   love

love *liberty*, or rather *licentiousness*; and are not willing to come under any bonds. They greedily grasp at any difficulty that seems to make never so little against religion; an evidence that they bear it no real good-will. They neither converse much with books, nor men, that may afford them satisfaction, in reference to their real scruples, which is proof enough they design not to be satisfied. They are light and jocular in their converse about the most serious matters; an evidence that their design is not to be informed. It is a good observation of the wise man, [Prov. xiv. 6.] *A scorner seeketh wisdom and findeth it not: but knowledge is easy to him that understandeth.* This is the real mystery of the matter with those gentlemen, whatever they may pretend.

I know they want not pretences, taking enough with the unthinking, whereby they would justify themselves in their infidelity. The principal one is, that they find it easy to load religion with abundance of difficulties, not easily, if at all, capable of solution. But after all, these gentlemen use those *objections* as the *sceptics* did of old, not so much to maintain any settled principle, no not their beloved one, whereof now we speak; as to create them work, and make sport with those who would seriously confute them, and to ward off blows from themselves, who have neither principles nor practice capable of a rational defence.

It is like indeed, that sometimes they may meet with such, who although they own religion, are yet incapable of defending it against such objections. But this is no wonder, since there are weak men of all persuasions. And their weakness is, or ought, not to be any real prejudice to the truth they maintain. Besides, every one may know that ignorance of any subject is fertile of doubts, and will start abundance of difficulties; whereas it requires a more full and exact acquaintance with the nature of things to solve them; and this falls not to every one's share.

Further, if this be allowed a reasonable exception against religion, that it is liable to exceptions not easy to be solved, it will hold as well good against all other sorts of knowledge, as against religion; yea, and I may add, it concludes much stronger; for the farther any subject is above our reach, the less reason we have to expect, that we shall be capable of solving every difficulty that may be started against it. There is no part of our knowledge, that is not incumbered with difficulties,

culties, as hard to be satisfyingly solved, as those commonly urged against religion. If this be a sufficient reason to question religion, that there are arguments which may be urged against it, not capable of a fair, or, at least, an easy solution; I doubt not, upon the same ground, to bring the gentlemen who maintain this, if they will follow out their principle, to reject the most evident truths, that we receive upon the credit of moral, metaphysical, and mathematical demonstrations; yea, or even upon the testimony of our senses. For I know few of these truths that we receive upon any of those grounds, against which a person of a very ordinary spirit may not start difficulties, which perhaps no man alive can give a fair account of; and yet no man is so foolish as to call in question those truths, because he cannot solve the difficulties which every idle head may start upon those subjects. I may give innumerable instances of the difficulties wherewith other parts of human knowledge are embarrassed: I shall only hint at a few.

That matter is divisible into, or at least consists of indivisible points, is with some a truth next to self-evident. That the quite contrary is true, and matter is divisible *in infinitum*, appears no less certain to many others*. But if either of them should pretend themselves capable of solving the difficulties, that lie against their respective opinions, it were sufficient to make all men of sense and learning doubt of their capacity and judgment: For the difficulties on both hands are such, that no ingenuous man that understands them, will pretend himself capable of giving a fair solution of those, which press that side of the question he is inclined to.

Again, whether we will, or will not, we must believe one side, and but one side, of the question is true; that either matter is divisible *in infinitum*, or not; that it consists of indivisibles, or not; these are contradictions. And it is one of the most evident propositions that the mind of man is acquainted with, that contradictions

---

* *Locke* on *Human Understanding*, edit. 5, pag. 207.—" I would " fain have instanced in our notion of spirit any thing more perplexed, " or nearer a contradiction, than the very notion of body includes in " it; the divisibility *in infinitum* of any finite extension, involving us, " whether we grant or deny it, in consequences impossible to be ex- " plicated, or made in our apprehensions consistent; consequences that " carry greater difficulty, and more apparent absurdity than any thing " that can follow from the notion of an immaterial substance."

tions cannot be true, or that both sides of a contradiction cannot hold. And yet against this truth, whereon much of our most certain knowledge depends, insoluble difficulties may be urged: For it may be pretended, that here both sides of the contradiction are true, and this pretence may be enforced by the arguments above-mentioned, which confirm the two opposite opinions, which no mortal can answer. Shall we therefore believe that contradictions may be true?

That motion is possible I am not like to doubt, nor can I, while I know that I can rise and walk; nor is he like to doubt of it, who sees me walk. And yet I doubt not the most ingenious of our atheistical wits would find himself sufficiently straitened, were the arguments of *Zeno Eleates* against motion well urged, by a subtle disputant. I shall offer one argument against motion, which I am fully satisfied will puzzle the most subtle adversaries of religion to solve satisfyingly. There are stronger arguments proving that matter is divisible *in infinitum* than any mortal can solve or answer, though I perhaps believe it untrue. And it is as certain as the sun is in the firmament, that if matter is divisible *in infinitum*, it consists of an infinite number of parts—(what some talk of indefinite is a shelter of ignorance, and if it is used any other way than as a shield to ward off difficulties for a while in a public dispute, the users cannot be excused either of gross ignorance, rooted prejudice, or disingenuity). This being laid down as proven, and proven it may be by arguments, which none living can satisfy, that matter is divisible *in infinitum*, and that consequently it contains an infinite number of parts. Nor is it less certain, that according to these conclusions laid down, if one body move upon the surface of another, as for instance, an inch in a minute's time, it must pass by an infinite number of parts; and it is undeniable, that it cannot pass one of that infinite number of parts without some portion of time. Now if so, what a vast portion of time will it require to make that little journey, which we know can be performed in a moment! Will it not evidently require an eternity! What difficulty can any urge, more difficult to be solved, against religion than this? And yet for all this he were a fool who would doubt of motion.

As to mathematical certainty, though many boasts are made of the firmness of its demonstrations; yet these may, upon this ground, be called all in question. And I nothing doubt, that if men's interests, real or pretended, lay as cross to them, as they

they are supposed to do to the truths of a religion, many more exceptions might be made against them, than are against those, and upon full as good, if not better reason. In justification of this assertion, I might proceed to demonstrate how trifling even the definitions of geometry, the firmest of all the mathematical sciences, are. Its definitions might be alleged, upon no inconsiderable grounds, trifling, nonsensical, and ridiculous. Its demands or postulates, plainly impracticable. Its axioms or self-evident propositions, controvertible, and by themselves they are controverted. Any one who would see this made good in particular instances, may consult (besides others) the learned *Huetius' Demonstratio Evangelica*, where, in the illustration of his definitions, axioms and postulates, he compares them with those of geometry, and prefers them to these, and shews they are incumbered with fewer difficulties than the other, though without derogating from the just worth and evidence of mathematical sciences. Besides what he has observed, I may add this one thing more, that those sciences deserve not any great regard, save as they are applied to the use of life, and in a subserviency to man's advantage. And when thus they are applied to practice, the difficulty is considerably increased, and they may easily be loaded with innumerable and insoluble inconveniences. For then, their definitions cease to be the definition of names, and are to be taken as the definitions of things that are actually in being. Their demands must not be practicable, but put in practice. And who sees not how many inextricable difficulties the practiser will be cast upon? The demonstration may proceed bravely so long as they hold in the theory, and mean by *Punctum, id cujus pars nulla est** ; and the same may be said of lines and surfaces, and all their figures ; without obliging us to believe that really there are any such things. But when we come to the practice, they must go further, and take it for granted, that there are such points, lines, surfaces and figures. This turns what was before only an explication of a name, into the definition of a thing. And therefore I am now left at liberty to dispute, whether there is any such thing ; or, whether indeed it is possible that there should be such. And who sees not now, that they are incumbered with as many difficulties as may perhaps be urged against any science whatsoever.

It

* " That which has no parts."

INTRODUCTION.

It were endless to enumerate the things we must believe, without being capable to resolve the difficulties about them. The veriest infidel must suppose that something is eternal, or all things are eternal, or that they jumped into being without any cause. Whichsoever he shall choose, he is led into a labyrinth of difficulties, which no mortal wit can clear. We must all own, that either matter and motion are the principle of thought; or, that there are immaterial substances which affect matter, and are strangely affected by what befals it. Whichsoever side any shall choose, he is cast upon inextricable difficulties. Much more might be said on this head; but what has been said is more than enough to shew, that if this course is taken, it saps the foundations of all human knowledge, and there is no part of it safe.

Besides, this way of questioning religion upon the pretence of difficulties lying against it, is contrary to the common sense of mankind, contradicts the practice of all wise men, and is inconsistent with the very nature of our faculties. For, if I have a clear unexceptionable and convincing proof for any truth, it is against all reason to reject it, because I have not so full and comprehensive knowledge of the nature and circumstances of the object, as is necessary to enable me to solve all difficulties that may occur about it: Yea, such is the nature of our faculties, that to justify in the opinion of the nicest inquirers after truth, nay, to extort an assent, clear proof is sufficient; whereas, to untie all knots, and solve all objections, perfect and comprehensive knowledge is absolutely needful; which man's condition allows him not to expect about the meanest things. And the more remote any thing lies from common observation, the less reason there is still to look for a fullness of knowledge and exemption from difficulties. If therefore men will turn sceptics in religion, to justify themselves, they must attempt the proofs whereon it is grounded. Sampson-like, they must grasp the pillars that support the fabric, and pull them down. If this is not done, nothing is done. And he that will undertake this, must have a full view of their force, and find where there strength lies: Now a serious view of this will be sufficient to deter any wise man from the undertaking.

In a word, this scepticism can yield no ease or satisfaction to a reasonable soul. For if a man shall think rationally, his reason will suggest to him, that though all religion at present seems uncertain to him, yet upon trial perhaps he may find the

grounds

grounds of religion fo evident, that he cannot withhold his affent. This will at leaft oblige him to a ferious inquiry into the truth. Next, in uncertainties (fuppofing, after ferious inquiry, he ftills thinks the truths of religion fuch) a prudent man will incline to what is moft probable. Finally, he will choofe and fteer fuch a courfe of life as will be fafeft, in cafe he fhall in experience afterward find, that there is a God, and a future ftate. All which fhew the folly of our fceptics, and, were it ferioufly confidered, would much mar their defign, which is thereby to juftify a licentious life.

Now we have confidered, and fufficiently expofed the two firft branches of the above-mentioned choice: and confequently every man muft find himfelf caft upon a neceffity of one of two. He muft either betake himfelf to *natural religion*, and fo turn *deift*; or he muft embrace the *fcriptures*, and turn *Chriftian*: For as to the *Jewifh religion*, it is not likely to gain many *converts*.

If therefore we are able to demonftrate the utter *infufficiency of natural religion*, in oppofition to the *deifts* who fet up for it, we reduce every man to this choice, that he muft be a *Chriftian* or an *atheift*; or, which is the fame upon the matter, a man of *no religion*; for an *infufficient religion* is in effect *none*. And to demonftrate this, that *natural religion* is utterly infufficient, that unaffifted reafon is not able to guide us to happinefs, and fatisfy us as to the great concerns of religion, is the defign of the fubfequent fheets. In them we have clearly ftated and endeavoured with clofenefs to argue this point. We have brought the pleadings of the learned lord *Herbert*, and the *modern deifts*, who do but copy after him, to the bar of *reafon*, examined their utmoft force, and, if I miftake it not, found them weak and inconcludent.

As for the occafion of my engagement in this controverfy, it was not fuch as commonly gives rife to writings of this nature. I undertook it with no defign of publication. I was provoked by no adverfary in particular. But every man being obliged to underftand upon what grounds he receives his religion, I ftudied the point for my own fatisfaction, and in compliance with my duty.

As for the reafons of my undertaking this part of the controverfy, I fhall not fay much. The only wife GOD, *who has determined the times before appointed, and made of one blood all nations of men that dwell on the earth, has appointed them the bounds of their habitation*, cut out different pieces of work for

for

them, cast them into different circumstances, and hereby exposed them to trials and temptations that are not of the same kind. As every man is obliged to cultivate in the best manner he can the bounds of land assigned to him, and defend his possessions; so every one is concerned to improve and defend after the best form he may, those truths, which his circumstances have obliged him to take peculiar notice of, and his temptations, of whatever sort, have endeavoured, or may attempt to wrest out of his hands.

Besides, we live in a warlike age, wherein every one must be of a party in matters of religion. And religion is a cause in which, when disputed, no man is allowed to stand neutral. As all are concerned to choose the right side, so every one is obliged to provide himself with the best armour his arsenal can afford, both for defending himself and others that own the same cause, and to annoy the common enemy. Nor is this work peculiarly confined unto those, who by office are obliged to it: For, *in publico discrimini est omnis homo miles* *.

Besides, it is well known, that the most bold attempt that ever was made upon revealed religion, since the entrance of Christianity into the world, has been made, in our day, by men, who set up for *natural religion*, and who have gone over from *Christianity* unto a *refined Paganism*, under the name of *Deism*. Two things they have attempted; to overthrow *revelation*, and to advance *natural religion*. The last work has been undertaken, I may without breach of charity boldly say it, not so much out any real affection to the principles or duties of natural religion, as to avoid the *odium* inevitably following upon a renunciation of all religion; and because they saw that men would not easily quit Christianity, without something were substituted in its room, that might at least have the name of religion. *Revealed religion* has been worthily defended by many, of old and of late, at home and abroad; but the *insufficiency of natural religion* has been less insisted on, at least in that way that is necessary to straiten an obstinate adversary. And several things incline me to think an attempt of this nature seasonable, if not necessary, at this time.

The times are infectious, and deism is the contagion that spreads. And that which has taken many, particularly of our unwary youth of the better quality, off their feet, and engaged them

---

* " In a time of public danger every man is a soldier."

them to espouse this cause, is the high pretence that this way makes to *reason*. They tell us, that their religion is entirely reasonable, and that they admit nothing, save what this dictates to them, and they endeavour to represent others as easy and credulous men. Now I thought it meet to demonstrate, for undeceiving of such, that none are more credulous, none have less reason upon their side, than they who set up for *rational religion*.

Again, we have stood sufficiently long upon the defensive part, we have repulsed their efforts against *revelation*. It seems now seasonable, that we should act offensively, and try how they can defend their own religion, and whether they can give as good account of it as has been given of Christianity. To stand always upon the defensive part, is to make the enemy doubt ours, and turn proud of their own strength.

The reasonableness of this will further appear, if we consider the quality of the adversaries we have to do with, and their manner of management. The enemies who have engaged revealed religion, sensible of their own weakness to defend themselves at home, and endure close fight, do commonly make inroads, where they expect none, or a faint resistance. They design not so much to conquer, as to disturb. Jest, buffoonery, or at best sophisms, and such little artifices, are the arguments they use, and the weapons of their warfare. The best way to make such rovers keep as home is, to carry the war into their own country, and to ruin those retreats they betake themselves to when attacked. They have seen what Christians can say in defence of *revealed religion*. It is now high time to see how they can acquit themselves on behalf of *natural religion*. It is easy to impugn. It is a defence that gives the best proof of the defender's skill, and says most for the cause he maintains.

I own indeed that most who have evinced the truth of revealed religion, have said something of the weakness of natural religion. But this has only been by the bye, and in a way too loose to straiten obstinate opposers, not to speak of the too large concessions that have been made them by some.

Finally, *natural religion* being the only retreat, to which the apostates from Christianity betake themselves, and whereby they think themselves secured from the imputation of plain *atheism*, it is hoped, that a full and convincing discovery of its weakness, may incline such as are not quite debauched, to look how they quit Christianity, and engage with that which, if this attempt is fuccefsful, muft henceforward pafs for *difguifed atheifm.*

It now only remains, that I offer fome account of the reafons that have induced me to manage this controverfy in a method fo far different from that which is commonly ufed. The reafons of this have been above infinuated, and I fhall not infift much further on them, left I fhould feem to detract from performances to which I pay a very great regard. The method fome have chofen, in managing this controverfy with the deifts, to me appears inconvenient. They begin with an endeavour to eftablifh the grounds of *natural religion,* and by the help of light borrowed from *revelation,* they carry the matter fo far, and extend natural religion to fuch a compafs, that it looks pretty complete-like; which has too evident a tendency to leffen its *real defects,* and make them *appear* inconfiderable.

Again, I am afraid that fome have gone near to give up the whole caufe. This fault I would be very loth to charge upon all. Many I know have dealt faithfully in it, and deferve praife. But how to excufe fome in this cafe I know not. One tells us that, " It is true indeed, that natural religion declares " and comprizes all the parts of religion, that are generally " and in all times either neceffary or requifite*!" And much more to the fame purpofe. This is much fuch another affertion of the weaknefs of natural religion againft the deifts, as the fame author gives us of the *perfection of the fcriptures,* in oppofition to the fame perfons in another place of his book. " I could," fays he, " prove, I think, by undenia- " ble, unavoidable inftances †," what Mr. Gregory of Oxford fays in his preface to fome critical notes on the fcriptures that he publifhed, viz. " That there is no author whatfoever that has " fuffered fo much by the hand of time as the Bible has." Is this the way to overthrow the fufficiency of natural religion, and to defend the fcriptures? This is not the only remark I could make upon this author, were it my defign. But this may let us fee how neceffary it is to deal a little more plainly with the afferters of natural religion.

Further, to adorn natural religion with the improvements borrowed from *revelation,* is the ready way to furnifh thofe who

---

* Difcourfe concerning Natural and Revealed Religion, by Stephen Nye, Part 2, Chap. 1, page 97.
† *Ubi fupra,* page 199.

who set up for its *sufficiency*, with pretences to serve their design, and to straiten themselves, when they come to shew its defects. And perhaps I should not mistake it far, if I asserted, that the strongest arguments urged by deists, have been drawn from unwary concessions made them by their adversaries.

And this is the more considerable, that the persons, with whom we have to do in this controversy, are, generally speaking, either of no great discerning, or small application; who have no great mind to wait upon the business, or look to the bottom of it. Now when such persons find many things granted, they are ready to think all is yielded, and so run away with it, as the cause were their own. That such concessions have done no good service, there is too much reason to believe. This I am sure of, it would have been long before the deists could have trimmed up natural religion so handsomely, and made it appear so *like a sufficient religion*, as some have done, who meaned no such thing.

Finally, the apostle Paul's method is doubtless most worthy of imitation, who, when he is to prove justification by faith, and enforce an acceptance of it, strongly convinces of sin, and the utter insufficiency of works for that purpose. The best way in my opinion, to engage men to close with *revealed religion*, is strongly to argue the *insufficiency* of *natural religion*.

As to the performance itself, and what I have therein attained, I am not the judge competent. Every reader must judge as he sees cause. I have not the vanity to expect that it should please every body. The vast compass of the subject, the variety of the purposes, the uncommonness of many, if not most of them, with respect to which I was left to walk in untrodden paths, and other difficulties of a like nature, with candid and judicious readers will go a great way towards my excuse in lesser escapes. As for the substance of the ensuing discourse, I am bold to hope, that upon the strictest trial it shall be found true, and pleaded for in words of truth and soberness.

AN

AN

INQUIRY

INTO THE

PRINCIPLES of the MODERN DEISTS.

CHAP. I.

Giving a short Account of the Rise, Occasions, and Progress of Deism, especially in England, the Opinions of the Deists, and the different Sorts of them.

THERE is no man, who makes it his concern to understand what the state of religion has, of late years, been, and now is, particularly in these nations, but knows that *deism* has made a considerable progress. Since therefore it is against those, who go under *this name*, that this undertaking is designed, it is highly expedient, if not plainly necessary, that in the entry, we give some account of the *occasions* and *rise* of *deism*, the principal opinions of the *deists*, and some other things that may tend to clear the matter discoursed in the subsequent sheets.

It is not necessary that we inquire more largely into the causes of that general defection in *principle* and *practice* from the *doctrine* of the *gospel* which now every where obtains; this has been judiciously done by others.

Nor will it be needful to write at length the *history* of *deism*. This I think impracticable, because the growth of this *sect* has been

been very secret, and they have generally disguised their opinions. And perhaps till of late, they scarce had any settled opinion in matters of religion, if yet they have. But though it were practicable, as it is not, yet it is not necessary to our present undertaking; and if it were attempted, would require more helps, and more leisure, besides other things, than I am master of.

One has of late written a pamphlet bearing this title, " An Account of the Growth of Deism in England *." The author, if he is not a deist, yet has done what in him lies to promote their cause, by setting off, with all the art and address he is master of, those things which, he says, have tempted many to turn deists, without any attempt to antidote the poison of them.

Another has wrote *Reflections* upon this pamphlet, wherein he has sufficiently shewn, that those alleged by the former author, were not sufficient reasons to justify any in turning deist. But I conceive that is not the main question. If he had a mind to disprove the other author, he should have made it appear, that the particulars condescended upon by his antagonist, had no real influence into this apostasy. Whether they gave a just cause for it, is another question. I am satisfied they did not. But neither do those *reasons* of this defection, condescended on by the *reflecter*, give a sufficient ground for it. Nor are there any reasons that can justify any in relinquishing Christianity. The inquiry in this case is not, What just grounds have the deists to warrant them in, or engage them to this defection? for all Christians own it impossible they should have any. But the question is, What has given occasion to any, thus to fall off from our religion? Now I conceive both these writers have hit upon several of the *true reasons* of this; though the first is apparently guilty of *deep imprudence*, I wish I might not say *malice*, against Christianity, in proposing those temptations, with all the advantage he could give them, and that without any antidote: For which and other faults he has been justly, though modestly, censured by the *reflecter*.

Although both of them has given some account of this matter, yet I conceive so much has not been said as may supersede a further inquiry, or make us despair of observing not a few things that have not had an inconsiderable influence, which are overlooked by both. Wherefore we shall in a few words propose

---

* Printed anno 1690.

propose our opinion of this matter. And in delivering it, we shall not pursue the design of any *party*, but make it evident that *all parties* have had their own accession to the *growth* of this *evil*. Though I am sensible that this account will fall heavy upon a *set* of men in particular, who have of late years claimed the name of the *Church of England*, though unjustly; if we take her Homilies, Articles, and the consentient judgment of her renowned bishops from the time of the Reformation to bishop Laud's time, for the standard of her doctrine*; and I see no reason why we ought not. I premised this to avoid any suspicion of a design to brand the Church of England, with an accession to the *growth of deism*. And even in speaking of that *set* of men, whom I take to be principally guilty, I would not be understood to speak so much of the *design* of the men, as of the *native tendency* of their *doctrine* and *practices*.

The many groundless, nay ridiculous pretences to *revelation*, and bold impostures of the Church of Rome, and of those who have supported that interest; their impudence in obtruding upon the world, doctrines cross to *reason* and *sense*, and principles of *morality* subversive of the *whole law of nature* †; their scandalous endeavour to bespatter the scriptures, and weaken their authority, on purpose to bring them into discredit, to make way for the designed advancement of their *wild traditions* into an equality with them, and to bring the world under a necessity of throwing themselves upon the care and conduct of their *infallible guide*, though they cannot yet tell us which is he; their gross and discernible hypocrisy in carrying on secular, nay impious and unjust designs, under the specious pretences of *holiness* and *religion*; their zeal for a *form* and *shew of religion*, a worship plainly *theatrical* ‡, while the lives of their Popes, Cardinals, Monks, Nuns, and all their highest pretenders to devotion have been scandalously lewd, even to a proverb §; the *immoral morality, atheistical divinity,* and *abominable practices* of the Jesuits, those zealous supporters and strongest props of the Popish interest, but in very deed the worst enemies of mankind, the subverters of all *true piety, morality,*

and

---

* See Bishop of Sarum's Explanation of the Thirty-nine Articles, on Art. 17; pag. 168.
†. Growth of Deism, pag. 5. Reflections on it, pag. 8.
‡ See Jesuit's Morals.
§ Clarkson's Practical Divinity of Papists.

and *government* in the world; thefe, I fay, together with many other evils of a like nature, every where obfervable in that church, have been, for a very long time too evident and grofs to be denied, or hid from perfons of any tolerable fagacity, living among them. And, by the obfervation of thofe and the like evils, continued in, approved, juftified, and adhered unto; and the cruelty of that church in deftroying all thofe, who would not receive, by wholefale, all thofe fhocking abfurdities, not a few who lived among them, and were unacquainted with the power of religion, that was ncceffary to engage them cordially to efpoufe the Reformed intereft, got their minds leavened with prejudices, and furnifhed with fpecious pretences againft all revealed religion; which they the more boldly entertained, becaufe they knew it was lefs criminal to turn *athieft* than *Proteftant* in places where the Popifh intereft prevailed.

Thefe prejudices once taken up, daily grew ftronger, by the obfervation of new inftances of this fort, and the conftancy of thofe of that communion in acting the fame part. And men of wit and learning, who foonest faw into this myftery, and had no inward bonds on them, failed not to hand about and cultivate thofe pretences to that degree, that many begun to own their apoftafy, if not openly, yet more covertly.

Not long after the beginning of the laft elapfed century, fo far as I can learn, fome in France and Italy began to form a fort of new a party. They called themfelves *Theifts*, or *Deifts*; unjuftly pretending that they were the only perfons who owned the *One true God*. And hereby they plainly intimated that they had rejected the name of *Chrift*. They rejected all *revelation* as *cheat*, *prieftcraft*, and *impofture*, pretending that there was nothing fincere in religion, fave what *nature's light* taught. However, being generally perfons too fond of a prefent life, and too uncertain about a future, they thought it not meet to put too much to the hazard for this their *pretended religion*. It was a refined fort of Paganifm which they embraced, and they were to imitate the Heathen philofophers, who, whatever their peculiar fentiments were in matters of religion, yet for peace's fake, they looked on it as fafe to follow the mode, and comply with the religious ufages that prevailed in the places where they lived. That which made this party the more confiderable was, that it was made up of men, who pretended to learning, ingenuity, breeding, and who fet up for *wits*. They pretended to write after the copy of the new philofophers, who

fcorned

scorned that philosophical slavery, which former ages had been under to Aristotle. They inculcated that credulity was no less dangerous in matters of religion than in matters of philosophy. And herein certainly they were not mistaken. But one may justly suspect, that at the same time, while they pretended to guard against easiness in believing, they have fallen into the worst *credulity*, as well as ruining *incredulity*. For none is so credulous as an atheist.

Much about the same time, some novel opinions began to be much entertained in Holland, in matters of religion. The broachers of them being men learned and diligent, carefully cultivated them, till they were ripened into something very near-akin to plain Socinianism, which is but one remove from deism. It was not long after, this when those new-fangled notions took footing in England and began to be embraced and countenanced by some *topping churchmen*, who, forgetful of their Articles, Homilies, and Subscriptions, and the conduct of their predecessors, carefully maintained, and zealously propagated this new divinity.

I shall not make bold to judge what the designs of those were, who appeared most zealous for these new notions: This is to be left to the judgment of him, who *searches the heart of the children of men, and will bring forth things that are now hid*. But there were not a few reasons to suspect that the Jesuits had a considerable hand in disseminating them, and that the others were their tools; though it is likely they did not suspect this. The Jesuits vaunted that they had planted the *sovereign drug* of Arminianism in England, which in time would purge out the *northern heresy* *. This it could not otherwise do, than by shaking men as to all principles of religion. And it is a known maxim, that *make men once atheists it will be easy to turn them papists*. The jealousies many discerning people had of this, were considerably increased when it was seen with what violence the abettors of this new divinity appeared against the more moderate part of the Church of England, as well as the Dissenters, upon the account of some *ceremonies*, owned by themselves as indifferent in their own nature; while at the same time, they expressed a great deal of tenderness, if not respect to the Church of Rome, and made proposals for *union* with her.

But

* Rushworth's Collect. Part 1, pag. 475. Letter by a Jesuit to the Rector of Brussels. See pag. 62, *ibid.*

But whatever there is as to this, it is certain that this divinity opens a door, and has given encouragement to that apoſtaſy from Chriſtianity, that has ſince followed, and ſtill increaſes, under the name of *deiſm*.

This divinity teaches us, that no more is neceſſary to be believed, in order to ſalvation, ſave what is confeſſed and owned by all that are called Chriſtians. *Dicunt ſe non videre unde, aut quo modo, præter pauca iſta, quæ apud omnes in confeſſo ſunt, alia plura adhuc neceſſaria eſſe oſtendi aut elici poſſit* * ; that is, " They ſee not how it can be made appear, that be-" ſides theſe few things, which are by them allowed, any o-" thers are neceſſary to ſalvation." Conſonantly hereto, they expreſsly deny any thing to be *fundamental* which has been controverted, or afterwards may be ſo †. In a word, they teach that we are not neceſſarily to believe any thing, ſave what is evident to us. And that only is to be reckoned evident, which is confeſſed by all, and to which nothing that has any appearance of truth can be oppoſed. Now after this, what is left in *Chriſtianity?* The *divinity*, the *purity*, the *pefection* and *ſufficiency* of the *ſcriptures*; the *Trinity, Deity of Chriſt, his ſatisfaction, the whole diſpenſation of the Spirit, juſtification by faith alone,* and all the *articles* of the *Chriſtian religion,* have been and are controverted. None of them therefore is neceſſary to ſalvation. Are not men left at liberty, without hazard of their ſalvation, to renounce all, ſave what is common to *Chriſtianity* with *natural religion?* and ſince even ſome of its moſt conſiderable articles about the *attributes* of GOD and his *providence, future rewards* and *puniſhments,* have been, or may be controverted, why may we not reckon them unneceſſary too? The *deiſts* have borrowed their *doctrine of evidence,* and oppoſed it to the *Chrſtian religion.* One of them tells us, " If our happineſs depends upon our belief, we " cannot firmly believe, till our reaſon be convinced of a ſuper-" natural religion ‡." And if the reaſons of it were evident, there could be no longer any contention about religion. How little does this differ from that divinity, which tells us, that GOD is obliged to offer us ſuch arguments to which nothing that has *an appearance of truth* can be oppoſed! And if this be wanting, they are not to be received as *articles of faith.* Now if after this

---

* Remonſtr, Apol. Fol. 12.
† *Ibi*, Cap. 24, Fol. 276; and Cap. 25, Fol. 283.
‡ Oracles of Reaſon, pag. 206. Letter by A. W. to C. Blount.

this the deists can but offer any thing that has an *appearance* of truth against Christianity, they are free to reject it *in cumulo*. This divinity reduces Christianity to *mere morality*. Nothing else is universally agreed to, if that be so. " The supposition " of sin, (says one that wore a mitre) does not bring in any " new religion, but only makes new circumstances and names " of old things, and requires new helps and advantages to im- " prove our powers, and to encourage our endeavours : And " thus the *law of grace* is nothing but a restitution of the *law of* " *nature**."

And further, lest we should think this morality, wherein they place the whole of Christianity, owes its *being* to the agency of the sanctifying Spirit, we are told, that " the Spirit of God, " and the grace of Christ, when used as distinct from moral a- " bilities and performances, signify nothing †." And a complaint is made of some, who fill the world " with a buz and " noise of the divine Spirit ‡." Hence many sermons were rather such as became the chair of a philosopher, teaching *ethicks*, than that of one, who by office is bound to *know* and preach *nothing save Christ and him crucified*. Heathen morality has been substituted in the room of gospel holiness. And ethicks by some have been preached instead of the gospel of Christ. And if any complaints were made of this conduct, though by men who preached the necessity of holiness, urged by all the gospel motives, and carefully practised what they preached in their lives, they were exposed and rejected, and the persons who offered them were reflected on as enemies to *morality;* whereas the plain truth of the case was, they did not complain of men being taught to be moral, but that they were not taught somewhat more.

After men once were taught that the controverted doctrines of religion were not necessary to salvation, and that all that was necessary thereto was to be referred to and comprehended under *morality*, and that there was no need of *regeneration*, or the sanctifying influences of the Spirit of Christ in order to the performance of our duty, it is easy to see how light the difference was to be accounted betwixt a *Christian* and an honest *moral Heathen*. And if any small temptation offered, how natural was

* S. Park's Defence of Ecclef. Poli. pag. 324.
† *Idem ibid*, pag. 343.
‡ Ecclef. Polit. pag. 57.

was it for men to judge that the hazard was not great, to step over from *Christianity* to *deism*, which is *Paganism a-la-mode*. And to encourage them to it, it is well known how favourably many used to express themselves of the state of the Heathens; little minding that the Christian religion represents them as *without God*, and *without Christ*, and *without hope, children of wrath*, and *dead in trespasses and sins*.

I need not stand to prove that this divinity is nearly allied to Socinianism. It is well known that they reckon the Socinians sound in the fundamentals, and therefore think them in no hazard, provided they live morally. Hence men have been emboldened to turn Socinians. And every body may see by what easy removes, one may from Socinianism arrive at *deism*. For my part I can see little difference betwixt the two. The deist indeed seems the honester man of the two; he rejects the gospel, and owns that he does so: The other, I mean the Socinian, pretends to retain it, but really rejects it. But I shall not insist any further in discovering the tendency of this *new divinity* to *libertinism* and *deism*, since others have fully and judiciously done it from the most unquestionable arguments and documents. And more especially, since in fact it is evident, that wherever this new divinity has obtained, Socinians and deists abound, and many who embrace it daily go over to them; which I take to be the surest evidence, if it be duly circumstantiate, of the tendency of this doctrine to encourage those opinions, and least liable to any just exception. And perhaps I might add, that few, comparatively very few, who own the contrary doctrine, have gone into this new way, where that divinity has not been entertained.

But to return whence we have for a little digressed, to the state of religion in England. No sooner were they advanced to *power* who had drunk in those opinions, but presently the doctrines that are purely evangelical, by which the apostles converted the world, the Reformers promoted and carried on our reformation from Popery, and the pious preachers of the Church of England did keep somewhat of the life and power of religion amongst their people: these doctrines, I say, began to be decryed; justification by the righteousness of Christ, which Luther called *Articulus stantis aut cadentis ecclesiæ* *, that redemption that is in him, even the *forgiveness of sins through faith*

---

* "An article by which the church must either stand or fall."

faith in his blood; the myſtery of the grace, mercy and love of God manifeſted in Chriſt; the great myſtery of godlineſs; the diſpenſation of the Spirit for conviction, renovation, ſanctification, conſolation and edification of the church, by a ſupply of ſpiritual gifts, and other doctrines of a like tendency, were, upon all occaſions, boldly expoſed, and diſcredited in preſs and pulpit. The miniſters who dared to avow them, from a conviction of the truth, the ſenſe of the obligation of their promiſes and ſubſcriptions to the Articles, were ſure to have no preferment, nay, to be branded with the odious names of *Calvaniſts, Puritans, Fanatics*, and I know not what.

The doctrines of *faith* were not regarded as belonging to the foundation of religion. The *morality* of the Bible was pretended the only thing that was neceſſary; and as much of the *doctrine*, as all, even Socinians, Quakers, and all the reſt were agreed in, were ſufficient. And if any oppoſed this, though in civil language and by fair arguments, they were ſure to be expoſed as enemies to *morality*; although their adverſaries durſt not put the conteſt on this iſſue with them, that he ſhould be reckoned the greateſt friend to morality who was moſt blameleſs in his walk, and ſhewed it the greateſt practical regard. They could exerciſe charity, forbearance, and love to a Socinian that has renounced all the fundamental truths of religion; but none to a poor *Diſſenter*, who ſincerely believed all the Doctrinal Articles; nay, even a ſober Churchman, who could not conſent to new unauthorized ceremonies, was become intolerable. So that men, at this time, might, with much more credit and leſs hazard, turn Socinian, or any thing, than diſcover the leaſt regard to truths contained in the Articles, owned by moſt of the Reformed churches, and taught by our own Reformers. This is too well known to be denied by any one who knows how things were carried on at that time and ſince *.

Further, whereas preachers formerly, in order to engage men to a compliance with the goſpel, were wont to preſs much upon them their guilt, the impoſſibility of ſtanding before God

in

---

* Any one that would be ſatisfied in the truth of this, muſt peruſe the ſermons and writings publiſhed by that party of old and of late, and the hiſtories of thoſe times, particularly *Ruſhworth's Collect.* the ſpeeches of the long Parliament, and later writings, and they will find documents more than enough. And they may conſult alſo *Honorii Regii's* Comment. *de ſtatu Eccleſiæ Anglicanæ.*

in their own righteoufnefs, their impotency, their mifery by
the fall, the neceffity of regeneration, illumination, the power
of grace to make them willing to comply, and that no man
could fincerely *call Chrift Lord*, and be fubject to him practi-
cally, *fave by the Holy Ghoft*; care was now taken to unteach
them all this, and to fhew them how very little they had loft by
the fall, if any thing was loft by it, either in point of *light* to difcern, or *power* and *inclination* to practife duty. They were
told how great length their *own righteoufnefs* would go, and
that it would do their bufinefs; they might fafely ftand before
God in it; or if there was any room for *Chrift's righteoufnefs*,
it was only to piece out their own, where it was wanting. In
a word, the people were told, what fine perfons many of the
Heathens were, who knew nothing of illumination, regeneration, or what the Bible was, and how little odds, if any at all,
there was betwixt *grace* and *morality*.

And, whereas a veneration for the Lord's day was a mean
to keep people under fome concern about religion, and that
day was fpent by faithful minifters, in preffing upon the confciences of their people, thofe new-contemned gofpel truths,
to the fpoiling of the whole plot; care was taken to difcredit
and bring it into contempt. Minifters, inftead of telling them
on that day, that they were too much inclined to fin, levity,
folly, and vanity, were commanded to deal with them as perfons too much inclined to be ferious; and inftead of preaching
the gofpel, they were required, under the higheft pains, to entertain them with a profane *Book of Sports*. And for difobedience many were ejected. And that they might be taught by
example as well as precept, a *Sunday's Evening Mafk* was publicly acted, where were prefent perfons of no mean note *.

Moreover, a ftate game being now to be played, the pulpit,
prefs, religion and all were made bafely to truckle to *ftate defigns*, and to the enflaving of the nations, by advancing the
doctrines of *paffive obedience, non-refiftance*, and *jure-divino-fhip*
of kings †; whereby men of religion were wounded to fee the
ordinances of Chrift proftituted to fuch projects, as were entirely
foreign, to fay no worfe, to the defign of their inftitution:
And men of no religion, or who were not fixed about it, were
drawn over to think it a mere cheat, and that the defign of it
was

* Rufhworth's Collect. Part 2, Vol. 1, pag. 459.
† Bifhop of Sarum on the Articles, Art. 7, pag. 152.

was only to carry on secular interest under specious pretences.

At length by those means, and some other things, which are not of our present consideration, concurring, confusions ripened into a civil war, whereby every one was left to speak, write, and live as he pleased.

Many who intended no hurt, while they upon honest designs inquired into, and laid open the faults of the topping clergy, did unawares furnish loose and atheistical men with pretences against the ministry. And what in truth gave only ground for a dislike of the persons faulty, was received by many as a just ground of prejudice against the very *pastoral*, as *priest-craft*, and all who are clothed with it, as a set of self-designing men.

The body of the people, who had been debauched by the example of a *scandalous clergy*, and hardened in sin by the intermission of all *discipline*, (which of late had only been exercised against the sober and pious who could not go into the measures that were then taken), the neglect of painful preaching, the *Book of Sports and Pastimes*, and who had their heads filled with airy and self-elating notions of man's *ability to good, free-will, universal grace*, and the like, and who now, when they much needed the inspection of their faithful pastors, were deprived of it, many of them, by the iniquity of the times, being forced to take sanctuary in foreign nations; the people, I say, by these things turned quite giddy, and broke into numberless sects and parties. Every one who had entertained those giddy notions was zealous, even to madness, for propagating them, and thought himself authorized to plead for them, print for them, and preach them. The office of the ministry, that had before been rendered contemptible by the suppression of the best preachers, and the scandalous lives of those who were mainly encouraged, was now made more so, by the intrusion of every bold, ignorant and assuming enthusiast. The land was filled with books of controvery, stuffed with unsound, offensive and scandalous tenets, which were so multiplied, as they never have been in any nation of the world, in so small a compass of time. The generality of the people being, by the neglect of a scandalous ministry, and the discouragement of those who were laborious, drenched in ignorance, were easily shaken by those controversial writings that were disseminated every where, and became an easy prey to every bold sectarian.

Many

Many of the better fort fet themfelves to oppofe thefe extremes, and from a deteftaton of them were carried, fome into one evil, fome into another; whereby the common enemy reaped advertage, and *truth* fuffered even by its defenders. Minifters who defired to be faithful, by the abounding of thofe errors, were forced to oppofe them in public; whereby preaching became lefs edifying, and difputes increafed, to the great detriment of religion.

The nation was thus crumbled into parties, in matters both civil and religious, the times turned cloudy and dark. Pretences of religion were dreadfully abufed on all hands to fubferve other defigns. And even the beft both of minifters and people wanted not their own fad failings, which evil men made the worft ufe of. The *word* and *providence* were ufed in favour of fo many crofs opinions and practices, that not a few began to run into that fame extreme, which fome in France and Italy had before gone into. And about this time it was that the learned *Herbert* began to write in favour of deifm: Of which we fhall have occafion to fpeak afterwards.

After the Reftoration, things were fo far from being mended, that they grew worfe. Lewdnefs and atheifm were encouraged at the court, which now looked like a little Sodom. The clergy turned no lefs fcandalous, if not more fo than before. Impiety was, as it were, publicly and with applaufe acted and taught on the ftage, and all ferious religion was there expofed and ridiculed. Yea, the pulpits of many became theatres, whereupon men affumed the boldnefs to ridicule ferious godlinefs, and the graveft matters of religion; fuch as communion with God, confeffion of fin, prayer by the Spirit, and the whole work of converfion. Controverfial writings were multiplied, and in them grave and ferious truths were handled in a jocular way. The fcriptures were burlefqued; and the moft important truths, (under pretence of expofing the Diffenters, to the great grief of all good men among them, and in the Church of England), were treated with contempt and fcorn. The pulpits were again proftituted to *ftate defigns* and *doctrines*; and the great truths of the gofpel, in reference to *man's mifery*, and his *recovery by Jefus Chrift*, were entirely neglected by many; and difcourfes of *morality* came in their place, I mean a morality that has no refpect to Chrift as its *end, author, and the ground of its acceptance with God*, which is plain *heathenifm*. The foberer, and the better part were traduced as enthufiaftical, difloyal disloyal hypocrites, and I know not what. And sometimes they on the other hand, in their own defence, were constrained to lay open the impiety, atheism, and blasphemous boldness of their traducers in their way of management of divine things. And while matters were thus carryed betwixt them, careless and indifferent men, especially of the better and most considerable quality, being debauched in their practice, by the licentiousness of the court, the immorality and looseness of the stage, were willing to conform their principles to their practice; for which this state of things gave them a favourable occasion and plausible pretences. Men whose walk and way looked like any thing of a real regard to religion, they heard so often traduced as hypocrites, fanatics, and I know not what, that they were easily induced to believe them to be such. They who taught them so, on the other hand, by the liberty they assumed in practice, convinced these gentlemen, that whatever their profession was, yet they believed nothing about religion themselves; and therefore it was easy to infer that all was but a cheat. Besides, the Popish party, who were sufficiently encouraged, while the sober Dissenters of the Protestant persuasion were cruelly persecuted, made it their business to promote this unsettledness in matters of religion. They found themselves unable to stand their ground in way of fair debate, and therefore they craftily set themselves rather to shake others in their faith, than directly to press them to a compliance with their own sentiments. And it is well known they wrote many books full of sophistry, plainly levelling at this, to bring men to believe *nothing*; as well knowing, that if they were once brought there, they would soon be brought to believe *any thing* in matters of religion.

On these and the like occasions and pretences, arose this defection from the gospel, which has been nourished by many of the same things which first gave it birth, till it is grown to such strength, as fills all well-wishers to the interest of religion with just fears as to the issue.

Nor was it any wonder that these pretences should take, (especially with persons of liberal education and parts, who only were capable of observing those faults which gave occasion for them), since the generality were prepared for, and inclined to such a *defection*, by a long continance under the external dispensation of the gospel, without any experience of its power, the prevalent love of lust, that makes men impatient of any thing that may

have

have the least tendency to restrain them from pursuing the gratification thereof; to which we may add the natural enmity of the mind of man against the mystery of the gospel.

There was another thing which at this time had no small influence,—the philosophical writings of Mr. Hobbs, Spinoza, and some others of the same kidney, got, one way or other, a great vogue amongst our young gentry and students, whereby many were poisoned with principles destructive of all true religion and morality.

By those and the like means, things are now come to that pass, that not a few have been bold to avow their apostacy from the Christian religion, not only in conversation, but in print. They disown the name of Christ, call themselves *deists*, and glory in that name. They have published many writings reflecting on the scriptures, and justifying themselves in rejecting them.

And we have just reason to suspect, that, besides those who do avow their principles, who are perhaps as numerous in these lands as any where else, there are many, who yet are ashamed to speak it out, who bear them good-will, and who want only a little time more to harden themselves against the *odium* that this way goes under, and a fair occasion of throwing off the mask, which they yet think meet to retain. Of this we have many indications.

Many have assumed an unaccountable boldness in treating things sacred and serious too freely in writing and conversation. They make bold to jest upon the scriptures, and upon every occasion to traverse them. When once men have gone this length, the veneration due to that blessed book is gone, and they are in a fair way to reject it.

Others have made great advances to this defection, by disseminating and entertaining reproaches against a standing ministry. It is known what contempt has been cast upon this order of men, whom God hath entrusted with the gospel dispensation, and who, by office, are obliged to maintain its honour. If this order of men fall under that general contempt, which some do their utmost to bring them to, religion cannot long maintain its station among us. When the principal means of the Lord's appointment are laid aside, or rendered useless, no other means will avail.

And hereon, further, there follows a neglect of attendance on the ministry of the word, which the Lord has appointed for

the

the edification of the church, and establishing people in the faith of the truth he has revealed to us therein. When this once begins to be neglected, men will soon turn sceptical and unconcerned about religion.

And further, it is very observable, that many are strengthened in this neglect, by principles calculated for this purpose; while the whole efficacy of preaching is made to depend, not on the *blessing* of Christ, whose institution it is, or the *influences* of his Spirit, which he has promised for setting it home on the hearers for their conviction, conversion, and edification, —but on the *abilities* and *address* of the preachers. It is natural to conclude, that it is better to stay at home and read some book, than to go to sermon, if the preacher is not of very uncommon abilities: Which is a principle avowed by many, and their practice suits their principles.

Besides, which is the true spring of the former, I am afraid *ignorance* of the nature of *revealed religion*, the design of its institutions, and all its principal concerns, is become more common than is usually observed, even amongst men of liberal education and the best quality. And hence many of them entertain notions inconsistent with their own religion, at first out of ignorance, and afterwards think themselves in honour engaged to defend them, although destructive to the religion they profess.

Add to all this, that *profanity* in practice has, like a deluge, overspread these lands. And where this once takes place, love to sin never fails to engage men to those principles, which may countenance them in the courses they love, and design to cleave to.

This seems plainly to be the state of matters with us at present. And we see but little appearance of any redress. The infection spreads, and many are daily carried off by it, both in England and Scotland. Though it must be owned that Scotland, as yet, is less tainted with that poison: But those of this nation have no reason to be secure, since many are infected, and more are in a forwardness to it than is commonly thought.

Having given this short, but I conceive, true account of the *rise* and *growth* of *deism*, it now remains that we consider, what these principles are which they maintain. The deists, although they are not perfectly *one* amongst themselves, yet do agree in two things: 1. They all reject *revealed religion*, and plainly maintain that all pretences to *revelation* are vain, cheat and imposture,

posture. 2. They all maintain that *natural religion* is sufficient to answer all the great ends of religion, and the only rule whereby all our religious practices are to be squared. The *first* of these assertions only tells what their religion *is not*, and expresses their opposition to all revelation, particularly to Christianity; which has been worthily defended and asserted against all their objections by many of late, and I shall not much insist in adding to what they have written to such excellent purpose. The *second* tells us what their religion *is*; and it is this we chiefly design in the following papers to debate with them. They have long been upon the *offensive* part, which is more easy; we design now to put them upon the *defensive*.

They who call themselves *deists*, although they thus far agree, yet are not all of one sort. I find them, by one of their own number, classed into two sorts, *mortal* and *immortal* *.

The *immortal* are they who maintain a *future state*. The *mortal*, they who *deny one*. It is with the *first* we are principally concerned; yet I shall in the subsequent chapter offer a few things with respect to the *mortal deists*. And in what I have to say of them I shall be very short; because I conceive, what has already been offered in the introduction, against this sort of men, might almost supersede any further discourse about them.

CHAP. II.

Mortal Deists who, and what Judgment to be made of them and their Sentiments.

THE *mortal deists*, who also are called *nominal deists*, denying a *future state*, are, in effect, *mere atheists*. This perhaps some may think a harsh judgment; but yet it is such as the deists themselves, who are on the other side, will allow.

One who owns himself a deist, thus expresses his mind,—
" We do believe, that there is an infinitely powerful, wise and
" good God, who superintends the actions of mankind, in or-
" der to retribute to every one according to their deserts: Nei-
" ther are we to boggle at this creed; for if we do not stick
                                                               " to

* Oracles of Reason, pag. 99.

"to it, we ruin the foundation of all human happiness, and are in effect no better than mere atheists *."

A further account of this sort of men we have given us by one, whom any may judge capable enough for it, who considers his way of writing, and the account he gives of himself. "I have observed some," says he, "who pretend themselves deists, that they are men of loose and sensual lives; and I make no wonder that they dislike the Christian doctrine of self-denial, and the severe threatenings against wilful sinners. You may be sure they will not allege this reason: But having read Spinoza and Hobbs, and being taught to laugh at the story of Balaam's ass, and Sampson's locks, they proceed to ridicule the reality of all miracles and revelation. I have conversed with several of this temper, but could never get any of them serious enough to debate the reality of religion,—but a witty jest, and t'other glass, puts an end to all further consideration †." These are mere sceptics and practical atheists, rather than real deists.

Now, it is to no purpose to debate with men of this temper. If they will listen to arguments, many have said enough, if not to convince them, (for I know it is not an easy matter to convince some men), yet to stop their mouths; and therefore I shall not offer any arguments,—only I shall lay down a few clear *principles*, and from them draw an *inference* or two, which will make it evident, what judgment we are to make of this sort of men.

The *principles* I take for incontrovertible are these which follow: 1. He deserves not the name of a *man* who acts not *rationally*; knowing what he does, and to what end. 2. No action which contributes not, at least in appearance, to *man's happiness* is worthy of him. 3. The happiness of a present life, which is all that these gentleman allow, consists in the enjoyment of things agreeable to *our nature*, and freedom from those that are noisome to it. 4. Man's nature is such, that *his felicity* depends not only on these things, which at present he has, or wants; but likewise on what is past, and what is future. A prospect of the one, and a reflection on the other, according as they are more or less agreeable, exceedingly increases his pleasure or pain. 5. The hopes of obtaining hereafter

---
* Letter to the Deists, pag. 125.
† Growth of Deism, pag. 5.

after *the good* we at prefent want, and of being freed from *evils* we fuffer by, mightily enhances the pleafure of what we poffefs, and allays the trouble that arifes from incumbent evils. 6. So ftrong is the defire every one finds in himfelf of a continuation in being, as cannot choofe but render the thoughts of *annihilation* very terrible and irkfome. 7. The practice of *virtue*, as it is the moft probable mean of attaining *future happinefs*, if any fuch ftate be, fo it is that which tends moft to perfect and advance man's nature; and fo muft give the moft folid and durable pleafure, even here in this life. 8. It is malicious to do what tends to the obftructing *another's happinefs*, when it cannot further *one's own*. Few men will queftion any of thefe, and if any do, it is not worth while to debate with him. Now from thefe we may fee,

1. It would contribute much to thofe gentlemen's *prefent felicity* to believe, (be it true or falfe) that there is a *future ftate of happinefs*, fince the hopes of immutable and endlefs blifs would be a notable antidote againft the uneafinefs of mind that arifes, not only from incumbent evils, but alfo from thofe we fear, and the inconftancy of our fhort-lived enjoyments.

2. The generality of mankind, efpecially where Chriftianity obtains, being already poffeffed of the profpect of *future happinefs*, which fupports them under prefent evils, arms them againft the troublefome reflections on paft troubles, and fears of the future; and moreover animates them in the practice of thefe actions whereby not only their own good, but that of the focieties wherein they live, is fignally promoted; all attempts to rob them of this hope are highly malicious, and import no lefs than a confpiracy aganft the happinefs of mankind, and the good of the fociety wherein they live: And therefore we may fay affuredly, that as thofe *mortal deifts* are much incommoded by their own opinion; fo their attempts for its propagation, muft be looked on as proceeding from no good defign to the reft of mankind.

Here perhaps fome of them may fay, that this opinion tends to liberate a great part of mankind from the difquieting fears of *future mifery*.

To this I anfwer, 1. I believe it true, that their fears of *future mifery* are uneafy to them; or they have but little hope of *future felicity*. Their way of living allows them none. But thefe fears proceed from confcience of guilt, and are the genuine refult of actions, equally deftructive to the actors, and the intereft of the reft of mankind. 2. Thefe fears have their ufe, and

and ferve to deter from fuch evils as are ruining to the perfons who commit them, and to human fociety. 3. While this opinion liberates a few of the worft of men, from thefe fears, which are a part of the juft punifhment of their villanies, and emboldens them to run on in thofe evils which ruin themfelves and others, it difpirits and difcourages the only ufeful part of mankind, by filling them with difmal thoughts of *annihilation*. 4. Nor can all that the deifts are able to do, liberate themfelves or mankind from thofe fears. The utmoft that they can pretend, with any fhew of reafon, is, that we have not ground to believe fuch a ftate. Will this make us fure that there is none? But of this we have faid enough in the introduction.

By what has been faid it is evident, what judgment we are to make of this fort of deifts. Their lives, writings and death, fhew them to be mere atheifts.

Vaninus, when firft he appeared and wrote his *Amphitheatrum Providentiæ Divinæ*, fet out for fuch an one that *believed a God*. But at length fpoke out plainly that *he believed none*, and was defervedly burnt for *atheifm* at Thouloufe, April 9, 1619. He confeffed there were twelve of them that parted in in company from Naples to teach their doctrine in all the provinces of Europe *.

Uriel Accofta wrote for this opinion, as himfelf tel's us in his *Examplar Vitæ Humanæ*, which is fubjoined to *Limburg's* conference with *Urobius* the Jew †. His laft action tells us what man he was. After he had made a vain attempt to fhoot his brother, he difcharged a piftol into his own breaft. This fell out about the twentieth or thirtieth year of the laft century. *So they live, and fo they die.*

Were this our defign, or if we faw any need of it, we might give fuch an account of the principles, practices, and tragical exits of not a few of this fort of perfons, as would be fufficient to deter the fober from following them. But what has been faid is fufficient to difcover the deftructive tendency of their *prime opinion*. And further we fhall not concern ourfelves with them, but go on to that which is mainly intended in this difcourfe.

CHAP.

---

* See Great Geographical Dictionary.
† Limburgi Præfatio & Refpons. Urielis Accoftæ Libro.

CHAP. III.

Wherein the Controversy betwixt us and the Immortal Deists is stated and cleared.

THE *immortal deists*, who own a *future state*, are the only persons with whom it is worth while to dispute this point about the *sufficiency of natural religion*. Before we offer any arguments on this head, it is necessary we state the question clearly; and it is the more necessary, that none of the deists have had the courage or honesty to do it. And here in the entry we shall lay down some things, which we think are not to be controverted on this occasion. And we shall, after these concessions are made, inquire what still remains in debate.

1. We look on it as certain, that all the world, in all ages, hath been possessed of some notion of a GOD, of some *power* above them, on whom, in more or less, they did depend; and to whom on this account, some respect is due. This Heathens have observed. *Cicero*, amongst others, hath long since told us, "That there is no nation so barbarous that owns not some god, that has not some anticipations or impressions from nature, of a God*." Nor is this any more, than what we are told, Rom. i. 19, 20, &c. that the Gentiles have some notions of *truth* concerning God, which they *hold in unrighteousness*; that God, partly by erecting a tribunal in their own breasts, which they cannot decline, though they never so much would, and partly by presenting to their eyes those visible works that bear a lively impress of his *invisible power* and *Godhead*, hath, as it were, forced upon them *the knowledge* of some part of that, which the apostle calls γνωϛὸν τȣ̃ Θεȣ̃, or *that which may be known of God*. Whence they all in some measure *knew God*, though they *glorified him not as God*.

The stories some have told us of nations that have no notion of a God, upon search are found false. And for some lewd persons, who have pretended to a settled persuasion, they are not to be credited. We have sufficient reason to look on them as liars, or at least, not admit them witnesses in this case.

2. I do think that the knowledge of some of the more obvious laws of nature, and their obligation, hath universally obtained.

---

* Cicero de Natura Deorum, Lib. 1.

tained *. The Gentiles, all of them, *do by nature those things, that is, the material part of those duties, which the law of nature enjoins, which shews the work of the law,* or some part of it at least, *to be written in their hearts,* since they do some things it enjoins. I do not think that this *writing of the law* imports *innate ideas,* or *innate actual knowledge,* which Mr. Lock hath been at so much pains to disprove †, with what success I inquire not now. Some think, that while he grants the self-evidence of a *natural propensity of our thoughts* toward some notions, which others call *innate,* he grants all that the more judicious intend by that expression. Others think that Mr. Lock's arguments conclude only the improbability of *innate ideas,* and that they are to be rejected, rather for want of evidence for them, than for the strength of what is said against them ‡. But whatever there is as to this, neither the apostle's scope nor words oblige us to maintain them. What is intended may be reduced to two assertions, viz. That men are born with such faculties, which cannot, after they are capable of exercising them, but admit the obligation and binding force of some, at least, of the laws of nature, when they are fairly offered to their thoughts; and, That man is so stated, that he cannot miss occasions of thinking of, or coming to the knowledge of those laws of nature. " Homines nasci cognitione
" aliqua Dei instructos, haud dicimus: Nullam omnino ha-
" bent, sed vi cognoscendi dicimus; neque ita naturaliter cog-
" noscunt atque sentiunt, insitam potentiam Deum cognos-
" cendi, ad cultum ejus aliquo modo præstandum, stimulantem,
" sponte se in adultis rationis compotibus, non minus certo &
" necessario quam ipsum ratiocinari, exerturam, unumquemque
" retinere, ratio nulla est cur opinemur cum sentiamus," says the learned Dr. Owen §.

3. It

---

* I inquire not whether they were acquainted with the proper and true grounds of the obligation of those laws they owned obligatory.
† Lock's Essay on Human Understanding, Book 1. Ch. 4. § 11.
‡ Becconsall of Nat. Relig. Ch. 6. § 1, 2.
§ Theologumen. Lib. 1. Cap. 5. Par. 2.—" We do not say that
" men are born with any actual knowledge of God, as they have
" no knowledge at all when they are born; but we say that they are
" born with a capacity of knowing him, and that they do not so natural-
" ly know as they feel this implanted capacity of knowing God, which
" stirs them up to worship him in some manner. And that this capa-

3. It is unquestionable, and has been sufficiently attested by the nations, and even by some of the worst of them, that man has a *conscience*, that sometimes drags the greatest and most obstinate offenders to its tribunal, in their own breasts, accuses them, condemns them, and in some sort executes the sentence against them, for their counteracting known duty, how little soever they know. A Heathen poet could say,

——*Prima est hæc ultio, quod se
Judice, nemo nocens absolvitur, improba quamvis
Gratia fallacis prætoris vicerit urnam* *.

4. We own that those laws of nature, which are of absolute necessity to the support of government and order in the world, and the maintenance of human society, are, in a good measure, knowable by the light of nature, and have been generally known.

5. We willingly admit that, what by tradition, and what by the improvement of nature's light, many of the wiser Heathens have come to know, and express many things excellently, as to the nature of God, man's duty, the corruption of nature, a future state, &c. and some of them have lived nearer up to the knowledge that they had than others: For which they are highly to be commended, and I do not grudge them their praise.

6. I look on it as certain, that the light of nature, had it been duly improven, might have carried them in these things, and others of the like nature, further than ever any went.

But after all these things are granted, the question concerning the *sufficiency of natural religion*, remains untouched.

For clearing this, it is further to be observed, that, when we speak of the sufficiency of natural religion, or those notices of God, and the way of worshipping him, which are attainable by the mere light of nature, without revelation, we consider it as a *mean* in order to some *end*. For by *sufficiency* is meant, that *aptitude* of a *mean* for compassing some *end*, that infers a necessary connection betwixt the *due use*, that is, such

" city will no less naturally and spontaneously exert itself in all adults
" that are possessed of reason, than that of reasoning itself, there is
" no reason why we should deliver as an opinion, as we feel it to be
" the case."

* " This is the first part of the punishment, that every guilty per-
" son is condemned by himself, although wicked interest should have
" overcome the integrity of his judge."

such an use of the mean, as the person to whom it is said to be *sufficient*, is capable to make of it, and the *attainment of the end*.

Now natural religion, under this confideration, may be afferted fufficient or not, according as it is looked at with refpect to one end, or another: For it is ufeful to feveral purpofes, and has a refpect to feveral ends.

1. It may be confidered with refpect to *human fociety*, upon which religion has a confiderable influence. " There could " never poffibly be any government fettled amongft atheifts, " or thofe who pay no refpect to a Deity. Remove God once " out of heaven, and there will never be any god's upon earth. " If man's nature had not fomething of fubjection in it to a " Supreme Being above him, and inherent principles obliging " him how to behave himfelf toward God, and toward the reft " of the world, government could have never been introduced, " nor thought of. Nor can there be the leaft mutual fecurity " between governors and governed, where no God is admitted. " For it is an acknowledging of GOD, in his fupreme judg- " ment over the world, that is the ground of an oath; and up- " on which the validity of all human engagements do depend," fays an excellent perfon [*]. And the famed Cicero expreffes himfelf very fully to the fame purpofe. Speaking of religion and piety, he fays,—*Quibus fublatis, perturbatio vitæ fequitur, & magna confufio, atque haud fcio, an pietate adverfus Deos fublata, fides etiam, & focietas humani generis, & una excellentiffima virtus, juftitia tollatur* [†]. If the queftion concerned this end, we might own natural religion fome way fufficient to be a foundation for human fociety, and fome order and government in the world: For it is in fact evident, that where revelation has been wanting, there have been feveral well formed governments. Though ftill it muft be faid, that they were obliged to *tradition* for many things that were of ufe, and to have recourfe to *pretended revelation*, where the *real* was wanting [‡].

Which

---

[*] See Ch. Wolfeley's Unreaf. of Atheifm, pag. 152, &c.

[†] De Natura Deorum, Lib. 1. mihi. pag. 5. "—Which being " taken away, a great diforder and confufion in life muft follow; and " I know not whether, after piety to the Gods is taken away, truth and " the focial affections, and juftice, the moft excellent of the virtues, " would not at the fame time be taken away."

[‡] See Amyrald on Relig. Part 2. Cap. 8.

Which shews revelation necessary, if not to the *being*, yet to the *well-being* of society.

2. Natural religion may be considered in its subserviency to God's *moral government* of the world; and with respect to this, it has several considerable uses, that I cannot enter upon the detail of. It is the measure of God's judicial proceedings, with respect to those of mankind who want revelation; and as to this, there is one thing that is usually observed, *that it is sufficient to justify God in punishing sinners*. That God sometimes, even here in time, punishes offenders, and, by the forebodings of their consciences, gives them dreadful presages of a progress in his severity against them, after this life, cannot well be denied. Now certainly there must be some *measure*, whereby God proceeds in this matter. Where there is no *law*, there is no *transgression*. Punishments cannot be inflicted, but for the transgression, and according to the tenor of a *law*. And this law, if it is *holy*, *just*, and *good* in its *precepts*, and *equal* in its *sanction*, is not only the *measure* whereby the governor proceeds in punishing offenders; but that which justifies him in the punishment of them. It is needless to speak of the grant of *rewards* in this case; because with respect to them, not only *justice*, but *grace* and *bounty* have place, which are not restricted to any such nice measures in the dispensation of favours, as *justice* is in the execution of punishments. Now if natural religion is considered with respect to this end, we say it is *sufficient* to justify God, and fully clear him from any imputation of injustice or cruelty, whatever punishments he may, either in time or after time, inflict upon mankind who want revelation. There are none of them come to age, who— 1. Have not fallen short of knowing many duties, which they might have known. 2. Who have not omitted many duties, which they knew themselves obliged to. And 3. Who have not done what they knew they ought not to have done, and might have forborn. If these three are made out, as no doubt they may be against all men, I do not see what reason any will have to implead God either of hardship or injustice.

There are I know, who think it very hard, that those natural notices of God and religion should be *sufficient* to justify God in adjudging those, who counteract them, to *future* and *eternal punishments*, while yet such an attendance to, and compliance with them as men are capable of, in their present circumstances, is not *sufficient* to entitle us to *eternal rewards*.

But

But if, in this matter, any injuſtice is charged upon God, who ſhall manage the plea? Shall they who tranſgreſs and contraveen thoſe notices do it? But what injuſtice meet they with, if they are condemned for not knowing what they might have known? not doing what they were obliged to do, and were able to do? and for doing what they might and ſhould have forborn? If all theſe may be laid to their charge, though there were no more, what have they to ſay for themſelves, or againſt God? They ſurely have no reaſon to complain. If any have reaſon to complain, it muſt be they who have walked up to the natural notices of God. But where is there any ſuch? We may ſpare our vindication till ſuch an one be found. Nor is it eaſy to prove that man's obedience though perfect, muſt neceſſarily entitle to eternal felicity. And he who ſhall undertake to implead God of injuſtice upon the account of ſuch a ſentence, as that we now ſpeak of, will not find it eaſy to make good his charge.

Were the difficulty thus moulded, That it is hard to pretend that theſe natural notices of God are ſufficient to juſtify God in condemning the tranſgreſſors of them to future puniſhments, while punctual complance with them is not ſufficient to ſave thoſe, who yield this obedience, from thoſe puniſhments, which the contraveeners are liable to for their tranſgreſſion,—though it were thus moulded, it would be a hard taſk to make good ſuch a charge. But I am not concerned in it; nor are any, who judge the perſons, who have gone fartheſt in this compliance, liable upon other accounts; becauſe they ſtill own their compliance ſo far available to them, as to ſave them from thoſe degrees of wrath, which deeper guilt would have inferred.

3. Other ends there are, with reſpect to which natural religion may be conſidered, which I ſhall paſs without naming, and ſhall only make mention of that which we are concerned in, and is aimed at in the preſent controverſy, and that is, the *future happineſs of man in the enjoyment of God*. This certainly is the *ſupreme* and *ultimate end* of *religion* with reſpect to *man himſelf*. For that the *Glory of God* is the *chief end abſolutely*, and muſt, in all reſpect, have the preference, I place beyond debate.

Now it is as to this end, that the queſtion about the ſufficiency of natural religion is principally moved. And the queſtion, in ſhort, amounts to this, Whether the notices of God and religion, which all men by the light of nature have, or at leaſt by the mere improvement of their natural abilities without revelation, may have, are ſufficient to direct them in the way to
eternal

eternal blessedness, satisfy them that such a state is attainable, and point out the way how it is to be attained; and whether by that practical compliance with those notices, which man in his present state is capable of, he may certainly attain to acceptance with God, please him, and obtain this eternal happiness in the enjoyment of him? The deists are for the affirmative, as we shall afterwards make appear, when we consider their opinions more particularly.

But before we proceed to offer arguments, it will be needful to branch this question into several particulars that are included in it, that we may the better conceive of, and take up the import of it, and how much is included and wrapt up in this assertion. The question which we have proposed in general, may be turned into these five subordinate queries:

1. Whether, by the mere light of nature, we can discover an eternal state of happiness, and know that this is attainable? Unless this is done, nothing in matters of religion is done. It is impossible that nature's light can give any directions as to the means of attaining future happiness, if it cannot satisfy us that there is such a state.

2. Whether men, left to the conduct of the mere light of nature, can certainly discover and find out the way of attaining it? that is, Whether, by the light of nature, we can know and find out all that is required of us, in the way of duty, in order to our eternal felicity? If the affirmative is chosen, it must be made appear by nature's light, what duties are absolutely necessary to this purpose; that those which are prescribed are indeed duties; and that they are all that are necessary in order to the attainment of the end, if they are complied withal. Although we should have it never so clearly made out, that there is a future state of happiness, yet if we are left at an utter loss as to the means of attaining it, we are no better for the discovery.

3. Whether nature's light gives such a full and certain discovery of both these as the case seems to require? Considering what a case man at present is in, to hope for an eternity of happiness, is to look very high: And any man, who in his present circumstances, shall entertain such an expectation, on mere surmises, suspicions and may-be's, may be reproached by the world, and his own heart, as a fool. To keep a man up in the steady impression, and expectation of so great things, conjectures, suppositions, probabilities, and confused general hints, are

PRINCIPLES OF THE MODERN DEISTS.

are not sufficient. Again, there are huge difficulties to be surmounted in the way to this blessedness, which are obvious and certain. Sensible losses are sometimes to be sustained, sensible pains to be undergone, and sensible dangers to be looked in the face. Now the question is, Whether is there such a clear and certain knowledge of these attainable, as the importance of the case, the stress that is to be laid on them, and the dangers that are to be encountered for them, requires? Certain it is, it will not be such notices as most please themselves with, that will be able to answer this end.

4. Whether the evidence of the attainableness of a future state of happiness, and of the way to it, is such as suits the capacities of all concerned? Every man has a concernment in this matter. The deists inquire after a religion that is able to save all, whereof every man, if he but please, may have the eternal advantage. Now then the question is, Whether the case is so stated, as that every man, who is in earnest, if he has but the use of reason, however shallow his capacity is, how great soever his inevitable entanglements and hinderances from close application are, may attain to this certainty about this end, and the way to it? For it must be allowed that there is a vast difference among men as to capacity. Men are no more of one measure in point of intellectual abilities, than in stature. That may be out of the reach of one, which another may easily attain to. Now, may as much be certainly known by the meanest capacity as is necessary for him to know? Again, all men have not alike leisure. That may be impossible to me, if I am a poor man, obliged to work hard to earn my own and family's bread, which would not be so if I had leisure and opportunity to follow my studies. Now, if these discoveries, both as to their truth, certainty and suitableness, are not such as the meanest, notwithstanding any inevitable hinderances he may be under, may reach, they will not answer the end.

5. Whether, supposing all the former, every man, however surrounded with temptations, and inveigled with corrupt inclinations, or other hinderances, which he cannot evite, is yet able, without any supply of supernatural strength, to comply so far with all those duties, as is absolutely needful in order to obtain this eternal happiness? Whatever our knowledge is, we are not the better for it, unless we are able to yield a practical compliance.

The deists have the affirmative of all these questions to make good.

good. How they acquit themselves in this, we shall see afterwards. The task, as any one may see, is sufficiently difficult. And I do not know, that any one of them who has yet wrote, hath given any evidence that they understood the state of the question in its full extent. They huddle it up in the dark, that the weakness of their proof may not appear. And perhaps they are not willing to apply their thoughts so closely to the subject, as is requisite, in order to take up the true state of the controversy.

The more remiss and careless they have been this way, we had so much the more to do to state the question truly betwixt us and them. And having done this, we shall next proceed to make good our part of it.

A *negative* is not easily proven, which puts us at some loss. It has been denied that it can in some cases be proven. But we hope, in this case, we are able to offer such reasons as will justify us in holding the *negative* in this debate. And we shall see next whether they are able to demonstrate the *affirmative*, and offer as good reasons for it, as we shall give against it. And it is but reasonable they should offer better, in a matter of so great concern.

CHAP. IV.

Proving the Insufficiency of Natural Religion, from the Insufficiency of its Discoveries of a Deity.

THOUGH it belongs to the asserters of the *sufficiency of natural religion*, to justify by argument their assertion, and we who are upon the *negative*, might supersede any further debate until such time, as we see how they can acquit themselves here; yet truth, not triumph, being the design of our engaging in the contest, that none may think we are without reason in our denial, and that we put them upon the proof, only to difficult them, we shall now by some arguments endeavour to evince the *insufficiency* of *natural religion*.

The first argument I shall improve to this purpose is deduced from the *insufficiency* of those *discoveries*, which the *light of nature* is able to make of God. Nothing is more plain than this, that religion is founded upon the *knowledge* of the *Deity*; and that our regard for him will be answerable to the knowledge
we

we have of him. That religion therefore which is defective here is lame with a witnefs: And if nature's light cannot afford fuch notices of the Deity, as are fufficient or neceffary to beget and maintain religion amongft men, then it can never with any rational man be allowed fufficient to direct men in religion.

Now, for clearing this argument, feveral things are to be difcourfed. And firft of all, it is requifite, that we ftate fuch a notion of religion in general, as may be allowed to pafs with all, who are, or can reafonably be fuppofed competent judges in fuch matters. Religion then, in general, may be juftly faid to import *that veneration, refpect or regard, which is due from the rational creature, in his whole courfe or life, to the fupreme fupereminently excellent Being, his Creator, Preferver,* LORD *or Governor and Benefactor.*

The *actions* of the rational creature, which may come under the notion of religion, are of two forts: Some of them do directly, properly and immediately import a regard or refpect to GOD as their *end*; which they are immediately and properly defigned to exprefs. Such acts are called *acts of worfhip*. And religion is more eminently thought to confift in thefe, and that not without reafon. Yea, by fome it is wholly, and againft all reafon, confined to them, and circumfcribed within thofe bounds. Again, there are other actions, which, though they have other more proper, direct and immediate ends, on account whereof they undergo various denominations, yet they alfo are, or may be, and certainly fhould be fubordinate to that, which, though it is not the proper, moft immediate, and diftinguifhing end of thefe actions, yet is the common and ultimate end, at which all a man's actions fhould be levelled. Now all the actions of a rational creature, which are of this laft fort, as referred to a Deity, and importing fomewhat of religion, may be termed acts of *moral obedience*. In fo far they are religious, and come within the compafs of our confideration, as they exprefs any refpect to God. And they exprefs and import regard to God, in as far as they quadrate with the moral law, which is the inftrument of God's moral government of the world; and therefore if they are right and agreeable to this rule, they may be termed acts of moral obedience, to diftinguifh them from thefe acts, which are folely and more ftrictly religious, and are called acts of worfhip.

But

But to speak somewhat more particularly of this regard that is due to God, it is as evident as any thing can, that it must be,

1. In its *formal nature* different from that respect, which we may allowably pay to any creature; that is, it must be given on accounts no way common to him with any of the creatures, but on account of those distinguishing excellencies, which are his incommunicable glory. None can reasonably deny this, since it must be allowed by all, that *religious respect* due to God, and *civil respect* due to creatures are different, and must be principally differenced by the grounds whereon the respect to the one or other is paid. Now the grounds whereon this homage is due unto the Deity, are, the supereminent, nay, infinite excellency of his nature and perfections, and his indisputably supreme, absolute and independent sovereignty over all his creatures, which stands eternally firm and unshaken, as being supported by that *supereminency of his excellency*, his *creation*, *preservation*, and *benefits*. Now none of these grounds are, in any degree, communicable to the creatures; and so to talk of a religious worship due to the creature, is to speak nonsense with a witness.

2. This veneration we give to God must be *intensively*, or as to degree, not only superior to that which we give to any creature, but even *supreme*. It is not enough, that we love God on accounts peculiar to him; but we must love him with a love superior to that which we give any creature, and *answerable* to those accounts, whereon we do love him. And the like may be said as to other instances. There is no need of insisting in the proof of this. Would our king be pleased, if we paid him no more respect than we do his servant? Is the distance betwixt God and the highest creature less considerable, than that which is betwixt a king and his meanest subject? Nay, is it not infinitely more? How can it then reasonably be expected that the same degree of respect we pay to the creatures, will find acceptance, or answer the duty we owe to the glorious and ever-blessed Lord God?

3. This veneration must be *extensively* superior to that paid to any of the creatures. Our regard to the Deity must not be confined to one sort of our actions, (those, for instance, which are religious in a *strict sense*, or more plainly, *acts of worship*); but it must run through every action of our life, inward and outward. Every action is a dependent of God's, and owes him homage.

homage. It is otherwife with men; for to one fort of men, we may owe refpect, in one fort of our actions, and owe them none in another. A child, in filial duties, owes his father *refpect*; as a fubject, he owes his governor *reverence*; and fo of other inftances of a like nature: But to no one creature is he, in *all refpects*, fubject, or obliged by every action to exprefs any regard. And the reafon is plain; he is fubject to none of them in all refpects wherein he is capable of acting. But, with refpect to God, the matter is quite otherwife: Whatever he has is from God, and to him he is in *all refpects* fubject, on him he every way depends. The power your father has over you, he derives from God, and it is God that binds the duties you are to pay your father on you; and therefore God is to be owned as *fupreme*, even in every act of duty that you perform to your father, your king, your neighbour, or yourfelf: for you are in all refpects *his*. While you are fubordinate on various accounts to others, yet ftill God is in every regard *fupreme* and *fovereign Lord* and *difpofer* of you and your actions, and therefore you owe him a regard, in every thing you think, fpeak or do. I think this plain enough.

I hope this account of the *nature of religion* in general, will not be found liable to any confiderable exceptions, it being no other than fuch as the firft view of the nature of the thing offers to any that ferioufly confiders it. And from this account it is evident, that religion is founded on the *knowledge of a Deity*. A *blind devotion* that is begot and maintained, either by profound ignorance of God, or confufed notions of him, anfwers neither man's nature, which is rational, and requires that he proceed in all his actions, efpecially thofe of moft moment, rationally, that is, with knowledge and willingnefs; nor will it obtain acceptance, as that which anfwers his duty, whereby he is obliged to ferve God with the beft and in the higheft way that his faculties admit him. The contrary fuppofition of Papifts is a fcandalous reproach to the *nature*, both of God and man; and an engine fuited only unto the felfifh defign of the villainous priefts, who, that they may have the conduct of men's fouls, and fo the management of their eftates, have endeavoured to hood-wink man, and make him brutifh, where he fhould be moft rational; and that they may have the *beft*, they make him prefent God with *the blind* and *the lame*, which his *foul abhors*.

This being, in general, clear, *that the knowledge of God is the foundation of all acceptable religion*, it is now proper to inquire re *what discoveries* of God are requisite to bring man to such religion, as has been above described, and to keep him up in practice of it. Now if we look seriously into this matter, I think we may lay down the following position, as clear beyond onal contradiction.

1. That *a particular knowledge of God is requisite to this purpose*, to beget and maintain this reverence for the Deity, which is undoubted due. It is not enough that we have some general ions, however extensive. To conceive of God in the general, that he is the best and greatest of beings, *optimus maximus*, is enough. The reason is obvious: we must have in every of actions, nay, in each particular action, that knowledge ich may influence and guide us to that respect, which is to him, in that sort of actions, or that particular one; but general notion having no more respect to one than another, I not do. It directs us no more in one than another, unless particulars that are comprehended under that general be examined to, and understood by the actor.

2. That *knowledge, which will answer the end, must be large and comprehensive.* This religion is not to be confined to one ticular sort of actions, but to run through all, and therefore re must be a knowledge, not merely of one or two pertions of the divine nature, but of all : not simply, as if God re to be comprehended, but of all those perfections and prerogatives of God, which require our regard in our particular ions, in so far as they are the ground of our veneration. for instance, to engage me to *trust* GOD, I must know his wer, his *care* and *knowledge*; to engage me to *pray* to him, must be persuaded of his *knowledge*, of his *willingness* and wer to assist me in the suit I put up; to engage me to *love* n, I must know the *amiableness* of his perfections; to engage to pay him *obedience*, I must know his *authority*, the *laws* has stamped it on, and that he has fixed a law to these particular actions, either more *general* or more *special*. Whence being evident, that different actions require different views God in order to their regulation ; and all a man's actions ing under rule, there must be a large and comprehensive iowledge of God to guide him in his whole course.

3. It being no less than an *universal religion* that is to be ught after, *the discoveries of God* wherein it must be founded, *ust be plain to the capacities of all mankind*; and that both to the *truth* of these discoveries and their *use*. It is certain
that

that all men are no more of the fame meafure of underftanding than they are in ftature. However important the difcovery is, if it is above my reach, it is all one to me as if it were not difcovered at all. To tell me of fuch a thing, but it is in the clouds, is to amufe and not to inftruct me. There may indeed, fuppofing an univerfal religion, be fomewhat of difference as to knowledge allowed, as to fome of the concernments of this religion, to perfons of more capacity and induftry, and who have more time; but it is calculated for the good of all mankind, the difcoveries muft be fuch, as all who are concerned may reach, as to all its effentials; for the meaneft have as much concernment in them as the greateft.

4. It is moft evident, that *thefe difcoveries* muft be *certain*, or come recommended by fuch evidence as may be *convincing and fatisfying to every mind*. Conjectural difcoveries, or furmifes of thefe things, built upon airy and fubtile fpeculations, are not firm enough to eftablifh fuch a perfuafion of truth in the foul, as may be able to influence this univerfal regard, over the belly of the ftrongeft inward bias and outward rubs.

5. *The evidence of thefe things muft be abiding*; fuch as may be able to keep up the foul in a conftant adherence to duty. It is not one day that man is to obey, but always; and therefore thefe difcoveries muft lie fo open to the mind at all times, as that the foul may by them be conftantly kept up in its adherence to duty. If from any external or internal caufe, there may arife fuch obftructions as may for one day keep man from thofe difcoveries, or the advantage of them; he may ruin, nay, muft ruin himfelf by failing in his duty; or at leaft, if he is not ruined, he is laid open to it.

6. Upon the whole it appears, that to found *natural religion*, or to introduce and maintain among men that regard which is due to the Deity, there is requifite fuch a *large, comprehenfive, certain, plain*, and *abiding difcovery*, as may have *fufficient force to influence to a compliance with his duty in all influences.*

Thus far matters feem to be carried on with fufficient evidence. We are now come to that which feems to be the *principal hinge*, whereon the whole controverfy, about the *fufficiency of natural religion*, turns; in fo far at leaft, as it is to be determined by this argument. Now this is, Whether nature's light can indeed afford fuch difcoveries of God, as are evinced to be neceffary for the fupport of religion? If it cannot, then it is found *infufficient*; if it can, then natural religion

gion is thus far acquitted from the charge laid against it. Now to attempt the decision of this question successfully, it is necessary that we state it right. It is not then the question, Whether *in nature* there is *sufficient objective light?* as the schools barbarously speak; that is, Whether in the works of creation and providence, which lie open to our view, or are the object of our contemplation, there are such prints of God, which, if they were all fully understood by us, are sufficient to this purpose? For the question is not concerning the works of God without us, but concerning us. The plain question is this, " Whether man can, from those works of God alone, without the help of revelation, obtain such a knowledge of God, as is sufficient to the purpose mentioned?"

Now the question being concerning *our power*, or rather the *extent* of *our power*, I know but four ways that can be thought upon to come to a point about it: Either,

1. By *divine revelation* we may be informed what *nature's light* unassisted can do. We would willingly put the matter on this issue: Our adversaries will not; so we shall leave it. Or,

2. Some apprehend that the way to decide this, is, to take our measures from the *nature of God*; and to inquire, When God was to make or did frame man, with what *powers* it was proper for him to endue him? or, with what *extent of power*, considering the infinite wisdom, goodness and power of the Creator? This way the deists would go. But, 1. It seems a little presumptuous for us to prescribe, or measure what was fit for God to do, by what appears to us fit to have been done. For when we have soared as high as we can, we must fall down again; for God's counsels are too deep for us, and if we should think this or that fit for God, yet he having a more full view of things, may think quite the contrary; and thus all that we can come to here in this way, is but a weak and presumptuous conjecture. 2. If in fact, what we think fit, or conjecture fit for God to have done, it be evident that God has not done; that he has given no such *power* or *extent of it*, as we judge necessary, our judgment is not only weakly founded, but plainly false; yea, and impious to boot: For if God has done otherwise, it is certain that the way which we prescribed was not best; nor can we hold by our own apprehension, whatever *shews* it is built on, without an implicit charge of folly against God. 3. Whatever we may pretend the wisdom of God requires to be done for, or given to man, if by no divine act

there

there is any evidence that he has fo done, though there be no proof of his having done the contrary, yet it weakens the evidence of all we can fay, if the thing is fuch in its nature, as would be known by experience, if exiftent; becaufe, in that cafe, the whole ftrefs of our argument leans upon a fuppofition that we are capable of judging of the wifdom of God, while it is certain, we have not all thofe circumftances under our view, which may make it really fit to act this way rather than that, or that way rather than this, which on the other hand he certainly has. This way then we cannot decide the cafe.

3. We may immediately perhaps judge of the *extent of man's ability* in this fort, by *a direct inquiry into the nature of the powers.* But this way is as uncertain as the former; for there is no agreement amongft the moft judicious about the *nature of thofe powers*, without endlefs controverfies. And all that are really judicious own fuch darknefs in this matter, that will not allow them to pretend themfelves capable to decide the queftion this way. It is little we know of the *nature*, or *powers*, or *actings* of fpirits : Nor do I believe that ever any perfon that underftands, will pretend to decide, the controverfy this way. Wherefore,

4. We muft, upon the whole, give over the bufinefs, or inquire into the extent of our ability by *experience*; and judge what man can do by what he has done. If not one has made fufficient difcoveries of God, it is rafh to fay that any one can by the *mere light of nature* make them : More efpecially it will appear fo, if we confider, that all mankind muft be pretended equally capable of thefe difcoveries, which concern their own practice. It is ftrange to pretend that all are capable of doing that which none has done. Further, thefe difcoveries are not of that fort that may be fufficient to anfwer their end, if one in one age fhall make fome fteps towards them, and another afterwards improve them : But it is neceffary that every one, in every age, and at every period of his life, have exact acquaintance with them, in fo far as is needful to regulate his practice in that period of his life. When I am in one ftation, I muft either fail in the refpect due to God, and fo lay myfelf open to *juftice*, or I muft know as much of God, as is requifite to influence a due regard in that ftation, or that part of my life that now runs; and therefore an univerfal defect as to thofe difcoveries muft inevitably overthrow the *pretended ability* of man to make thefe difcoveries, and confequently the *fufficiency of*

of nature's light to beget or maintain religion, which cannot be supported without them.

Now for clearing this matter, it is to be confidered, that what we are upon is a *negative*, and it belongs to thofe who affirm *man able to make fuch difcoveries of God*, to fhow by whom and where thefe difcoveries have been made, or to produce thofe *notices* of God that are built on the *mere light of nature*, that are *fufficient* to this purpofe. Now none of them dare pretend this has been done, or, at leaft, fhew who has done it, or make the attempt themfelves; and therefore we might take it as confeffed, that it is not to be done.

But if it is ftill pretended, that this has been done, though without telling us by whom, or pointing to thefe difcoveries where we may find them;

I anfwer, How fhall we know this? May we know it by the effects of it, in the lives of thofe, who either have had no other light fave that of *nature*, as it was with the philofophers of old before Chrift, or who own none other fave that of *nature*, as the deifts and others who rejected Chriftianity? Truly if we judge by this rule, we are fure the *negative* will be much confirmed? For it is plain that thofe notions of a God, which were entertained by the philofophers of old, influenced none of them *to glorify him as God*. The vulgar Heathens were void of any refpect to the *true God*; nay, by the whole of their practice bewrayed the profoundeft ignorance, and moft contemptuous difregard of him. The philofophers, not one of them excepted, whatever *notions* they had of a Deity, and whatever length fome of them went in *morality, upon other inducenents*, yet fhewed nothing like to that *peculiar, high and extenfive refpect to the one true God* which we now inquire after. We may bid a defiance to the deifts, to fhew us any thing like it in the practice even of a Socrates, a Plato, a Seneca, or any others of them. Their virtue was plainly built upon another bottom. It has been judicioufly obferved by one of late, that there was little notice taken of God in their *ethicks*; and I may add, as little regard in their *practice*. Nor are the lives of our deifts, or others fince, any better proof of the *fufficiency* of the *natural notices* of God, to beget and fupport a due veneration for him.

If the deifts decline this trial of the *fufficiency* of thofe *difcoveries* of a God, by their influence upon *practice*, then we muft look at them in themfelves. And here we muft have recourfe, either to thofe who had no acquaintance with the *fcripture*

ture revelation; or to those who have given us accounts of God amongst ourselves; who though they own not the scriptures to be from God, yet have had access to them, for the improvement of their own notions about God. The last sort might be cast, as incompetent witnesses in this case, upon very relevant grounds. But we shall give our enemies all that they can desire, even as to the advantage they may have this way, that they may see our cause is not wanting in *evidence* and *certainty*.

We begin then with those who have been left to the *mere light of nature*, to spell out the letters of God's name, from the works of *creation* and *providence*, without any acquaintance with the more plain scripture account of God. Now what we have to say as to them, we shall comprize in a few observations.

1. As for the attainments of the *vulgar Heathens*, there is no place for judging of them otherwise than by their *practice*. They have consigned nothing to writing, and so we have no other way to guess at their opinions in matters of *religion*, but either by their *practice*, or by ascribing to them the principles of those, who in their respective countries, had the disposal of these matters. Whichsoever way we consider the matter, it must be owned that the vulgar Heathens were stupidly ignorant as to the truths of religion. If we make their *practice* the measure of judging, which in this case is necessary, none can hesitate about it. If we make the principles and knowledge of their leaders the standard, whereby we are to judge of their attainments, and make a suitable abatement, because scholars must always be supposed to know less than their masters, I am sure the matter will not be much mended, as the ensuing remarks will in part clear.

2. As to the philosophers, if I had time and opportunity to present in a *body* or *system* all that has been said, not by one of them, but by all the best of them put together, it would put any one that reads, to wonder, that they, "who were such giants," as an excellent person speaks, " in all other kinds of literature, " should prove such dwarfs in divinity, that they might go to " school to get a lesson from the most ignorant of Christians that " know any thing at all *." Any one that will but give himself the trouble to peruse their opinions about God, as they lie scattered in their writings, or even where they are proposed to more advantage by those, who have collected and put them together,

* See Char. Wolseley's Reasonableness of Scripture Belief.

gether, will soon be convinced of how low a stature their divinity was, and how justly the apostle Paul said, that by *their wisdom they knew not God*. All their knowledge of God was no more than plain and gross ignorance, of which the best of them were not ignorant, and therefore Thales, Solon, Socrates, and many others, spoke either nothing of God at all, or that which was next to nothing. And it had been well for others, if they had done so too; what they spoke, not only falling short of a sufficient account, but presenting most abominable and misshapen notions about God; of which we have a large account in *Cicero de Natura Deorum* *.

3. Besides that endless variety amongst different persons, in their opinions about a Deity, which is no mean evidence of their darkness, even the very same persons, who seem to give the best accounts, are wavering and uncertain, say and unsay, seem positive in one place, and immediately in the very next sentence seem to be uncertain and fluctuating. Thus it is with them all, and thus it usually is with persons who are but groping in the dark, and know not well how to extricate themselves.

4. They who go furthest, have never adventured to give any methodical account. They wanted materials for this; and therefore give but dark hints here and there. *Cicero*, who would make one expect such an account, while he inscribes his book *De Natura Deorum*, yet establishes scarce any thing; but spends his time in refuting the opinion of others, without daring to advance his own †.

5. They who have gone furthest, are too narrow in their accounts, they are manifestly defective in the most material things. They

---

* Cicero, Lib. 1. P. 4. *Qui vero Deos esse dixerunt, tanta sunt in varietate ac dissentione constituti, ut eorum molestum sit annumerare sententias. Nam de figuris Deorum & de locis atque sedibus & actione vitæ, multa dicuntur*, &c.—" But those who have affirmed that there are " Gods, have gone into so great a variety and difference of opinion, that " it is difficult to enumerate their sentiments, for many things are said " by them concerning the shapes of the Gods, their places, habitations, " and manner of life."

† De Natura Deorum, Lib. 2. *An, inquit, oblitus es quod initio dixerim, facilius me talibus de rebus, quod non sentirem quam quod sentirem dicere posse.*—" Have you forgot that I told you at the beginning, that " I could more easily tell what I did not think, than what I thought, " of these matters!"

PRINCIPLES OF THE MODERN DEISTS.

They are all reserved about the number of the Gods. It is true the best do own that there is one *Supreme*; but then there is scarce any of them positive that there are no more Gods save one. No not Socrates himself, who is supposed to die a martyr for this truth, durst own this plainly. And while this is undetermined, all religion is left loose and uncertain; and mankind cannot know how to distribute their regard to the several deities. Hence another defect arises, and that is about the *super-eminency* of the *divine excellencies*. Although the Supreme Being may be owned superior in order; yet the inferior deities being supposed more immediate in their influence, this will substract from the Supreme Deity much of his respect, and bestow it elsewhere. Moreover, about God's *creating power* their accounts are very uncertain, few of them owning it plainly. Nor are any of them plain enough about the *special providence* of God, without which it is impossible to support religion in the world.

6. As their accounts are too narrow, so in what they do own they are too general. But will this maintain religion? No, by no means. But there must be a particular discovery of these things. Well, do they afford this? Nay, so far are they from explaining themselves to any purpose here, that industriously they keep in dark generals. The *divine excellencies*, unless it be a few negative ones, they do seldom attempt any explication of. His *providence* they dare not attempt any particular account of. The extent of it to all particular actions is denied by many of their schools, owned distinctly by few, if any; but particularly cleared up by none of them*. The *laws* whereby he rules men are no where declared. When some of them are insisted on in their *ethicks*, the authority of God in them, which is the only supreme ground of obedience, and that which alone can lay any foundation for our acceptance in that obedience at God's hand, is no where taken notice of. The *holiness* of the divine nature, which is the great restraint from sin, is little noticed, except where some of the more abominable evils are spoke of. The *goodness*

---

* ——*Doctrinam de providentia rerum particularisive gratia a veteribus (quatenus ex eorum libris qui extant, collegi potest) remissius credi observamus*: Herbert de Veritate, pag. 271, 272.—" We observe that " the doctrine of universal providence and particular grace was but " faintly believed by the ancients, so far as can be collected from " their books."

goodnefs of God as a *rewarder*, is not by any of them cleared up. And yet upon thefe things the whole of religion hangs, which by them are either wholly paffed over, or mentioned in generals, or darkened by explications that give no light to the generals; at leaft, and for moft part, are fo far from explaining, that they obfcure, nay corrupt them, by blending pernicious falfhoods with the moft valuable truths.

7. The difcoveries they offer are not for the moft part proven, but merely afferted. Their notions are moft of them learned from tradition, and they were, it would feem, at a lofs about arguments to fupport them. Where the greateft certainty is required, leaft is found.

8. Where they do produce arguments, as they do fometimes, for the being and providence of God in general, they are too dark and nice, both in matter and manner, to be of any ufe to the generality of mankind.

To have produced particular inftances for the juftification of each of thefe obfervations, would have been too tedious. Any one that would defire to be fatisfied about them, may be fully furnifhed with inftances, if he will give himfelf the trouble to perufe *Cicero de Natura Deorum, Diogenes Laertius's Lives of the Philofophers*, or *Stanley's Lives*; but efpecially the writings of the feveral philofophers themfelves concerning this fubject. Nor will this tafk be very tedious, if he is but directed to the places where they treat of God: For they infift not long on this fubject, and the better and wifer fort of them are moft fparing.

When I review thefe obfervations, which occurred by my reading the works of the Heathens, and their opinions concerning God, I could not but admire the grofs inadvertancy, to give it no worfe word, of the deifts, (and more efpecially of the late lord Herbert, who was a man of learning and application) who pretend that the knowledge of thofe general attributes of God, his greatnefs and goodnefs, vulgarly expreffed by *Optimus Maximus*, are fufficient: Since it is plain from what has been faid, 1. That *this general knowledge* is of no fignificancy to influence fuch a peculiar, high and extenfive, practical regard to the Deity, as the notion of religion neceffarily imports. Of which even Blount was, it feems, aware, when he confeffes in his *Religio Laici*, that there is a neceffity that his articles muft be well explained. 2. It is plain that the philofophers, and confequently the common people, did not underftand well the meaning of thofe articles,

cles, or of thofe general notions concerning God, at leaft, in any degree anfwerable to the *end* we now have in view.

I dare fubmit thefe obfervations, as to their truth, to any impartial perfon, who will be at pains to try them, upon the granting of a twofold reafonable demand. 1. That he will confult either the authors themfelves, or thofe, who cannot be fufpected of any bias, by their being Chriftians, which I hope deifts will think juft; fuch as Cicero, Diogenes Laertius, &c. or thofe who have made large collections, not merely of their *general fentences* concerning God; but of their explications. In which fort Stanley excels. 2. I require that, in reading the authors, that they do not lay hold on a *general affertion*, and fo run away, without confidering the whole of what the authors fpeak on that head. The reafons why I make thefe demands, are, firft, fome perfons defigning, for one end or other, to illuftrate points in Chriftianity with quotations from Heathen authors, take up *general expreffions*, which feem congruous with, or may be the fame, which the fcripture ufes, without confidering how far they differ, when they both defcend to a particular explication of thofe general words. Again, fome Chriftians, writing the lives of philofophers, and collecting their opinions, are milled by favour to fome particular perfons, of whom they have conceived a *vaft idea*, and therefore either fupprefs or wreft what may detract from the perfon they defign to magnify. M. Dacier, for inftance, has written the life of Plato: but that account is the iffue of a peculiar favour for that philofopher's notions in general; and it is evidently the aim of the writer to reconcile his fentiments to the *Chriftian religion*. A work that fome others have attempted before. To this purpofe Plato's words are wrefted, and fuch conftructions put on them, as can no other way be juftified, but by fuppofing that no material points of the Chriftian religion could be hid from Plato, or his mafter Socrates. And yet after all, Plato's grofs miftakes, and that in matters of the higheft import; yea, and fuch of them, as are fuppofed, generally, to lie within the reach of nature's light, are fo obvious and difcernible, that the evidence of the thing extorts an acknowledgment. To give but one inftance; after the writer has made a great deal ado about Plato's knowledge of the *Trinity**, a ftory which hath been oft told, but never yet proven, it is plainly acknowledged, that he fpeaks of the *Three Perfons*
of

---

* M. Dacier's Life of Plato, pag. 141.

of the *Deity* as of *three Gods*, and *three different principles*; which is, in plain terms, to throw down all that was built before, and prove that Plato knew neither the *Trinity*, nor the *one true God*. Finally, general fentences occur in thofe authors, which feem to import much more knowledge of God, than a further fearch into their writings will allow us to believe they had: For any one will quickly fee, that in thofe general expreſſions, they fpoke as children that underſtood not what they fay, or at leaſt, have but a very imperfect notion of it. And though this may feem a fevere reflection on thefe great men; yet I am fure none fhall impartially read them, who will not own it juſt.

But now, to return to our fubject, this *sufficient discovery* of God not being found amongſt thofe, who were ſtrangers to the fcrptures and Chriſtianity, let us next proceed to confider thofe, who have had accefs to the fcriptures, and lived fince the Chriſtian religion obtained in the world. And here it muſt be owned, that fince that time philofophers have much improven natural theology, and given a far better account of God, and demonſtrated many of his attributes from reafon, that were little known before, to the confufion of atheiſts. From the excellent performances of this kind, which are many, I defign not to detract. I am content that a due value be put on them: but ſtill I am for putting them only in their own place, and afcribing no more to them, than is really their due. Wherefore, notwithſtanding what has been now readily granted, I think I may confidently offer the few following remarks on them.

1. We might juſtly refufe them, as no proper meafure of the *ability* of *unaſſiſted reafon*, in as much as it cannot be denied, that *the light*, whereby thofe difcoveries have been made, was borrowed from the fcriptures: of which none needs any other proof than merely to confider the vaſt improvement of knowledge, as to thofe matters, immediately after the fpreading of Chriſtianity, which cannot, with any fhew of reafon, be otherwife accounted for, than by owning that this light was derived from the fcriptures, and the obfervation and writings of Chriſtians, which made even the Heathens afhamed of their former notions of God. But not to infiſt on this.

2. Who have made thofe improvements of natural theology? Not the Heathens or deiſts. It is little any of them have done this way. The accurate fyſtems of natural theology have come from Chriſtian philofophers, who do readily own that the fcripture

ture points them, not only to the notions of God they therein deliver, but alfo to many of the *proofs* likewife, and that their reafon, if not thus affifted, would have failed them as much, as that of the old philofophers did them.

3. It is worthy our obfervation, that fuch of the Chrftians, who favour the deifts moft, fuch as the Socinians and fome others, do give moft lame and defective accounts of God. They who lean much to *reafon*, their reafon leads them into thofe miftakes about the *nature* and *knowledge* of God, which tend exceedingly to weaken the *practical influence* of the notion of a God. And we have reafon to believe that the deifts will be found to join with them, in their grofs notions of God, as ignorant of the *free actions* of men, before they are done, and as not fo particularly concerned about them in his *providence*, with many fuch-like notions, which fap the foundations of all practical regard to God.

4. But let the beft of *thefe fyftems* be condefcended on, they cannot be allowed to contain *fufficient difcoveries* of God. For it is evident beyond contradiction, that they are neither full enough in explaining what they in the general own, nor do they extend to fome of thofe things which are of moft neceffity and influence to fupport *practical religion*. They prove a *providence*, but cannot pretend to give any fuch account of it, as can either encourage or direct to any dependence on, truft in, or practical improvement of it. And the like might be made appear of other perfections. Again, they cannot pretend to any tolerable account of the remunerative bounty, the pardoning mercy and grace of God, on which the whole of religion, as things now ftand, entirely hangs. Can they open thefe things fo far as is neceffary to hold up religion in the world? They who know what religion is, and what they have done, or may do, will not fay it.

5. In their proofs of thefe truths, there muft be owned a *want of that evidence*, which is requifite to compofe the mind in the perfuafion of them, and eftablifh it againft objections. Let fcripture light be laid afide, which removes objections; and let a man have no more to confirm him of thofe truths fave thefe arguments, the difficulties daily occurring from obvious providences will jumble the obferver fo, that he will find thefe proofs fcarcely fufficient to keep him firm in his affent to the truths; and if fo, far lefs will they be able to influence his practice fuitably againft temptations to fin. Now this may arife, not fo much from the *real weaknefs* of the arguments, which

may

may be conclusive, as from this, that most of them are rather drawn *ab absurdo*, than from any clear light about the nature of the object known; and hence there comes not that light along, as to difficulties, which is necessary to remove them. And though these arguments silence in dispute, and close the adversary's mouth; yet they do not satisfy the mind. Moreover, some of no mean consideration, have pretended that many of these demonstrations, even as to some of the most considerable attributes of God, are inconclusive: Particularly they have asserted, that the *unity* of God was not to be proven by the *light of nature*, nor *special providence*. But not to carry the matter thus far, it is certain that the force of these demonstrations must lie very secret, that such persons, who owned the truths, and bore them good-will, yet could not find it.

Much more might be said on this head, but I am not willing to invalidate these arguments, or even to shew all that might, perhaps, not only be said, but made appear against them. But whatever there is as to this, it is certain that the discoveries of God by nature's light being small, are easily clouded, by entangling difficulties arising from the dark occurrences of providence, and the natural weakness and unstaidness of our minds, which are always to be found in matters sublime, and not attended with strong evidence. And attention in this case will increase the darkness, and force on such an acknowledgment as Simonides made to Hiero, the tyrant of Syracuse, That " the longer he thought about God, the more " difficulty he found to give any account of him."

6. They must, whatever be allowed as to their validity in themselves, be owned to be of no use to the generality, nay, to the far greater part of mankind. No man who knows them, and knows the world, will pretend that the one half of mankind is able to comprehend the force of them. And so they are still in the dark about God; which quite everts the whole story about the sufficiency of the natural discoveries of a Deity.

7. It is plain, that there is no serving God, walking with or worshipping of him, without thoughts, and serious ones too, of him. Now his nature and excellencies are infinite, how then shall we conceive of them? Our darkness and weakness will not allow us to think of him as he is, and conceive those perfections as they are *in him*. And to conceive otherwise is dangerous. We may mistake in other things without sin; but to frame wrong, and other conceptions of God and his excellecies, than the truth of
the

the thing requires, is dangerous and sinful; for it frames *an idol.* Now though this difficulty may be easy to less attentive minds; yet it will quite confound persons who are in earnest, and understand what they are doing, in their approaches to God. Nor can ever the minds of such be satisfied in our present state, otherwise than by God's telling us, how we are to conceive of him, and authorizing us to do it in a way of condescension to our present dark and infirm state.

8. I cannot forbear to notice, as what wants not its own weight in this case, though in condescension we did a little wave arguments drawn from the *practical influence of truths*, that however great the improvements, as to notions of truths concerning the nature of the Deity may of late have been, yet the *effects* of *these notices* in their highest improvement, have been far from recommending them, as *sufficient* to *the end* we have now in view. *This natural theology* has rather made men more *learned* than more *pious*. Where scripture *truth* has not been received in its *love* and *power*, men have seldom been bettered by their improvements in natural theology. But we see in experience, that they who can prove most and best in these matters, evidence least regard to the Deity in their practice.

I shall add one observation more, which at once enforces the argument we are upon, against *the sufficiency of natural religion*, and cuts off a pretended retortion of it, against the Christian religion; and it is this: The religion the deists plead for, and are obliged to maintain, is a religion that pleads acceptance on its own account, which has no provision against *guilt* and *escapes*, as shall be demonstrated hereafter; a religion which consequently must be *more perfect*, and so requires a *more exact knowledge* of the Deity in order to its support: whereas, the Christian religion is one which is calculated for man in his *fallen state;* and the *fall* is every where in it supposed, and a gracious provision made against *defects* in *knowledge,* and *unallowed practical escapes.*

CHAP. V.

Proving the Insufficiency of Natural Religion from its Defectiveness as to the Worship of GOD.

THE argument we are to improve against the *sufficiency of natural religion* in this chapter, might have been considered as a branch of the foregoing: But, that we may be more distinct, and to shew a regard unto the importance of the matter, we shall consider it as a distinct argument by itself.

Now therefore, when we are to speak of the *worship* of God, it is not of that inward veneration that consists in acts of the mind, such as esteem, fear, love, trust, and the like; but of the outward, stated, and solemn way of expressing this *inward veneration*. That there should not only be an inward regard to the Deity in our minds, influencing the whole of our outward deportment; but th t besides, there should be fixed, outward, and solemn ways of exercising and expressing these inward actings, seems evident beyond any reasonable exception,—

.1. From the general agreement of the world in this point. All the world has owned some worship necessary. Every nation and people had their peculiar way of worship[*]. It is true, most of them were ridiculous, many of them plainly wicked, and all of them vain; but this makes not against the thing in general; only it bespeaks the darkness of nature's light, as to the way of managing in particulars, that which in general it directs to.

2. The deists themselves own this much. Herbert in his treatise, *de Religione Gentilium,* confesses it a second branch of the generally received religion, for which he pleads, *that God is to be worshipped.* It is true, in his next, while he tells us that virtue and piety were owned to be the *principal means* of *worshipping* him, he would seem to preclude us from the benefit of the former acknowledgment. But yet he dares not assert, that this which he condescends on was the *only way,* and so pretend the worship we speak of *unnecessary*: But being to hold forth *the sufficiency of this natural religion,* he was loth to speak any more of that, which would lead him, if he had considered it, unto a discovery of its nakedness. But others of the deists do own the necessity of such a worship, and pretend prayer and praise sufficient to

this

---

[*] Herbert de Veritate, pag. 271, 272.

this purpofe, as he alfo doth in his other treatifes, particularly *de Veritate**.

3. The fame reafons which plead for inward acts, peculiarly directed to this end, plead for outward veneration likewife. If we have minds capable of this inward veneration, fo are we capable of outward expreffions; and are under the fame obligation to employ thofe latter forts of powers to the honour of God, that binds us to the former. Nor is there more reafon why, befides that tranfient regard we ought to pay him in all our actions, there fhould be inward acts peculiarly defigned to exprefs our inward veneration, than that there fhould be outward ftated acts, peculiarly defigned for the fame purpofe.

4. *The nature of fociety pleads loudly for this.* Mankind as united in focieties, whether leffer, as families, or greater, as other focieties, depend entirely on God; and therefore owe him reverence, and the expreffion of it in fome joint and fixed way. Public benefits require public acknowledgments: And this fort of dependence on, and fubjection to the Deity, fhould certainly have fuitable returns.

5. It is incontrollably evident, that many in the world do fhake off all regard to the Deity, and walk in an open defiance to him, and thofe laws which he has eftablifhed. Certainly therefore, it is the duty of fuch as keep firm, openly to teftify their dependence on and regard to the Deity, which is not fufficiently done by the performance of thofe things, which are materially according to the appointment of God. For what regard to God there is, influencing to thofe outward acts, cannot be clearly difcerned by on-lookers, who know not but fomewhat, befide any regard to the authority of the lawgiver, may be at the bottom of all. It is therefore neceffary that there be public, folemn actions, directly and plainly importing our avouchment of a regard to him, in oppofition to thefe affronts that are publicly offered to him.

6. *This worfhip* is neceffary in order to maintain and cherifh that *inward veneration*. It is well known, however much we are bound to it, yet the fenfe of this obligation, and that veneration

itfelf

---

* Herbert de Veritate, pag. 272. *Nos interea externum illum Dei cultum (fub aliqua religionis fpecie) ex omni feculo regione, gente evicimus.*— "In the mean time we have proved this external worfhip of God, un- "der fome appearance of religion, from every age, country, and na- "tion."

itself to which we are obliged, is not so deeply rivetted upon our minds, but it needs to be cherished, and the habits strengthened by actings. It is not so easy for men to do this by inward meditation, who for most part are little accustomed to this way, and can indeed scarce fix their minds in this inward exercise at all, especially if they have no fixed way of exercising it, but are left at liberty to choose their own way. Religion therefore must go out of the world, or, there must be stated and fixed ways of exercising it. This is easily justifiable from experience, which shews, that where once public worship is disregarded, any other sort of respect to the Deity quickly falls of its own accord.

7. *It is necessary for the benefit of human society.* The foundations of human society are laid upon the notion of a God, and the sacredness of oaths, and the fixed notions of right and wrong, which all stand and fall together. Nor is there any way of keeping that regard to those things, which are the props of human society, without such a worship of God, as that we plead for. This all the lawgivers were of old satisfied about, and took measures accordingly.

8. If religion has any *valuable end*, then certainly this must be one main part of it, to lead man to *future happiness*; which cannot, with any shew of reason, be alleged to consist in any thing besides *the enjoyment of* God. And it is plainly ridiculous to suppose, that mankind can be kept up in any fixed expectation of, or close pursuit after this, if not animated and encouraged by some, nay frequent experiences of commerce betwixt him and the Deity here. And it is foolish to pretend, that this is otherwise to be had, in any degree answerable to this end, in any other way than in the way of designed, fixed, solemn and stated worship.

Now this much being said in the *general* for clearing the necessity of such *a worship*, and the importance of it in *religion*; it remains that we prove *the light of nature insufficient* to direct us as to *the way* of it. And this we conceive may be easily made appear from the ensuing grounds.

1. The manifest mistakes all the world fell into, who were left in this matter to the conduct of the mere light of nature, abundantly evince the incompetency of nature's light for man's direction, with repect to the worship of God. Every nation had their own way of worship, and that stuffed with blasphemous, unworthy, ridiculous, ungrounded, impious and horrid rites and usages; of which there are innumerable accounts every where to be met with. We can no where in the Heathen world find any
worship

worship that is not manifestly unworthy of, and injurious to the glorious God. Surely *that light* that suffered the world to lose their way so evidently, must be sadly defective. Their worship was every where such, even where wise men were the instituters of it, that it could not satisfy any person who had any true notion of God: and was the scorn of the wise and discerning. Nor can it with any shew of reason be pleaded, that these defects and enormities are to be charged, not on the *defectiveness of nature's light*, but the *negligence* of those who did not use it to that advantage it might have been used; since it has been above proven, that the only way we can judge what nature's light can do, is by considering what it *has done* somewhere or other. And these enormities did every where obtain: they were not peculiar to some places; but wherever men were left to the mere light of nature, there they fell into them.

2. These ways of worship, viz. *prayer* and *praise*, which are condescended upon by the deists, and seem in general to have the countenance of reason; yet, as they are discovered by nature's light, can no way satisfy. Be it granted that nature's light directs to them in general, and binds them on us as duty; yet it must be allowed, that this is not enough; for the difficulty is, how we shall in *particular* manage them to the *glory of God*, and our *own advantage*. The duty is stated in the general, and when we begin to think of compliance with it, we find the light of nature, like the Egyptian task-masters, set us our work, and demand *brick*, while yet it allows us *no straw*. What endless difficulties are we cast in, about the matter of our prayers and praises? What things shall we pray to God, and praise him for? How shall we be furnished with such discoveries of the nature, excellencies, and works of God; and what things are proper for us, as may be sufficient to guide us in our prayers and praises, and keep us up in a close attendance on these duties in the whole tract of our lives, without wearying or fainting? Are we, because we know not what is good or ill for us, to hold in mere generals, as the best of the philosophers thought? If so, will the mind of man, for so long a tract of time, be able to continue in this general way, without nauseating? Or, shall we descend to particulars? If so, how shall materials be furnished to us for such particular addresses, who know so little of God's works, or our own wants? Again, who shall teach us the way and manner of praying and praising, which will be acceptable to God? Shall every one's fancy be the rule? If there be a

fixed

fixed rule, Which, and where is it? Again, What security have we from the mere light of nature, as to the success and acceptance of these duties? It will be to no advantage to except, that God requires of us no more than he has directed us in; for this is to beg the main question. Were it once granted, that no more is required than what nature's light directs to, there might be some countenance for this plea, that what it gives no directions in, will not be insisted upon by God; but this is plainly refused, and so the difficulties remain. Nor is it to more advantage to pretend, that the substance being agreed to, God will not insist upon circumstances of worship: for the difficulties objected respect not merely the circumstances, but the very substantial parts of these duties. As to what may be pretended of the *influence of the hopes of eternal life*, toward the keeping up men in an attendance on duties; as to the particular manner of the performance of which, and the grounds of acceptance, they are entirely in the dark. This plea shall be fully considered afterwards. And as it is obvious, that no general supposal of benefit can for any long tract of time keep men steady in the performance of actions, about the nature and acceptance of which they are in doubt; so, it shall be made appear there is no ground from the mere light of nature for any such hope of future felicity, as can relieve in this case.

3. The plain confession of the more thoughtful, wise and discerning of the Heathen world, plainly proves this[*]. The followers of the famed Confucious in China, though they own that there is one supreme God, yet profess themselves ignorant of the way in which he is to be worshipped, and therefore think it safer to abstain from worshipping, than err in the affirmation of improper honour to him. Plato in his second Alcibiades, which he inscribes " Of Prayer," makes it his business to prove, " That we know not how to manage prayer;" and therefore concludes it " safer to abstain altogether, than err in " the manner." Alcibiades is going to the temple to pray, Socrates meets him, dissuades him, and proves his inability to manage the duty, of which he is at length convinced; whereupon Socrates concludes, " You see, says he, that it is " not at all safe for you to go and pray in the temple—I am " therefore of the mind, that it is much better for you to be " silent.—And it is necessary you should wait for some person
" to

---

[*] Hornbeck de Conversione Gentilium, Lib. 5. Cap. 6. pag. 47.

"to teach you how you ought to behave yourſelves, both to-
"wards the gods and men. To which Alcibiades ſaid, And
"when will that time come, Socrates? And who is he that
"will inſtruct me? With what pleaſure ſhould I look on him?
"To which he replies, He will do it who takes a true care
"of you. But methinks, as we read in Homer, that Minerva
"diſſipated the miſt that covered Diomedes, and hindered him
"from diſtinguiſhing a God from a man; ſo it is neceſſary,
"that he ſhould in the firſt place ſcatter the darkneſs that co-
"vers your ſoul, and afterwards give you theſe remedies that
"that are neceſſary to put you in a condition of diſcerning
"good and evil ; for at preſent you know not how to make a
"difference. Alcibiades ſays, I think I muſt defer my ſacri-
"fice to that time. Socrates approves—You have reaſon, ſays
"he ; it is more ſafe ſo to do, than run ſo great a riſk *. The
"famed Epictetus was ſo much of the ſame mind, that he knew
"no way but to adviſe every one to follow the cuſtom of their
"country in worſhip †." Upon the ſame account Seneca rejects all this worſhip. And memorable is the confeſſion of Jamblichus, a Platonic philoſopher, who lived in the fourth century—" It is not eaſy to know what God will be pleaſed with,
"unleſs we be either immediately inſtructed by God ourſelves,
"or taught by ſome perſon whom God hath conversed with, or
"arrive at the knowledge of it by ſome divine means or other ‡."
Thus you ſee how much theſe great men were bemiſted in this
matter, and may eaſily conclude what the caſe of the reſt of
mankind was.

4. The very nature of the thing ſeems to plead againſt the *ſufficiency of reaſon* in this point: For it ſeems plainly to be founded on the cleareſt notions of nature's light, that the wor-
ſhip of God is to be regulated by the *will* and *pleaſure* of God; which, if he reveal not, how can we know it? Hence it was that the Heathens never pretended *reaſon*, but always *revelation* for their worſhip. The governors all of them did this. And Plato tells us, " That laws concerning divine matters muſt be
" had from the Delphick Oracles §".

Much

---

* We have the ſame account of Socrates and Xenophen; of which Stanley, pag. 75.
† Epictet. Enchirid. Cap. 38.
‡ Seneca Epiſ. 95. Jambl. de Vita Pythag. Cap. 28.
§ Plato de Legibus.

Much more might be said on this head, were it needful: but I am apprehensive this is a point that the deists will not be fond to dispute with us; not only because they are no great friends to *this worship,* but because they can say so little on this head, which has any shew of reason: of which their famed leader *Herbert* was sufficiently aware, when he tells us in his third article, *That virtue is the principal worship of God;* whereby he owns, that there is indeed another part of, which he dare not name, because he knows not what to say about it.

CHAP. VI.

Proving the Insufficiency of Natural Religion, from its Defectiveness as to the Discovery wherein Man's Happiness lies.

NEXT to the *glory of God,* the indisputably *supreme end* of man, and of the whole creation, of which I am not now to discourse, *the happiness of man,* is, past all peradventure, *his chief end.* Yea, perhaps, if we speak properly, except as abovesaid, it is his *only end.* For whatever man is capable of designing, is comprehended under this, being either what doth, or at least is judged to contain somewhat of *happiness* in it, or what is supposed to contribute to that wherein satisfaction is understood to consist. Every thing a man aims at, is either aimed at *as good* in itself, or contributing to *our good.* The first is a part of *our happiness*; the last is not in proper speech so designed, but the *good* to which it contributes, and that still is as before a part of *our happiness.* If religion is therefore any way useful or sufficient, it must be so with respect to this end. And since religion not only claims some regard from man, but pleads the preference to all other things, and demands his *chief concern,* and his being employed about it as the *main business* of his life, it must either contribute more toward this end, than any thing else, nay be able to lead man to this end, otherwise it deserves not that regard which it claims, and is indeed of little, if any use to mankind. If then we are able to evince that natural religion is not *sufficient* to lead man to that happiness, which all men seek, and is indeed the *chief end* of man, there will be no place left for the pretence of its sufficiency, in so far as it is the subject of this controversy betwixt the deists and us. And this we conceive

may

may be made appear many ways. But in this chapter we shall confine ourselves to one of them.

If nature's light is not able to give any tolerable discovery of that wherein man's happiness lies, and that it may by him be obtained, then surely it can never furnish him with a religion that is able to conduct him to it. This cannot with any shew of reason be denied. It remains therefore that I make appear, that *nature's light is not able to discover wherein man's happiness lies, and its attainableness.* Now this I think is fully made out by the following considerations:

1. They who, being left to the conduct of the mere light of nature, have sought after *that good* wherein man's happiness is to be had, could not come to any agreement or consistency among themselves. This is a point of the first importance, as being the hinge whereon the whole of a man's life must turn; the spring which must set man a going, and give life to all his actions, and to this they must all be directed. This, if any other thing ought to be easily known; and if nature's light is a sufficient guide, it must give evident discoveries of. But, methinks, here is a great sign of a want of this evidence; great men, learned men, wise philosophers and industrious searchers of truth have split upon this point, into an endless variety of opinions; insomuch that Varro pretends to reckon up no less than 288 different opinions. May I not now use the argument of one of the deists, in a case which he falsely supposes to be alike, and thus in his own words argue upon this point, (only putting in, *the discoveries of nature's light about happiness, or the evidence of those discoveries,* in place of the *evidence of the reasons of the Christian religion,* against which he argues): " If the " discoveries of it were evident, there could be no longer any " contention or difference about the chief good; all men " would embrace the same and acquiesce in it: no prejudice " would prevail against the certainty of such a good*." " It is " every man's greatest business here to labour for his happiness, " and consequently none would be backward to know it. And, " if all do not agree in it, those marks of truth in it are not visi- " ble, which are necessary to draw an assent†." But whatever there is in this, it is a most certain argument of darkness, that there is so great a difference, where the searchers are many, it

is

* Oracles of Reason, pag. 205.
† *Ibid,* pag. 201.

is every one's interest to find, and the business and search is plied with great application.

2. The greatest of the philosophers have been plainly mistaken in it. They espoused opinions in this matter, which are not capable of any tolerable defence. Solon, the Athenian lawgiver, defined them " happy who are competently furnished " with outward things, act honestly, and live temperately *." Socrates held, that there was but one *chief good*, which is *knowledge*, if we may believe Diogenes Laertius in his life Aristotle, if we may take the same author's words for it, places it in *virtue, health*, and *outward conveniency*, which no doubt was his opinion, since he approved Solon's definition of the *chief good* †; and herein he was followed by his numerous school. Pythagorus tells us, that the " knowledge of the per- " fections of the soul is the chief good." It is true, he seems at other times to speak somewhat differently; of which we may speak afterwards. Zeno tells us, that it lies in " living " according to nature." Cleanthes adds, that " according to " nature is according to virtue." Crysippus tells us, that it is " to live according to expert knowledge of things which hap- " pen naturally‡." It is needless to spend time in reckoning up innumerable others, who all run the same way, placing happiness in that which is not able to afford it, as being finite, of short continuance, fickle and uncertain. It is not my design to confute those several opinions. It is evident to any one, that they are all confined to time, and upon this very account fail of what can make us happy.

3. They who seem to come some nearer the matter, and talk sometimes of *conformity to God* being the *chief good*; that it is *our end* to be like God, and the like; as Pythagoras and some others §; but especially Plato, who goes further than any of the rest ‖; yet cannot justly be alleged to have made the discovery, because we have not any account of their opinions clearly delivered by themselves, but hints here and there gathered up from their writings, which are very far from satisfying us as to their mind. Besides they are so variable, and express themselves so differently, in different places, that it is hard to find their mind; nay I may add, they are, industriously and of design obscure. This Alcinous the Platonic philosopher, tells us plainly enough in his
Doctrine

---

* Stanley, pag. 26. Life of Solon, Cap. 9. † Stanley, pag. 540.
‡ *Ibid*, pag. 462. § *Ibid*, pag. 541. ‖ *Ibid*, p. 192. Cap. 8.

Doctrine of Plato, which is inferted at length in *Stanley's Lives*. He fays, " that he thought the difcovery of the *chief good* was not " eafy, and if it were found out, it was not fafe to be declared." And that for this reafon, he did communicate his thoughts about it but to very few, and thofe of his moft intimate acquaintance. Now the plain meaning of all this, in my opinion is, that he could not tell wherein man's *happinefs* confifts, or what *that* is which is able to afford it : or at moft, that though one way or other in his travels, by his ftudies or converfe, he had got fome notions about it; yet he did not fufficiently underftand them, and was not able to fatisfy himfelf or others about them, and that therefore, he either entirely fuppreffed, or would not plainly fpeak out his thoughts, leaft the world fhould fee his ignorance, and that though his words differed, yet in very deed he knew no more of the matter than others. For to fay, that, upon fuppofition that his difcoveries had been fatisfying, as to truth and clearnefs, and that he was capable to prove and explain them, they were not fit to be made known to the world, is to fpeak the groffeft of nonfenfe; for nothing was fo neceffary to be known, and known univerfally, as the *chief good*, which every one is obliged to feek after. To know this, and conceal the difcovery, is the moft malicious and invidious thing that can be thought of. And rather than charge this on Plato, I think it fafer to charge ignorance on him. He fpeaks fomewhat liker truth than others, while he tells us, " That happinefs confifts in the knowledge of the chief good ; " that philofophers, who are fufficiently purified, are allowed, " after the diffolution of their bodies, to fit down at the table of " the Gods, and view the field of truth ; that to be made like " God is the chief good ; that to follow God is the chief good." Some fuch other expreffions we find. But what does all this fay? Does it inform us that Plato underftood our happinefs to confift in the *eternal enjoyment of God?* Some, who are loth to think that Plato miffed any truth of importance which is contained in the fcripture, think fo : But for my part, I fee no reafon to convnce me from all this that Plato underftood any thing tolerably about the *enjoyment of God*, either in time or after time, or that he was fixed and determined wherein the happinefs of man confifts, or that really any fuch ftate of future felicity is certainly attainable. All this was only a heaven of his own framing and fancy, fitted for philofophers; for the being of which, he could give no tolerable arguments. And all this account fatisfies me no more that Plato underftood wherein happinefs confifts, than

the

the following does, that he knew the way of reaching it, which I shall transcribe from the same chapter of *Alcinous's doctrine of Plato:* " Beatitude is a good habit of the genius, and this simi-
" litude to God we shall obtain, if we enjoy convenient nature,
" in our manner, education and sense, according to law, and
" chiefly by reason and discipline, and institution of wisdom,
" withdrawing ourselves as much as is possible from human
" affairs, and being conversant in these things only which are
" understood by contemplation: the way to prepare, and as it
" were, to cleanse the demon that is in us, is to initiate our-
" selves into higher disciplines; which is done by music,
" arithmetic, astronomy and geometry, not without some res-
" pect of the body, by gymnastic, whereby it is made more
" ready for the actions both of war and peace." I pretend not to understand him here: But this I understand from him, that one of three is certain, either he understood not himself, or had no mind that others should understand; or that he was the most unmeet man in the world to instruct mankind about this important point, and to explain things about which the world was at a loss. When men speak at this rate, we may put what meaning we please upon their words.

4. It is plain that none of them have clearly come to know themselves, or inform others that *happiness is not to be had here;* that it *consists in the eternal enjoyment of God after time;* and that *this is attainable.* These are things whereabout there is a deep silence, not so much as a word of them, far less any proof. If ever we were to expect such a thing we might look for it from those who have not merely touched at this subject by the bye, and in dark hints, but have discoursed of *moral ends* on set purpose, such as Cicero and Seneca. Cicero frequently tells that he designed to enrich his native country with a translation of all that was valuable in the Greek philosophers, he had perused them for this end, and thus accomplished, he sets himself to write of *moral ends*, which he does in five books. Here we may expect somewhat to the purpose: But if we do, we are disappointed. The *first* book sets off Epicures's opinion about *happiness* with a great deal of rhetoric. The *second* overthrows it. The *third* represents the Stoic's opinion. And the *fourth* confutes it. The *fifth* represents and asserts the Peripatetic's opinion, which had been as easily overthrown as any of them. And this is all you are to expect here, without one word of God, the *enjoyment of him*, or any thing of that kind, which favours of a life after this.

Seneca

Seneca writes again a book *de Vita Beata* confifting of thirty-two chapters. Here we may find fomewhat poffibly. And indeed if one fhould hear him ftate the queftion, as he does in his fecond chapter he would expect fome great matters from him. *Quæramus quid optime factum fit, non quid ufitatiffimum: Et quid nos in poffeffione felicitatis æternæ conflituat, non quid vulgo, veritatis peffimo interpreti, probatum fit. Vulgus autem tam chlamydatos, quam coronam voco**. What may we not now expect? But after this, I affure you, you are to look for no more words about eternity, nor any thing more, but a jejune difcourfe in pretty fentences, about the Stoic's opinion, reprefenting that a man would be happy, if his paffions were extinct, and he was perfectly pleafed with the condition he is in, be it what it will. Now after this, who can dream that *nature's light* is fufficient to fatisfy here? Is every man able to difcover that which philofophers, the greateft of them, after the greateft application, failed fo fignally about, that fcarcely any of them came near it, and none of them reached it?

5. Nor will it appear ftrange, that the Heathen philofophers of old fhould be fo much at a lofs about *future happinefs*, to any one who confiders how difficult, if not impoffible it muft be for any, who rejects revelation, and betakes himfelf to the mere light of nature, to arrive at the wifhed for, and neceffary affurance of eternal felicity after this life, even at this prefent time, after all the great improvements, which the rational proofs of a future ftate have obtained, fince Chriftianity prevailed in the world. If nature's light, now under its higheft improvements, proves unable to afford full affurance, and ftill leaves us to fluctuate in uncertainty about future happinefs; no wonder that they fhould be in the dark, who were ftrangers to thefe improvements.

That the arguments for a future ftate, fince Chriftianity obtained, have received a vaft improvement from Chriftian divines and philofophers, cannot modeftly be denied. The performances of Plato and Cicero, on this point, which were the beft among the ancients, are, when compared with our late Chriftian writers, but like the trifles of a boy at fchool, or the rude effays

---

* " Let us inquire what is beft to be done, and not what is moft
" common; and what puts us in poffeffion of eternal felicity, and not
" what is approved by the vulgar,—the worft judges of truth. By the
" vulgar I mean the rich and great men, as well as the mob."

says of a novice, in comparison to the most elaborate and complete performances of the greatest masters; if they bear even the same proportion. He who knows not this, knows nothing in these matters. Yea, to that degree have they improven those arguments, that it is utterly impossible for any man, who gives all their reasons for the continuance of the soul after death, with their answers to the trifling pretences of the opposers of this conclusion, a fair hearing and due consideration, to acquiesce rationally in the contrary assertion of *atheists* and *mortal deists*; or not to favour, at least this opinion, as what is highly probable, if not absolutely certain.

But after all, if we are left to seek assurance of this from the *unassisted* light of nature, that *certainly God has provided for, and will actually bestow upon man, and more especially man who is now a sinner, future and eternal felicity*, we will find ourselves plunged into inextricable difficulties, out of which the light of nature will find it very difficult, if not impossible to extricate us. It is one thing to be persuaded of the future separate subsistence of our souls after death, and another to know in what condition they shall be; and yet more to be assured, that *after death our souls shall be possessed of eternal happiness.* It is precisely about this last point that we are now to speak. The arguments drawn from nature's light will scarce fix us in the steady persuasion of future and eternal felicity. There is a great odds betwixt our knowledge of future punishments, and the grounds whereby we are led to it, and our persuasion of future and eternal rewards. Upon inquiry the like reasons will not be found for both. Our notices about eternal rewards, when the promises of it contained in the scriptures are set aside, will be found liable to many objections, hardly to be solved by the mere light of nature, which do not so much affect the proofs advanced for future punishments. Besides, since the entrance of sin, its universal prevalence in the world, and the consequences following upon it, have so long benighted man, as to any knowledge that he otherwise might have had about eternal happiness, that now it will be found a matter of the utmost difficulty, if not a plain impossibility, for him to reach assurance of eternal felicity by the mere light of nature, however improven.

The pleas drawn from the *holiness* and *justice* of God, say much for the certain punishment, after this life, of many notorious offenders, who have wholly escaped punishment here; especially

especially as they are strengthened by other collateral considerations clearing and enforcing them.

But, whether the pleas for future and eternal rewards, from the justice and goodness of God, on the one hand; and the sufferings of persons really guilty of sin, but in comparison of others virtuous, on the other; will with equal firmness conclude, that God is *oblig*ᵉ*d* to, or certainly *will*, reward their *imperfect* virtue, and compensate their sufferings, may, and perhaps not without reason, be questioned.

That it is congruous that virtue should be rewarded, may perhaps easily be granted. But what that reward is, which it may from divine justice or bounty claim, it will not be easy for us to determine, if we have no other guide than the mere light of nature. The man who perfectly performs his duty is secured against the fears of punishment, and has reason to rest fully assured of God's acceptance and approbation of what is every way agreeable to his will. He has a perfect inward calm in his own conscience, is disturbed with no challenges, and has the satisfaction and inward complacency, resulting from his having acquitted himself according to his duty: His conscience assures him he has done nothing to provoke God to withdraw favours already given, or to withhold further favours. And though he cannot easily see reason to think God obliged, either to continue what he freely gave, or accumulate further effects of bounty upon him, or to protract his happiness to eternity; yet he has the satisfaction of knowing, that he hath not rendered himself unworthy of any favour. This reward is the necessary and unavoidable consequence of *perfect obedience.*

But this comes not up to the point. That which the light of nature must assure us of is, That virtuous men, on account of their virtue, may claim and expect, besides this, a further reward, and that of no less consequence than eternal felicity. Now, if I mistake it not, when the promise of God, which cannot be known without revelation, is laid aside, the mere light of nature will find it difficult to fix upon solid grounds, for any assurance as to this. Many thorny difficulties must be got through. Not a few perplexing questions must be solved. If it is said that the justice of God necessarily obliges him, besides that reward necessarily resulting from perfect obedience, (of which above), further to recompence, even the most exact and perfect performance of our duty, antecedently to any promise given to that effect, with future and eternal felicity; it

may

may be inquired, How it shall be made appear that virtue, suppose it to be as perfect as you will, can be said to *merit*, and to merit so *great* a reward? May not God, without injustice, turn to *nothing* an innocent creature? Sure I am, no mean nor incompetent judges have thought so [*]. Where is the injustice of removing or taking away what he freely gave, and did not promise to continue? Is it modest or safe for us, without the most convincing evidences of the inconsistency of the thing, to limit the power of God, or put a *cannot* on the Almighty? And does not the very possibility of the annihilation of an innocent creature, in a consistency with justice, though God, for other reasons, should never think fit to do it, entirely enervate this plea? If God, without injustice may take away the *being* of an innocent creature, how is it possible to evince, that in justice, he must reward it with *eternal happiness*? Again, if we may, for our virtue, claim eternal felicity, as due in justice, may it not be inquired, What exercise of virtue,—for how long a time contiued,—is sufficient to give us this title to eternal rewards? If the bounty and goodness of God is insisted on, as the ground of this claim, the plea of justice seems to be deserted. And here again it may be inquired, Whether the goodness of God is necessary in its egress? Whether the bounty of God ought not to be understood to respect those things which are absolutely at the giver's pleasure to grant or withhold? Whether, in such matters, we can be assured that bounty will give us this or that, which, though we want, is not in justice due, nor secured to us by any promise? Further, it may be inquired how far must goodness extend itself as to rewards? Is it not supposable, that it may stop short of eternal felicity, and think a less reward sufficient? Of so great weight have these, and the like difficulties appeared to not a few, and those not of the more stupid sort of mankind, that they have not doubted to assert boldly, that even innocent man, without revelation, and a positive promise, could never be assured of eternal rewards. And how the light of nature can disengage us from these difficulties, were man perfectly innocent, I do not well understand.

But whatever there is of this, the *entrance of sin* and the consideration of man's case as involved in *guilt*, has cast us upon new

---

[*] See the Excellency of Theology, &c. by T. H. R. Boil, pag. 25, 26, 27, &c. and Consid. about the Recon. of Reason and Rel. by T. E. pag. 21, 22.

new and yet greater difficulties. From this present condition wherein we find all mankind without exception involved, a whole shoal of difficulties emerge, never, I am afraid, to be removed by *unassisted reason.*

Now, it may be inquired, what obedience is it that can entitle us to eternal felicity? If none save that which is *perfect* will serve, who shall be the better for this reward? Who can pretend to this perfect or sinless obedience? If *imperfect* obedience may; how shall we be sure of this? How shall he who deserves punishment, claim, demand and expect reward, a great reward, yea; the greatest reward,—eternal happiness? If the goodness of God is pleaded, and it is said, that though we cannot expect in *strict justice* to have our *imperfect obedience* rewarded; yet we may hope it from the *bounty* of God? Besides, what was above moved against this, in a more plausible case, when we were speaking of *innocent man,* it may be further inquired, whether, though infinite bounty might deal thus graciously with man, if he were *perfectly* righteous, it may not yet withhold its favours, or at least stop short of eternal felicity, with the best among sinners? Again, what *degree* of imperfection is it that will prejudge this claim? What may consist with it? Who is good in that sense, which is necessary to qualify him for this expectation? Is there any such person existent? What way shall we be sure of this? Is it to be measured by outward actions only, or are inward principles and aims to come in consideration? Who can know these save God? If it be said, we can know ourselves to be such: I answer, how shall we maintain any confidence of future, nay eternal rewards, while conscience tells that we deserve punishment? What if by the mere light of nature we can never be assured of forgiveness? How shall we then by it be sure of eternal rewards? If we are not rewarded here, how can we know but that it has been for our sins that good things have been withheld from us? May not this be presumed to be the consequence of our known sins, or more covert evils, which self-love has made us overlook? If we suffer, yet do we suffer more than our sins deserve, or even so much? If we think so, will we be sustained competent judges of the quality of offences, and their demerit, which are done against God, especially when we are the actors? To whom does it belong to judge? If ye meet with some part, for ye can never prove it is all, of demerit or deserved punishment of your sins here, will this conclude that ye shall be exempted from suffering what further God may in justice think due to them, and you on their account hereafter? What security have ye that ye shall escape with what is inflicted on you here? And not only so, but instead of meeting with what ye further deserve, obtain rewards which ye dare scarcely say ye deserve? If God spare at present a noted offender, who cannot without violence to reason be supposed a subject meet for pardon or for a reward, and reserve the whole punishment due to his crimes, to the other world; but in the mean while, sees meet to inflict present punishment on thee, though less criminal, perhaps to convince the world, that even lesser offenders shall not escape; if, I say, he deal thus, is there no way for clearing his justice, but by conferring eternal happiness on thee? Why, if he inflict what further punishment is due to thee, in exact proportion to thy less atrocious crimes; and punish the other with evils proportioned to his more atrocious crimes, and make him up by the severity of the stroke for the delay of the punishment; if, I say, thus he do, I challenge any man to tell me where the injustice lies? And may not the like be said as to any other virtuous person, or whom thou supposest to be such, who meets with sufferings?

Nor do less perplexing difficulties attend those other pleas for future happiness to man, at least, in his present condition; which are drawn from God creating us capable of future happiness, implanting desires, and giving us gusts of it: All which would be given in vain, if there was no happiness designed for man after time.

But how by this we can be secured of eternal happiness, I do not well see. Nor do I understand how the difficulties which may be moved against this, can be resolved. It may be inquired, Whether this desire of happiness, said to be implanted in our natures, is really any thing distinct from that natural tendency of the creature to its own perfection and preservation, which belongs to the being of every creature, with such difference as to degrees and the manner, as their respective natures require? If it is no more than this, it must be allowed essential to every rational creature: And if every rational creature has an essential attribute, which infers an obligation on God to provide for it eternal happiness, and put it in possession of this felicity, if no fault intervene, doth it not thence necessarily, follow, that God cannot possibly, without injustice, turn to nothing any innocent rational creature; nay, nor create any one, which it is possible for him again to annihilate without injustice? For if we should suppose it possible for God to do so,

and

and thus without injuſtice fruſtrate this defire, where is the force of the argument? And is it not a little bold to limit God thus? I need not enter into the debate, Whether there is any ſuppoſable cafe, wherein infinite wiſdom may think it fit to do ſo? That diſpute is a little too nice: For on the one hand, it will be hard for us to determine it poſitively, that infinite wiſdom muſt, in any cafe we can ſuppoſe, think it fit to deſtroy or turn to nothing an innocent creature; and on the other hand, it is no lefs rafh to affert, that our not knowing any cafe, proves that really there is none fuch known to the only wife God. Befides, if we allow it only poffible, in a confiſtency with juſtice and veracity, for God to do it, I am afraid the argument has loſt its force. Further, it may be inquired, Whether the rational creature can in duty defire an eternal continuation in being, otherwife than with the deepeſt ſubmiffion to the ſovereign pleaſure of God, where he has given no poſitive promife? If ſubmiffion belongs to it, all certainty evanifhes, and we muſt look elfewhere for affurance of eternal happinefs. A defire of it, if God fee meet to give it, can never prove that certainly he wll give it. If it is faid, that the creature without ſubmiffion or fault may infiſt upon and claim eternal happinefs; I do not fee how this can be proven.

But again, do not thefe defires refpect the whole man, confiſting of foul and body? Doth not death diffolve the man? Are not thefe defires apparently fruſtrated? How will the light of nature certainly infer from thofe defires, guſts, &c. that the whole man fhall have eternal felicity, while we fee the man daily deſtroyed by death? Can this be underſtood without revelation? Does the light of nature teach us that there will be a refurrection? I grant, that without the fuppofal of a future exiſtance, we cannot eaſily underſtand what end there was worthy of God for making fuch a noble creature as man: But while we fee man, on the other hand, daily deſtroyed by death, and know nothing of the refurrection of the body, which is the cafe of all thofe who reject revelation, we fhall not know what to conclude, but muſt be toffed in our own minds, and be at lofs how to reconcile thofe feeming inconſiſtencies: Which gave a great man occaſion to obferve, "That there can be no "reconciliation of the doctrine of future rewards and punifh- "ments, to be righteoufly adminiſtered upon a fuppofition of "the feparate everlaſting fubfiſtence of the foul only *." And

for

* Dr. Owen on Heb. vi. ver. 1, 2. Vol. 3, pag. 21.

for proof of this, he infists on several weighty considerations, which I cannot transcribe.

But, should we give up all this, Will this desire of happiness prove that God designed it for man, whether he carried himself well or not? If it prove not that sinful man may be happy, or that eternal happiness is designed for man, who is now a sinner, what are we the better for it? Are we not all more or less guilty? What will it help us, that we were originally designed for, and made capable of future felicity, if we are now under an incapacity of obtaining it? Do we not find that we have fallen short of perfect obedience? And can those desires assure us that God will pardon, yea reward us, and that with the greatest blessing which innocent man was capable of? Moreover, before we end this discourse, I hope to make it appear, that by the *mere light of nature* no man can assuredly know that *sin shall be pardoned*; and if so, it is vain to pretend, that we can be assured of eternal felicity in our present condition. They who have sinned less and suffered more in this life, shall not be so severely punished in that which is to come, as they who have sinned more grievously and escaped without punishment here, this reason assures us of: But it can scarcely so much as afford us a colourable plea for eternal rewards, to any virtue that is stained with the least sin. The scriptures make mention of a happiness promised to innocent man upon perfect obedience; and of salvation to guilty man upon faith in JESUS CHRIST. Beside these two I know no third sort. As to the last, the light of nature is entirely silent, as we shall see afterwards. Whether it can alone prove the first is a question: But that man in his present condition cannot be better for it, is out of question.

6. Were it granted that these arguments are conclusive, yet the matter would be very little mended: For it is certain, that these arguments are too thin to be discerned by the dim eyes of the generality, even though they had tutors who would be at pains to instruct them. Yea, I fear that they rather beget suspicions than firm persuasions in the minds of philosophers. They are of that sort, which rather silence than satisfy. Arguments *ab absurdo*, rather force the mind to assent, than determine it cheerfully to acquiesce in the truth as discovered. Other demonstrations carry along with them a discovery of the nature of the thing, which satisfies it in some measure. Hence they have a force, not only to engage, but to keep the soul steady

in

PRINCIPLES OF THE MODERN DEISTS. 125

in its adherence to truth; but thefe oblige to implicit belief as it were, and therefore the mind eafily wavers and lofes view of truth; and is no longer firm, than it is forced to be fo, by a prefent view of the argument. If learned men were always obfervant of their own minds, and as ingenuous as the Auditor is in Cicero, in his acknowledgment about the force of Plato's arguments for the *immortality of the foul* *, they would make fome fuch acknowledgment as he does. After he has told, that he has read oftener than once Plato's arguments for the *immortality of the foul*, which Cicero had recommended in the foregoing difcourfe as the beft that were to be expected, he adds, " *Sed* " *nefcio quomodo, dum lego affentior: cum pofui librum, & me-* " *cum ipfe de immortalitate animorum cæpi cogitare, affentio om-* " *nis illa elabitur* †." In like manner might others fay, When I pore upon thofe arguments I affent; but when I begin to look on the matter, I find there arifes not fuch a light from them, as is able to keep the mind fteady in its affent. More efpecially will it be found fo, if we look not only to the matter, but to the difficulties which offer about it. Yet this fteadinefs is of abfolute neceffity in this cafe, fince a refpect to this muft be fuppofed always prevalent, in order to influence to a fteady purfuit. The learned Sir Matthew Hale obferves, that, " It is ve-
" ry true, that partly by univerfal tradition, derived probably
" from the common parent of mankind, partly by fome glim-
" merings of natural light in the natural confciences, in fome,
" at leaft, of the Heathen, there feemed to be fome common
" perfuafion of a future ftate of rewards and punifhments. But
" firft it was weak and dim, and even in many of the wifeft of
" them overborn; fo that it was rather a fufpicion, or at moft,
" a weak and faint perfuafion, than a ftrong and firm convic-
" tion: And hence it became very unoperative and ineffectual
" to the moft of them, when they had greateft need of it;
" namely, upon imminent or incumbent temporal evils of great
" preffure. But, where the impreffion was firmeft among them,
" yet ftill they were in the dark what it was."

7. It is further to be confidered, that it is not the general perfuafion that there is a ftate of future happinefs and mifery, which
can

* Cicero Tuf. Queft. Lib. 1.
† " But I know not how it happens, that although I affent to him
" as long as I am reading, yet when I have laid down the book, and
" begun to think with myfelf of the immortality of the foul, all that
" affent vanifhes."

can avail *; but there muſt be a diſcovery of that happineſs in its nature, or wherein it conſiſts; its excellency and ſuitableneſs, to engage man to look on it as his chief good, purſue it as ſuch, perſevere in the purſuit over all oppoſition, and forego other things, which he ſees and knows the preſent pleaſure and advantage of, for it. Now, ſuch a view the light of nature can never rationally be pretended to be able to give: If it is, let the pretender ſhew us where, and by whom ſuch an account has been given and verified; or let him do it himſelf. And if this is not done, as it never has, and I fear not to ſay never can be done; it would not mend the matter, though we ſhould forego all that has been aboveſaid, (as was above inſinuated), which yet we ſee no neceſſity of doing.

8. I might here tell how faintly the deiſts uſe to ſpeak upon this head. Though upon occaſion, they can be poſitive; yet at other times they ſpeak modeſtly about the being of a future ſtate of happineſs, and tell us, " That rewards and puniſhments hereaf-
" ter, though the notion of them has not been univerſally receiv-
" ed, the Heathens diſagreeing about the doctrine of the immor-
" tality of the ſoul, may yet be granted to ſeem reaſonable, becauſe
" they are deduced from the doctrine of providence,—and that
" they may be granted parts of natural religion, becauſe the wiſeſt
" men have inclined to hold them amongſt the Heathen †,",&c. and now do in all opinions. And as they ſeem not over certain as to the being of future rewards and puniſhments, ſo they plainly own they can give no account what they are. " *Quæ vero, qualis,*
" *quanta,* &c. *hæc vita ſecunda vel mors fuerit ob defectum condi-*
" *tionum ad veritatus iſtius conformationem poſtulatarum,* ſciri
" nequit," ſays the learned *Herbert* ‡.

CHAP.

---

* Herbert de Veritate, pag. 59.
† Orac. of Reaſon, pag. 201.

‡ *De Ver.* pag. 57. *& Alibi ſæpius.*—" But what, of what kind,
" and how great, this ſecond life or death ſhall be, can not be known,
" for want of thoſe conditions that are required for the confirmation of
" the truth of it."

CHAP. VII.

Nature's Light affords not a sufficient Rule of Duty. Its Insufficiency hence inferred.

THERE is certainly no other way of attaining happiness, than by pleasing God. Happiness is no other way to be had, than from him, and no other way can we reasonably expect it from him, but in the way of *duty* or *obedience*. Obedience must either be with respect to these things which immediately regard the honour of the Deity, or in other things. The *insufficiency of natural religion as to worship*, has been above demonstrated. That it is wanting as to the latter, viz. these duties which we called, for distinction's sake, *duties of moral obedience*, is now to be proven. That man is subject to God, and so in every thing obliged to regulate himself according to the prescription of God, has been above asserted, and the grounds of this assertion, have been more than insinuated. Now if nature's light is not able to afford a complete directory as to the whole of man's conduct, in so far as the Deity is concerned, it can never be allowed sufficient to conduct man in religion, and lead him to eternal happness: While it leaves him at a loss as to sufficient rules for universal virtue, which even deists own to be the principal way of serving God and obtaining happiness. It is one of the principal things to which this is to be ascribed, and whereon man's hopes must reasonably be supposed to lean, if he is left to the mere conduct of the light of nature. Now the insufficiency of nature's light in this point will be fully made appear, from the ensuing considerations; some of which are excellently discoursed by the ingenious Mr. Lock in his *Reasonableness of Christianity, as delivered in the Scripture**. If he had done as well in other points as in this, he had deserved the thanks of all that wish well to Christianity : But so far as he follows the truth we shall take his assistance, and improve some of his notions, adding such others, as are by him omitted, which may be judged of use to the case in hand.

1. Then we observe, that no man left to the conduct merely of nature's light, has offered us a *complete body of morality*. Some parts of our duty are pretty fully taught by philosophers and politicians

* Reas. of Christ. pag. 267.

ticians. "So much virtue as was neceffary to hold focieties toge-
"ther, and to contribute to the quiet of governments, the civil
"laws of commonwealths taught, and forced upon men that liv-
"ed under magiftrates. But thefe laws, being for the moft part
"made by fuch, who have no other aims but their own power;
"reached no further than thofe things that would ferve to tie men
"together in fubjection; or at moft, were directly to conduce
"to the profperity and temporal happinefs of any people. But
"*natural religion* in its full extent, was no where, that I know
"of, taken care of by the force of natural reafon. It fhould feem
"by the little that hitherto has been done in it, that it is too hard
"a thing for unaffifted reafon to eftablifh morality in all its
"parts, upon its true foundations, with a clear and convincing
"light*." Some parts have been noticed, and others quite omitted.
A complete fyftem of morality in its whole extent has never been
attempted by the mere light of nature, much lefs completed.

2. To gather together the fcattered rules that are to be met
with in the writings of *morality*, and weave thefe fhreds into a
competent *body of morality*, in fo far as even the particular direction of any one man would require, is a work of that im-
menfe labour, and requires fo much learning, ftudy and attention, that it has never been performed, and never like to be performed, and quite furmounts the capacity of moft, if not of
any one man. So that neither is there a complete body of morality given us by any one. Nor is it ever likely to be collected
from thofe who have given us parcels of it.

3. Were all the moral directions of the ancient fages collected, it would not be a fyftem that would be any way ufeful to
the body of mankind. It would confift for moft part of enig-
matical, dark and involved fentences, that would need a commentary too long for vulgar leifure to perufe, to make them intelligible. Any one that is in the leaft meafure acquainted
with the writings of the philofophers will not queftion this. Of
what ufe would it be to read fuch morality as that of Pythagoras,
whofe famed fentences were, "Poake not in the fire with a
"fword; ftride not over the beam of a balance; fit not upon
"a bufhel; eat not the heart; take up your burthen with help;
"eafe yourfelf of it with affiftance; have always your bed-
"clothes well tucked up; carry not the image of God about
"you

* Reaf. of Chrift. pag. 268.
† Diog. Laert. Life of Pythagoras.

"you in a ring," &c. Was this like to be of any use to mankind? No surely, some of them indeed speak more plain, some of them less so; but none of them sufficiently plain to be understood by the vulgar.

4. Further, were this collection made, and, upon other accounts, unexceptionable; yet it would not be sufficiently full to be an universal directory. For, 1. Many important duties would be wanting. Self-denial, that consists in a mean opinion of ourselves, and leads to a submitting, and passing from all our most valuable concerns, when the honour of God requires it, is the fundamental duty of all religion, that which is of absolute necessity to a due acknowledgment of man's subjection and dependence; and yet we shall find a deep silence in all the moralists about it. Which defect is the more considerable, that the whole of our apostacy is easily reducible to this one point, *an endeavour to subject the will, concerns and pleasures of God to our own*. And no act of obedience to him, can, without gross ignorance of his nature, and unacquaintedness with the extent of his knowledge, be presumed acceptable, which flows not from such a principle of self-denial, as fixedly prefer the *concerns* of God's glory to all other things. Again, what duty have we more need of, than that which is employed in forgiving enemies, nay in loving them? We have frequent occasions for it. If we are not acquainted that this is duty, we must frequently run into the opposite sin. But where is this taught among the Heathens? Further, where shall we find a directory as to the *inward frame* and *actings* of our minds, guiding us how to regulate our thoughts, our designs? Some notice is taken of the outward behaviour; but little of that which is the *spring* of it. Where is there a rule for the direction of our thoughts as to *objects* about which they should be employed, or as to the *manner* wherein they are to be conversant about them? These things are of great importance, and yet by very far out of the ken of unenlightened nature. Divine and spiritual things were little known, and less thought of by philosophers. 2. As this system would be defective as to particular duties of the highest importance; so it would be quite defective as to the grounds of those duties which are enjoined. It is not enough to recommend duty, that it is useful to us, or the societies we live in. When we act only on such grounds, we shew some regard to ourselves, and the societies whereof we are members; but none to God. Where are these cleared to be the *laws* of God? Who is he that presses obedience upon the consciences of men,

from the confideration of God's *authority* ftamped upon thefe laws he prefcribes? And yet without this, you may call it what you will; obedience you cannot call it. It is well obferved by Mr. Lock,—" Thofe juft meafures of right and wrong, which " neceffity had any where introduced, the civil laws prefcrib- " ed, or philofophers recommended, ftood not on their true " foundations. They were looked on as bonds of fociety, and " conveniencies of common life, and laudable practices: But " where was it that their obligation was thoroughly known, " and allowed, and they received as precepts of a law, of the " higheft law, the law of nature? That could not be without " the clear knowledge of the lawgiver, and the great rewards " or punifhments for thofe that would not, or would obey. But " the religion of the Heathens, as was before obferved, little " concerned itfelf in their morals. The priefts that delivered " the oracles of heaven, and pretended to fpeak from the gods, " fpoke little of virtue and a good life. And on the other fide, " the philofophers who fpoke from reafon, made not much " mention of the Deity in their ethicks *."

5. Not only would this rule be defective and lame; but it would be found *corrupt* and *pernicious*. For, 1. Inftead of leading them in the *way*, it would in many inftances lead them *afide*. We fhould have here Epictetus binding you to *tempo- rize*, and " worfhip the gods after the fafhion of your coun- " try †." You fhould find Pythagoras " forbidding you to " pray for yourfelf to God ‡." becaufe you know not what is convenient. You fhould find Ariftotle and Cicero commending *revenge* as a *duty*. The latter you fl ould find defending Bru- tus and Caffius for *killing* Cefar, and thereby authorizing the murder of any magiftrates, if the actors can but perfuade them- felves that they are tyrants. Had we nothing to conduct us in our obedience and loyalty, but the fentiments of philofophers, no prince could be fecure either of his life or dignity. You fhould find Cicero pleading for *felf-murder*, from which he can never be freed, nor can any tolerable apology be made for him. Herein he was feconded by Brutus, Cato, Caffius, Seneca and others innumerable. Many of them practifed it; others ap- plauded of their fentiments in this matter. You may find a large

* Reafonablenefs of Chriftianity, pag. 278.
† Epict. Enchirid. Cap. 38.
‡ Diog. Laert. Vit. Pyth. pag. 7.

PRINCIPLES OF THE MODERN DEISTS. 131

large account in Mr. Dodwel's *Apology for the Philosophical Performances of Cicero* prefixed to Mr. Parker's tranſlation of his book *de Finibus*. And you may find the deiſts juſtifying this in the preface to the *Oracles of Reaſon*, wherein Blount's killing of himſelf is juſtified. Of the ſame mind was Seneca, who expreſsly adviſes the practice of it. We ſhould here find *cuſtomary ſwearing commended**, if not by their precepts, yet by the examples of the *beſt moraliſts*, Plato, Socrates, and Seneca. In whom numerous inſtances of oaths by Jupiter, Hercules, and by beaſts, do occur. In the ſame way we ſhould find *unnatural luſt recommended†*. Ariſtotle practiſed it. And Socrates is ſoully belied, if he loved not the ſame vice. Whence elſe could *Socratici Cinædi* come to be a proverb in Juvenal's days. *Pride and ſelf-eſteem* were among their *virtues*. Which gives me occaſion to obſerve, that this one thing overturned their whole morality. Epictetus, one of the beſt of all their moraliſts, tells us, " That the conſtitution
" and image of a philoſopher is to expect good, as well as fear
" evil, only from himſelf ‡." Seneca urgeth this every where—
" *Sapiens tam æquo animo omnia apud alios videt, contemnitque,*
" *quam* Jupiter: *Et hoc ſe magis ſuſpicit, quod* Jupiter *uti illis*
" *non poteſt, ſapiens non vult §.*" And again, " *Eſt aliquid*
" *quo ſapiens antecedat Deum. Ille naturæ beneficio, non ſuo,*
" *ſapiens eſt* ‖. *Incomptus vir ſit externis & inſuperabilis, mira-*
" *torque tantum ſui* **." " Price and ſelf-eſteem was a diſeaſe
" epidemical amongſt them, and ſeems wholly incurable by any
" notions that they had. Some arrived to that impudence to
" compare themſelves with, nay, prefer themſelves before their
" own gods. It was either a horrible folly to deify what they
" poſtponed to their own ſelf-eſtimation, or elſe it was a ſtupendous

---

* Seneca de Ira, Lib. 3. Cap. 15.
† Diog. Laert. Vita Ariſt. Lib. 5. pag. 323.
‡ Epict. Ench. Cap. 27.
§ Seneca, Epiſt. 73.—" A wiſe man beholds and deſpiſes all things
" that he ſees in the poſſeſſion of others, with as eaſy a mind as Ju-
" piter himſelf. And in this he admires himſelf the more, that Jupi-
" ter cannot uſe thoſe things which he deſpiſes, whereas the wiſe
" man can uſe them, but will not."
‖ *Id.* Epiſt. 53.—" There is ſomething in which a wiſe man excels
" God, as God is wiſe by the benefit of his nature, and not by his
" own."
** *Id. de vita Beata,* Cap. 8.—" Let a man be incorruptible and
" incorrigible be external things, and an admirer of himſelf alone."

"dous effect of their pride to prefer themselves to the gods
"that they worshipped. Never any man amongst them propo-
"sed the honour of their gods as the chief end of their ac-
"tions, nor so much as dreamed of any such thing; it is evident
"that the best of them in their best actions reflected still back to
"themselves, and determinated there, designing to set up a pil-
"lar to their own fame*." That known sentence of Cicero,
who speaks out plainly what others thought, will justify this severe censure given by this worthy person, *Vult plane virtus
honorem: Nec virtutis ulla alia merces* †. Were it needful, I
might write volumes to this purpose, that would make one's flesh
tremble to read. They who desire satisfaction in this point,
may find it largely done by others. I shall conclude this first
evidence of the *corruption* of their *morality*, with this general
reflection of the learned Amyrald in his *Treatise of Religions*;
"Scarce can there be found any commonwealth amongst those,
"which have been esteemed the best governed, in which some
"grand and signal vice has not been excused, or permitted, or
"even sometimes recommended by public laws ‡. 2. Not only did they enjoin *wrong* things; but they enjoined what was
right to a *wrong end*, yea even their best things, as we heard
just now, aimed at their own honour. We have heard Cicero
to this purpose telling plainly *that honour was their aim.* Or
what the poet said of Brutus killing his own sons when they intended the overthrow of the liberty of their country,

Vicit amor patriæ laudumque immensa cupido §,

is the most that can be pleaded for most of them. Others are
plainly blasphemous, as we have heard from Seneca, designing
to be above God by his virtue. At this rate this philosopher
talks very oft: " Let philosophy," says he, " minister this to me,
" that it render me equal to God ||." To the maintenance of
this, their notions about the soul of man contributed much;
stiling it a piece clipt from God ʼΑποσπασμα τῦ Θεῦ, or a part of
God,

---

* Sir Char. Wolseley's Reason of Scripture Belief, pag. 118.
† *Cicero de Amicitia.*—" Virtue certainly will have honour, nor is
" there any other reward of virtue."
‡ See instances to this purpose in a discourse of Moral Virtue, and
its difference from Grace, pag. 225.
§ " The love of his country, and his immense desire of praise, over-
" came him."
|| Seneca, Epistle 48.

God, τῦ Διὸς Μερ☉, as Epictetus fpeaks. Horace calls it *divinæ particula auræ*. Cicero in his *Somnium Scip*. tells us what they thought of themfelves, *Deum fcito te esse*—" Know " thyfelf to be a God." And accordingly the Indian Brachmans vouched themfelves for Gods. And indeed they, who debafed their Gods below men, by their abominable characters of them, it was no wonder to find them prefer themfelves to them. Nor did any run higher this way than Plato. Let any one read his arguments for the *immortality of the foul*, and if they prove any thing, they prove it *a God*. Thus they quite corrupted all they taught, by directing it to wrong ends. 3. This fyftem would corrupt us as to the *fountain of virtue* and its *principle*, teaching us to truft ourfelves, and not depend on God for it. We have heard fome fpeak to this purpofe already; and Cicero may well be allowed to fpeak for the reft. " *A Deo tantum* " *rationem habemus: Bonam autem rationem aut non bonam a* " *nobis**." And a little after, near the clofe of his book, after he has owned our external advantages of learning to be from God, he fubjoins—" *Virtutem autem nemo unquam acceptam Deo retulit,* " *nimirum recte: Propter virtutem enim jure laudamur, &* " *in virtute recte gloriamur, quod non contingeret, fi id donum* " *a Deo, non a nobis haberemus*†." Thus we fee how corrupt they were in this point, and it is here eafily obfervable whence they were corrupted as to their chief end. He that believes that he has any thing that is not from God, will have fomewhat alfo that he will not refer to him, as his chief end. 4. The corruption of this fyftem, would in this appear, that it would be *full of contradictions*. Here we fhall find nothing but endlefs jars; one condemning as abominable, what another approves and praifes: Whereby we fhould be led to judge neither right, rather than any of them. A man who, for direction, will betake himfelf to the declarations of the philofophers, goes into a wild wood of uncertainty, and into an endlefs maze, from which
he

---

* Cicero de Natura Deorum, Lib. 3. P. mihi, 173.—" We have " only reafon from God, but we have good or bad reafon from our-" felves."

† " But nobody ever acknowledged that he was indebted to God for " his virtue, and certainly with good reafon; for we are juftly praifed " on account of our virtue, and we juftly boaft of it, which could not " be the cafe, if we had that as a gift from God, and not from our-" felves."

he should never get out. Plenty of instances, confirming these two last mentioned observations, might be adduced. If the reader desire them, I shall refer him to Mr. Lock's *Essay on Human Understanding*, Book 1. Chap. 3. Parag. 9. where he may see it has been customary with not a few nations, to expose their children, bury them alive without scruple, fatten them for the slaughter, kill them and eat them, and dispatch their aged parents: yea some, he will find, have been so absurd, as to expect paradise as a *reward of revenge*, and of *eating abundance of their enemies*. Whether these instances will answer Mr. Lock's purpose, I dispute not now. I design not to make myself a party in that controversy. But I am sure such fatal mistakes, as to what is good and evil, are a pregnant evidence of the insufficiency of nature's light to afford us a complete rule of duty. If they, who were left to it, blundered so shamefully in the clearest cases, how shall we expect direction, as to these that are far more intricate?

6. Be this system never so complete, yet it can never be allowed to be a rule of life to mankind. This I cannot better satisfy myself upon, than by transcribing what the ingenious Mr. Lock has excellently discoursed on this head. " I will suppose there
" was a *Stobeus* in those times, who had gathered the *moral say-*
" *ings* from all the *sages* of the world. What would this amount
" to, towards being a steady rule, a certain transcript of a law,
" that we are under? Did the saying of Aristippus, or Confucius,
" give it authority? Was Zeno a lawgiver to mankind? If
" not, what he or any other philosopher delivered, was but a
" saying of his. Mankind might hearken to it or reject it as
" they pleased, or as it suited their interest, passions, principles,
" or humours. They were under no obligation: The opinion
" of this or that philosopher, was of no authority. And if it
" were, you must take all he said under the same character.
" All his dictates must go for law, certain and true; or none of
" them. And then if you will take the moral sayings of Epicu-
" rus (many whereof Seneca quotes with approbation) for pre-
" cepts of the law of nature, you must take all the rest of his
" doctrine for such too, or else his authority ceases: So no more
" is to be received from him, or any of the sages of old, for parts
" of the law of nature, as carrying with them an obligation to be
" obeyed, but what they prove to be so. But such a body of
" ethicks, proved to be the law nature, from principles or reason,
" and reaching all the duties of life, I think no body will say
" the

"the world had before our Saviour's time." And I may add, nor to this day has, by the mere light of nature. "It is not enough," continues he, "that there were up and down scattered sayings "of wise men, conformable to right reason. The law of nature "was the law of conveniency too: And it is no wonder these "men of parts, and studious of virtue, (who had occasion to think "of any particular part of it) should, by meditation, light on "the right, even from the obfervable conveniency and beauty "of it, without making out its obligation from the true prin- "ciples of the law of nature, and foundations of morality." More he adds judiciously to this purpose; but this is enough. And hence it is plain, that such a system of morality would, if collected, at best be only a collection of problems, which every man is left at liberty to canvass, dispute, or reject; nay more, which every man is obliged to examine as to all its parts, in so far as it prescribes rules to him, and not to receive, but upon a discovery of its truth from its proper principles.

7. It is then plain that every man is left to his own reason to find out his duty by. He is not to receive it upon any other authority than that of reason, if revelation is rejected. He must find out therefore, in every case, what he is to do, and deduce its obligation from the principles of the law of nature. But who sees not, that the most part of men have neither leisure nor capacity for such a work? Men may think duty easy to be discovered now, when Christianity has cleared it up. But Mr. Lock well observes, "That the first knowledge of those truths, which have "been discovered by Christian philosophers, or philosophers since "Christianity prevailed, is owing to revelation; though as soon as "they are heard and considered, they are found to be agreeable "to reason, and such as can by no means be contradicted. Every "one may observe a great many truths which he receives at first "from others, and readily assents to, as consonant to reason, which "he would have found it hard, and perhaps beyond his strength "to have discovered himself. Native and original truth, is not "so easily wrought out of the mine, as we who have it delivered "ready dug and fashioned into our hands, are apt to imagine. "And how often at fifty, and threescore years old, are thinking "men told, what they wonder how they could miss thinking "of? Which yet their own contemplations did not, and possibly "never would have helped them to. Experience shews, that the "knowledge of morality, by mere natural light (how agreeable "soever it be to it), makes but a slow progress and little advance
"in

" in the world: Whatever was the caufe, it is plain in fact, that
" human reafon, unaffifted, failed men in its great and proper
" bufinefs of morality."

8. As it is unqueftionably certain, that the moft part of mankind are not able, by their own reafon to frame a complete body of morality for themfelves, or find out what is their own duty in every particular inftance. (I fhall not fpeak of any man's being obliged to difcover what belongs to other people's duty, left our antagonifts fhould fufpect I defigned to open a door for priefts, a fet of men and an office which they mortally hate). I fpeak only of what is every one's duty in particular. And I fay it is evident, that the moft part of mankind are unable to find this, which is not to be done, but by fuch ftrains of reafoning, and connexion of confequences, which they have neither leifure to weigh, nor, for want of capacity, education and ufe, fkill to judge of; and as I fay, they are unable for this, fo I fear this tafk will be found too hard for the ableft philofophers. Particular duties are fo many, and many of them fo remote from the firft principles, and the connexion is fo fubtile and fine fpun, that I fear not to fay that it muft efcape the piercing eyes of the moft acute philofophers: and if they engage in purfuit of the difcovery, through fo many and fo fubtile confequences, they muft either quit the unequal chace, or lofe themfelves inftead of finding truth and duty. And if we allow ourfelves to judge of what fhall be, by what has been the fuccefs of fuch attempts, I am fure this is more than bare guefs.

9. It is further to be obferved, that no tolerable progrefs could be made herein, were it to be done before advanced years. But it is certain, that youth, as well as riper age, is under the *law of nature*, and that that age needs clear difcoveries of duty the more, that in it irregular paffions and inclinations are more vigorous, and it is expofed to more temptations than any other part of a man's life; and befides, it wants the advantages of experience, to fortify it againft the dangerous influence of them, which advanced years are attended with. Now it will be to no purpofe to me, to find out fome years hence what was my duty before, as to obedience; for now the feafon is over. The law may difcover my *fin*, but can never regulate my *practice*, in a period of my life that is paft and gone. Every man muft have the knowledge of each day's duty in its feafon. This is not to be had from the light of nature. If we are left at a lofs in our younger years, as nature's light will have us, we may be ruined

ruined before knowledge come. Much fin muft be contracted, and ill habits are like to be very much ftrengthened before any ftop come : yea, they may be fo ftrong, that the foundation of inevitable ruin may be laid.

Finally, knowledge is requifite before acting; at leaft, in order of nature it is fo, and muft, at leaft in order of time, be contemporary. Action gives not always time for long reafoning and weighing fuch trains of confequences, as are requifite to clear duties from the firft principles of nature's light, and enforce their obligation. And therefore man left to it, is in a miferable plight, not much unlike to the cafe of the Romans, *Dum deliberant Romani capitur Saguntum* *: While he is fearching for duty, the feafon is loft; and the difcovery, if it comes, arrives too late to be of any ufe.

It is in vain for any to pretend, that the knowledge of duty is connate to the mind of man. Whatever may be pretended as to a few of the firft principles of morality, and it is but a very few of which this can be alleged, yet it is certain, it can never be without impudence extended to the thoufandth part of the duties we are bound to in particular cafes. General rules may be eafy; particular ones are the difficulty, and the application of generals to circumftantiated cafes is a hard tafk. It is but with an ill grace pretended, that thefe duties are felf-evident, and the knowledge of them innate or connate, call it what you pleafe, to the mind of man; which the world has never been agreed about; which wife men, when the faireft occafions offered of thinking on them, could not difcern; which philofophers, upon application and attention, cannot make out from the principles of reafon. The reafon why the knowledge of any truth is faid to be innate, is, becaufe, either the mind of man is ftruck with the evidence of it on its firft propofal, and muft yield affent, without feeking help from any principles of a clearer evidence; or becaufe its dependence on fuch principles is fo obvious, that the conclufion is fo plainly connected with fuch principles, that it is never fooner fpoke of, than its connexion with them, and fo its truth, appears. Of the firft fort few duties can be faid to be. And if they were of the laft fort, any perfon of a tolerable capacity would be able to demonftrate them upon attention. Now how far it is otherwife in this cafe, who fees not?

Upon

---

* " While the Romans were deliberating, Saguntum was taken."

Upon the whole I muſt conclude, that nature's light is not ſufficient to give us *ſuch a law* or *rule* as may be a *ſure guide* to thoſe who deſire to go right, ſo that they need not loſe their way or miſtake their duty, if they have a mind to know it, nor be uncertain whether they have done it.

It will not relieve the deiſts to pretend, that ſome of the exceptions above mentioned may be retorted upon Chriſtians, and improven againſt the ſcriptures: For nothing but ignorance of the true ſtate of the queſtion can give countenance to this pretence. The ſcriptures are a rule provided by ſovereign grace for fallen man, and by *infinite* wiſdom are adjuſted to God's great deſign of recovering man to the praiſe of his own grace, in ſuch a way as may *ſtain the pride of all glory*. They are ſufficient as an outward mean, and do effectually conduct man to that happineſs deſigned for him, under the influence of the aſſiſting grace provided for him, and in the uſe of the means of God's appointment. They provide a relief againſt any unavoidable defects in his obedience, and direct to the proper grounds of his acceptance in it: But men who pretend nature's light is able to guide to happineſs, are obliged to ſhew that it affords us a rule of duty; which of itſelf, without the help of any ſupernatural aſſiſtance, either as to outward means or inward influences, may be able to lead man to the obedience required; and this obedience muſt be ſuch, as anſwers our original obligation, and upon account of its own worth, is able to ſupport, not only a hope of aceptance but of future, nay eternal rewards. For ſuch as are left to nature's light, can neither pretend to any ſuch outward means, nor inward aſſiſtance, nor any ſuch relief againſt defects in knowledge or practice, as the ſcriptures do furniſh us with. Nature's light lays no other foundation for hopes of acceptance or reward, ſave only the worth or perfection of the obedience itſelf. And this, if it is duly conſidered, not only repels the pretended retortion, but gives additional force to the foregoing argument.

CHAP. VIII.

Proving the Inſufficiency of Natural Religion from its Defects as to ſufficient Motives for enforcing Obedience.

IT is warmly diſputed in the ſchools, whether *rewards* and *puniſhments* be not ſo much of the *eſſence* of a law, and ſo included in its notion, that nothing can properly be ſtiled law

which

which wants them? I defign not to make myfelf a party in thofe difputes. But this much is certain, that laws and government are relatives; they mutually infer and remove each other. There is no government properly fo called, that wants laws, or fomewhat that is the meafure and ftandard of its adminiftration. And there are no laws where there is no authority and government to enjoin them. Whence this plainly refults, that obedience, if it does no more, yet it certainly entitles to the protection of the government. And difobedience, not only deprives of any title to that, but lays open to fuch further feverities, as the government fhall have power to execute and fee meet to ufe for its own prefervation, againft violaters of its conftitutions. But further, to wave this difpute, the nature of man, which proceeds not to actions fave upon knowledge, makes this much certain, That whatever he may be fuppofed to be obliged to in ftrict duty, yet really in fact, he ufes not to pay any great regard to laws which are not enforced by motives or inducements, that may be fuppofed to work with him, as containing difcoveries of fuch advantages attending obedience, and difadvantages following difobedience, as may powerfully fway him to confult his duty as well his intereft, by yielding obedience. If then natural religion is found unable to difcover thofe things which ordinarily prevail with man to obey, and carry him over any obftructions which lie in the way, it can never be fuppofed fufficient to lead man to happinefs: For man is not to be driven, but led; he is not to be led blind-folded, but upon rational views of duty and intereft. That natural religion is in this refpect *exceedingly defective*, is the defign of this difcourfe to demonftrate. All thofe motives, which ufually have any influence, may, I think, be brought under the following heads. 1. A full view of the authority of the lawgiver and his laws. 2. A profpect of prefent benefit by obedience. 3. A profpect of future rewards for it. 4. Fear of punifhment in cafe of difobedience. And 5. Examples. Now, as I know no motive which may not eafily without ftretch be refolved into one of thofe, fo, if I make it appear that nature's light is lame as to each of them, I think I have gone a great way to difprove its fufficiency to happinefs. Well, let us effay it.

1. The great inducement to obedience is *a clear difcovery of the authority of the lawgiver*, and laws thence refulting. This is not perhaps, properly fpeaking, a motive, as it is oft ufed: for in very deed this is the formal reafon of obedience; a regard
whereto

whereto gives any action the denomination of obedience, and
entitles to the law's protection, and other advantages; yet certain
it is, that this should have the principal influence, from the
ground just now laid down, and therefore we shall here speak of
it. It will prevail far with man to obey the law of nature, if
nature's light clearly discovers how much the lawgiver deserves
that place; how well he is qualified for it; how indisputable
his title to the government is, and how far he has interposed his
authority; that the stamp of it is on these laws, to which we
are urged to be subject; that they bear a plain congruity to his
sublime qualifications; that he is concerned to have them obeyed;
observes the entertainment they meet with; entertains a
respect for the obedient, and resents disobedience. If we are
left in the dark, as to all or most of these, it will exceedingly
weaken our regard to the law. And that this is plainly the case,
is now to be made appear. 1. It goes a great way toward the
recommendation of any law to be fully satisfied as to the qualifications
of the framer. But how dark is nature's light here?
It discovers indeed his power and greatness: But its notions of
his wisdom, justice, clemency and goodness are exceedingly
darkened, by the seemingly unequal distributions of things here
below, the innumerable miseries, under which the world
groans, and other things of a like nature; that truly very few
if left merely to its conduct, would reach any such discoveries
of those glorious properties, as would influence any considerable
regard to those laws he is supposed to make.

I dispute not now what may be strictly known and demonstrated
of God, by a train of subtle arguments. For I would
not be understood so much as to insinuate the want of *objective
evidences* of the *wisdom* and *goodness of the Deity.* Our question
respects not so much these, as *man's power* of discerning
them. It is not absolutely denied, that there are many and
pregnant evidences of these attributes in the works of creation
and providence; our question is only, Whether there is such
evidence of those perfections, especially in God's moral government
of the world, every where appearing, as may be able
effectually to influence the practice, and affect the mind of man
in his present state, notwithstanding of any obstructions arising,
either from the inward weakness of his faculties, or the works
of God from without, which to the darkened mind of man
may have a contrary appearance? And that which I contend
is, That such is the state of things, so they go in the world, and

so

so blind are men's eyes, that there is not so near and clear evidence of these things, in what is discernible by the most of men, as may strike strongly, affect powerfully, and have a lively influence to quicken to practice. If our governor is near, if he is daily conversant with us, if we have daily indisputed evidences of his goodness, wisdom, justice, clemency, and other qualifications fitting for government, without any actions that may seem to be capable of a contrary construction, or even of a dubious one, this enforces a regard to his commands. On the contrary, if he is little known, if his way of management is hid from us, if there are instances, which however possibly they may be just, yet have a contrary appearence to us, this weakens regard and quite confounds. And this is plainly the case as to God, with men left to the mere conduct of nature's light, not through any defect on God's part, but through the darkness of the mind of man in his present state; and this is the more considerable, that we use to be more sensible of what evil any is supposed to do us, than of what good we may receive from them. Now since this observation is of use to prevent mistakes, I desire it may be carried along through the rest of our remarks.
2. It works powerfully, and strongly excites to obedience, if the indisputableness of the lawgiver's title, and the grounds whereon it leans are clearly known. Now as to God, the grounds of his title to the legislative as well as executive power, are the super-eminent excellency of his nature, rendering him not only fit, but the only fit person for it; his creation of all things, and thence resulting, propriety in them as his creatures, such as his preservation of them in being, his providential care and inspection, and the many benefits he bestows on them. But we have heard already, how dim the discoveries of God's super-eminent excellencies are, which the light of nature affords. As to his creation, it was disputed among the learned and quite overlooked by the vulgar, amongst those who were left to nature's light, as baron Herbert well observes and clears. As to his close influence in their preservation, it could not be noticed or known, where the other was overlooked. His providential care and inspection, which perhaps, as to its power of influencing, would go the greatest length, if it can be proven by the light of nature; yet cannot certainly by it be explained, and truly is so darkened by many obvious occurrences in the external administration of the world, that past all peradventure, it can never suitably affect men, who have no other discoveries of it,

it, than the light of nature affords. As to God's benefits, though they are many, yet they did not affect so much, because they were conveyed by the intervention of such second causes as did arrest, instead of helping forward the short-sighted minds of men, and detained them in contemplation of the servant who brought the favour, whereas they should have looked further, to him who sent it; so they should have done, but so they did not. Again, some of their most valuable benefits, their virtues, they denied God to be the author of, as we have heard above from Seneca, Cicero and Epictetus. And finally, some of them were inclinable to think, that the benefits were more than countervailed by the evils we labour under. Thus were the minds of men darkened, and so they had continued, if we had been without *revelation*. 3. It is of much force to influence obedience, if we have a clear and satisfying discovery of his government in those laws; that is, that he who is thus qualified for, and rightfully possessed of the government, has made such laws, and stamped his authority on them. However great ideas we have of his excellency and title to give laws; yet this will have no weight, if we are not clearly satisfied that these are *his* laws. Now how palpably defective nature's light is here, has been fully made out in the last chapter. 4. It will have no small force, if we had a clear knowledge, that these laws are in their matter fully congruous to the qualifications we desire in a lawgiver, such as wisdom, goodness, justice, clemency, and the like. But as these attributes are either not known or darkly known by the light of nature; so the impress of them on the laws of nature has not been discovered, nor is it discoverable: for I doubt not but it might easily be made appear, that the whole frame of the laws of nature are adapted to the nature of man as innocent, and indued with sufficient power to continue so, which is not the case with him now. And therefore how to reconcile these laws to the notions of God and man is a speculation, as of the last consequence, so of the greatest difficulty, which had never been got through, if God had not vouchsafed us *another guide* than nature's light. 5. If the lawgiver is certainly known to have a great regard to his laws, and to take careful inspection of the observation of them; this will be a strong inducement to regard them. But here nature's light is no less dark, than as to the rest. The whole face of things in the world seem to have so contrary an aspect, that we could never see clearly through this matter, if, without revelation, we

were

were left to judge of God by the mere light of nature. The abounding of sin, prosperity of sinners, sufferings of the best, and the like, led some to deny God's providence and government entirely; others of the better sort doubted of it, as Claudian elegantly represents his own case, lib. 1. *contra Rufinum.*

> *Sæpe mihi dubiam traxit sententia mentem,*
> *Curarent superi terras, an ullus inesset*
> *Rector & incerto fluerent mortalia casu.*
> *Nam cum dispositi quæsissem fœdera mundi.*
> *Præscriptosque mari fines, annisque meatus,*
> *Et lucis, notisque vices: Tunc omnia rebar*
> *Consilio firmata Dei———*
> *Sed cum res hominum tanta caligine volvi*
> *Adspicerem, lætosque diu florere nocentes,*
> *Vexarique pios: Rursus labefacta cadebat*
> *Religio caussæque viam non sponte sequebar*
> *Alterius, vacuo quæ currere semina motu*
> *Affirmat magnumque novas per inane figuras*
> *Fortuna, non arte, regi: quæ numina sensu*
> *Ambiguo vel nulla putat, vel nescia nostri.**

I know that Claudian got over this by *Rufinus's* death, but such providences have not always the like issue, and I only adduce his words as a lively representation of the strait. Yea, to so great a height came these doubts, that it is to be feared that many were carried to the worst side. It is certain the best of them were so confounded with those occurrences, that they could not spare reflections full of blasphemy upon
Providence.

---

* " I had often my mind distracted with doubt, whether the gods took care of the world, or whether there was no governor in it, and the affairs of mortals fluctuated under uncertain chance. For when I had enquired into the laws of the world, as disposed into order, and the bounds that are prescribed to the sea, and the course of the year and the succession of day and night, then I thought that these things were established by the wisdom of God. But again when I saw that the affairs of men were involved in so great darkness, that the wicked flourished in joy for a long time, and that the godly were harrassed. Religion being weakened, expired, and I against my will followed the tract of another opinion, which supposed that the seeds of things have a blind motion, and that new forms of things are directed through an immense void, by chance, and not by art, and which supposes that the deities have either an ambiguous sense or none at all, and that they know nothing of us."

Providence. The famed Cato's laſt words may ſcarcely be excuſed for this crime. Finally, it is certain, that there was ſo much darkneſs about this matter, that none of them all paid a due regard to God.

I ſhall now leave this head, after I have obſerved one or two things; and the firſt of them is, That however ſome of theſe truths above mentioned may poſſibly be made out by a train of ſubtle arguments; yet ſuch arguments, however they may draw an aſſent from a thinking man, not only tranſcend the capacity of the vulgar, but fail of exciting and affecting even the moſt philoſophical heads. For to draw forth our active powers into action, the inducements muſt ſhine with a light, that may warm the mind as it were, not only diſſipating doubts about the reality of what it obſerved, but alſo ſhewing its excellency. Upon this occaſion I may not impertinently apply to the philoſophers, what Plautius ſays of comic poets,

> *Spectavi ego pridem comicos ad iſtum modum*
> *Sapienter dicta dicere, atque illis plaudier*
> *Cum illos ſapientes mores monſtrabant populo:*
> *Sed cum inde ſaum quiſque ibant diverſi domum,*
> *Nulus erat illo pacto, ut illi juſſerunt*.

"I have often ſeen, that after the comic poets have ſaid "good things, and that they have been applauded for them "while they taught good manners to the people, as ſoon as they "were got home, no body was the better for their advice." The other thing I obſerve, is, that any defect as to the knowledge of the lawgiver is ſo much the more conſiderable than any other, that a regard to the lawgiver is that which gives the formality of obedience to any action, and therefore the leſs knowledge there is of him, the leſs of obedience, properly ſo called, there will be. Thus far we have cleared how little nature's light can do for enforcing obedience from the diſcoveries it makes of the lawgiver.

2. A ſecond head of motives to duty is *preſent advantage*. Now if nature's light is able to prove, that obedience to the law of nature is like to turn to our preſent advantage, either

---

* Le Clerk *Parrhoſiana*, page 52.

as to profit or pleasure, this would be of weight: But it is needless to insist on this head; for who sees not, that there is but little to be said as to many duties here? Are they not to cross our present inclinations? And for any thing that nature's light can discover, diametrically opposite to our present interest and honour; I mean according to the notions generally entertained of those things in the world? So it is but little that it can say upon this head. How often are we so situated, that in appearance nothing stands in our way to pleasure, honour or profit, but only the command? It were easy to enlarge on this head; but since it will not be readily controverted I wave it. And indeed it were of no consideration, if present losses were otherwise compensated by future advantages.

3. If nature's light can give a full view of *future rewards*, then this will compensate present disadvantages, and be a strong inducement to obedience. But the discovery, if it is of any use, must be clear and lively, that it may affect and excite, as has been above observed. Well, what can nature's light do here? Very little, as has been above fully demonstrated, when we discoursed of the *chief end*. It remains only now that we observe that evils and disadvantages discouraging from duty are present, sensible, great, and so affect strongly: wherefore if future rewards have not somewhat to balance these, they cannot have much influence. Now it has been made sufficiently evident, that all which nature's light has to put in the balance, to encourage the mind to go on in duty, against present, sensible, certain and great discouragements, is at most, but a dark, conjectural discovery of rewards, or rather suspicion about them, after time, without telling us what they are, or wherein they do consist. Will this ever prevail with men to obey? No it cannot. The prospect of future rewards was not that which prevailed with the most moral amongst the heathens of old. Their knowledge of these things, if they had any, was of little or no use or influence to them, as their excitement to virtue.

4. Nature's light is no less defective as to the discovery of *punishments*: For however the forebodings of guilty consciences, a dark tradition handed down from generation to generation, and some exemplary instances of divine severity, have kept some impressions of punishments on the minds of many in all ages; yet it is well known, that those things were ridiculed by most of the philosophers, the poet's fictions made

them contemptible, and the daily inftances of impunity of finners here, weakened the impreffions. Befides, evils that follow duty, and loffes fuftained, are fenfible, prefent, certain, known, and fo affect ftrongly, and therefore are not to be balanced by punifhments, which are not, or rather, at leaft, are rarely executed in time, and whereof there is little diftinct evidence after time. For be it granted that the juftice and holinefs of God render it incredible that fo many tranfgreffors as efcape unpunifhed here, fhould get off fo; yet certain it is, that nature's light can no way inform what punifhment fhall be inflicted.

5. Nature's light can never point us to *examples* which may have any influence. There are but few of thofe who wanted revelation, even of the philofophers, who were not tainted with grofs vices. We have ftrange ftories told of a *Socrates*; and yet after all, he was but a forry example of virtue. He is frequently by Plato introduced fwearing. He is known to have bafely complyed with the way of worfhip followed by his own country, which was the more impious, that it is to be fuppofed to be againft the perfuafion of his confcience; yea we find him with his laft breath, ordering his friend to facrifice the cock he had vowed to Efculpaius. M. Dacier's apology for him is perfectly impertinent. He is accufed of impure amours with Alcibiades, and of proftituting his wife's chaftity for gain. It is evident that in the whole of his conduct, he fhews but little regard to God. Such are the *examples* we are to expect here. We might give full as bad account of the *famed Seneca*, were it neceffary to infift on this head not to mention others of lefs confideration.

Now to conclude, how fhall we by nature's light be prevailed on to obey, while it gives fo unfatisfying difcoveries of the law and lawgiver? Can fhew fo little of prefent or future advantage by obedience, or difadvantage by difobedience? Nor can it offer any examples that are worth following.

It is certain that the experience of the world juftifies this account. What means it, that inftances of any thing like virtue are fo rare where revelation obtains not? Sure it muft fay one of two, if not both; that either nature's light prefent no *inducements* fufficient to influence *practice*, or that man is *dreadfully corrupt*: The deifts may chufe which, or both, and let them avoid the confequences if they can.

It had been eafy to have faid a great deal more on this head.

The

The subject would have admitted of confiderable enlargement; but this my defign will not allow. I intend to keep clofe to the argument, and run out no further than is of neceffity for clearing the force of that. And where the cafe is plain, as I take it to be here, I content myfelf with touching at the heads which clear the truth under debate.

CHAP. IX.

Shewing the Importance of knowing the Origin of Sin to the world, and the Defectivenefs of Nature's Light as to this.

IT is not more clear that the fun fhines, than that the *whole world lies in wickednefs*. The creation groans under the weight of this unweildy load, which lies fo heavy upon it, that it is the wonder of all who have any right notions of the juftice or holinefs of God, that it is not funk into nothing, or exquifite mifery before now. The Heathens made bitter complaints of it. And indeed if their complaints had been left upon themfelves, and had not been turned into accufations of the holy God, none could have wondered at them, or condemned them. For it is manifeft to any one who will not ftop his ears, put out his eyes, ftifle his confcience, forfwear and abandon his reafon, that *the world is full of fin*, what nation or place is free of idolatries, blafphemies, the raging of pride, revenge, perjuries, rapes, adulteries, thefts, robberies, murders, and other abominable evils innumerable? And who fees not, that all thefe are the effects of ftrong, prevailing, univerfal and contagious corruptions and depraved inclinations; from a fhare of which, no man can juftly pretend himfelf free? And if he fhould, any one who ftrictly cbferves his way, may eafily implead him, either of grofs ignorance or difingenuity.

To know how things came to this pafs with the world, and trace this evil to its fountain, is a bufinefs of great importance to religion. Yea, of fo much moment is it, that one can fcarcely tell how any thing like religion is to be maintained in the world, without fome competent knowledge of it.

1. If this is not known, we can never make any right eftimate of the *evil of fin*. If men were by their original conftitution, without their own fault, made of fo wicked or infirm a nature, as that either they were inclined to it, or unable

ble to resist temptations, amongst the throng of which they were placed, it is impossible for them to look upon sin as so detestable an evil as really it is; or blame themselves so much for it, as yet they are bound to do. If it is quite otherwise, and man was orignally upright, and fell not into this case, but by a fault justly chargeable on him, it is certain, that quite other apprehensions of sin should be maintained. Now such as men's apprehensions are about the evil of sin, such will their care be to avoid it, prevent it, or get it removed. And who sees not, that the whole of religion is easily reducible to these things?

2. If the *origin of sin* is not understood, man can never understand what he is obliged to in the way of duty. If we derive this weakness, wickedness and depraved inclination from our first constitution, we can never look on ourselves as obliged to such an obedience, as the rectitude, holiness, and purity of the divine nature, seems to render necessary. And if we are uncertain as to this, we shall never know how far our duty extends. And if we know not what is required of us, how can we do it? To say we are bound to obey as far as we can, is to speak nonsense, and what no way satisfies the difficulty: For this leaves us to judge of our own power, opens a door to man to interpret the law as he pleases, and charges God with such folly in the frame of the law, as we dare scarcely charge on any human lawgiver.

3. Without the knowledge of the *origin of sin*, we can never know what measures to take, in subduing our *corrupt inclinations*. If we know not of what nature they are, how they come to be interwoven with our frame, and so much of a piece with ourselves, we shall not know where to begin attempts for reformation, or if it be practicable to eradicate them. And yet this must be done, otherwise we cannot with any shew of reason project happiness. But the rise of corruption being hid, we shall neither know what it is to be removed or where to begin our work, nor how far success to attempts of this kind may reasonably be hoped for. And of how destructive consequence this is to all religion is easily seen.

4. If the *origin of sin* is not known, we will be at a loss what thoughts to entertain of God's *holiness*, *justice* and *goodness*, yea and his *wisdom* too. If our natures were originally burdened with those corrupt inclinations so twisted in with them, as now we find them; or if we were so infirm, as

not

not to be able to refift a throng of temptations, among which we were placed, we will fcarcely be able to entertain fuch a high regard for God's holinefs, goodnefs and wifdom in our make, or of his juftice in dealing fo by us. And if we fuppofe otherwife, we will ftill be confounded by our darknefs about any other way we can poffibly think of, whereby things were brought to this pafs, and mankind fo univerfally precipitated into fo miferable a cafe.

5. If the *origin of evil* is not known, we fhall never be able to judge what *eftimate* God will make of fin, whether he will look on it as *fo evil* as to demerit any deep refentment, or otherwife.

6. Hereon it follows, that the whole ftate of our affairs with God, will be quite darkened and become unintelligible. We fhall not know whether he fhall animadvert fo heavily on us for our fins, as to ruin us, or fo flightly pafs over them, as not to call us to an account. If the latter is fuppofed *obedience* is *ruined*; confidering what man's inclinations and temptations are: who will obey, if no ruin or hurt is to be feared by fin? If the former is fuppofed, our *hope* is *ruined*. We fhall not know what value God will put on our obedience, if this is not known; whether he will not reject it for the finful defects cleaving to it. Nor fhall we know whether he will pardon us, or upon what terms, if we know not what thoughts he has of fin. And this we know not, nor can we poffibly underftand, unlefs we know how it came, and came to be fo twifted in with our natures.

Finally, hereon depends any tolerable account of the *equity of God's proceedings*, at leaft of his goodnefs in dealing fo with the world, fubjecting it to fuch a train of miferies. If any thing of fin is chargeable juftly upon man's make and firft conftitution, it will be much to clear his juftice, but harder to acquit his goodnefs in plaguing the world fo. If otherwife, it will be eafy to juftify God: but how then were men brought to this cafe?

Thus we have fhortly hinted at thofe grounds that clear the importance of the cafe. An enlargement on them would have made the dulleft underftand, that without fome fatisfying account of the origin of evil, all religion is left loofe. The judicious will eafily fee it. It now remains that we make appear the *infufficiency of nature's light*. To clear this point, it is evident if we confider,

1. That

1. That moſt of the wiſe men of the world have paſſed over this in ſilence, as a ſpeculation too hard and high. The effects of it were ſo ſenſible, that they could not but notice them, as the Egyptians did the overflowing of their Nile. But when they would have traced theſe ſtreams up to their ſource, they were forced to quit it as an unequal chace. The reaſon whereof is ingeniouſly, as well as ſolidly given by the judicious Dr. Stillingfleet, " The reaſon was, ſays he, as corruption in-
" creaſed in the world, ſo the means of inſtruction and know-
" ledge decayed; and ſo as the phenomena grew greater, the
" reaſon of them was leſs underſtood: The knowledge of the
" hiſtory of the firſt ages of the world, through which they
" could alone come to the full underſtanding of the true cauſe
" of evil, inſenſibly decaying in the ſeveral nations; inſo-
" much that thoſe who are not at all acquainted with that hiſtory
" of the world, which was preſerved in ſacred records among
" the Jews, had nothing but their own uncertain conjectures to
" go by, and ſome kind of obſcure traditions, which were pre-
" ſerved among them, which, while they ſought to rectify by
" their interpretations, they made them more obſcure and falſe
" than they found them.*

2. Others who would needs appear more learned, but were really leſs wiſe, offered accounts, or pretended to ſay ſomewhat, rather to hide their own ignorance, than explain what they ſpoke of. So obſcure are they, that nothing can be concluded from what they ſay, but that they were ignorant, and yet ſo diſingenuous and proud that they would not own it. Among this ſort Plato is reckoned, and with him Pythagoras, who tell us, " that the principle of good is unity, finity, quieſ-
" cent, ſtreight, uneven number, ſquare, right and ſplendid; the
" principle of evil, binary, infinite, crooked, even, long of
" one ſide, unequal, left, obſcure.†" Plutarch as is noted by Dr. Stillingfleet, ſays, that the opinion of Plato is very obſcure, it being his purpoſe to conceal it; but he ſaith in his old age, in his book *de Legibus*, ὃ δὲ 'αινιγμων εὐε συμβολι ὡς without any riddle and allegory, he aſſerts the world to be moved by more than *one principle*, by two at the leaſt; the one of a *good and benign nature*, the other *contrary* to it, both in its nature

* Origines ſacrae, lib. 3. cap. 3. ſect. 8.
† Origines ſacrae, ibid. ſect. 11.

nature and operations τὸν μὲν ἀγαθερον ειναι, τηνδε ἐναντιαν ταύτη ἡ τῃν ἐναντίων δημιεργεν.

3. Another, and perhaps the greater part, did plainly give the moſt abſurd and ridiculous, not to ſay blaſphemous accounts of this matter. Some pretending all the vitioſity inherent in matter, which they ſuppoſed not created. The folly as well as wickedneſs of this opinion, is well laid open by the judicious perſon laſt quoted. This was what Plato aimed at, as Dr. Stillingfleet clears from Numenius, a famous Syrian Platonic philoſopher, who is thought to have lived in the ſecond century, who giving an account of Pythagoras and Plato's opinions, ſays, Pythagoras ait, " *Exiſtente providentia, mala quoque neceſſario* " *ſubſtitiſſe propterea quod ſylva ſit & eadem ſit malitia prædita:* " *Platonemque idem Numenius laudat, quod duas mundi ani-* " *mas autumet; unam beneficentiſſimam; malignam alteram ſcil.* " *Sylvam. Igitur juxta Platonem mundo bona ſua Dei, tan-* " *quam patris liberalitate collata ſunt; mala vero matris ſylvæ* " *vitio cohæſerunt*[*]*. " The plain caſe is, they thought God and matter eternally co-exiſtent, and that vitioſity was inherent in matter, and that God could not mend it. To this purpoſe Maximus Tyrius a Platonic philoſopher, who lived in the ſecond century, ſpeaks, " That all the evils that are in the " world, are not the works of art, but the affections of mat- " ter[†]." Seneca ſays, " *Non poteſt artifax mutare materiam*[‡]." This way the Stoicks went. Though they who have ſtudied them, pretend that there was ſome difference betwixt Plato's opinion and theirs. They who would deſire a more full account both of theſe opinions, and the abſurdity and impiety of them, may have it from Dr. Stillingfleet, but a great many of the philoſophers plainly maintained two anti-gods, the one good and

---

[*] " Although that there is a Providence, evils neceſſarily exiſt in " the world, becauſe matter exiſts in it, which is naturally the cauſe " of evil. And Rumenius commends Plato who thought that there " were two ſouls of the world, the one moſt beneficent, and the other, " viz. matter, malicious. Therefore according to Plato, the good things " that are in the world, are conferred on it as it were by the liberality " of its father, but the bad things that are in it, originate from the vi- " tioſity of matter, which is its mother."

[†] Max. Tyr. Ser. 25.

[‡] Seneca de Provid. " The workman cannot change the nature of " the matter on which he works."

and the other evil. The Persians had their Oromasdes, to whom they ascribed all the good, and Arimanius, on whom they fathered all their evils. How many run this way, any one may learn from Plutarch's discourse of Isis and Osiris, and judge whether he himself was not of the same mind. What was it that drove those great men on such wild conceits, which are so absurd that they are not worth confuting? Nothing else but their darkness about the rise of sin. And how dismal were the consequences of those notions and of this darkness? What else drove so great a part of the world to that madness, to worship even the Principle of evil? Was it not this, that they entertained perverse notions about the origin of evils, both of sin and punishment?

4. Not to insist on those absurd opinions, the latter accounts we have of this matter, by persons who reject the scriptures, after they have taken all the help from them they think meet though they are more polished, are not one whit more satisfactory. For clearing this we shall offer you the most considerable of this sort that have occurred to us. We shall begin with Simplicius a Phrygian philosopher who lived in the fifth century, and was a great opposer of the scriptures. He in his commentary upon the 34th chapter of Epictetus, speaks thus, " The soul of man is *nexus utriusque mundi*, in the
" middle between those more excellent beings, which remain
" above (which he had taught to be incapable of sin) with
" which it partakes in the sublimity of its nature and under-
" standing, and those inferior terrestrial beings, with which it
" communicates through the vital union which it hath with the
" body, and by reason of that freedom and indifferency which
" it hath, it is sometimes assimilated to the one, sometimes to
" the other of those extremes. So that while it approacheth
" to the nature of the superior beings, it keeps itself free from
" evil; but because of its freedom, it may sometimes sink down
" into those lower things, and so he calls the cause of evil
" in the soul, its voluntary descent into this lower world, and
" immersing itself in the feculency of terrestrial matter." much more he adds; but it all comes to this, " That because of the
" freedom of the will of man, nothing else can be said to be
" the author of evil, but the soul." We have likewise an account from the Oracles of Reason much to the same purpose.

A. W.

* Comment. in Epict. Cap. 34.

A. W. a deist in a letter to Sir Charles Blount answering an objection of Sir Charles Wolseley's, against the sufficiency of natural religion, gives this account: " This generally acknow-
" ledged lapse of nature, that it came, may be discovered by
" natural light; how it came, is reasonable to conclude with-
" out revelation, namely, by a deviation from the right rule of
" reason implanted in us; how he came to deviate from this
" rule, or lapse, proceeds from the nature of goodness, ori-
" ginally given us by our Creator, which reason tells us to be
" an arbitrary state of goodness only ; therefore not a necessary
" goodness to which our natures were constrained. In short
" our fall proceeds from our not being able to reason rightly on
" every thing we act, and with such beings we were created :
" For all our actions are designed by us to some good which
" may arise to us ; but we do not always distinguish rightly
" of that good: we often mistake *bonum apparens* for the
" *bonum reale*. *Decipimur specie recti*. The *bonum jucun-*
" *dum* for want of right reasoning, is preferred to the *bonum*
" *honestum*; and the *bonum vicinum*, though it be less
" in itself, often carries it before the *bonum remotum*, which
" is greater in its own nature. No man ever held that we
" could *appetere malum qua mulum**; and therefore I will not
" grant him a total lapse in our natures from God. For we
" see many born with virtuous inclinations; and though all
" men at sometimes err, even the best, in their actions, it
" only shews that we were not created to a necessitated good-
" ness. It is enough to prove no fatal lapse, that many are
" proved, through the course of their lives, more prone to do
" good than evil, and that all men do evil, only for want of
" right reasoning ; because the will necessarily follows the last
" dictate of the understanding†." The next and last whom we shall mention, is the learned Herbert, whom the rest do but copy after. Thus then he accounts for it; " *Quod ad ma-*
" *lum culpæ spectat, hoc quidem non aliunde provenire, quem*
" *ab arbitrio illo omnibus insito,* `ingenitoque, quod tanquam*
" *bonum*

---

* " An apparent good for a real good.—We are deceived by the
" appearance of rectitude.—A pleasing good is preferred to an honour-
" able good, and a near to a distant one, but we cannot desire evil as
" evil."

† Oracles of Reason, pag. 197.

"*bonum eximium Deus optimus maximus nobis largitus est; ex quo etiam a belluis magis quam ipso intellectu distinguimur: quum tamen ades ancipitis sit naturæ, ut in utramque partem flecti possit, fit ut in malum sæpe propendeat & dilabatur; cæterum per se est beneficium plane divinum, ejusque amplitudinis & præstantiæ, ut citra illud, neque boni esse possemus: ecquis enim boni aliquid efficere dicitur, nisi quando in adversam partem datur optio? Hinc igitur malum culpa accidere, quod nobilissima anima facultas, in sequiorem sua sponte partem, nulloque cogente traducatur detorqueaturque**.*

These three accounts, in several respects, run the same way. It were easy however to set them by the ears in some considerable particulars, and perhaps, to shew the inconsistency of the several authors with themselves, on these heads: but this is not my design to spend time on things, whereby truth will not gain much; as, perhaps, they contain the sum of what reason can say on the head, so we shall now shew how very far they are from satisfying in the case. The substance of them may be reduced to these three propositions:

1. That Man's body sways the soul, to which it is joined, to things suitable to itself, which are evil. This Simplicius more than insinuates.

2. That as reason is the guide of the will, which necessarily follows its last dictate; so the will's inclination to evil flows from our not being able to reason rightly. This the Oracles of Reason give plainly as a response in the words now quoted.

3. The will is *ancipitis naturæ**, perfectly indifferent, equally capable

---

* De Religione Gentilium. Cap. 13. pag. 164.—" With regard to the evil of sin, this arises from no other source than our natural freedom of will, which God the best and the greatest has bestowed on us as a distinguished blessing, and by which we are distinguished from the brutes even more than by reason itself. But as this blessing is of so ambiguous a kind, that it may be turned either way, it happens that it often inclines to evil and goes astray. Yet in itself it is certainly a divine blessing, and of such an extent and excellency, that without it we could not be good. For who is ever paid to do any good, unless when he had it in his choice to act in a different manner? The evil of sin therefore proceeds from hence, that the most noble faculty of the soul, of its own accord, and without any one forcing it, is drawn away and turned to the wrong side."

† Of a doubtful nature.

capable of, and fwayed to evil and good. This all the three concur in. It is like a nice balance which ftands even, but is eafily fwayed to either fide.

But now it is eafy to multiply difficulties againft this account, and fhew how it no way clears, but rather involves the matter more. And,

1. I would defire to know whether that inferior part, the body, or terreftrial part of man, call it which you will, fways to any thing, not fuited to its original frame and perfection, or not? If it aims at nothing, bends or inclines to nothing, but what is perfective of itfelf, I defire to know how that can be faulty? How can this body be made a part of a compofition, wherein it is faulty for it, to aim at what is truely perfective of its nature? How can it be criminal for the foul to aim at enobling and fatisfying the capacities of that, which is fo nearly united to itfelf? How is it confiftent with the wifdom of God, to unite two beings, the one whereof cannot reach its own perfection without hurt to the other? If it is faid, that it inclines to what contributes not to its own perfection; then I defire to know how it came to be fo depraved as to have a tendency to its own detriment? How was it confiftent with the wifdom of God to make it fo? How was it confiftent with the goodnefs of God to affociate it when fo made, with another more noble being to which it muft prove a burden; yea, which muft fway to that, which proves the ruin of the whole compofition? And how can man be blamed for doing that, to which his nature inevitably muft carry him? For if he is thus compounded, his body, earthly part, or lower faculties fway to evil; his will is equally inclinable to both; and, in this cafe, how can the compofition be otherwife, than depraved? For my part I fee not how it could be otherwife; or how God can juftly punifh it for being fo, upon the fuppofition laid down.

2. If it be afferted that we are not, by our original conftitution able to reafon rightly, in what concerns our own duty, as we have heard from the Oracles of Reafon; then I defire to know if we are not neceffitated by our very make and conftitution to err? If we are to believe, what the fame Oracle utters, that the will muft follow neceffarily the underftanding; then I defire to know, if we are not neceffitated to fin? If things are thus and thus, we muft either believe them to be, or believe that this Oracle gives a falfe refponfe; then I defire to know how God could make us neceffarily evil? How can he punifh us for it?

it? Can this be reconciled with the reſt of this doctrine, about the arbitrary ſtate of man's goodneſs? I might aſk not a few other queries, but perhaps theſe will ſuffice.

3. If the will be, in its own nature, perfectly free and indifferent, then I deſire to know, whether there is any thing in that compoſition, whereof it is a part, or to which it is joined, or any thing in the circumſtances wherein man is placed, ſwaying it to the worſt ſide? If there is any thing either in man's conſtitution or circumſtances, ſwaying him wrong; then I deſire to know, is there any thing to balance them? Whether there is or is not any thing to keep him even? I would deſire to know how any thing came to be in his conſtitution, to ſway him wrong? If there is any thing to balance theſe inducements to ſin, or inclinations, then man is perfectly indifferent ſtill: and about this we ſhall ſpeak anon. If there is a will, equally capable of good and evil, and man has ſomewhat in his conſtitution or circumſtances, at leaſt ſwaying him to evil, then I deſire to know how it was poſſible for him to evite it? If he has nothing determining him more to evil than to good, or if any thing that inclines to evil is balanced, by other things of no leſs force determining and ſwaying him to good, then many things may be enquired: how comes it to paſs, that though man is equally inclinable to good or evil, that almoſt all men chooſe evil? Yea I need not put an almoſt to it. It it a ſtrange thing to ſuppoſe all men equally diſpoſed to good or evil, and yet none chooſe the good.

4. I do not know how this notion of man's liberty, which is eaſily granted to be in itſelf, if the notion of it is rightly ſtated, a perfection, will take with conſiderate men, that it conſiſts in a perfect indifferency to good or evil: for if this is a neceſſary perfection of the rational nature, without which it cannot be called good, as Herbert clearly aſſerts, in his words above quoted; then I aſk, what ſhall become of thoſe natures unalterably good, of which Simplicius talks? Is it abſurd to ſuppoſe, that there may be ſuch? Are they, if they be, leſs perfect, becauſe uncapable of that which debaſes and depraves them? Is God good, who has beyond diſpute no ſuch liberty as this? Is an indifferency to commit ſin or not to ſin, a great perfection? If it be, is it greater than not to be capable of ſinning? They may embrace this notion of liberty who will, and fancy themſelves perfect, I ſhall not for this reckon them ſo.

5. This account of man as equally inclined to good or evil, is

either an acount of man's cafe as he now is, or as at firft made: If man is now otherwife, to wit, inclined more to evil than good, how came he to be fo? This is the difficulty we defire to be fatisfied about. If this be the cafe he was made in, and ftill continues in, then, I fay, it is utterly falfe, and contradictory to the ears, eyes and confcience of all the world. Who fees not that man is plainly, ftrongly, and I may add univerfally, inclined to evil? The wifer heathens have owned it. And it is plainly made out againft the moft impudent denier. Hierocle's words, as I find them tranflated by an excellent perfon, are memorable to this purpofe. " Man, fays he, is of his own motion inclined " to follow the evil and leave the good. There is a certain ftrife " bred in his affections; he hath a free will which he abufeth, " binding himfelf wholly to encounter the laws of God. And " this freedom itfelf is nothing elfe, but a willingnefs to admit " that which is not good, rather than otherwife*." This is a true ftate of the matter from a heathen.

6. The fuppofition of man's being made perfectly indifferent is injurious to God, who cannot be fuppofed, without reflection on him, to have put man in fuch a cafe. The leaft that can be faid, preferving the honour due to the divine excellencies, is that God gave a law to man, fuitable to the rectitude of his own nature and to man's happinefs and perfection; that he endued him with an ability to know this law, the obligations he lay under to obey it, and the inducements that might have fortified him in his obedience againft the force of any temptation which he might meet with. If this be not afferted, it will not be poffible to keep God from blame, which all that own him, are concerned to take care of: for how could he bind man to obey a law, which he did not make known to him, or at leaft gave him a power to know? If he laid him open to temptations, and made him incapable of difcovering what might antidote their force, if he would ufe it, what fhall we think of his goodnefs? Further, we muft own that the will of man was made inclinable, though not not immutably fo, to its own perfection: how elfe was it worthy of its author? Finally, we muft own that man had no affection or inclnation in him, that was really contradictory to that law which he was fubjected to, and which tended to his happinefs and perfection. If this is denied, then I afk, were not thefe inclinations finful? Was that being worthy of God, that had no tendency

* Hierocles Carmin. Aur. Tranfl. Reaf. of Script. Belief, pag. 146.

tendency to its own perfection? But on the contrary, what was inclinable to its own ruin?

7. This being the least, that can without manifest reproach to the wisdom, goodness and justice of the Creator, be supposed in favour of man's original constitution; I desire to know, is this the case still, or is it not? If it is not, then how came it to be otherwise? How comes man originally to be worse now, than at first? How is this consistent with the deist's principles, that there is no lapse? If it be asserted, we are in the same state still, how then comes all the world to be full of wickedness? How is this reconcileable with the experiences and consciences of men, that assured them of the contrary?

8. If it is thought enough to resolve all this, as to actual failings, into the choice of man; yet what shall we say as to that darkness as to duty, which we heard the deists confessing, in their Oracles of Reason? How came that inability to reason rightly, which we have before demonstrated man under, and which our adversaries will own! Again, how come we to have vitious inclinations so strongly rooted in our natures! Strong they are; for they trample upon our light, the penalties of laws divine and human; yea and the smartings of our own conscience. The drunkard and unclean person finds his health ruined, and yet in spite of all this, his inclination makes him run on in the vice that has ruined him: and the like is evident in other cases innumerable. Deeply rooted they are: they are some way twisted in with the constitutions of our body, and no less fixed in our souls. So fixed they are, that, though our own reason condemns them, it cannot remove them. Though sometimes fear restrains them as to the outward acts; yet it cannot eradicate the inclination. Instruction and all human endeavours cannot do it. A famed Seneca that understood so much, who undertook to teach others, and perhaps has spoke and writ better than most of the heathens; yet by all his knowledge and all his endeavours, owns this corruption so deeply rooted in himself, that he expected not to get rid of it. *Non perveni ad sanitatem, ne perveniam quidem: delinimentis magis quam remedia podagræ meæ compono contentus si rarius accedit, & si minus terminatur.** 9. Not

---

* "I am not come to a sound state, nor shall I ever arrive at it. I am composing palliatives rather than remedies for my gout, being content if it attacks me more seldom, and proves less violent."

9. Not only so, but further, how come these inclinations to be born with us? Grow up with us? That they are so, is evident. We no sooner begin to act, than to act perversely. We no sooner shew any inclinations, than we shew that our inclinations are evil. Yea, among Christians, where there are many virtuous persons, who give the best example, the best instruction, and use the best discipline for the education of their children in virtue; yet we see the children discover inclinations so strong, as are not to be restrained by all these endeavours, much less eradicated: and, so early are they there, that they cannot be prevented by the most timeous care.

10. It will not help the matter to tell us, that there are some born with virtuous inclinations. For 1. If all are not so, the difficulty remains. How came these to be born otherwise, of whom we have been speaking! How came their frame to be different from, nay and worse than that of others! Are they under the same law? If so, why have they more impediments, and less power of obedience? 2. We would be glad to see the persons condescended on, that are void of vitious inclinations, that we might ask them some questions. You say you are born with virtuous inclinations. Well, but have you no ill inclinations? If you are no drunkard, adulterer, &c. yet have you no inclination to pride, prodigality, neglect of God, covetousness, or somewhat like? I fear the man that can answer plainly in the negative here, will not be easily found. And till we see him, we deny there is any such. 3. To confirm this, several persons, whom the world has looked on as virtuously inclined from their infancy, have, when seriously acquainted with Christianity, owned that they were as wickedly inclined as others; only by the help of their constitution, they were not so much prompted to those evils, which are most obobserved and condemned in the world. And this account has been given by persons of judgment, whose capacity, nor ingenuity cannot reasonably be questioned. Finally, the ground whereon A. W. pronounces against an universal lapse, viz. That we cannot *appetere malum qua malum*†, is ridiculous: For this is a thing perfectly inconsistent, not only with the due exercise, but the very nature of our rational faculties: And if notwithstanding this impossibility of any man's desiring

† Desire evil as evil.

ing evil as evil, so many are deeply corrupted, no imaginable reason can be assigned, why all may not be so, without supposing that we can *appetere malum qua malum*.

To conclude then, it is upon the whole evident, that reason can never trace this matter to its proper source. Our consciences condemn us indeed, and so acquit the Deity. But without revelation we can never understand upon what grounds we are condemned by ourselves, nor how the Deity is to be justified; and so this sentence of our consciences involves the matter more, and encreases the difficulty. It is not from any distinct view of the particular way how we come to be guilty, and how God comes to be free of blame, that conscience is led to this sentence. And therefore, how to come to any satisfaction about the matter, that may liberate us from the inconveniencies abovementioned, which are really subversive of all religion, and can reasonably be supposed available to us, reason can never satisfy us.

Since these gentlemen, with whom we have to do, find it their interest to deny any lapse, I shall, to what has been said, add a short, but judicious and solid confirmation of this, from a person of a more than ordinary reach, I mean Dr. How: who, after he has quoted many testimonies from Heathen authors, proving this lapse, reasons for it, and confirms it further from arguments not easily to be answered: His words run thus, " If we consider, can
" it be so much as imaginable to us, that the present state of man
" is his primitive state, or that he is now such as he was at first
" made? For neither is it conceivable, that the blessed God
" should have made a creature with an aversion to the only im-
" portant ends, whereof it is naturally capable: Or particu-
" larly that he created man, with a disaffection to himself; or,
" that ever he at first, designed a being of so high excellency,
" as the spirit of man to trudge so meanly, and be so basely
" servile to terrene inclinations; or, since there are manifestly
" powers in him, of a superior and inferior sort and order, the
" meaner should have been by original institution framed to
" command; and the more noble and excellent, only to obey
" and serve; as every one that observes, may see the common
" case with man is.

" And how far he is swerved from what he was, is easily
" conjecturable by comparing him with the measures, which
" shew what he should be. For it cannot be conceived for
" what end laws were ever given him; if at least we allow
" them

" them not to be the measures of his primitive capacity, or de-
" ny him ever to have been in a possibility to obey. Could
" they be intended for his government if conformity to them
" were against or above his nature ? Or were they only for
" his condemnation ? Or for what, if he was never capable of
" obeying them ? How inconsistent were it with the goodness
" of the blessed God, that the condemnation of his creatures
" should be the first design of his giving them laws! And with
" his justice, to make his laws the rule of punishment, to whom
" they could never be the rule of obedience and duty ! Or
" with his wisdom, to frame a system and body of laws, that
" should never serve for either purpose ! And so be upon the
" whole useful for nothing. The common reason of mankind
" teacheth us to estimate the wisdom and equity of lawgivers,
" by the suitableness of their constitutions to the genius and
" temper of the people for whom they are made ; and we com-
" monly reckon nothing can more slur and expose a govern-
" ment, than the imposing of constitutions, most probably im-
" practicable, and which are never likely to obtain. How
" much more incongruous must it be esteemed to enjoin such
" as never possibly could ! Prudent legislators, and studious of
" the common good, would be shy to impose upon men, under
" their power, against their genius and common usages, nei-
" ther easily alterable, nor to any advantage ; much more ab-
" surd were it, with great solemnity, and weighty sanctions, to
" enact statutes for brute creatures: and wherein were it
" more to purpose, to prescribe unto men strict rules of piety
" and virtue, than to beasts or trees, if the former had not
" been capable of observing them, as the latter were not *."
I believe the deists will not easily overthrow this nervous discourse.

CHAP. X.

*Proving Nature's Light unable to discover the Means of obtain-
ing Pardon of Sin, or to shew that it is attainable.*

THAT *all have sinned* is sufficiently clear from the foregoing discourse. That it is of importance to understand the
rise of sin, and that nature's light is unable to trace its original,

* Dr. How's Living Temple, Part 2, pag. 121, 122.

nal, has been likewise evinced. But all this were indeed of less consideration, if nature's light could assure us of pardon, or direct as to the means whereby it may be obtained. But here it is no less defective, than as to the former. That we are all guilty of sin even the deists do acknowledge; the Oracles of Reason own that all men at sometimes err, even the best, in their actions. And the evidence of it is such, that none can get over the truth, if he is not plainly resolved to deny what is most evident. Now this being the case, that we have all transgressed, it is of the highest importance to know whether God will pardon us, or upon what terms he will do it? If he punish us, what a case are we in? How can they who fear punishment expect rewards! But because this is a difficulty of no small importance, and the deists, since they see they cannot clear it, make their business to obscure the importance of the case, and render it more involved; we shall, therefore,

I. State the case, and clear the importance of it.
II. Discover the weakness of nature's light about it.
III. Speak fully to a particular exception about repentance.

Sect. I.
Wherein the Importance of the Difficulty is stated.

IF the deists should allow sin to be so great an evil, as we pretend it is, it would exceedingly embarrass them; therefore they labour to smooth the matter by telling us, that either it is no evil, or one of not so great consideration, as is commonly imagined: but the wildness and unreasonableness of this attempt will be easily shewn, by a consideration of the evil of sin. It is not my design to write largely on this head, but only to condescend on a few of those considerations, whereon we insist for proving sin to be *exceeding sinful:* which, although they are built on rational grounds, yet we are led to them by the assistance of revealed light.

1. Sin is a *transgression* of a *law*, the highest law, the law of the supreme and righteous Governor of the world. *Where there is no law there is no transgression.* And such as the law is, such is the transgression. There is no more just way of measuring the evil of sin, than by considering the law it violates. The law bears the impress of the highest authority, that of the Supreme Ruler of the universe. Every transgression must therefore import, if not a contempt, yet certainly a want of

of due regard to this authority, which, how criminal it is in man, who is as to being, prefervation and well-being, every way dependent, is eafily underflood. Moreover, this law is not a mere arbitrary appointment, but fuch as is the neceffary refult of the nature of God and man ; and therefore the violation of it, imports no lefs, than an accufation of the rectitude of God's nature, whence the law refults ; and charges unfuitablenefs thereto, upon the nature of man, as being fo made, that, without wrong to itfelf, it cannot be fubject to the rule of God's government. And who fees not how deeply this reflects on God?

2. Sin contradicts the great defign of man's being. *God made us and not we ourfelves.* It is blafphemy to allege, that infinite wifdom made fo noble a creature as man without defign. Nor can it reafonably be pretended, that the chief aim of God in making him was any other, than his having the felf-fatisfaction of having acted as became him, and having made a work every way worthy of his wifdom and holinefs. And fince man alfo was capable of propofing defigns, it is foolifh to imagine, that God either could or would allow him to make any other his chief end than the pleafure of God ; or acting fo as to make it appear that he was every worthy of his Author. But when man fins he plainly counteracts what God defigned, and he was obliged to defign ; for he pleafes not God, but himfelf ; and this is doing what in him lies to fruftrate God of the defign he had in his work, and dabafe the being and powers given him for the honour of God by employing them againft him, and ufing them in contradiction to his declared will.

3. Sin mifreprefents God. The works of God bear an imprefs of God's wifdom and power. Man only was made capable of reprefenting his moral perfections, his holinefs, juftice, truth, and the like. But when he fins, he not only fails of his duty, but really mifreprefents God his maker, as one who approves fin, that is directly crofs to his will, which is ever congruous to the holinefs of his nature ; or, at leaft, as one, who either wants will or power to crufh the contraveener ; and fo he is reprefented either as unholy, or impotent ; or one, who can tamely allow his will to be counteracted by a creature that he has made and fuftains. But what horrid reflections are thefe on the holy God ?

4. Sin accufes God of want of wifdom and goodnefs in appointing laws which were not for his creature's good, and he could not obey without detriment ; of envy, in barring the creature

ture by a law, from that which is neceſſary to his happineſs; of inſufficiency, to ſatisfy the creature he has made, while he is obliged to ſeek for that elſewhere, which is not to be found in him, in the way of obedience; and of folly, in making ſuch a law, as cannot be expected to be obeyed, in regard the creature ſubjected to it, gains more by breaking than by keeping of it.

Finally, to crown all, ſin dethrones God, and ſets the creature in his room. The honour of God's law and authority, and the ſinner's good, are wickedly ſuppoſed to be inconſiſtent, and the latter is preferred. The will of the Creator and creature croſs one another, and the creature's will is preferred. The friendſhip, favour, and ſufficiency of Deity is laid in balance againſt ſome other imaginary good, and deciſion is given againſt God. Theſe are a few of the many evils of ſin. They are not ſtrained ones. This is not a rhetorical declamation againſt ſin, wherein things are unjuſtly aggravated to raiſe odium againſt it; but a plain account of a few of the evils of it, which yet is infinitely ſhort of what the caſe would admit. But who can fully repreſent the evil that ſtrikes againſt infinite goodneſs, holineſs, juſtice, wiſdom, and ſupreme authority? Who can unfold its aggravations, ſave he who knows what God is, and what he is to man, and what man is, and how many ways he is dependent on, ſubject, obliged and indebted to God? Well therefore may ſin be ſaid to have an infinity of evil in it.

The deiſts, to evade the difficulties ariſing from this evil of ſin, take different courſes. Some plainly deny any ſuch thing as evil, or that there is any thing morally good or bad. Thomas Aikenhead, who was executed at Edinbrugh, January 8, 1697, for his blaſphemies, in his paper he delivered from the ſcaffold, tells us what his thoughts were in in this matter, and upon what grounds they were built. When in his rational inquiries he came to conſider, whether we were capable of offending God, he tells us, " That after much " pondering and ſerious conſideration, he concluded the nega- " tive." The famed Mr. Hobbs was not of a very different mind, for he plainly aſſerts, " That there is nothing good or " evil in itſelf, nor any common laws conſtituting what is " naturally juſt or unjuſt: but all things are to be meaſured " by what every man judgeth fit, where there is no civil go- " vernment; and by the laws of ſociety, where there is one." And elſewhere, " Before men entered into a ſtate of civil go- " vernment, there was not any thing juſt or unjuſt, foraſ-
" much

"much as juſt and unjuſt are the relatives of human laws; every action being in itſelf indifferent." And whether Spinoza was not of the ſame mind, is left to thoſe to judge, who have time and leiſure to trace his meaning, in his obſcure and deſignedly involved way of writing. But ſurely this propoſition in his atheiſtical ethicks looks very like it, "*Si homines liberi naſcerentur (liber autem eſt juxta Spinozam, qui ſecundum ductum vel ex ductu rationis agit) nullum boni & mali formarent conceptum, quamdiu liberi eſſent.*" Mr. Hobbs has been learnedly confuted by many, ſuch as Dr. Cumberland, Mr. Tyrell, and almoſt all who write of the law of nature. Spinoza has likewiſe been examined by Wittichius and many others. The firſt, viz. Thomas Aikenhead, his grounds I ſhall purpoſe and examine.

The firſt in his own words runs thus, "I thought, ſays he, a great part of morality, if not all, proceeded *ex arbitrio hominum*†, as of that of a kingdom, or commonwealth, or what moſt men think convenient for ſuch and ſuch ends, and theſe ends are always terminated upon being congruous to the nature of things; now we ſee that according to men's fancies things are congruous or incongruous to their natures, if not to the body, yet to the thinking faculty."

The ſum of this confuſed diſcourſe, which probably he learned from Hobbs, amounts to this; God has fixed no law to our moral actions, by which they are to be regulated. Theſe which are called moral laws, are only the determinations of governments, or the concurring judgment of men, concerning what they think meet to be done for their own ends. That which ſome judge meet and congruous, others may find unſuitable to their nature and ends, and ſo are not obliged to obey. But 1. Are not all theſe ungrounded aſſertions, whereof no proof is offered, but the author's deluded fancy? Has it not been irrefragably demonſtrated by as many as diſcourſe of moral good and evil, that antecedently to any government among men, we are under a law, the law of nature, and that this is the will of God. 3. If all theſe had kept ſilence, does not the thing itſelf ſpeak? What can be more evident, than that there is a law of nature, and that this is the law of God? We are certain,

* "If men were born free (and he is free according to Spinoza, who acts according to the guidance of reaſon) they would form no conception of good or evil, as long as they were free."
† "From the will of man."

tain, that we are made of rational natures, capable of laws and government. We are no lefs fure that God made us, and made us fo. It is felf-evident, that to him who made us, it belongs to govern, and difpofe of us to thofe ends for which we were made. And we by our very beings are bound to obey, fubmit, and fubject ourfelves to his will and pleafure, who made us and on whom we every way depend, and therefore his will, if he make it known, is a law, and the higheft law to us. Again, it is clear that this reafon, if we attend to it, tells us that fome things are to be done, and fome things left undone; fuch as thefe, that we are to ferve, love, obey and honour him that made us, upholds us, and on whom we every way depend; that we are to carry toward our fellow-creatures, as it becomes thofe, who have the fame original with us, who are fubjected to the fame rule, are obliged to purfue the fame ends; and that we are to difpofe of ourfelves, as the author of our nature allows us. Thefe are all, if not felf-evident, yet next to it, and eafily deducible from principles that are fo. Further, the reafon that is implanted in us by God, tells us fo, we are to take what it leads us to, while duly ufed, as the will of God, and fo a law to us. " For whatever judgment " God makes a man with, concerning either himfelf, or other " things, it is God's judgment, and whatever is his judgment " is a law to man ; nor can he neglect or oppofe it without " fin, being in his exiftence made with a neceffary fubjec- " tion to God. Such and fuch dictates being the natural ope- " rations of our minds, the being and effential conftitution of " which, in right reafoning, we owe to God; we cannot " but efteem them the voice of God within us, and confe- " quently his law to us [*]."

What he tells us of men's different apprehenfions, about what is right or wrong makes nothing to the purpofe. That only fhews that in many inftances we are in the dark as to what is good and evil, which is granted ; but will not infer that there is no fixed meafure of good and evil. In many general truths, all who apply themfelves to think, underftand the terms, and have the truths propofed, do agree. And perhaps, all that is knowable of our duty by the light of nature, is deducible from fuch principles of morality, as all rational men who have them fairly propofed to them, muft affent to. And deductions from

---

[*] Sir Charles Wolfeley's Scripture Belief, pag. 32, 33.

from laws, when duly made, are of equal authority with the principles from which they are inferred. And finally, when men, in purfuance of their perverfe natures, follow what is crofs to thofe dictates of reafon, they are condemned by their confciences, which fhews them under the obligation of a law, and that acting in a congruity to their natures as corrupt, is not the ftandard they are obliged to walk by, fince their own reafon checks them for doing it. They who would defire to have this matter fully difcourfed, may read others who have done it defignedly, of whom there is great plenty.

His fecond reafon runs thus: " Alfo we do not know what " is good or evil in itfelf, if not thus; whatfoever can be at- " tributed to God, that is good; and what cannot, is evil. " And we know not what can be attributed to God, but fuch " things as by a deduction we afcribe to him, we call perfect, " and fuch as we deny to be in him, we call imperfect, and fo " we moft ignorantly commit a circle. There is no other no- " tion of things in themfelves good or evil."

It is much harder to find the fenfe of thefe words, if they have any, than to anfwer the argument. The defign of it is to prove that there is no ftandard whereby we may judge what is good and what is evil. The force of the argument amounts to this, that there is no way how we come to know any thing to be good, but by this, that it may be afcribed to God. But we cannot know whether it is to be afcribed to God, unlefs we know that it is perfect or good.

This is thin fophiftry, which I might eafily expofe, were it to any purpofe to difcover the weaknefs of that, which its au- thor was afhamed of and difowned. As to the firft propofition. " That there is no other way to know whether any thing be good ar evil, but this, that it can or cannot be afcribed to God."
1. The complex propofition is falfe; for there are other ways whereby we may know things to be good or evil. And this holds whether we take it in a phyfical or a moral fenfe. We know that to be morally good which God enjoins us to do. We know the will of God in fome inftances, from the nature God has given us; and from thefe inftances our reafon can in- fer others. As to phyfical good, we know things to be good or perfect, by acquaintance with the nature of things, and by the felf-evident notions of perfection : for there are fome things, fuch as dependence, fubjection, and the like, which without any reafoning about the matter, we underftand to be imperfect

or perfect. As soon as we underſtand the terms, and know that a perfection is that which it is better for any being to have than to want : and then what theſe particular words, dependence, ſubjection, &c. ſignify. This alone overthrows his whole argument. 2. The maxim which he fixes as a ſtandard, That is good which may be aſcribed to God, and that is not good which may not be aſcribed to him; if it is taken in its full extent, it is falſe as to moral good, of which the only queſtion is : for it is certain, that it is good for man to be a dependent, a ſubject, &c. which cannot be aſcribed to God. If it is taken in a phyſical ſenſe, it is not to the purpoſe ; and beſides, it would even in this ſenſe need ſome caution.

As to his other propoſition, " That we cannot otherwiſe know what is to be aſcribed to God, than by knowing that it is good or perfect," it can ſcarcely be ſuppoſed to ſpeak of good in a moral ſenſe ; and in any other ſenſe it is impertinent. If it is underſtood in a moral ſenſe it is likewiſe falſe, for we may know that things which are not in their own nature moral perfections, belong to God, ſuch as power, omnipreſence, &c. If it be underſtood in any other ſenſe, we have nothing to do with it.

The next head that he adds is, " That all men will confeſs
" that any thing may be morally evil and good alſo, and con-
" ſequently any thing decent or indecent, moral or immoral.
" Neither, though there were things in themſelves evil, (if
" we do not apprehend other things inſtead of them) can we
" have any inclination thereunto ? Otherwiſe the will could
" wiſh evil."

But 1. Who will grant him (in any other ſenſe that will be ſubſervient to his purpoſe) that all actions are indifferent ? I know none but men of his own principles. 2. As for what he pretends, that we cannot incline to that which is in its own nature evil, unleſs it be under the notion of good, I ſee not what this ſays for him ; it is enough that we can do that action which is evil and prohibited, yea, and which we know is prohibited, to conſtitute ſin and make the ſinner deeply guilty.

But not to inſiſt any further on this inconſiderable trifler, whoſe undigeſted notions ſcarce deſerve the conſideration we have given them ; and much leſs did they become the awful gravity of the place where they were delivered. There are others of the deiſts who think it not ſafe to venture thus far : becauſe in effect this overthrows all religion and eſtabliſhes

plain

plain atheifm: yet they mince the matter and leffen fin as much as they can.

Herbert goes this way, telling us the finner's excufe, that " 1. *Homines funt natura fua fragiles peccatoque obnoxii.* " 2. *Peccata hominum non tam in Dei contumeliam, quam in* " *propriam utilitatem, fub boni alicujus apparentis obtentu fieri* " *plerumque; ac licet in eo homines fallerentur, nihil tamen in-* " *fenfo in Deum animo patratum effe**." That is, " Men are by " nature frail and liable to fin: and they do not fin out of con- " tempt of God, but for their own profit, while fin appears " under the fhew of good. And although in this men are de- " ceived, yet there is nothing done with any ill defign againft " God."

A. W. in his letter to Charles Blount, pleads, " That though " the offence is committed againft an infinite being, we are but " finite creatures, who commit fin †."

But now, as to the firft of thefe reafons or excufes, I fear, if it plead any thing, it cafts the fault over on God. Are we to excufe ourfelves from our frailty? Well, either we are made fo frail that we are not able to obey, or we are not; if we are able to obey, then where is the excufe when God requires no more of us than what he gave us power to perform? If we are not able, then how came God to fubject us to a law we were not able to obey? If we have rendered ourfelves unable, is not this our fault?

As to the fecond, " that we do not fin out of contempt of the Deity, but for our own advantage." I anfwer, 1. The princi- ple that the finner goes on, according to this apology made for him, viz. That the thing he does, though it croffes the law of God, yet makes for his own advantage, is highly injurious to, and blafphemous againft God: for it fuppofes that God has bar- red man from what contributes to his happinefs, and fuppofes that more advantage is to be had by difobedience, which is a high aggravation of the fault. 2. I will not grant him, that there is no oppofition in the heart to God. What though there be not plain, declared, direct and open hoftility; yet there is an alienaton of affection, averfion from converfe with, and a ne- glect of God to be found with all in more or lefs, of which their actions are a fufficient proof.

* De Relig. Gentilium, Cap. 5. pag. 199.
† Oracles of Reafon.

As to the third, " that an offence, though againſt an infinite God, is leſſened by the conſideration of the ſinner's being finite ;" I anſwer, 1. This excuſe pleads for all ſin alike: for let the ſinner ſin never ſo deeply, yet he is finite ſtill. 2. If this be well conſidered, it is perfectly ridiculous: for the meaſure of ſin, its greatneſs is not to be taken this way, but the contrary; for provided the object againſt whom it is committed is infinite, the meaner the perſon is that commits it, the greater ſtill is the fault.

But in very deed, all theſe attempts to extenuate ſin, as they are uſeleſs to ſinners, who are not judged by man, but God, and not to be dealt with according to the eſtimate he makes, but that which God makes of ſin; ſo likewiſe they ſmell rank of the want of a due regard for the honour of the Deity, and are of the worſt conſequences to the world, ſince they tend to encourage ſin, open a door to impiety, and embolden ſinners to go on in courſes they too much incline to. Beſides, ſuch excuſes for ſin do but ill become perſons who make ſuch an horrible out cry againſt the doctrine of ſatisfaction upon all occaſions, as having a tendency to make forgiveneſs cheap in ſinner's eyes, and to embolden men to ſin without fear. May not the charge be here retorted? Who gives the greateſt encouragement to ſin, he that aſſerts the neceſſity of a ſatisfaction, or he who extenuates ſin to that degree as to encourage the ſinner to hope he may get off without a ſatisfaction? I ſhall, to what has been ſaid, ſubjoin a few words from a late diſcourſe. If the quotation ſeem long, the excellency of it will eaſily excuſe it; beſides, it is ſo full to the purpoſe, and leads ſo directly to that which is the deſign of what has hitherto been ſaid. " Furthermore,
" it is to be conſidered, that the rights of the divine govern-
" ment; the quality and meaſure of offences committed againſt
" it; and when or upon what terms they may be remitted; or
" in what caſe it may be congruous to the dignity of that go-
" vernment, to recede from ſuch rights, are matters of ſo
" high a nature, that it becomes us to be very ſparing in ma-
" king any eſtimate about them, eſpecially a diminiſhing one.
" Even among men, how ſacred things are majeſty and the
" rights of government? And how much above the reach of a
" vulgar judgment? Suppoſe a company of peaſants that un-
" derſtand little more than what is within the compaſs of their
" mattock, plough and ſhovel, ſhould take upon them to judge
" of the rights of their prince, and make an eſtimate of the
" meaſure

"measure of offences, committed against the majesty and dig-
"nity of government, how competent judges would we think
"them? And will we not acknowledge the most refined hu-
"man understanding as incompetent to judge of the rights of
"the divine government? Or measure the injuriousness of the
"offence done against it, as the meanest peasant to make an
"estimate of these matters in a human government? If only
"the reputation be wronged of a person of a better quality,
"how strictly is it insisted on, to have the matter tried by his
"peers, or persons of an equal rank, such as are capable of under-
"standing honour and reputation! How would it be resented,
"that an affront put upon a nobleman, should be committed to
"the judgment of smiths and coblers, especially if they were
"*participes criminis**, and as well parties as judges?
"When the *regalia*† of the great Ruler and Lord of heaven
"and earth are invaded, his temple violated, his presence
"despised, his image torn down thence and defaced: Who
"among the sons of men are either great, or knowing, or in-
"nocent enough to judge of the offence and wrong? Or how
"fit it is, that it be remitted without recompence? Or what re-
"compence would be proportionable? How supposable is it, that
"there may be congruities in this matter, obvious to the divine
"understanding, which infinitely exceed the measure of ours‡."

From what has been said, it is easy to understand the importance of the case. All mankind are involved in sin, lie under
this dreadful guilt, and that not in one, but in many instances.
Now if they are not sure that it may be removed, and know
not in what way this is to be done; they must either not take
up the case, or they must be under continual disquietments,
dread the issue, and fear divine resentments. They can never
expect any rewards for obedience, and consequently they must
languish in it, and so all religion that can be available is lost.

Sect. II.

Shewing the darkness of Nature's Light as to Pardon.

THE importance of the case being thus cleared, we now proceed to demonstrate the insufficiency of nature's light to help
out

---

* "Sharers in the crime."
† "Royal prerogatives."
‡ Dr. How's Living Temple, Part 2. pag. 237, 238, 239.

out of this strait. And that we may without fear assert it so, is evident from the ensuing considerations:

1. That light which failed men so far, as to a discovery of the strait, is not likely to help them out of it. If we understand not where the difficulty lies, and how great it is, we are never likely to solve it. Now it is undeniable, that a great part of the world understood not the evil of sin, or of how vast a consequence it was to be assured about the pardon of it. The prevalent darkness of their minds about the nature, holiness and justice of the Deity; their own natures and relation to him; their ignorance of the nature of sin; the commonness of it in the world; their strong inclinations to it, and other things of a like nature, kept them from apprehending the difficulty of the case. But above all, the best moralists amongst the philosophers, such as Socrates and Plato, seemed utterly unconcerned. And the reason is plain, their pride blinded them so, that they idolized their own virtues, and made no reckoning of their sins.

2. They who had a little more concern about sin, saw somewhat of the difficulty of this matter, but found themselves at a loss what way to relieve themselves: and therefore they had recourse, some to philosophy, music and mathematics, for the purgation of their souls; and others to lustrations, sacrifices and diverse washings, and I do not know what other fancies, which had no manner of foundation in reason, no suitableness to the nature of the difficulty, no divine warrant, and therefore were never able to satisfy the conscience, as to the sinner's acceptance with God, and the removal of the guilt. These being only the productions of their own imaginations, notwithstanding of all these, their fears continued, and they remained under apprehensions that even death should not terminate their miseries, as Lucretius himself sings,

—— At mens sibi conscia facti,
Prœmetuens adhibet stimulos, terretque flagellis,
Nec videt interea, qui terminus esse malorum
Possit, nec qui sit penarum denique finis,
Atque eadem metuit magis hæc in morte gravescant*.

3. They who either thought somewhat deeper of the case, or at least, seemed to do so, especially at times when the impressions

* " But the mind conscious to itself of actual guilt, by fearing pu-
" nishment applies stings to itself and terrifies itself with whips: nor

pressions they had of divine justice were quickened by some terrible plagues or judgments, had recourse to things that were so far from relieving, that they really increased the guilt, I mean that abominable custom of human sacrifices. This cruel custom almost universally obtained in the world, if we may believe either profane or sacred records; of which Dr. Owen in his treatise of *Vindictive Justice* gives many instances. They not only sacrificed men, but even multitudes of them. The instances of this kind in the sacred records are known. As to others, Ditmarus quoted by Dr. Owen tells us, " That the Normans and " Danes, every year in the month of January did sacrifice to " their gods ninety-nine men, as many horses, dogs and " cocks*." Clemens Alexandria quoted by the same author, tells what the usage of the nations in this matter was, and on what occasion.—" *Jam vero cum civitates & gentes tanquam* " *pestes invasissent, sæva postularunt libamina; & Aristomenes* " *quidem Messenius, Ithometæ Jovi, Trecentos mactavit, se tot* " *& tales rite sacrificare existimans, in quibus etiam Theom-* " *pompus rex Lacedæmonum erat, præclara victima. Tauri au-* " *tem populi, qui habitabant circa Tauricam Chersonesum, quos-* " *cunque hospites apud se ceperint, Dianæ Tauricæ eos statim* " *sacrificant (inde inhospitalia littora). Hæc tua sacrificia Eu-* " *ripides in scena tragice decantat†.*" Here are no less than three hundred sacrificed at once, and among them a king. Here are strangers sacrificed. And any one that will read there will find how usual it was to sacrifice their children and nearest relations. The custom is barbarous, and fully speak out the despair of men awakened to a serious consideration of sin, and the darkness

" does it see in the mean time how any bounds can be set to its suf-
" ferings, nor what will at last be the end of its punishment, and fears
" lest these same sufferings should grow more grievous at death."
* Dr. Owen de Justitia Vindicatrice, Cap. 4. page 69.
† " But when, like the plague, they had over-run all states and na-
" tions, they required cruel offerings. Aristomenes the Messenian sacri-
" ficed three hundred men to Jupiter Ithometes, among whom like-
" wise was Theopopyus king of the Lacedemonians, an illustrious vic-
" tim. And the Tauri a nation in Crim Tartary, whenever they
" caught any strangers among them, they immediately sacrificed them
" to Diana Taurica, whence their shores were proverbially stiled in-
" hospitable. Euripides relates these sacrifices of yours in a tragical
" manner on the stage."

darkness of nature's light. If it could have pointed to any other thing that could quiet the conscience, civilized nations, such as those among whom this custom did prevail, would never have had recourse to it.

4. It is no wonder that men should be brought to such straits; for they wanted the knowledge of many things, that were of absolute necessity to make them once so much as understand what a case they were in. They knew not, nor, as has been proven could they know the rise of sin, and therefore could not know what estimate to make of it, nor what God would make of it. They knew neither the extent of the mercy nor justice of God, without which it was impossible to determine in the case.

5. The questions that must be resolved before the mind of a sinner, that once understands his state, can be satisfied, are so many, so intricate, and so palpably above the reach of unenlightened reason, that it is foolish to pretend that nature's light will or can satisfy the mind of any man in the case. Men may pretend what they will, who either do not take up the case, or who are otherwise themselves satisfied by divine revelation; but they who seriously, and without partiality or prejudice view the case, will have other thoughts. Who will give me rational satisfaction as to those and the like questions? Whether, considering the greatness of sin, the justice, wisdom and holiness of God, and the honour of his government, it is consistent to pardon any sin? If it be, whether he will pardon all, many or few sins? What, or what degrees of sin he will forgive? Whether he will pardon without any reparation for the honour of his laws or not? Upon what or what terms he will do it? If he require reparation, what reparation, and by whom is it to be performed? How shall we know that he has pardoned? If he pardon, whether will he remit all punishment due to sin, or how much? Whether will he merely pardon, or will he over and above re-admit the sinner to grace, and as entire favour as before he sinned? Whether will he not only pardon, but reward the sinner's imperfect obedience? Unless all of these are resolved, the difficulty is not loosed. And who will undertake to resolve them and give rational satisfaction that understands the case.

6. These questions are not only above the reach of man; but they belong not to him to judge and decide them. The offence is committed against God. He alone understands what the contempt of his authority, the disorder brought into his government by sin, and the disobedience of his creature amounts unto: what

is

is fit to be done in the cafe, he alone is judge, at his tribunal it is to be tried. Man is too ignorant, too guilty, and too partial in his own favour to be allowed to judge? Now where are the decifions of God in the cafe to be found? Are they legible in the works of creation or providence, or confciences of men? In the works of creation it cannot be pretended. The works of providence afford innumerable inftances of his juftice, fome of his forbearing finners, even while they continue in their fin, and loading them without outward effects of his bounty; But where is the finner, of whom we can fay, God has forgiven him? Or faid that he will forgive? The confciences of men read them fometimes fad lectures of juftice; but never, if they be not informed from revelation, any of forgivenefs.

7. All the pretences that are offered for relief in this cafe, are abfurd, vain and infignificant. They are all reducible to this one head, That God is infinitely merciful; but this gives not the leaft relief. For,

1. I afk, muft God then of neceffity exercife mercy, or is the egrefs and exercife of this mercy neceffary? If it is not, but ftill remains arbitrary, and in the pleafure of God whether he will pardon or not; then I inquire, where is the relief pretended? Does it not all evanifh? Are we not as much at a lofs as before, whether he will pardon, or how far, or upon what terms? If it is neceffary in its egrefs, then I inquire, how is this reconcileable with the notion of mercy, that feems to refpect voluntary and undeferved acts of favour fhown to them, to whom God was not obliged to fhow any? How is this reconcileable to or confiftent with juftice, which is exercifed in punifhing finners? By what arguments can this be made appear? Whence is it that there are fo many acts of juftice, and no inftances known to, or knowable by the light of nature, of God's having pardoned any?

2. Mercy is either unlimited in its egrefs or it is not. If it is limited and cannot be exercifed, but upon fuch and fuch provifos as make the exercife of it confiftent with God's averfion to fin, and with the regard he has for the authority of his laws, the concern he has for the honour of his government, and his juftice, wifdom and holinefs, then we are where we were before: For who can tell whether it be confiftent with thefe things to pardon? In what cafe and upon what provifos: if it is not limited to any fuch qualifications, then I defire to know, how this is reconcileable to his nature? How is fuch mercy confiftent with any exercife of juftice at all? What account can be

given

given of the direful effects of justice, whereof the world is full? By what means can it be reconciled to the holiness of God's nature to pardon impenitent sinners? What need is there for any to guard against sin, since upon this supposition, all sin shall be forgiven?

3. Is infinite mercy universal in its extent? If it is not, then I desire to know, what sins, what sinners shall be pardoned? How shall any know whether his sins are the sins that are to be pardoned? If it is universal in its extent, and all sins must be pardoned; then is there not a door opened for all sin? How can this be proven? Why have we no evidence of this in God's providential dealing? Whence have we so many evidences of the contrary? If it is said that mercy must in more or less be exercised toward all, then I inquire, who tells us so? How far shall it be exercised? Will it pardon all or part? Upon what terms? Will it not only pardon, but remunerate the guilty?

4. I inquire who are the proper objects of mercy? Or what is requisite to constitute the proper object of it? Amongst men, the proper object of that mercy which belongs to governors, is not sin and misery. To spare and pardon upon this score only, is a plain vice in men especially in governors. But the object of mercy is such sin and misery, as is consistent with the honour and good of the governor, government and the governed to pardon. Now, if it be thus in this case, then I see nothing, but we are where we were, and are plunged into all our difficulties; and why it should not be thus, I see no reason. For there is no man who knows what God is, what sin is, what justice is, that will say it is consistent with the honour, justice, wisdom and holiness of God to pardon impenitent sinners, going on in their sins. And when they say, that his mercy only requires him to pardon penitent sinners, then this plainly says, that the exercise of his mercy is confined to those who are its proper objects, that is, not to miserable sinners, for the impenitent are most so; but to those whom he may spare, in a decorum to his government and congruity to his other perfections. And indeed this is what cannot in reason be denied: and when it is granted, then it remains a question, not yet decided, nor indeed determinable by reason, whether repentance alone is sufficient to this purpose?

5. The case of justice and mercy are quite different as to their egress: For justice has respect to a fixed rule, an universal rule, and requires that regard be had to it, in dealing with all that are under that rule: whereas mercy only is conversant about

par-

particular instances, according to the wisdom and pleasure of him in whom it resides.

6. The infiniteness of either of these attributes, neither requires nor admits, that there be infinite numbers of instances of either: but that the acts of justice and mercy be such as becomes the infinite nature of God, when it is proper to exercise them, or when the wisdom, holiness, justice or mercy of God require that they be exercised.

But the deists object, 1. " That upon supposition that God will " not pardon sin, there is no use of his mercy*." I answer, we do not say he will not pardon sin; but we say, nature's light cannot tell whether he will pardon it or not, or what is the case wherein mercy takes place. We own its use, but we say, nature's light cannot tell when and how it is proper to exercise it.

Again, it is pretended, " That God is infinitely merciful, then " he must as the least of its operations pardon the greatest of " sins†." This is plainly denied, and we have told wherefore above.

It is further pretended, " That justice has done its business, " when it has condemned the sinner, and then mercy brings him " off ‡:" but this is gross ignorance. It belongs as much to justice to take care that its sentence be executed, as to see it passed.

Again, it is urged, " That though God be infinitely just as well " as merciful, yet his justice is only as inherent, not as extensive " as his mercy toward us: for we are punished only according to " our deservings, but mercy is shown us above our deservings §." The first part is false. The very contrary assertion, viz. that justice is more extensive, is true, as has been cleared above, if we respect the number of objects. The proof of it is a plain sophism. For 1. It is not true that mercy bestows its effects, which in their nature are above our deservings, to more persons than justice gives its effects, which are according to desert. 2. The effects of mercy are not more above deserving, than the effects of justice are according to it. 3. The effects of justice are with infinite exactness proportioned to deservings. And all that can be said is, that the effects of mercy are suited to the nature of infinite mercy, not that they are given to infinite number of persons, or infinite degrees.

Further, it is pretended, " That God with whom we have to " do, is a Father who will not animadvert severely upon his pe-
" nitent

* Aikenhead's Speech.   † Ibid.   ‡ Ibid.
± A. W. in his Letter, Oracles of Reason.

" nitent fon"." I anfwer, as he is a father, fo he is a righteous judge. Forther, though he be a father, yet he is not fuch a father as men are, infirm, liable to failings, that needs his children, that may give them occafion or temptation to offend, that is of the fame nature with them. And hence no firm argument can be inferred from any thing that is known in this matter by the light of nature. Befides, the meaneft offence againft God is more atrocious, than the greateft offence againft one's natural father. For which neverthelefs there is no forgivenefs, but punifhment without mercy, by the law of nations and nature.

Finally, all thefe are but generals, that may well raife fufpicions in the minds of men, but can never give particular fatisfaction to any one man, as to his cafe, or any one of the particular difficulties that have been mentioned. They no more fatisfy, than thofe notions that generally prevailed, of the placability of the Deity, which had their rife at firft from revelation, were continued by the neceffity of finners, who having challenges for fin, behooved to take fanctuary fome where, and handed down by tradition: But being general, and leaving men at a lofs about the means of atoning the Deity, were really of no ufe if not to keep men from running into downright defpair, and keep them up in attendance upon fomewhat that looked like religion; but whereon the minds of fuch as really underftood any thing of the cafe, could never find fatisfaction.

There is only one thing that feems of any moment, that is objected to all this; and that is, that nature's light which difcovers the fore, difcovers a falve for it, to wit, repentance, to which we fhall anfwer in the following fection, that is peculiarly defigned to confider this.

SECT. III.

Wherein it is inquired whether Repentance is fufficient to atone for Sin? How far Nature's Light enables to it? What affurance Nature's Light gives of Pardon upon Repentance.

IT now remains that we confider the only exception, which is of moment, and that is, that repentance is a fufficient atonement, that nature's light difcovers this, and fo we are

§ Blount's Relig. Laici, pag. 69. Herbert de Relig. Gen. pag. 199.

not left without relief. This is the more confiderable that feveral Chriftians, yea divines of great note, and fome of them defervedly of high efteem, have feen meet, in compliance with their feveral hypothefes in divinity, to drop affertions that feem to favour this. We fhall firft propofe their opinions, who affert this, and then confider it.

The deifts go all this way as one man. I fhall offer one for all, and it is Charles Blount, who not only fpeaks the fenfe, but tranflates the very words of the learned lord Herbert. He tells us then, " That repentance is the only known and
" public means, which on our part is required for fatisfying
" the divine juftice, and returning to the right way of ferving
" God*." And for clearing this, he premits to it thefe enfuing confiderations, " 1. That he that judgeth man is his Father,
" and doth look on him as a frail creature, obnoxious to fin.
" 2. That he generally finds men fin, rather out of frailty,
" than out of any defire to offend his divine Majefty.
" 3. That if man had been made inwardly prone to fin, and
" yet deftitute of all inward means to return to him again,
" he had been not only remedilefs in himfelf, but more mi-
" ferable, than it could be fuppofed an infinite Goodnefs did
" at firft create, and doth ftill perpetuate human kind.
" 4. That man can do no more on his part, for the fatisfying
" of divine juftice, than to be heartily forry and repent him
" of his fins, as well as to endeavour, through his grace, to
" return to the right way, from which through his tranfgref-
" fion, he had erred : or if this did not fuffice for the making
" of his peace, that the fupreme God by inflicting fome tem-
" poral punifhment in this life, might fatisfy his own juftice.
" 5. That if temporal punifhment in this life, were too lit-
" tle for the fin committed, he might yet inflict a greater
" punifhment hereafter in the other life, without giving eternal
" damnation to thofe, who (if not for the love of goodnefs)
" yet, at leaft, upon fenfe of punifhment, would not fin eter-
" nally. Notwithftanding, fince thefe things may again be
" controverted, I fhall infift only upon that univerfally ac-
" knowledged propofition firft laid down†." This propofition, with the explications, he tranflates from Herbert, only has made fome fmall additions.

It

* Religio Laici, pag. 68, 69, 70.
† Herbert de Relig. Gentil. pag. 199.

It is no wonder to see those speak so; but it is a little more odd to hear Christians talk so. One who would seem very zealous for Christianity tells us, " That the God of " patience and consolation, who is rich in mercy, would " forgive his frail offspring, if they acknowledge their faults, " disapproved the iniquity of their transgressions, begged his " pardon, and resolved in earnest to conform their actions " to this rule, which they owned to be just and right: this " way of reconciliaton, this hope of atonement, the light " of nature revealed to them.——He that made use of this " candle of the Lord, (viz. reason) so far as to find his duty, " could not miss to find also the way to reconciliation and " forgiveness, when he had failed of his duty*." Much more speaks he to the same purpose.

But it is stranger to hear divines speak so. And yet we find one telling us, " That the same light of nature, which de- " clares to us our duty, dictates to us, when we have failed " in that duty, to repent and turn to God with trusting to " his mercy and pardon, if we do so and not else. We " do find it legible in our hearts, that God is good and wise- " ly gracious to pity our infirmities, to consider our lost " estate, and necessary frailty, as that there is a God, and " any worship that is at all due to him †."

To the same purpose the learned Baxter speaks in his Reasons of the Christian Religion, Part 1. Chap. 17. Dr. Whichcot in his sermon on Acts xii. 28. and others too large to quote.

But now, with all due deference to those great names, I shall take leave to offer the following remarks, wherein I shall clear my own mind, and offer the reasons on which I dissent from them.

1. I observe that the deists speak more uncertainly about this matter; whereas these Christian writers seem more positive. The deists seem not to want their fears that repentance may not serve the turn, and therefore they seem willing to admit of temporal punishments, and even punishments after time, only they have not will to think of eternal punishments; as we heard from Herbert and Blount, who both speak in the same words on this head. But the Christian writers are positive. And I am jealous the reason is not, that they saw farther into the light of nature

* Locke's Reasonableness of Christianity, pag. 255, 256.
† Mr. Humphrey's Peaceable Disquisitions, Chap. 14. pag. 57.

ture than the deists; but that they lean more firmly to the scripture revelation, which assures us that penitent sinners shall be forgiven. Though I must add, the scripture no where says that penitent sinners shall be forgiven upon their penitence, as that which is sufficient to atone the justice of God. And to speak plainly, however confident those worthy persons are, that they have read this doctrine in the book of nature, I dare be bold to affirm that they had either failed in the discovery, or stammered a little more in reading their lesson, if they had not learned it before-hand out of the book of the Scriptures; though the thing seems, when they have read it there, to approve itself so much to reason, that reason cannot but assent to it. It is well observed by one of those authors, with whom we now manage this debate, " That when truths are once known to us, though
" by tradition, we are apt to be favourable to our own parts, and
" ascribe to our own understanding the discovery of what, in
" truth we borrowed from others, or, at least, finding we can
" prove, what at first we learned from others, we are forward to
" conclude it an obvious truth, which, if we had sought, we could
" not have missed. Nothing seems hard to our understandings,
" that is once known; and because what we see with our own
" eyes, we are apt to overlook, or forget the help we had from
" others, who first shewed and pointed it out to us, as if we
" were not at all beholden to them for that knowledge; for
" knowledge being only of known truths; we conclude our
" faculties would have led us into it without any assistance; and
" that we know these truths by the strength and native light
" of our own minds, as they did, from whom we received them
" by theirs, only they had the luck to be before us. Thus
" the whole stock of human knowledge is claimed by every
" one, as his private possession, as soon as he (profiting by
" other's discoveries) has got it into his own mind; and so it is;
" but not properly by his own single industry, nor of his own
" acquisition. He studies, it is true, and takes pains to make a
" progress in what others have delivered, but their pains were
" of another sort, who first brought those truths to light, which
" he afterwards derives from them. He that travels the roads
" now, applauds his own strength and legs, that have carried
" him so far, in such a scantling of time, and ascribes all to
" his own vigour, little considering how much he owes to their
" pains, who cleared the woods, drained the bogs, built the
" bridges, and made the ways passable; without which he
" might have toiled much with little progress. A great many

things

"things which we have been bred in the belief of from our cra-
"dles (and are notions grown familiar, and as it were natural to
"us, under the gospel) we take for unquestionable obvious truths
"and easily demonstrable, without considering how long we
"might have been in doubt, or ignorance of them, had reve-
"lation been silent. It is no diminishing to revelation, that
"reason gives its suffrage too to the truths revelation hath
"discovered. But it is our mistake to think that because
"reason confirms them to us, we had the first certain know-
"ledge of them from thence, and in that clear evidence we
"now possess them*." How applicable this excellent discourse is to the case in hand, will appear from what we design to subjoin on this head. Though after all, that which the
scripture delivers, and reason confirms in this case, is not,
"That repentance is sufficient to atone the justice of God, or
"that God will pardon a penitent sinner, merely on the ac-
"count of his penitence," which the deists' case requires. The
scriptures plainly teach the contrary, and those learned persons,
or some of them at least who own them, believe according to
the scriptures, the contrary, which makes a considerable difference betwixt them and the deists; though in this case, they
seem to speak the same things. But that which the scripture
asserts, is, " That penitence is a qualification suitable to a sin-
"ner to be pardoned, and that it is not suitable to the wisdom
"and justice of God to pardon one, who is not sorry for for-
"mer offences, and resolves to obey for the future*." Reason
confirms this indeed, but it is not to the purpose.

2. But to come a little more close to the purpose; this repentance, which is pretended to be sufficient, consists of two
parts, *sorrow for the offence*, and *a return to obedience*. This
last part, *a return to obedience*, what is it? Nothing, but
only a performance of the duties we were antecedently bound
unto by the law of creation, which only receives a new denomination from its relation to an antecedent deviation, or
sin. This denomination adds no new worth to it, nor does
the relation whereon it is founded. Wherefore we can never
reasonably suppose, that there is any great matter in this,
that can atone for the transgression. It is well if it obtains
approbation as a part of our duty. But no reasonable man
can pretend that it atones for any part of our sin.

3. Though

* Locke's Reasonableness of Christianity, pag. 279, 280, 281.

3. Though nature's light difcovers our obligation to that duty, which now, becaufe fin preceded, muft be called a return; yet it is a queftion, if nature's light is able to bring a finner, that has once gone away, to fuch a return as is neceffary. For 1. We have above proved that nature's light is defective as to motives to obedience, as to the difcovery of particular duties, and much more is it defective as to motives to a return: becaufe there is more required to encourage a finner to come back, who has once offended, than to engage him to continue. There is a difcouragement arifing from fear of punifhment, and falling fhort of any reward he might have expected, upon the account of his fin to be removed, and that is not eafily done, as fhall be fhown. 2. Befides, not only difcouragements lie in the way of a return, but crofs inclinations, averfions from duty, and inclinations to fin. Now I am not fatisfied that nature's light can remove, or direct how to remove thefe; of which we may fpeak more fully in the next chapter. So that as for this part of repentance we neither fee of what ufe it is as to atonement, nor do we find it clear that nature's light can bring any to it.

4. The ftrefs of the bufinefs then muft lean on this forrow for by-gone tranfgreffions, that is the other part of the compofition. But here I am fure it will be readily granted, that every fort of forrow for fin will not ferve. If one is only grieved for the lofs he has fuftained, the hazard he has run himfelf into, and the evil he has to fuffer, or fears at leaft for his offence; this can be available to no man. Wherefore though nature's light may bring a man to this, and has oft done it, yet this fignifies nothing in the cafe.

5. The forrow, that only can be pretended, is that which arifes purely, or at leaft, principally from concern for the difhonour done to God. Now as to this forrow, it is to be obferved, that it is not any action of ours done in obedience to any command: but it is a paffion, in its own nature uneafy, as all forrow is, though fuitable to a finner, and, upon the fuppofition, that he is fo, ufeful perhaps. And it refults from the joint influence of prevailing love to God, his law and authority, and a clear conviction of fin's having injured his honour, and our being, on this account, obnoxious.

6. It is not eafily to be granted that nature's light can bring any man to this forrow. Since 1. It is evident that the temper men are naturally of, is quite contrary to that which

gives

gives rife to such a sorrow. We are naturally averse from God, as shall be made appear afterwards, and are not under the influence of any such prevalent love to him, and it is not easy to prove that nature's light is able to remove this natural aversion of the heart from God : but of this more in the next chapter. 2. God can never appear amiable to a sinner, if he is not revealed as one ready to forgive. We cannot be sorrowful for our sin, if we are not seriously convinced that we have sinned, and see the demerit of sin. If we are convinced that we have sinned, and deserve punishment, we cannot have prevalent love to God, which is requisite to give life to this sorrow, make it run in the right channel, and proceed on those accounts, which will make it acceptable to God, or available to us, unless he appear to us as ready to forgive, which nature's light doth not discover.

7. I doubt if nature's light calls us to repentance. I allow that there are several things obvious to nature's light, which may be said to drive us to repentance, because they serve to discover to us these things whereon this sorrow follows, bind the obligation on us to that duty, which, because of the preceding sin is called a return, and serve as arguments to enforce the compliance, provided we had a call or invitation to return, I mean a new call. For clearing this, we are to observe that, were man innocent, and guilty of no fault, and had his obedience no imperfection necessarily cleaving to it, and were he under no such inconveniency as might make him dread wrath, or fear his obedience might be rejected ; in in that case a discovery of the obligation he lies under to duty were a call and invitation sufficient, as securing him, at least as to to the acceptance of his duty. But where there are those things in his case, sin and imperfection cleaving to the duty, and the performer chargeable with guilt on both those accounts, in order to engage him to duty, there is requisite a new call or invitation, securing him against those grounds of fear, and giving him ground to expect acceptance. Now it is such a call as this, that only can bring the sinner to repentance. And this we deny that nature's light gives; though we own that it discovers many things, that may be said in some sense, to lead to repentance : Because, upon supposition of such an invitation, they are improveable as arguments to enforce compliance with duty. Thus, if God invite me back again, his goodness discovered in the works of creation and providence, invites to go to him, and

and all the direful evidences of his anger against sinners persuade the same thing: and therefore may be said to lead, or rather drive to repentance; because they have a tendency that way in their own nature, and are capable of such an improvement: But still it is only upon the foregoing supposition.

8. To make this matter yet a little more clear, I grant tthatthe light of nature discovers sinful man to be still under an obligation to obey God. As long as God is God, and man his creature, man is under a tie to subjection, and God has a right to man's obedience. This obedience to which man is bound, after once he has sinned, must be called a return. Further, the light of nature teaches, that if man had yielded perfect obedience, he should not have done it in vain. Acceptance, at least, he should have had, and what other reward the goodness of God thought meet. And that man sustains a great loss by sin, that interveens betwixt him and his expectations from the goodness of God, and besides, exposes him to the hazard of his just resentment, which, if it is seen, as by nature's light in some measure it may be, will occasion sorrow. Further, nature's light will teach that the more deeply we sin, the more we have to fear, and therefore out of fear and a regard to our own interest and expectation of being freed from those severer judgments, which a progress in sin draw on men, may be induced to return. Now all this nature's light discovers: but neither is this sorrow, which favours of some regard to ourselves, but of little or none to God; nor this return, which is not that cheerful, cordial obedience that God requires and accepts, of any avail in the case. No man, that knows what he says, will pretend, that such a sorrow or such a return is sufficient to atone the justice of God for by-gones, or even obtain acceptance for itself, which has so much of love to self, and so little of that which respects God.

9. But the repentance that is available in this case is a sorrow, flowing from prevalent love to God, and grieving, if not only, yet principally for the wrong done to God, and a cheerful following of duty upon prospect of God's being a rewarder of it. Now to call or to make up a sufficient invitation to a sinner, to such a repentance, it is requisite that 1. God be represented in such a way, as a sinner that sees himself guilty, can love him, delight in him, and draw near to him. But this he can never be, if he is not represented as one with whom certainly *there is forgiveness*. 2. It requires further, that God be represented as one, who will accept of sinners' obedience, notwithstanding of

their defert of wrath for former difobedience, and this requires ftill that he be a God that forgives. 3. Further, it is requifite, that he be reprefented as one, that will accept of obedience, not only from one that has finned, but that implies fin and imperfection in it. Now this cannot be, if he is not known to be one that is *plenteous in mercy and will abundantly pardon.* Now I fay the light of nature gives no fuch difcovery of God: and therefore gives no call or fufficient invitation to this repentance.

10. Nor will it help out here, to fay, that the light of nature doth reprefent God as placable, one who may be pacified: for, fhould I grant that it does fo, yet this cannot invite to fuch an obedience, fo long as 1. It is left a queftion, whether he be actually reconciled, or pofitively determined to forgive? 2. Efpecially confidering, that he has not pointed to, and pofitively declared on what terms he will be appeafed. Yea 3. Since moreover he has given no vifible inftance, knowable by the light of nature, that he has forgiven any particular perfon. But 4. On the contrary, the world is full of the moft terrible effects of his difpleafure, and thefe falling moft heavily on the beft, even thofe who go fartheft in a compliance with duty. In a word, thefe dark notions of a placable God, which yet is the utmoft that unenlightened reafon can pretend to, are utterly infufficient to bring any of the children of men to that repentance we are now in queft of; it is fo funk, and as it were quite obfcured by crofs appearances. And all that can reafonably be faid, is, that in the providence of God there is fuch a feeming contrariety of good and evil, that men know not what to make of it, but are toffed by contrary appearances. And of this we have a fair acknowledgment by one, who, befides that he was a perfon of great learning, was not only a great ftickler for the natural difcoveries of this placability, but one of the firft broachers of it, being led to it by the peculiar hopothefis he maintained and advanced in divinity, I mean the learned Amyrald. After he has afferted the natural difcoveries of this placability, and alleged that they lead to repentance, yet fubjoins—" But " there are (fays he) motions in the corrupt nature of man " which fruftrates the effect, if God did not provide for it in " another manner (that is, by revelation). For man flies from " the prefence of God through fear of punifhment, and cannot " hinder the prevalence of it in his foul, fo that as a man af" frighted beholds nothing ftedfaftly, but always imagines new " occafions of terror, and reprefents hideous phantafms to him-
" felf;

"self; so we are not able to allow ourselves leisure to consider
"attentively this dispensation of the goodness of God towards
"the wicked, nor thereby to assure ourselves of obtaining mercy
"and pardon. As a lewd wretch, whose conscience bears him
"witness of many heinous crimes, though he should perceive some
"connivance in the magistrate for a time, and his judge shew
"him some countenance, cannot but be distrustful of him, and
"suspect that he does but defer his punishment to another time,
"and assuredly reserves it for him; especially if he hath an
"opinion that the magistrate is not such an one as himself, but
"abhors the wickednesses committed by him. Now are we
"universally thus principled, that as we have those whom we
"fear, so we never bear good will toward them of whom
"we have some diffidence. And the distrusting the good
"will of any one being a step to fear, is likewise by the same
"reason, a degree of hatred; unless the distrust proceed to such
"a measure as to be an absolute fear; for then the coldness
"of affection is turned into perfect hatred. Wherefore man
"thus distrusting the good will of God towards him, conse-
"quently can have but a very slight affection to him; yea, he
"will even become his enemy, in as much as the distrust in
"this case will be extremely great*." Thus far he goes. Now
methinks this quite overthrows the placability he had before asserted discoverable by the light of nature, at least as to any use
it can be supposed of for assuring sinners of pardon, or inviting
them to repentance.

11. But to go a step further, I cannot see that the light of nature
is able to give us any assurance of this placability. Where is
it in the book of nature that we may read this truth, that God
is placable? Is it in the works of creation? No, this is not pretended. Nor can it be, they were all absolved and finished before the entrance of sin, and cannot be supposed to carry on them
any impressions of placability to sinners. Is it in the works of
providence? Yes, here it is pretended. And what is it in the works
of providence that is alleged to evince this placability? Is it that
God spares sinners for some time, and not only so, but bestows
many outward good things on them, whom he spares? Yes, this
is that whereon the whole stress of the business is laid. But I
cannot see the force of this to assure us that God is placable.
For 1. It is certain that the nature of the things do not infer
certainly

* Amyrald of Religions, Part 2. Chap. 17. pag. mihi, 253, 254.

certainly any such thing. Forbearance is not forgiveness: nor does it intimate any design to forgive. It may be exercised, where there is a certain design aud fixed purpose of punishing. And what relation have a few of those outward things, whereby love or hatred cannot be known, unto peace and reconciliation with God? It is, I know, pretended, that even this forbearance is a sort of forgiveness, and that all the world sharing in it, are in some sort forgiven. So Mr. Baxter says. If this learned person or any other has a mind to extend the notion of pardon so far as to include even reprieves under that name, we cannot hinder: but it is certain, that no abatement of the punishment, far less the dissolution of the obligation, which is that ordinarily meant by pardon, do necessarily follow upon, or is included in a delay of punishment. The slowness in execution, which may proceed upon many grounds, hid in the depth of divine wisdom from us, may be more than compensated by its severity when it comes. *Leaden feat*, as some have used the expression, *may be compensated by iron hands*. And when men have seriously weighed outward good things, which are thrown in greatest plenty in the lap of the most wicked, and are full of vanity and commonly ensnare, they can see but very little of any mercy designed them thereby. And if any inference toward a placability is deducible, which I profess I cannot see, I am sure that it is far above the reach of not a few, if not most of mankind, to make the deduction and trace the argument. And so it can be of no use to them. 2. All those things are consistent with a sentence standing unrepealed and never to be repealed, if either scripture, which tells us that God *exercises much long suffering*, and gives plenty of good things to the *vessels of wrath*; or reason, which assures us that persons continuing obstinate to the last in sin, cannot evite judgment, may be believed. 3. As there is nothing in the nature of the things that can ascertain us of God's placability, much less is there any in the condition of the person, to whom this dispensation is exercised. Were these bestowed on the most virtuous, or were there an increase of them, as persons proceeded in virtue, and came nearer and nearer to repentance; or were there on the other hand a continued evidence of wrath and implacability towards obstinate sinners, this then would seem to say somewhat. But all things are quite contrary, the worst have the most of them, and the best have commonly least of them. What will the sinner say, that God is inviting me by this goodness to virtue? No, if I should

turn

turn virtuous I might rather expect to be worse dealt with. That is a bootless way for any thing I can see in it. Does not the scripture and experience tell us, that thus things go, and that such use sinners have made of this dispensation? And so dark is it, that even they who had God's mind in the word to unriddle the mystery, have been shaken at it so far, that they have been upon the brink of apostasy, while they saw the way of sinners prosper, and that they *who hate God were exalted.* How then can unenlightened reason draw such inferences as these learned men pretend? Although I have a great veneration for these learned men; yet if it would not appear presumptuous in one so far below in all respects, to censure his superiors, I would take the liberty to say, that in this matter they are guilty of a double mistake: First, In that they measure men's abilities by a wrong standard. What such men as they may trace by reason, many men are under not only a moral, but even a natural incapacity to discover. It is certain, besides that vast difference which is in the capacities of men, from different education and circumstances, whence it is morally impossible for one who wants that education, and other occasions and advantages which another has, to go that same length and trace these discoveries, which the other who had education and occasion may do: there is likewise vast difference even in the natural abilities of men (whether that arises from their bodies or souls I dispute not now, nor is it to the purpose; for if from either it is still natural) so that one has not a natural capacity to trace the truths that others may, who have better natural abilities: and so it is naturally impossible for the former to make the discoveries which the other may. And I fear not to add, that if any such inferences may be drawn from these premises, as those learned persons pretend, yet many are under a natural impossibility; and the most under insuperable moral incapacity of tracing those discoveries. And if it be allowed that any man, without his own fault, is under an incapacity of making such deductions, about the placability of God, from these dispensations of providence, which I think cannot modestly be denied, the whole plea about placability will prove not only unserviceable to the deists, but, if I mistake it not, unmeet to maintain that station for which it is designed, in the hypothesis of the learned asserters of this opinion. Another mistake I think those persons guilty of, is, that men whose minds are not enlightened by revelation, may possibly trace those discoveries, which

they

they who are guided by it may read in the book of nature. 4. I add, if thefe things whereon they infift, as difcoveries of this placability in God, ferve to raife any fufpicions of that fort in the minds of men, and this is the moft that can be reafonably pretended, for demonftration they do not amount unto, they are quite funk by the contrary evidences of God's feverity; which muft have fo much of force, in as much as they moft commonly befall the moft virtuous, which heightens the fufpicion. And befides, as we heard Amyrald obferve, the minds of finners, who are convinced in any meafure of fin, who are yet the only perfons that will think themfelves concerned in this matter, are much more inclined to entertain fufpicions than good thoughts of him, whom they have offended, and who, as their confciences affure them, hates their offences. 5. That which puts the cope-ftone upon our mifery, and concludes us under darknefs, is that nature's light has no help to guide us over thefe difficulties laid in our way, from any known inftances of any perfons led to repentance by thefe means, or pardoned on their repentance. So that upon the whole, I cannot fee fufficient evidence of this placability in the light of nature.

12. If it is alleged here, that if God had no defign of mercy in fparing the world, it is perfectly unintelligible why he did it. In anfwer to this, it is to be obferved, that we do not fay that God had no defign of mercy in fparing the world, but that this his forbearance of the world is not a fufficient proof and evidence of this defign; and that nature's light can give no fatisfying account of the reafon of this difpenfation of God. So dark was this to fuch as had no other light but that of reafon, that the moft part laid afide thoughts of it as a thing above their reach; and the more thoughtful knew not what judgment to make, but were confounded and perplexed in their thoughts. They underftood not what occount was to be made of God's producing fo many fucceffive generations of men, and toffing them betwixt love and hatred, hope and fear, by fuch a ftrange mixture of good and evil; effects of his bounty and evidences of his anger. Yea fo far were they confounded, that fome of them came the length to fet God afide from the government of the world. No lefs a perfon than Seneca introduces God, telling good men, " That he could not help their calamities." And Pliny accufes God, under the notion of *nature*, of no good defign. " *Naturam, quafi magna & feva mercede contra tanta* " *fua munera ufum; ita ut non fatis fit æftimare, parens melior* " *homini,*

" *homini, an triſtior noverca fuerit;*" *id eſt,* " Nature has ſo
" cruelly counterbalanced its largeſt gifts with horrible evils,
" that it is hard to ſay, whether it is not a ſad or cruel ſtep-mother
" rather than a kindly parent to man." So that in faƈt, men were
thus ſpared and left in this dark condition, as to the reaſons of
God's diſpenſations, is evident from experience. The reaſons
of this conduƈt are to be ſought in the depth of the wiſdom and
ſovereign juſtice of God. Chriſtians who are found in the faith,
will own, that all who belonged to the eleƈtion of grace could
not have come into being, if the world had not been thus ſpared.
They will own that the world could not have been preſerved in
any order, without theſe effeƈts both of bounty and ſeverity,
whereby ſome reſtraint was put on the luſts of men, and ſome
government kept up among them, and they were kept from
running to ſuch a height in ſin, as would have made it impoſſible for God, with any conſiſtency to his juſtice, holineſs or wiſdom to have preſerved the world, till his deſign in its preſerva-
tion was reached. And it may be ſaid further, for the ſatisfaction of Chriſtians (for the deiſts have no concern in this account, which is bottomed on the revelation they deny). That if
God had ſeen meet to make all that belonged to Adam's covenant at once, they could not have refuſed to conſent to the
placing their happineſs on that bottom whereon he placed it in
the tranſaƈtion with Adam, and could not have condemned
God for executing the ſentence upon all immediately upon the
breach of it. And therefore I think they have no reaſon to
quarrel God's keeping them out of hell for a while. Further,
God in his wiſdom, by leaving ſo many in this dark caſe for ſo
many ages, has let them ſee the ſhortneſs of their wiſdom to diſ-
entangle them from that miſery, whereunto by ſin they were involved. It was *in the wiſdom of God,* that *the world by wiſdom knew not God.* Finally, this ſhould make us welcome the
goſpel, which only can diſpel the darkneſs we are under, as to
the whole ſtate of matters betwixt God and us, and lead us to
life and immortality, and mercy, pardoning mercy, which the
dim light of nature could never diſcover to us.

Now if we conſider what has been above diſcourſed, it will
be found that we have made conſiderable advances towards a
deciſion of that which is in debate.

We have cleared what that repentance is, which with any
ſhew of reaſon can be pretended available in the preſent caſe.

We have evinced that the placability of God, of which ſome
talk

talk, were it difcoverable by nature's light, is not fufficient to bring men to this repentance.

Further, we have made it appear, that the evidences of this placability brought from nature's light are not conclufive.

But were all this given up, which we fee no caufe to do, the principal point is ftill behind, viz. " Whether nature's light can " afcertain us that all penitent finners fhall be pardoned upon " their repentance." This the deifts maintain, and we deny. Their affertion, " that the light of nature affures us that peni- " tent finners upon their repentance fhall affuredly be for- " given," is that which we fhall next take under confideration, and demonftrate to be groundlefs, falfe and abfurd, by the enfuing arguments.

1. I reafon againft it from the nature of pardon. Forgivenefs or pardon is a free act of God's will. It is a freeing of the finner from the obligation he lies under to punifhment, by virtue of the penal fanction of that righteous and juft law which he has violated. All divine laws are unqueftionably equal, juft, and righteous, and their penal fanctions are fo too. Certainly therefore God may juftly inflict the punifhment contained in the fanction of the law upon the tranfgreffors; and confequently, we may without fear infer, that to relieve him from that penalty is a moft free act, to which God was not neceffarily obliged. And indeed, though all this had not been faid, the thing is in itfelf clear; for we can frame no other notion of forgivenefs than this, " That it is a voluntary and free act of grace, which remits the punifhment, and loofes the finner from that punifhment he juftly deferved, and which the lawgiver might juftly have inflicted on him." Now this being clear, we infer, that fuch acts cannot be known otherwife than, either by revelation, that is God's declaring himfelf exprefsly to this purpofe, or by the deed itfelf, fome pofitive act of forgivenefs, which is the effect of fuch a purpofe. The deifts difown and deny any revelation. And for any effect declarative of fuch a purpofe, we fhall challenge the world to produce it. There never was, nor is any one perfon, of whom we can certainly affirm, upon the information only of nature's light, that God has forgiven him, either upon repentance or without out. And if there were fuch perfons, it would not bear the weight of a general conclufion, that becaufe God has done it to them, therefore he will do it to all, in all other inftances.

2. I reafon againft this fuppofed conftitution from the extent

tent of it, that God will pardon all penitent finners. If this is not faid, he pardons none upon their penitence: for if any penitent finner can be fuppofed to remain unpardoned, why may not all? Befides, if a penitent finner is punifhed, then it muft be upon fomewhat elfe than penitence, that he who is pardoned obtains remiffion. For if mere penitence had been fufficient, a penitent could not have fuffered. Now if all penitent finners are forgiven, and nature's light affures them that they fhall be forgiven, then the extent of this conftitution is very large. For, 1. It makes void the penal fanction of the law as to all fins, however atrocious they are, if the finner is only a penitent. 2. It extends to all ages, places, and generations of men, that ever have been, or fhall be in the world. 3. It reaches to all forts of perfons, even thofe who are in a capacity to introduce the greateft diforders into the government of the world, as well as the meaneft offenders. Well then, the deifts muft maintain that it is thus enacted, and this act or conftitution is in all this extent publicly declared by the light of nature, fo that all may know it. 4. It reaches to all fins, paft, prefent, and to come; they fhall all be forgiven, if the finner does only repent. Now againft fuch an extenfive conftitution, we offer the following confiderations:

(1.) All wife governors, who have any regard to the honour of their laws, authority, and governments, ufe to be very fparing in indemnifying tranfgreffion. And no wonder they fhould; for wife and juft rulers are not wont to enact penalties, but in proportion to offences. And therefore a paffing eafily from them tends to make tranfgreffion cheap, and weaken the conftitution, and fo diffolve the government. Now God is no lefs tender of the honour of thofe laws, which enact nothing but what is the tranfcript of his own righteous nature, and the oppofite whereof he has the deepeft abhorrency of, as contrary to the fame. And can we then reafonably fuppofe him to be fo lavifh of forgivenefs as to eftablifh it in fo ftrange an extent? I believe it will be hard for any thinking man to judge fo.

(2.) In all well ordered governments pardon is a particular act of grace, reftricted to fome time, place and perfon; yea and crimes too: and therefore is never extended fo univerfally as here it is, and if it is to the purpofe, muft be afferted. So that the common reafon of mankind declares againft fuch a conftitution: for what is or may be pretended of impenitent sinners being excluded, is in very deed, no restriction of the law indemnifying transgressors of whatever sort, that are but willing to be indemnified. For impenitent sinners are they only who have no will to be pardoned, or who will not accept of favour. Now to indemnify all that are willing to be pardoned is a very odd constitution. And before I ascribe this to the wisdom of the great Ruler of the world, I must see better reasons than I am ever like to see in this case.

(3.) No wise government ever enacted pardon of such an universal extent, without further security for the honour of the government, into a perpetual and standing law. Pardon and acts of grace are a part of the sovereignty of the governor: and however he may make them very extensive sometimes; yet he always reserves it so in his own power, that it shall afterwards be voluntary and free to him to forgive or not as he shall see cause.

(4.) Such a constitution is especially irreconcileable with wisdom and equity, if it is extended to transgressions not yet committed; for in that case it looks like an invitation to sin.

(5.) And this binds more strongly, if the persons are strongly inclined to sin.

(6.) More especially such a constitution is never to be reconciled with wisdom, if it is universally made known and published without any provision made for the securing of the honour of the law, against any abuse of such grace. Now I desire to know if nature's light discovers such an act and declaration of grace. Where is there any care taken, or any provisos inserted in the declaration that can evidence the regard which God has for his laws, and secure against the abuse of such kindness? Indeed the scripture discovery of mercy to penitent sinners, on account of Christ's satisfaction, fully removes all those difficulties which otherwise, so far as I can see, are never to be removed: And therefore I can never see how such a declaration could be made without the concomitant discovery of a satisfaction to justice, and reparation of the honour of the lawgiver and law, and security against abuse of grace. Remarkable to this purpose are the words of the learned and judicious Dr. How: " That
" prince would certainly never be so much magnified for his
" clemency and mercy, as he would be despised by all the
" world, for most remarkable defects of government, that
" should not only pardon whosoever of his subjects had offend-
" ed

"ed him, upon their being sorry for it; but go about to pro-
"vide, that a law should obtain in his dominions, through all
"after time, that whosoever should offend against the govern-
"ment, with whatsoever insolency, malignity and frequency,
"if they repented, they should never be punished, but be taken
"forthwith into highest favour. Admit that it had been con-
"gruous to the wisdom and righteousness of God, as well as his
"goodness, to have pardoned a particular sinner, upon repent-
"ance, without satisfaction; yet nothing could have been more
"apparently unbecoming him, than to settle an universal law
"for all future time, to that purpose, that let as many as would,
"in any age to the world's end, affront him never so highly,
"invade his rights, trample on his authority, and tear the con-
"stitution of his government, they should upon their repentance
"be forgiven, and not only not be punished, but be most high-
"ly advanced, and dignified." Thus far he. In the subsequent paragraph he learnedly and judiciously shews the difference in the gospel proposal of mercy to offenders, from this supposed case of forgiveness without satisfaction.

3. I inquire, whether is it possible that there may be any crime so atrocious, that it may be possible for God, in a congruity with his perfection, to punish, notwithstanding of the intervention of repentance? If there may be any such, then certainly it is not merely on account of repentance that sin is pardoned: and so a penitent cannot always be sure of forgiveness. Further, considering how grievous and sinful every transgression of God's law is, how can I be sure what sins are pardonable upon repentance and what not? If it is not possible for God to punish any penitent, then 1. I would inquire what so great matter is there in repentance, that can bind God up from vindicating his honour against affronts already offered? 2. To what purpose was the penal sanction since, in the case it was designed? For when the law is transgressed, it may not possibly take place but the execution is inconsistent with the nature of God. 3. How will this impossibility ever be proven? Repentance hath nothing in it so great to infer it: for in repentance no more can be alleged but a return to duty antecedently due. And as to this, we are unprofitable servants. And Christ has told us what reason tells us also, that we deserve no thanks for it. And as for the other part, sorrow for by-gones, it is the necessary result of that regard

* Living Temple, Part 2. pag. 327.

gard to the Deity, and knowledge of our own fin, that is likewife our own duty. Now what is there, in all this, that fhould be fuppofed to be of fo great worth, that it muft inevitably ftop the courfe of juftice?

But here it may be objected, not only by deifts, but fome, who are very far from favouring them, " That God cannot caft " away from his love and felicity any foul, which truly loveth " him above all, and which fo repenteth of his fin, as to return " to God in holinefs in heart and life.*"

I anfwer, 1. The fuppofition that a finner convinced of fin can repent without fome fecurity given as to pardon, can love God above all, and fo repent, as to turn to holinefs in heart and life, appears to me impoffible. Much lefs is it poffible that an unconvinced finner can repent. The reafon is plain, a clear conviction of fin inevitably lays us under the deepeft fear of God, and dread of punifhment from him, which not only cafts out that love, but draws on hatred, or at leaft, ftrong averfion; as we heard the learned Amyrald well obferve in the words before quoted. Now it is certain, that fuppofe one impoffibility, twenty will follow. 2. If the thing is not impoffible, which I think it is, yet certainly it is a cafe that never happened, and is never like to happen. 3. Suppofing it poffible, it is a very bold affertion, that no crime, how atrocious foever, would juftify the inflicting of the penalty contained in the righteous fanction of the law. 4. Much lefs then is it hard to fuppofe that it would juftify God's denying any reward to the finner, that he has fo finned. And if it is granted that penitence does not neceffarily reftore to a profpect of reward, all religion and encouragement to it is loft. I cannot forbear quoting again the accurate and judicious Dr. How's words, who after he has fhown that our offences againft God incomparably tranfcend the meafure of any offence that can be done by one creature againft another, prefently fubjoins, " Yea, and as it can never be thought con- " gruous, that fuch an offence againft a human governor, " fhould be pardoned, without the intervening repentance of " the delinquent; fo we may eafily apprehend alfo the cafe to " be fuch, as that it cannot be fit, it fhould be pardoned on that " alone, without other recompence †:" whereof if any fhould doubt, I would demand, is it, in any cafe, fit, that a penitent delinquent

---

* Baxter's Reafons of Chrift. Relig. Part 1. pag. 184, 188.
† Living Temple, Part 2. pag. 240.

quent againſt human laws and government ſhould be puniſhed, or a proportionable recompence be exacted for his offence notwithſtanding? Surely it will be acknowledged ordinarily fit; and who would take upon him to be the cenſor of the common juſtice of the world in all ſuch caſes! Or to condemn the proceedings of all times and nations, whereſoever a penitent offender hath been made to ſuffer the legal puniſhment of his offence, notwithſtanding his repentance? How ſtrange a maxim of government would that be, That it is never fit that an offender, of whatſoever kind, ſhould be puniſhed, if he repent himſelf of his offence! And ſurely, if ever, in any caſe, ſomewhat elſe than repentance be fitly inſiſted on as a recompence, for the violation of the ſacred rights of government, it may well be ſuppoſed much more ſo in the caſe of man's common delinquency and revolt from God.

4. I reaſon againſt this poſition, from the conſideration of the imperfection of this repentance, which, as it takes place amongſt ſinful men, is guilty of a double imperfection. Our ſorrow and our return are imperfect, in reſpect of degrees. Our relation to God and his to us requires the higheſt, the moſt perfect love and the moſt cordial obedience. No leſs will anſwer our obligations. And our ſorrow, if it is required, muſt be ſuppoſed likewiſe to be ſuch as reſults neceſſarily from ſuch a love. Now what can be more evident than this, that none of the children of men love God as they ought, and, with that intention and vehemency, which anſwers their original obligation? And conſequently their ſorrow and obedience can never come up to it: for they being the reſult of this love, can never go beyond the principle, which influences them. Again, our return is liable to another imperfection, even a frequent interruption. The caſe is not thus, that we only once, through infirmity, make an eſcape; but even after our ſuppoſed return, it muſt be allowed that there will be after-deviations. And hence it becomes a queſtion, how can we expect acceptance in our returns? How can our repentance, which anſwers not the demands of the law, and our ties to duty be accepted for itſelf? And if ſo, much more may it be a queſtion, how can it be allowed ſufficient to atone for other tranſgreſſions, yea, how can it be ſufficient to atone for tranſgreſſions, which it takes no notice of? For there are ſuch ſins as by the light of nature we are never likely to reach the conviction of; and therefore it is impoſſible we ſhould ſorrow for them, or repent of them? However men may pleaſe themſelves

selves with a fancy of the sufficiency of their repentance; yet a sinner, that understands his own case, will never be able to satisfy his own conscience in this matter.

I know it is pleaded, " That we have a harder province
" to administer than even the angels themselves; they not ha-
" ving so gross a body as we have, nor exposed to so much evil
" as we are. But God he knoweth our frame, and upon that
" account is not extreme to mark what is done amiss. A crea-
" ture, as a creature, is finite and fallible: and yet we are
" not the most perfect of God's creation. Now, for fallible to
" fail, is no more than for frail to be broken; and mortal to
" die. Where there is finite and limited perfection, there
" is not only a possibility, but a contingency to fail, to err, to
" be mistaken, not to know and to be deceived, And where
" the agent is such, there is place for repentance. Re-
" pentance is that which makes a finite being failing, capa-
" ble of compassion. If repentance did not take effect, it
" would be too hazardous for a creature to come into be-
" ing. If upon a lapse, an error, or mistake, we should be
" undone to eternity, without all hope of recovery; who would
" willingly enter upon this state*?" Thus speaks Dr. Wichcot.

To this plausible discourse we answer, Either this reasoning proceeds upon the state of things, according to the covenant of grace, and respects them who have laid hold on it, or it does not. If it does proceed on this footing, we say it helps not the deists: but if, as it seems, it be extended further, then I shall make the following remarks on it. 1. Although we have here many things prettily said, yet I cannot but deeply dislike the discourse, because it aims at the extenuation of sin, and pleads its excuse from our frailty. Now, besides that this bears hard upon the Author of our constitution, as if he had made it unequal to the laws he imposed on it, it is a foolish argument, because the case may be as much exaggerated on the other hand by the representing the greatness of the lawgiver, the equality of the laws, and the ability of man, at least in his first make to obey. And the one will not signify more to give us hope of forgiveness on our repentance, than the other will to make us despair of it. 2. It seems to reflect on God's different conduct with the angels that sinned, who had no place allowed them for repentance:

* Dr. Whichcot's select Sermons, Part 2. Serm. 2d, on Acts xiii. 38. pag. 322, 323.

pentance: for their frame was finite, and so frail and failable. The little difference from the grossness of our bodies, if man is not supposed corrupt, and his body inclined to evil, makes no difference that can satisfy; for still we were under no necessity of sinning from our constitution, if it is not supposed to be corrupt. But to pretend that man was made corrupt, carries our frailty too far, to make it God's deed. We cannot plead in excuse, any defects in our constitution, that God put not there. 3. It condemns all human laws that spares not penitent transgressors. If it be said, that they are under a necessity to do it; I answer, whence does this necessity arise? Is the honour of the divine law less dear to him, and of less consideration than the honour and rights of human constitutions and governments? But further, I desire to know, will necessity justify the punishment of the penitent? If not, then here it doth not justify: if it doth, who will assure me that there is not as great a necessity for this course in divine as human governments; at least in some instances? And if in any instance the punishment of a penitent may take place, who will condescend where it may, and where not? How likewise can it be said that penitence secures pardon? Further, 4. I say directly to the argument, If divine laws are as much adjusted to man's power, as the constitutions and laws of human government are, (and that they behoved to be so, with respect to his power in his first constitution has been made appear) then it is no more hazardous to come into being, than to enter into human society, where frail man may, for a word or a deed, forfeit his own life to justice and all the advantages of it, and beggar his posterity, and that without any prospect of relief by his repentance. If it be said, that the punishments are greater in this case; I grant it: so are the laws too, and consequently the transgressions; and so likewise are the advantages of obedience; and without an injurious reflection on God, it cannot be denied that the laws are, as well at least, attempered to man's abilities wherewith he was created and subjected to them. 5. I do not see how it can be injustice to inflict a just punishment upon transgressors, and such of necessity, that is, which is included in the sanction of the divine laws. Nor does repentance make that execution unjust; which, without it, is allowed not only just, but indispensibly necessary. This I might largely shew, but others have done it before*.

5. The

* See Specimen Refutationis Crellii, pag. 100, 101, & sequ.

5. The falsehood of this proposition may be further evidenced from the nature of the juftice of God, that feems necessarily to require that sin be punished. For clearing this, I shall make the ensuing observations: in doing which we shall aim at such a gradual progression as may set the matter in the best light.

(1.) Justice strictly taken, is "that virtue of the rational nature, whose business it is to preserve, maintain, and be a guardian of the rights of rational beings." It is commonly defined a "constant and abiding or fixed will of giving to every one what is their right or due." Whence it has been debated, whether in man there is any such thing as self-justice; because, according to this account of justice, it seems to be restricted to the rights of others. And this restriction has countenance given to it from that common maxim, that *volenti non fit injuria**, which is founded in this, that a man is supposed capable of parting, without wrong, with his own rights, and consequently is not capable of injustice towards himself. It is true, man has no rights, which he may not deprive himself of by his own consent. Yet since man has such rights, though they are but derived ones, as also his being is, as he cannot deprive himself of without fault, I see not but even such a thing as self-justice may take place among men: but whatever the case be as to men, there is certainly in God to be allowed such a thing as self-justice. For clearing of which, I observe,

(2.) That God, being the fountain of all rights, has certainly rights, which he can by no means deprive himself of. He has a right of dominion over the creature, and to the creature's subjection, that he cannot part with. As long as there is a rational creature it is, by its being, inevitably subject to its Creator, and he cannot part with that right he has to govern it. "With "the supreme Proprietor, there cannot but be unalienable "rights, inseparably and everlastingly inherent in him: for it "cannot be, but that he, who is the fountain of all rights must "have them primarily and originally in himself; and can no "more so quit them, as to make the creature absolute and independent, than he can make the creature God†." Hence inevitably there must be allowed self-justice, which is nothing else, save that fixed determination of the divine will, not to

part

---

* "No injury is done to one who is willing."
† Living Temple, Part 2. pag. 270.

part with what is his own unalienable right, and consequently to maintain it.

(3.) This justice, in order to maintain God's right of government, obliges him to enact penal laws as the measure of the creature's subjection and obedience. A subject cannot be without laws. And where the creature is capable of transgressing, laws cannot be such without penalties. Without these, they were rather counsels or advices, than laws; and the person to whom they are given is left at will to be subject, or not. And if God should thus leave the creature without a penalty, then upon transgression, the transgressor has slipt entirely out under the dominion of God; for he is not actively, in that instance, subject to God. And neither is he passively subject, if there is no penalty. So that by this means God has forfeited or lost his right, which is impossible. There is no other imaginable tie of subjection, but either the precept or the penal sanction of the law, whereby rational creatures, as to their moral dependence can be bound. Now if God part with the one, by remitting the penalty, or enacting laws without it, and man cast off the other by disobedience, the creature is, at least thus far, independent. Which how absurd it is, is easy to see. Wherefore, in case the creature is made, we cannot but suppose a law must be made to it. And if the creature is capable of violating that law, there must, for preserving that right, which God has to the creature's subjection, be a penalty annexed to that law. Whence it seems evident, " that God did owe it to himself pri-
" marily, as the absolute Sovereign and Lord of all, not to
" suffer indignities to be offered him, without animadverting
" upon them, and therefore to determine he would do so*."

(4.) The creature being made, justice requires that it should be under such a law as is enacted with a penalty, and such a law being now enacted, there seems to arise a double necessity for the execution of the law, in case of transgression. The one arising from the reason of the law, the other from the law itself: Since upon the grounds already laid down, the law was necessary; the same grounds enforce the execution of the law: for when the case falls out, for which the law was provided, it is not merely the law or constitution itself, but the execution of it that secures the end. When the creature disobeys, he has in so far renounced an actual dependence on, and subjection to the lawgiver and law: and therefore it seems of necessity that either as to these actions he is not subject, or he must be subject to the penalty.

* Living Temple, pag. 271.

penalty. Again, as the reason of the law enforces the execution, so does the law itself. For the law being once made, justice requires that its honour be secured either by obedience, or by the subjection of the transgressor to the punishment.

(5.) To proceed yet further, if the law is not executed, the design, even the principal design of punishment in this case, is not reached. It is not the only or main design of punishment or penal sanctions to reclaim the offender, or benefit by-standers, or secure the community. It is true, the penal sanction, or law enacting the penalty, is of use to deter from transgressing, and so is of use to the community, and all under the government, but the execution, if the sanction is punishment after this life, is of no advantage to the offender, nor is it instructive to by-standers, or the rest of the community, who do not see it: wherefore these are not the principal ends of punishment. Though it is be observed, that any public intimation that the penalty shall not be inflicted, could not but be of the worst consequence to the community, as rendering it vain as to all that use which it has of deterring persons who are under the law from sin. Yet I say, these are not the principal ends of punishment; but the satisfaction of the Lawgiver. For the case is not here, as it is in human governments, where the governor and government are both constituted for the good of the governed, which therefore must be the chief aim of all laws: but on the contrary, the governed are made, and the laws made, and penalties enacted for the Governor, who made all things for *himself*. And consequently, the principal design of punishment is the securing and vindicating his honour in the government. Nor is this any such thing as answers to private revenge amongst men.
" But that wherewith we must suppose the blessed God to be
" pleased in the matter of punishing, is the congruity of the thing
" itself, that the sacred rights of his government over the world
" be vindicated, and that it be understood how ill his nature
" can comport with any thing that is impure, and what is in
" itself so highly incongruous, cannot but be the matter of his
" detestation. He takes eternal pleasure in the reasonableness
" and fitness of his own determinations and actions; and re-
" joices in the works of his own hands, as agreeing with the
" apt, eternal schemes and models, which he hath conceived
" in his own most wise and all-comprehending mind: so that
" though he desireth not the *death of sinners*, and hath *no de-*
" *light* in the *sufferings* of his afflicted creatures, which his
" immense

" immense goodness rather inclines him to behold with com-
" passion ; yet the true ends of punishment are so much a grea-
" ter good, than their ease and exemption from the sufferings
" they had deserved, that they must rather be chosen, and
" cannot be eligible for any reason, but for which also they
" are to be delighted in, i. e. a real goodness, and conduci-
" bleness to a valuable end inherent in them."

(6.) As justice in a strict sense, of which hitherto we have spoken, as it denotes that rectitude of the divine nature, which is conversant about, and conservative of the divine rights, pleads for penal laws and punishment; so likewise justice in a large sense, as it comprehends all his moral perfections, holiness, wisdom, faithfulness, &c. and answers to that which is amongst men called universal justice, pleads for the same : for so taken, it comprehends his holiness and perfect detestation of all impurity ; in respect whereof, he cannot but be perpetually inclined to animadvert with severity upon sin; both because of its irreconcileable contrariety to his holy nature, and the insolent affront, which it therefore directly offers him ; and because of the implicit and most injurious misrepresentation of him which it contains in it, as if he were either kindly or more indifferently affected towards it : upon which accounts, we may well suppose him to esteem it necessary for him, both to constitute a rule for punishing it, and to punish it accordingly ; that he may both truly act his own nature, and truly represent it. Again it includes, thus taken, his governing wisdom, which requires indispensibly that he do every thing in his government so as he may appear like himself, and answerably to his own greatness ; so as to secure a deep regard for his government, and all the parts of the constitution. In respect whereof, it might be shown, that the punishment of sin, or the execution of the penal laws solemnly enacted is necessary. Wisdom takes care that one attribute do not quite obscure another, and will not allow that he gratify mercy to the detriment of justice. Again, it includes his faithfulness and sincerity, which seem pledged in enacting the penalty for its execution. How is it consistent with them to enact such severe penalties, if he may remit them without any reparation made for the wrong done? Any one that would see more to this purpose, besides others who have discoursed of Vindictive Justice, may peruse the learned Dr. How's Living Temple, Part 2. Chap. 6 and 7, who has learnedly discoursed and improven this
subject :

subject: to whom we own ourselves indebted for much light in this matter.

Thus it seems evident, that whether we take the divine justice in this last and largest notion, as it is comprehensive of all the perfections of the Deity, or in the former and strict notion as it imports a virtue, whose province it is to take care of the preservation of the incommunicable rights of the Deity, and vindicate their honour; it seems necessarily to forbid the remission of sin without the punishment of the transgressor, or a reparation of the injured honour of the Deity.

If it is alleged, that by repentance the sinner returns to his subjection, and so the honour of God's goverment is repaired. I answer, that upon supposition of the sinner's return being a sufficient reparation of the honour of the Deity, there would indeed be no necessity of punishment: but this is the question, and the objection begs what is in question. The principles now laid down, shew that justice, however taken, must take care to preserve and vindicate God's honour in case of transgression. The penal sanction of the law tells us, that the punishment of the transgressor is that which wisdom and justice have fixed on, as proper for this end. There is no alternative, punishment or repentance. The law makes only mention of punishment. When therefore the objectors say that repentance is sufficient, we deny it. They do not prove it, nor can they. God, to whom alone it belongs to determine what is necessary for the vindication of his own honour, must determine the reparation; we cannot. Yea, it were presumption in angels to do it. God has fixed upon punishment: if he allow of any thing else, the light of nature does not tell it. Nor is there any thing in the nature of repentance, as has been above cleared, that can induce us to think it is sufficient to this purpose. The most virtuous, who must be supposed the penitents, if there are any such, meet with as heavy punishments in this life as any, which shews, at least, that God looks not upon their penitence as satisfaction.

6. Against this proposition we reason thus, Every man is endued with a power to repent when he pleases, or he is not. To assert the latter, were to yield the cause; for it matters not to the sinner, whether repentance be a sufficient atonement or not, if it be not in his power to repent. Besides, it is a question in this case of considerable difficulty, whether it is consistent with the perfections of God to give this power, till once his honour

honour is secured by a suitable reparation for the injury done it by sin. If it is in the sinner's power to repent when he pleases, then again I insist,

Either God without impeachment of his justice may inflict the punishment contained in the sanction of the law on the sinner, notwithstanding of his repentance, or he may not. If he may, then the deists can never without revelation be sure that he will not inflict the punishment, which is what we say : nor will it mend the matter, that though God, without impeachment of his justice, may punish the repenting sinner, that he cannot do it without injuring his mercy : for what is contrary to of one God's attributes, is so to all. And moreover, the justice of God in particular requires that each of the divine attributes have their due.

But if it be said, that God cannot in justice punish the repenting sinner; then I desire to be satisfied, if this does not evacuate and make void the penal sanction of the law? For if every man hath a power to repent when he pleases, and this repentance stops the execution of the sentence, I do not see but any may offend without hazard.

All that can be said is, that God may surprize man in the very act of sinning, or so soon after it, that he shall not have time to repent, and so man's hazard is sufficient to deter him from sin.

But to this I answer, that the consideration of this hazard can never have much influence on man, to make him refuse the gratifying of his senses, in which he finds so much pleasure, so long as in the ordinary conduct of providence he sees that God very rarely takes that course of snatching away sinners in the very act of sin, or so soon after, as to preclude repentance. It is not so much what God may do, as what he ordinarily does, that is of weight to determine men, especially when they have so strong motives to persuade them to the contrary, as the impetuous cravings of unruly lusts are known to be.

This argument gives us a clear view how much the deist's notion of pardon upon mere repentance favours sin ; and how unreasonable the outcries of Herbert and Blount, repeated *ad nauseam*, against the maintainers of satisfaction really are. They say, the doctrine of satisfaction makes sin cheap. But whether do they who say that sin cannot be pardoned without the sinner's repentance and satisfaction, or they who assert repentence alone sufficient, make sin cheapest ?

7. I further argue against this doctrine, that this constitution, grant or allowance of repentance, in case of transgression, is either co-eval to the law, and has its rise as the law hath, in the relation betwixt God and man and their natures, as being a necessary result of them; or it is a posterior establishment, and an act of free and gracious condescendence in God, to which he was not necessarily obliged. If this last is said, then I say, this could not be known, but by a revelation or some deed of God, expressive of his mind in this matter. The first is denied by the deists; and we desire them to produce the work of providence whereon it is legible, that God without any reparation to his justice for the injury done him by sin, will pardon the sinner upon his penitence and admit him to bliss. For though we should admit that some works of providence singly taken, without observing others which have a contrary aspect, have somewhat like an intimation of a placability, which we see but little reason to do; yet we deny positively that there is any that specifies the terms, or particularly condescends on repentance, as that whereon he will be pacified and reconciled to sinners. And if any will pretend to draw this from them, I wish they would essay it, and let us see of what form their procedure will be: perhaps they may prove that it is not consistent with God's attributes to pardon an impenitent sinner: but if they think thence to infer, that therefore it is consistent to his attributes to pardon one merely upon his penitence, they may make good the consequence if they can; they will find it harder than it appears.

If the former is said, that this constitution is co-eval with the law, and is as much a necessary result of the nature of God and man, and their mutual relation, as the law itself; besides what has been said to demonstrate the folly of it, let these three things be considered:

(1.) The deists do, and are obliged to say, that man is not now from his birth more corrupt than he was at first.

(2.) Man at his original was, and consequently according to them, still is endued with power sufficient perfectly to know and obey the law he is subjected to. To say that he was subjected to a law, which he was not able to know or obey, is to accuse the Deity of folly and injustice; as has been made appear.

(3.) The law to which man is subjected, is exactly suited to God's great design, his own glory and man's happiness.

These

These being granted, I conceive it evident, 1. That nothing can be said more injurious to the glorious perfections of God, than that any of them gives ground of hopes, far less assurance of impunity to man, if he break these laws, which are equally suited to promote God's glory and his own good, and which he wanted neither power to know nor obey. 2. Such a grant would be of no less dangerous consequence to man, because it could be of other use, than to tempt to a violation of those laws, which it is so much his interest to obey.

But some may say, it would be discouraging to man to think he were undone, if he disobeyed in the least. I answer, this could be no reasonable discouragement if he was possessed of power perfectly to know and obey the law he was subjected to.

Again, it may be said, that it was necessary there should be such an encouragement to man; because, though he was entrusted with sufficient power to know and obey the law of God ; yet he was for trial exposed to a great many strong and forcible temptations to disobedience.

For answer to this ; suppose two men equally able to know and obey the law ; the one knows he may obtain pardon on repentance, the other believes himself irrecoverably lost if he transgress ; I desire the objector, on supposition that both were attacked with a temptation equally strong, to answer me seriously, 1. Which of those two would in all probability soonest yield ; he that saw a probability of escape or he that saw none ? 2. Since the keeping of the law was highly advantageous to both, which of the two is in the best state ; he who has this strong motive to obedience, that he is ruined if he disobey, or he that hath this encouragement and enforcement of the temptation to disobedience, that he may disobey and escape ? Nor will they evade by saying, that this constitution was knowable before, but was not taken notice of till sin fell out : for if it might be known, all the inconveniencies mentioned will follow. Besides, if it was taken notice of after the first sin, it might be a temptation to all succeeding transgressions.

In fine, if this allowance of repentance be said to have the same rise with the law, and be equally necessary from the nature of God and man and their mutual relation ; it is a plain dispensation with the law, and that equally made public, being notified in the same way as the law is; which how it is consistent with the wisdom, holiness, and justice of God, I know not.

8. To

8. To add no more on this head, if this ſtory about the ſufficiency of repentance lies ſo open to the light of nature, whence was it that it was ſo little diſcerned? The name of it, in the ſenſe and to that uſe we now ſpeak of, ſcarce occurs among the ancients, if we may believe Herbert, who read them all with great diligence, and with a deſign to find what was for his purpoſe. Speaking of their ſins, he ſays, "*Neque igitur mihi dubium eſt, quin eorum pænituerit Gentiles, quæ tot mala accerſerunt, licet rarius quidem pænitentiæ verbum inter authores, eo, quo jam uſurpatur ſenſu, reperiatur*.*" Why does not he doubt of it? The reaſon he goes on is, becauſe they uſed ſacrifices. But I ſuppoſe for this very reaſon ſome do doubt if they thought repentance ſufficient: but of this more by and by. The philoſophers neither taught nor practiſed it. It is true, Periander one of the wiſe men of Greece, had this for his ſaying, Αμαρτων μεταβολευε, " Repent of thy ſins;" that is, poſſibly, leave them off. For who can tell us whether he had a right notion of repentance, or of what avail he thought it? Seneca ſays, *Quem penitet peccaſſe pene eſt innocens* †. This is ſpoken with his uſual pride that made him think little of ſin. But where is the perſon that taught repentance, or offered to evince it ſufficient to atone the Deity? Moſt of them contemptuouſly diſregarded it. We find nothing like it in their beſt moraliſt's practice: but on the contrary, they were ſo puffed up with their virtues, that they made no account of their ſins. The prieſts taught not this doctrine, for they inculcated ſacrifices as neceſſary to atone the Deity. And if we may believe no incompetent judge, both prieſts and people were perſuaded that repentance is is not ſufficient to atone the Deity. It is Ceſar who tells us, that, " *Pro vita hominis niſi vita hominis reddatur non poſſe deorum immortalium numen placari arbitrantur Galli* ‡." To which we might add many more teſtimonies to the ſame purpoſe. Nor do we find any thing like this diſcovery among

---

* Herbert de Relig. Gentil. pag. 198.—" Nor is it therefore a doubt with me that the Gentiles repented of thoſe crimes which brought ſo many evils upon them, although the word repentance, in that ſenſe in which it is now uſed, ſeldom occurs in their authors."

† " He who repents of having ſinned is almoſt innocent."

‡ Cæſar de Bello Gal. Lib. 6. See Outramus de Sacrificiis, Lib. 1. Cap. 22.—" The Gauls are of opinion that the Majeſty of the immortal gods cannot be appeaſed unleſs the life of a man be given for the life of another."

among them; which is very strange in a matter of importance, if it was so clearly revealed. That which is most like what they would be at, is what we find in Ovidius—

> *Sæpe levant pœnas, ereptaque lumina reddunt*
> *Quem bene peccati penituisse vides. Et alibi,*
> *Quamvis est igitur meritis indebita nostris,*
> *Magna tamen spes est in bonitate Dei* *.

But this is nothing to the purpose: how many of the poets' notions, and particularly this one, were traditional? How evidently were their notions of all things about the gods suited to their own fabulous stories of the clemency of the gods. And besides, we have no assurance that he understood what we do by repentance. Nor indeed could he. But of this more anon.

Objections considered.

IT remains now that we take notice of some considerable objections that are made against what hitherto has been discoursed by different persons, on different views and principles.

I. Say some, if the case is so apparent *that all have sinned,* and the relief is so hid, that nature's light could not discern it; whence is it that all men run not to despair and take sanctuary here? Whence is it that religious worship was universally continued in the world? Yea, whence is it that such a worship universally obtained, that seems founded on the supposition of a placable God?

To this specious argument we answer, that many things there are in nature, whereof we can give no satisfying account. And if there should prove something in morality too, not to be accounted for, it were not to be wondered at. But not to insist on this, I answer directly. A fair account may be given of this otherwise than by admitting what we have overthrown upon so many clear arguments. Towards which, we shall make the following attempt: 1. The natural notices of a Deity, that are inlaid in the minds of men, strongly prompted them to worship some one or other. From this natural obligation they could not shake
themselves

---

* De Ponto Lib. 1. Eleg. 1. 7.—" You see that he who duly re-
" pents of his offence, often alleviates his punishment, and restores
" his lost light.——Although therefore it is not due to our merits,
" yet there is great hope in the goodness of God."

themselves loose. 2. Their ignorance and darkness as to the real horror of the case, made them think little of sin, and consequently apprehend that it would not prove such an obstruction to acceptance, as really they had reason to apprehend it was. 3. All who allow of revelation, own that the revelation of forgiveness, as well as the means of obtaining it, was twice universal in the days of Adam and Noah. 4. Though this revelation was in so far lost by the generality of mankind, that it could not be useful to its proper end, yet somewhat of it remained still in the world, and spread itself with mankind. 5. All sorts of men found their interest and account in keeping it up. The priests who engrossed the advantage of the religion of the world, found their gain in it. The politicians who aimed at the good of society, found it useful to their purpose. The poets who aimed at pleasing, found it capable of tickling the ears of a world involved in sin. And the people whose consciences were harrassed with guilt of atrocious crimes, found some sort of relief. And what all found some benefit by, was not likely quite to be lost. The philosophers seeing the strait of the case, saw that they could not make a better of it, and so acquiesced. 6. Their profane conceptions of the deities, as if they were persons that allowed or practised their evils, did help forward. The gods which their own fancy had framed, they could cast into what mould they pleased, as it best suited their interest or inclinations. 7. Satan who acted a very visible part among them, and bore sway without controul, no doubt had a deep hand in the matter, and could variously revive, alter and manage the tradition, natural notices and interests of men, so as to make his own advantage of them. Other things might be added, shewing the concernment of the holy God in this matter, which I shall wave for some reasons that are satisfying to myself. But what is said, I conceive sufficient to blunt the edge of the objection. I shall only subjoin the words of the learned Amyrald, who after he has owned the natural discoveries of placability; but withal shown their uselessness, and that they had no influence nor could have, in the words formerly quoted, at length he moves this same objection that we have here proposed, and returns the answer, which we shall now transcribe, though it is somewhat long, the rather because it comes from a person not only of great learning, but one who owned placability might be demonstrated by the light of nature, and yet denies that it was the foundation of the religion that was to be found in the world.

world. " But perhaps, (fays he,) it will here be demanded,
" whence then came it to pafs that all nations have each of
" them had its religion ? And why are not all men diffociated
" inftead of hanging together in religious fociety ? To which
" I antwer, that the mind of man is never agitated with the
" fame emotions, nor conftant in the fame thoughts; the fame
" paffion not always poffeffing him, nor the fame vice. They
" take their turns, or fucceed and mingle one with another.
" Two things therefore have hindered that men, though pof-
" feffed with fear, have not abandoned all fervice of the Deity,
" —profanenefs and pride : God permitting the profanenefs of
" fome and the prefumption of others to temper the terror
" of confcience. Firft, profanenefs ; becaufe not weighing
" fufficiently how much God abominates vice, and how inex-
" orable his juftice is, they often have flattered themfelves with
" this thought, that he fcarce takes any notice of fmall of-
" fences, and fuch as are in the intention and purpofe only, that
" is, in the affections of the will and not in actions really ex-
" ecuted. Moreover, they thought he was not much incenfed,
" but with crimes that turn to fome notable detriment to the
" commonwealth, or carry fome blot of infamous improbity.
" Although mafculine luft was either juftified or excufed, or
" tolerated by the moft civilized people of Greece. And they
" were fometimes fo befotted in their devotions, that they
" thought not but crimes of the greateft turpitude with no great
" difficulty might be expiated by their facrifices, luftrations, reli-
" gious proceffions, myfteries and bacchanel folemnities. On the
" other fide, prefumption ; becaufe not fufficiently acknow-
" ledging how much they owed to the Deity, they imagined
" that their good works, their offerings, and the exercife of
" that fhadow of virtue, which they purfued, might counter-
" vail the offences they committed : fo that were they bal-
" anced together, there might be hope not only to avoid pu-
" nifhment, but moreover to obtain recompence. Upon which
" ground it was that Socrates being near his end, and dif-
" courfing of the immortality of the foul, fpeaks largely of his
" hope, (in cafe the foul be not extinguifhed with the body)
" to go and live with Hercules and Palamedes, and the other
" perfons of high account. But as to afking God pardon of the
" offences he had committed, he makes no mention at all of it ;
" becaufe though he fpoke always diffemblingly of himfelf, he
" had in the bottom of his foul great opinion of his own vir-
" tue

" tue, and made no great reckoning of his vices, from which
" notwithstanding he was no more exempt than others. And
" had his life been of such purity, that the eyes of men could
" not discern a blot in it (although some have written infamous
" matters of him) yet when the account is to be made up with
" God, there needs another perfection of virtue than that of
" his to satisfy so exact a justice. But yet further, oftentimes
" these two vices of profaneness and presumption have met to-
" gether in the same subject, and lulled men with vain hopes
" into absolute supinity. Whence the excess of fear hath been
" retrenched, which would otherwise have at last turned into
" despair, and consequently not only dissipated all communion
" in religion, but likewise ruined all human society. For fear
" restraining man on the one side from absolute contemning the
" Deity by profaneness, on the other side, profaneness and pre-
" sumption hindered it from precipitating men into that furious
" despair which would have overthrown all, and caused more
" horrible agitations in the mind of man, than ever the most
" outragious bacchides were sensible of. So that by the mix-
" ture, vicissitude and variation of these diverse humours has
" religion been maintained in the world. But it is easy to judge
" how sincere that devotion was, which was bred of fear, (a
" passion that is naturally terminated on hatred) self-presump-
" tion, and misapprehension of the justice of God. Whereas
" the certain knowledge of the remission of sins, of which the
" special revelation from heaven can only give us assured hope,
" is a marvellous powerfully attractive to piety, out of gratitude
" towards so inestimable a goodness*."

II. Some object against what has been proven, That God is good, compassionate and kind ; and that natures of any excellency take pleasure in exercising mercy, compassion and kindness, and with difficulty are brought to acts of severity.

I answer, 1. The goodness, kindness, mercy and compassion of God are a pretty subject for men to declaim and make harangues about. But when they are made, they are little to the purpose ; for they are easily answered by a representation of the justice and holiness of God. And the difficulty is not touched, unless men can shew how these seemingly jarring attributes may be consistent. 2. The inferences men must draw from such representations of the nature of God, are such as will

cross

* Amyrald of Relig. Part 1. Chap. 7. pag. 254, 255, 256.

cross the experience of mankind who want revelation, and see many effects of his bounty, goodness, forbearance and patience, but none of his pardoning mercy; and many of his justice and holy severity. Wherefore we may leave this subject and proceed, though much might be said to clear how little all this is to the purpose. But we conceive this is apparent from what has been above discoursed.

III. It is said, " That the very command of God to use his appointed means for men's recovery, doth imply that it shall not be in vain; and doth not only shew a possibility, but so great a hopefulness of success to the obedient, as may encourage them chearfully to undertake it, and carry it through*."

In answer to this, I have above cleared, that men are still obliged to obey; that there are many things, of which several are by him mentioned in the subsequent sections of that chapter, whence these words are quoted, which might be improven to excite man to a cordial compliance, in case there were a new, clear and plain invitation to a return with hope of acceptance. And I admit, that to deny this, as he says, in the words immediately proceeding those now quoted, were to make earth a hell. Yea further, so long as men are out of hell, there is still a possibility in the case: but that there is any such invitation given, or assurance of a hopeful issue, or means directly and specially instituted by God as means of recovery, knowable by men left to the mere light of nature, I deny: because I see not the shadow of a proof and evidence to the contrary that has been offered.

IV. It is alleged by the same author, That God's commanding us to *forgive* others, encourages us to expect *forgiveness* at his hand.

To this I say, 1. The learned person owns, " That from from this it doth not follow, that God must forgive all, which he bindeth us to forgive, for reasons he had before expressed." 2. I say, that this, the command of God to forgive others, lies not so open to the view of nature's light, as that every one can discern it. And besides, it admits of many exceptions, for ought that unassisted nature can discover. 3. It is restricted to private persons, and is not to be extended to public injuries done against government. 4. When it is found to be our duty by nature's light, we are brought to see it by such reasons as

these

* Baxter's Reasons of Christ. Relig. Part 1. Chap. 17. §. 9. pag. 186.

these, That we need the like favour at their hands, that we are frail, &c. which gives us ground to be jealous that the like is not to be expected at his hand, with whom these things have no place, which are the reason of the law to us. So that from this, as it is discoverable by nature's light, no sure inference can be drawn.

V. It is objected, That sacrifices and all the religious services amongst the Heathens, were only symbolical of a good life and repentance*.

To this I say, 1. If this were true, Herbert and the deists are much in the wrong to the priests who urged the use them, as men who neglected to inculcate repentance. For any thing I can see they were more commendable than the philosophers, who neither taught nor practised repentance, and vilified sacrifices. But 2. This is a scandalous falsehood; for there is nothing more evident, than that by the sacrifices they designed to atone the deities, and expected that they should be accepted in place of the offerers, and their death be admitted instead of what they had deserved themselves. See abundance of testimonies given to this by him to whom we referred, when we quoted Cesar's testimony to this purpose; I mean Outram. What, I pray, meant the custom that prevailed, not only among the Jews, but Heathens, of offering their sacrifices with solemn prayers to God, that all the plagues which they or their country had deserved, might light on the head of the victim; and so they themselves escape? And hereupon they thought that all their sins did meet upon it, and defile it to that degree, that none who had touched it dared to return home till they had washed and purified themselves. Suidas reports of the Greeks, " *Quod,*
" *ei, qui malis averruncandis quotannis destinatus erat, sic im-*
" *precabantur, fis περιψημα nostrum, hoc est, salus & redemptio.*
" *Atque ita illum in mare projiciebant, quasi Neptuno sacrum*
" *persolventes†.*" Servius tells us, " *Massilienses, quoties pesti-*
" *lentia laborabant, unus se ex pauperibus offerebat, alendus*
" *anno integro publicis & purioribus cibis. Hic postea, orna-*
" *tus verbenis & vestibus sacris, circumducebatur per totam ci-*
" *vitatem*

* See A. W. Letter, Oracles of Reason.
† " They cursed the person who was yearly appointed for averting
" misfortunes, in this manner, " Be thou our atonement," that is,
" our safety and redemption; and so they threw him into the sea, as
" performing a sacrifice to Neptune."

"*vitatem cum execrationibus, ut in ipsum reciderent mala totius civitatis; & sic projiciebatur**." But we have stayed too long in refuting this mad and ungrounded conceit.

VI. Some, to prove that the works of providence, particularly his forbearance to sinners and bounty to them, do call men to repentance without the word, urge the apostle's words, Rom. ii. 4. *Or despisest thou the riches of his goodness and forbearance, and long-suffering, not knowing that the goodness of God leadeth thee to repentance?* To this we answer,

1. Divines, and these not a few, nor of the lowest form, do understand this whole context of the Jews; and they urge reasons for it that are not contemptible. If this opinion hold, no more can be drawn from these words, than what has been already granted without any prejudice to our cause, viz. that this dispensation, where persons are otherwise under a call to repentance, gives time to repent, and enforceth the obligation of that call they are under.

2. But to cut off all pretence of any plea from this scripture, we shall take under our consideration the apostle's whole discourse, from the 16th ver. of the 4th chap. to the 4th ver. of the 3d, and give a view of these words, and other passages insisted on to the same purpose, with a special eye to the apostle's scope in the discourse, and the particular design of every passage. And this we shall undertake, not so much out of any regard to this objection in particular, but to obviate the abuse of several passages of this discourse of the apostle, by one with whom we shall have just now occasion to debate almost every verse in this second chapter. If therefore our solution of the apostle's discourse seem a little tedious at present, this disadvantage will be compensated by the light it will contribute for clearing many of the ensuing objections.

The apostle Paul, Rom. i. 16. had asserted, that the *gospel is the power of God to salvation to every one that believes, to the Jew first and also to the Greek,* that is, it is the only powerful mean of salvation to persons of all sorts; neither Jew nor Greek can be

saved

---

* " As often as the Massilians were afflicted with the pestilence, one of the poor offered himself, who was to be nourished for a whole year with clean victuals, at the public expence, after which being adorned with vervains and sacred garments, he was led round the whole city with execrations, that the misfortunes of the whole city might fall upon him, and thus he was cast out."

saved by any other mean. In the 17th verse, he advances an argument for proof of this assertion, which is plainly this, that revelation, which exhibits *the righteousness of God*, which is the only righteousness that can please God, and on the account whereof he accepts and justifies sinners; and which exhibits *this righteousness*, not upon slender or conjectural grounds, but *from faith*, that is, upon the testimony of the *faithful God*, who can neither be deceived nor deceive us, proposes this righteousness to our faith, as the only powerful mean of salvation: but it is the *gospel* only that doth reveal this righteousness of God *from faith*, or upon the credit of divine testimony unto *faith:* therefore the gospel is the only powerful mean of God's appointment.

This is plainly the apostle's argument; and if we consider it, we will find it to comprize three assertions; 1. That the *righteousness of God* revealed in the gospel, and received by *faith*, is that, on the account whereof, sinners are accepted with and justified before God. This is one branch of his first proposition, which he designs to explain and confirm afterwards at length. Here he only confirms it by hinting a proof of it from the prophet Habakkuk's words, *the just shall live by faith*, that is, faith receiving the righteousness of God revealed in the promise, is the foundation of all the godly, their hopes of pardon, peace with God, grace to support under trials, and a merciful deliverance from them. As it is by these things they live in troublesome times, so it is the acceptance of this righteousness, that gives them any right to these advantages. 2. His first proposition implies this assertion, that this righteousness of God revealed in the gospel, is the *only* effectual mean of acceptance with and justification before God; or, that there is no other way wherein any of the children of men may obtain those advantages, save this way of accepting by faith the righteousness of God, upon the credit or faith of his testimony; this is the other branch of his first proposition. 3. The apostle asserts in this argument, that the gospel doth reveal this righteousness of God; on which, and on which only, acceptance with and justification before God are to be obtained, *from faith to faith.* This is the apostle's assumption or second proposition.

The apostle having hinted for the present, at a sufficient proof of the first of these assertions, as has been said, passes it. He lays aside likewise the third of these assertions, designing to clear it afterwards, and addresses himself to the proof of the second in

the

the enfuing difcourfe from chap. i. ver. 18. to chap. iii. ver. 20. or thereabout.

The propofition then which our apoftle fpends the whole context under confideration in proof of, is, " That there is no other way whereby a finner can obtain juftification before, or acceptance with God, but by faith:" Or that " neither Gentiles nor Jews can be juftified before God by their own works." This he demonftrates, Firft, Againft the Gentiles in particular, from chap. i. ver. 18. to chap. ii. ver. 16. according to our prefent fuppofition, or conceffion of his adverfaries. Next, He proves the fame in particular againft the Jews, chap. ii. to ver. 8. of chap. iii. And from thence to the clofe of his difcourfe he demonftrates the fame in general againft all mankind whether Jews or Gentiles.

First, Then, he demonftrates againft the Gentiles in particular, that they cannot be juftified before God by *the works* they may pretend to have done in *obedience* to the *law of nature*, by the enfuing arguments, which we fhall not reduce into form; but only propofe the force of them, by laying down in the moft natural and eafy order, the propofitions whereof they do confift.

1. The apoftle infinuates, ver. 18. that the Gentiles had fome notions of truth concerning God, and the worfhip due to him from the light of nature, ver. 18. though they imprifoned them: and what here he infinuates, he directly proves ver. 19, 20.

2. He afferts, that they did not walk anfwerably to thefe notices, but detained them *in unrighteoufnefs*; that is, they fuppreffed, bore them down, and would not allow them that directive power over their practices which they claimed; but in oppofition to them went on in fin. This he had intimated in general, ver. 18. and he proves it, ver. 21, 22, 23.

3. He proves, that *the wrath of God, is revealed from heaven*, efpecially by inftances of fpiritual plagues, the moft terrible of all judgments, againft them for their counteracting thofe notices of truth. This he alfo intimated, ver. 18. and proves it, ver. 24, 25, 26.

4. He fhews, that the Gentiles being thus, by the juft judgment of God, given up and left to themfelves, did run on from evil to worfe in all forts of abominations; and thereby did render their own condemnation the more fure, inevitable and intolerable. This he does from ver. 26, to 32.

5. To

5. To confirm this further, ver. 32. he shews that the fact cannot be denied, in regard that they both practised those evils themselves, and made themselves guilty by their virtual approbation of them in others: nor could it be excused, since they could not but know, if they attended to the light of nature, that such grofs abominations are *worthy of death*.

6. The apostle having in the last verse of chap. i. mentioned this aggravation of their sins, that they were against knowledge, takes occasion thence to proceed to a new argument, whereby he at once confirms what he had said about their sinning against knowledge, chap. i. ver. 32. and further evinces his main point, that they must inevitably be condemned by a new argument, which he lays down in the ensuing assertion, either expressed or insinuated.

(1.) He takes notice, that the Gentiles, if he speaks of them, do themselves practise those things, which they judge and condemn others for.

(2.) He takes it for granted, as well he may, that he who condemns any practice of another, doth confess that that practice in itself is worthy of condemnation.

(3.) He hereon infers, that the Gentiles do practise those things, which according to their own acknowledgment, are in themselves worthy of condemnation. Now this conclusion directly fixes upon them the aggravation mentioned in the close of the proceeding chapter, viz. That they know the things they do to be *worthy of death*. And this sufficiently clears the connection.

(4.) He argues again, that the judgment of God being always according to truth, he will certainly condemn all, who do things that in truth are worthy of condemnation, ver. 2.

(5.) Hereon by an inevitable consequence, ver. 3. he concludes, that God will certainly condemn the Gentiles, which is the main point.

(6.) As an inference from the whole, he concludes, that as any prospect of escape is vain, so they are precluded from all excuse, or shadow of ground for reclaiming against the sentence of God, which by their own acknowledgement proceeds only against practices, that are in truth worthy of condemnation.

7. The apostle having thus locked them up, as it were, under unavoidable condemnation, proceeds ver. 4. to cut off their retreat to that, wherein some of them took sanctuary.

They

They concluded, that God, who did forbear them, while they went on in sin, and allowed them to share so deep in his goodness, would not punish them so severely. To cut off this plea, the apostle first taxes them as guilty of a grievous abuse of this dispensation, while they drew encouragement from it to go on in sin. 2. He argues them of gross ignorance of the genuine tendency of this dealing of God. To argue thus, " God spares me and is good to me, therefore I may safely sin against him, and hope for his impunity in committing known sin against him," is mad and unreasonable. Reason would say, " God forbears me, and so gives me time; he adds to former obligations I lay under to obey him by loading me with new kindnesses, therefore I should be the more studious to please him, and avoid these things which I know will be offensive to him, and be ashamed for former offences." This by the way is the full import of that expression, *The goodness of God leading to repentance.* But of this more anon. 3. Hereon ver. 5. he infers that their abuse of this dispensation and their not returning to obedience, or answering the obligations laid on them increases their guilt, and so lays up materials for an additional libel, and a more highly accented punishment, ver. 5.

Having thus shortly given an account of the scope and meaning of the words, I shall next lay down a few short observations clearly subversive of any argument that can be drawn from them.

(1.) None can say, that the persons, who were under this dispensation did, in fact, understand it to import a call to repentance. The apostle accuses them of ignorance of this, and of abusing it by drawing encouragement from it, that they should escape punishment, though they went on in sin.

(2.) It is plain, the apostle's scope led him to no more, but this, to evince, that this dispensation afforded them no ground to hope for impunity, no encouragement to proceed in a course of known sin, that it did aggravate the guilt of their continuance in such sins, and enforce the obligations they otherwise were under to abstinence from them, and the practice of neglected duties. This is all the words will bear, and all that the scope requires.

(3.) The apostle is proving, as we have clearly evinced above, that the persons, with whom he is now dealing, without recourse to the gospel revelation, are shut up from all access to justification

fication before God, acceptance with him, pardon and falvation; certainly therefore he cannot in this place be underftood to intend that thefe perfons were under means fufficient to lead them to that repentance, upon which they might be affured of forgivenefs and peace with God.

(4.) This fame apoftle elfewhere appropriates the call to repentance unto the gofpel revelation, Acts xvii. 30. fpeaking to the Heathens at Athens, he fays, *the times of this ignorance God winked at; but now commandeth all men ev ry where to repent.* Here it is plain, that men left to the light of nature, are left without this call, until the gofpel come and give this invitation.

(5.) Wherefore we may from the particular fcope of this verfe, the general fcope of the apoftle's difcourfe, and his plain declarations upon other occafions, conclude, 1. That the repentance he here intends, is not that repentance to which the promife of pardon is in the gofpel annexed; but only an abftinence from thefe evils, which their confciences condemn them for, and the return to fome fort of performance of the material part of known, but deferted duty. Frequent mention is made of fuch a repentance in fcripture; but no where is pardon promifed upon it. 2. This leading imports no more, but that the difpenfation we fpeak of difcovers this return to be duty, and gives fpace or time for it.

(6.) To confirm what has been now faid, it is to be obferved, that our apoftle acquaints, that this forbearance and goodnefs is exercifed towards *the veffels of wrath fitted to deftruction*, Rom. ix. 22. which fufficiently intimates that this difpenfation of itfelf gives no affurance of pardon to thefe who are under it, but is confiftent with a fixed purpofe of punifhing them. Yet without this affurance, it is impoffible there fhould ever be any call to repentance, that can be available to any of mankind, or anfwer the hypothefis of thofe with whom we have to do.

8. In the clofe of ver. 5. the apoftle introduces a difcourfe of the laft judgment for two ends: Firft, To cut off thofe abufers of God's goodnefs from all hopes of efcape. He has before fhewed that they have ftored up fins, the caufes of wrath; and here he fhews there is a judgment defigned, wherein they will reap as they have fown. Thus the words following are a confirmation of the foregoing argument, and enforce the apoftle's main fcope. Secondly, He does it for clearing the righteoufnefs of God from any imputation that the difpenfation he had been fpeak-

ing

ing of, viz. his forbearance and goodnefs towards finners, might tempt blind men to throw upon it: and this he does by fhewing that this is not the time of retribution, but that there is an open and folemn diftribution defigned, wherein God will fully clear his righteoufnefs. To thefe two ends is this whole account of the laft judgment fuited. He tells them that there is a *day of wrath and of the revelation of the righteous judgment of God*. While he fpeaks of *the revelation of the righteous judgment of God*, he tacitly grants that by this difpenfation of forbearance, the righteoufnefs of God's judgment is fome way clouded or under a vail: but withall he intimates that there is a definite time, a *day* fixed for its manifeftation; and that this day will prove a *day of wrath*, that is, a day wherein the vindictive juftice of God will fignally manifeft itfelf, in punifhing fuch finners as they were with whom he deals. In fhort, he acquaints them, that the defign of this day is *to reveal the righteous judgment of God*, that is, to manifeft to the conviction of angels and men, the righteoufnefs of God's proceedings toward the children of men, particularly as to rewards and punifhments. It will be *righteous*, and therefore fuch finners as they fhall not efcape. It will be *revealed* to be fuch; and fo all ground of calumny will be taken away. To clear this, he gives an account of the concernments of that judgment, in fo far as it is to his purpofe; wherein,

(1.) He teaches, that there will be an open retribution of rewards and punifhments, God will *render*, &c.

(2.) He fhews, that God will proceed in this retribution upon open and inconteftible evidence. He will *render according to works*. The perfons who are to be punifhed fhall, to the conviction of on-lookers, be convicted by their *works of impiety*; and the piety of thofe to whom the rewards are given, fhall in like manner be cleared.

(3.) He acquaints them, that the diftribution fhall be fuitable to the character of the perfons, the nature and quality of their works. He will render *according to their works*; that is, evil to the evil; good to the good. This is all that is intended by κατα *fecundum*, or *according:* the meaning is not that he will render according to the merit of their works. For though I own that God will punifh according to the juft demerit of fin; yet that is not intended here by this phrafe *according* to works: for the word in its proper fignification intimates, not ftrict or univerfal proportion betwixt the things connected

nected by it; much less doth it particularly import, that the one is the meritorious cause of the other; but the word is, in all languages, commonly taken in a more lax signification, to denote any suitableness betwixt the things connected by it. So our Lord says to the blind men, Matth. xix. 29. *According to your faith be it unto you.* Who will say that any faith, but especially such a lame one as we have reason to think they had, did merit that miraculous cure; or that it was every way suitable unto it? Since then the word of itself does not import this, it cannot be taken so here, unless either other scriptures determine us to this sense, or something in the context fix this to be the meaning of it. To take it in this sense as to rewards, is so far from having any countenance from other scriptures, that it is directly contrary to the whole current of them. And when the word is taken in this sense, then the scriptures plainly tell us that we are not *saved* or *rewarded by* or *according* to our *works of righteousness*, but *according to his mercy through Jesus Christ*, Tit. iii. 5, 6. Nor is there any thing in the text or context to incline us to take it in this sense, but much on the contrary to demonstrate that this is not the meaning, at least with respect to rewards: for to say, that the reward shall be given us according to our works, that is, for our works, as meritorious of it, flatly contradicts the apostle's scope, which is to prove, that all mankind, Jews and Gentiles, do by their works merit only condemnation, and that none can expect upon them absolution, much less reward. Besides, the works here principally intended are not all our works, nor these, which if any had, would have the fairest pretence to merit, viz. the inward actings of grace, faith, love, &c. but outward works that are evidences of the inward temper and frame of the actors. This is evident from the word itself, from the particular instances elsewhere condescended upon, when the last judgment is spoken of, and from the design of this general judgment.

(4.) He shews, that this retribution will be universal, *to every one*, &c.

(5.) He illustrates further the righteousness of it, ver. 7. by characterizing the persons who are to be rewarded, they are such as *do well*, that is, whose actions openly speak them good, and evidence the honesty of the principle whence they flow; they *continue in well doing*, their walk is uniform and habitually good; flowing from a fixed principle, and not from an external accidental cause; they continue patiently in this course, in opposition

to

to all discouragements; nor do they aim at worldly advantage, but at that *glory, honour* and *immortality*, which God sets before them. None but they, who are perfectly such, shall have a reward, if it is sought for, according to the tenor of the covenant of works: and in this sense not a few, nor they obscure interpreters, do take the words; as if the apostle had said, if there be any among you, who have perfectly obeyed, ye shall be rewarded: but whereas I have cleared that none of you are such, ye are cut off from any expectation of reward. But if the sincerity of obedience is only intended, then the meaning is that God will of his grace, according to his promise, and not for their works, give the reward to the sincerely obedient; and thereby will openly evince his righteousness, in dealing with them exactly according to the tenor of the covenant, to which they belong; so that no person, who has any just claim to reward founded upon either covenant, shall want it.

(6.) To clear the glory of God's righteousness further, he specifies the reward, viz. *eternal life*, a reward sufficient to compensate any losses they have been at, evidence God's love to holiness, and his regard unto his promises.

(7.) He, in like manner, clears the matter further, by giving a description ver. 8. of the persons, who are to be condemned, which evinces the apparent righteousness of the sentence to be passed against them. They are such against whom it will be made evident, that they have been *contentious*, that is, that they have opposed and suppressed the truths they knew, stifled convictions, and *detained them in unrighteousness:* such as have *not obeyed the truth*, or walked up to their knowledge, but have obeyed *unrighteousness*, following the inclinations of their corrupt hearts. As if the apostle had said, the persons who are to be rewarded are of a character that ye can lay no manner of claim to, but your character is perfectly that of those who are to be condemned.

(8.) He specifies the punishment, *indignation and wrath*.

(9.) To fix the truth and importance of this deeper upon their minds, he repeats and enlarges upon this assertion, ver. 9, 10. thereby assuring them that the matter is infallibly certain, and to give a further evidence of the *righteousness of God*, he adjects a clause and repeats it twice over, viz. *first to the Jew and also to the Gentile*, wherein he shews the impartiality of God's proceedings. He will not suffer one soul, who has any just claim to reward, to go unrewarded, be he Jew or Gentile. He will not allow one sinner, to whom punishment belongs, to escape unpunished. The Jews' privileges shall not save them, if guilty, but judgment shall begin first at the house of God; nor shall the bare want of privileges prejudge the Gentiles.

(10.) To confirm this, he adduces an argument from the nature of God, ver. 11. viz. that with him there is *no respect of persons*, that is, no unjust partiality toward persons, upon considerations, that do not belong unto the rule, whereby the cause is to be tried.

(11.) To strengthen this and obviate objections, ver. 12. he asserts, that God will proceed impartially in judging them according to the most unexceptionable rule. He will condemn the Jews for their transgressions of that law, which he gave to them. He will condemn the Gentiles, not for the transgression of the written law, which they had not, but for their sins against the law of nature, which they had. And so neither of them shall have ground to except against the rule, according to which God proceeds with them.

(12.) Hence he takes occasion, ver. 13. to repel an objection or plea of the Jews, who might fancy that they should not be punished or perish, to whom God had given the privilege of the written law. To cut of this plea he tells them, that where persons expect justification by the law, it is not the *knowledge* of the *law*, or *hearing* of it, but *obedience* to it that will be sustained. Here he does not suppose that any shall be justified by *doing the law*; nay, he proves the contrary. It is manifestly his design, in the whole discourse, to do so: but he shews that the plea of the Jews, that they had the law, is insufficient; as if he had said, be it granted, that justification is to be had by the law; yet even upon that supposition, ye have no title to it, unless ye perfectly obey it. The law pleads for none, but those who do so. And since none of you do thus obey it, as shall be evinced anon, ye must perish, as I said, ver. 12.

(13.) Whereas the Gentiles might plead, it would be hard treatment if they should be *condemned*, since they were *without the law*; he demonstrates that they could not except against their own condemnation upon this ground, because although they wanted the written law, yet they had another law, viz. that of *nature*; for the breaches of which they might justly be condemned. That they had such a law he proves against them, ver. 14, 15. *First*, From their practice: he tells them that by the guidance of mere nature they did the *works of the law*, that

is

is, they performed the material part of some of the duties which the law enjoins, and thereby evidenced acquaintance with the law, or as he words it, *they shew the work of the law written in their hearts*, that is, the remainders of their natural light, or reason, performs the work of the law commanding duty, and forbidding sin. *Secondly,* He proves that they have such a law from the working of their conscience. He whose conscience accuses him for not doing some things, and approves him for doing other things, knows that he was obliged to do the one and omit the other, and consequently has some knowledge of the law. This is the apostle's scope, ver. 14, 15. So that *for,* in the beginning of ver. 14. refers to and renders a reason of the first clause of ver. 12. that they who had *sinned without law,* viz. the written law, *shall perish without law,* that is, not for violating the written law, which they had not.

(14.) Having removed these objections, he concludes his account of the last judgment, ver. 16. wherein he gives them an account, 1*st,* To whom it belongs originally to judge, it is God. 2*dly,* Who the person is to whom the visible administration is committed, it is Jesus Christ. 3*dly,* What the matter of that judgment is, or what will be judged, it is the *secrets of hearts.* Although works will be insisted upon as evidences for the conviction of on-lookers, of the righteousness of God in his distribution of rewards and punishments; yet the *secrets of men* will also be laid open, for the further confusion of sinners, and justification of the severity of God against them.

Secondly, Now the apostle having proven, that the Gentiles are all under condemnation, and so cannot be justified by any works they can do; and having likewise removed some exceptions of the Jews that fell in his way, he proceeds next directly to prove the same against the Jews in particular, and answers their objections from chap. ii. ver. 17. to chap. iii. ver. 8. inclusive.

To prove this charge against the Jews, he makes use only of one argument, which yet is capable of bearing the weight of many conclusions or inferences. To understand this, we must take notice, that the apostle here is dealing with the Jews, who sought to be *justified* by *works.* And,

1. By way of concession, he grants them several privileges above the Gentiles from ver. 17. to ver. 20. inclusive, viz. That they were *called Jews;* that they had *the law,* on which they rested, and pretended some peculiar interest in God, as,

being externally in covenant with him, ver. 17. of which they *boasted*; that they had some knowledge of the *law*, and pretended themselves capable of guiding others. This he grants them in a variety of expressions, ver. 18, 19, 20. By which the apostle secretly taxes their vanity, and insinuates, that whatever they had in point of privilege, they abused it.

2. The apostle charges them with a practical contradiction to this their knowledge, and this he makes good against them, particularly against their highest pretenders, their teachers, 1. By condescending on several instances, wherein they were guilty and appealing to their consciences for the truth of them, ver. 22, 23. which I shall not infist in explaining. 2. He proves it further by a testimony of scripture, ver. 24. wherein God complains, that their provocations were such, as tempted the Gentiles to *blaspheme his name*.

This is the argument, the conclusion he leaves to themselves to draw. And indeed it will bear all the conclusions formerly laid down against the Gentiles. Whatever their knowledge was, they were not *doers*, but *breakers* of the *law*, and so could not be *justified* by it, ver. 13. but might expect to perish for their transgressions of it, according to ver. 12. They sinned against knowledge, and so deserved as severe resentments as the Gentiles, chap. i. ver. 32. They could not pretend ignorance; for they taught others the contrary, and so were without excuse, chap. ii. ver. 1.

The apostle next proceeds to answer their objections. The first whereof is brought in, ver. 25. The short of it is this, the Jews pretended they had *circumcision*, the seal of God's covenant, and so claimed the privileges of it. This objection is not directly proposed, but the answer anticipating it is introduced as a confirmation or reason enforcing the conclusion aimed at, viz. That they could not be justified by the law: and therefore it is, that we find the casual particle *for* in the beginning of the verse. This much for the manner wherein the objection is introduced. To this objection the apostle answers,

1. By a concession; *circumcision verily profiteth if thou keep the law*, that is, if thou perfectly obey the commands, then thou mayest in justice demand the privileges of the covenant, and plead the seal of it, as a pledge of the faithfulness of God in the promises.

2. He answers directly by shewing, that this seal signified

just

just nothing as to their claim of a legal righteousness, because they were *breakers of the law*. *But if thou be a breaker of the law, thy circumcision is made uncircumcision.* The short of the matter is this; this seal is only a conditional engagement of the faithfulness of God: it does not say, thou shalt get the privileges whether thou perform the condition or not: so that by this means, if the condition is not performed, ye have nothing to ask, and ye are as remote from a claim to the reward, as they who want the seal.

3. The apostle, to illustrate and confirm what he had said about the unprofitableness of circumcision in case of transgression, shews, that a Gentile upon supposition that it were possible, obeying the law, but wanting the seal of the covenant, would have a better title to the privileges promised, than a Jew, who had the seal, but wanted the obedience, ver. 26. *Therefore if the uncircumcision keep the righteousness of the law,* that is, if a Gentile should yield that obedience the law requires, *shall not his uncircumcision, be counted for circumcision?* That is, shall not he, notwithstanding he wanteth the outward sign of circumcision, be allowed to plead an interest in the blessings promised to obedience, and to insist upon the faithfulness of God for the performance of the promises made to the obedient, of which circumcision is the sign? The reason of this is plain, circumcision seals the performance of the promise to the obedient; the Gentile obeying has that, which is the ground whereon the faithfulness of God is engaged to perform the promise, viz. obedience, and so a real title to the thing promised, though he wants the outward sign: whereas the disobeying Jew has only the seal, which secures nothing, but upon the condition of that obedience, which he has not yielded. This is only spoken by way of supposition, not as if any of the Gentiles had yielded such obedience: for he has plainly proven the contrary before. The apostle's reason is this, circumcision is an engagement for the performance of the promise to the obedient. The disobedient Jew has therefore no title to the promise; whereas the Gentile that obeys having that obedience to which the promise is made, has a real right to it, and so might expect the performance of it, as if he had the outward seal.

4. To clear yet further the unprofitableness of circumcision without obedience, the apostle, upon the foresaid supposition, shews, that the Gentile obeying would not only have the better title;

but

but his obedience would contribute to clearing the justice of God, in condemning the disobedient Jew, ver 27. *And shall not uncircumcision which is by nature, if it fulfil the law, judge thee, who by the letter and circumcision doest transgress the law,* that is, if a Gentile wanting circumcision and the security thereby given, with the other advantages which the Jews have, discover the inexcusableness of your disobedience, who have the *letter* and *circumcision*, or the written law, that is, who have a clearer rule of duty and a plainer promise.

5. To remove entirely the foundation of this objection, the apostle clears the real design of circumcision, and the character of the person to whom the advantages do belong, ver. 28, 29. wherein he shews negatively, that the Jew to whom the promises do belong is not every one who belongs to that nation, or is outwardly a Jew; and that the circumcision, to which the promises are absolutely made, is not the *outward circumcision*, which is *in the flesh*, ver. 28. ; but positively, that the Jew, to whom the promised blessings belong, is he who is a *Jew inwardly*, that is, who has that inward frame of heart which God requires of his people; and the circumcision, to which blessings are absolutely promised, is that inward renovation of heart which is the principle of the obedience required by, and accepted of God, ver. 29.

This objection being removed out of the way, the apostle proceeds to answer an instance against what he has now said in the three or four first verses of the 3d chap. The objection is proposed ver. 1. and is in short this, By your reasoning, would the Jews say, we have no advantage beyond the Gentiles, and circumcision is utterly unprofitable. To this he answers,

1. By denying flatly what is asserted in the objection, declaring, notwithstanding of all this, the Jews had every way the advantage.

2. Lest this should appear a vain assertion, he clears it by an instance of the highest consequence, viz. that they had *the oracles of God*, which the Gentiles wanted, wherein that relief against transgressions, which the Gentiles were strangers to, is revealed, as he expressly teaches afterwards, ver. 21. As if the apostle had said, Though ye Jews fail of obedience, and so are cut off from justification by the law as a covenant of works, yet ye have a righteousness revealed to you in the law and the prophets, ver. 21. to which the sinner may betake himself for relief; this the Gentiles who want the law and prophets know nothing of. 3. He

3. He clears that this is a great advantage, notwithstanding that many of the Jews were not the better for it, ver. 3. thus at once anticipating an objection that might be moved, and confirming what he had said. *What if some did not believe,* that is, though some have fallen short of the advantages of this revelation, shall we therefore say it was not in itself a privilege? Nay, it is in itself a privilege, and they by their own fault in not believing, have forfeited the advantages of it to themselves only; *for shall their unbelief make the faith of God without effect?* That is, assuredly believers will not be the worse dealt with for the unbelief of others; but they will obtain the advantage of the promises.

We have insisted much longer upon this context than was designed, but we hope that they who consider that the apostle's arguments and his whole purposes, are directly levelled at that which is the main scope of these papers, will not reckon this a faulty digression. And besides, we shall immediately see the usefulness of this, in order to remove the foundation of a great many objections drawn from this context by Mr. Humfrey; some of whose notions we shall consider after we have removed one objection more, and it is this:

VII. The words of the apostle Paul to the Athenians, Acts xvii. 27. are made use of to this purpose. The apostle tells them in the preceding words, that the God whom he preached, was he who *made the worlds, hath made of one blood all nations of men, for to dwell on all the face of the earth, and hath determined the times before appointed, and the bounds of their habitation; that they should seek the Lord, if happily they might feel after him and find him, though he be not far from every one of us: for in him we live and move and have our being.* The sum of what is pleaded from this testimony amounts to this, that men left to the light of nature are in duty bound to *seek the Lord; that God is not so far from them,* but he may be found; and that if they will *feel* after him, that is, trace these dark discoveries of him, in the works of creation and providence, they may *happily find him.*

For answer to this we say, 1. No word is here to be stretched further than the occasion and scope of the apostle requires and allows. 2. The occasion of this discourse was, that Paul being at Athens, saw that city set upon the worship of idols, and overlooked the one true God, which moved him with wrath, and gave occasion to this discourse; the evident scope whereof is to shew, that they were to blame, that they overlooked the true God, and gave that worship to idols, which was only to be given to God. For convincing them of this, 3. He shews, that the true God, by his works of creation and providence had in so far discovered himself, that if by these works they sought after the knowledge of him, they might find him so far, or know so much, as to understand that he alone was the true God, to whom divine worship was due. 4. He owns, that indeed these discoveries were but dark, to wit, in comparison of the discoveries he had made of himself in the word; which is sufficiently intimated by that expression of *feeling after him*, they might *find him*, so far as to deliver them from that gross idolatry and neglect of him they were involved in. Here is all that the scope holds out: but he does not say, that they might find him, so as to obtain the saving knowledge of him by these works of providence; but on the contrary he tells us, *that God winked at the times of ignorance*, that is, seemed as if he did not notice men, and in his holy and sovereign justice left them to find by their own experience, which by any means they had, that they could not arrive to the saving knowledge of God; though they might, as has been just now said, have gone so far as to disentangle themselves from that gross idolatry for which he now reproves them. He does not say, that God then called them to saving repentance, gave them any discovery of his purpose of mercy, and thereon invited them to peace and acceptance: but on the contrary, he tells, *that now he calls all men every where to repent*, ver. 30. which sufficiently intimates that they had not that call before. In a word, it is not that seeking or finding of God, or that nearness to God which is here intended, that elsewhere the scripture speaks of, when it treats about men's case who are living under the gospel, and have God in Christ revealed, and the gospel call to turn, to seek after and find him to their own salvation; as the scope of the place fully clears. Any one that would see this place fully considered, may find it done by the learned Dr. Owen, in that accurate, though short digression concerning *universal grace*, inserted in his *Theolog. Pantodap.* pag. 33. There likewise is that other scripture, Acts xiv. ver. 15, 16, 17. largely considered. On which I shall not now insist, seeing there is nothing in it that has the least appearance of opposition to what we have asserted, if not that God is there said, *not to have left himself without a witness* among the nations, in as much as he

did

did good to them, gave fruitful seasons, &c. This is granted: but these necessaries of life are no witness that God designed for them mercy and forgiveness, as has been made appear above, and as the Spirit of God tells us there; *for God suffered them to walk in their own way.*

VIII. Some allege that there is a law of grace connatural to man in his lapsed state, and that in substance it is this, That God will pardon sinners upon their repentance: and they tell us, that this law of grace is as much written in the heart of lapsed man, as the law of nature was written in the heart of innocent man. To this purpose speaks Mr. Humfrey in his *Peaceable Disquisitions**, and that with such an air of confidence, as might make one expect better proof than he has offered.

We shall just now examine Mr. Humfrey's arguments. As to the notion itself of a connatural law of grace written in the hearts of all mankind in this lapsed condition, we look upon it as absolutely false. It contradicts scripture, reason and experience. My design excuseth me from the use of scripture arguments. Experience I need not insist upon, after what has been already said. Reason will not allow us to call any law connatural to man, save upon one of these three accounts; either because we are born with actual knowledge of it; or, because it lies so open and is so suited to our rational faculties, that any man, who has the use of reason, can scarce miss thinking of it, at least, refuse his assent to it, when it is proposed to him; or, finally, because it is nearly connected with notions and principles that are self-evident, and is easily deducible from them. Now this discovery of mercy to sinners merely upon repentance is connatural in none of these senses. I know no truth that is connatural in the first sense. The ingenious Mr. Locke has said enough against this†. In the second sense, it is not connatural. Who will tell me, that this is a self-evident proposition, while so great a part of the more knowing and judicious part of mankind, not only refuse their assent to it, but reject it as a plain untruth? Yea, I doubt if any man that understands the case, and knows nothing of the satisfaction of Christ, will give his assent to it. In this last sense it is not connatural; for if it were so, it were easily demonstrable by these self-evident principles, to which it is nearly allied: which when Mr. Humfrey shall have demonstrated from these principles

---

* Peace. Disquis. Chap. 4. pag. 56.
† Essay on Human Understand. Lib. 1.

principles, or any other for him, we shall then consider it; but this I am apprehensive will never be done. In a word, all these truths, which with any tolerable propriety of speech can be called connatural, if they are not self-evident, are yet such as admit of an easy demonstration. And it is foolish to call any truth connatural, unless it is such, as either needs no proof, or is easily demonstrable. This is sufficient to overthrow this notion.

Before we consider the arguments which Mr. Humfrey advances for his opinions, I shall offer to the reader a more full view of it in his own words. He then asserts, "that there is "a connatural law of grace written in the heart of man, that "is, that this law of lapsed nature, this law of grace, or re- "medving law, is written in the heart of man in regard of "his fallen nature, no less than the law of pure nature itself "was. The law of nature, (says he) as I take it, is the dic- "tates of right reason, declaring to us our duty to God, to "ourselves and to our neighbours; and the light of the same "reason will dictate to us, when we have failed in that duty "to repent and turn to God, with trusting to his mercy and "pardon if we do so, and not else. We do find it legible in "our hearts, that God is good and wisely gracious to consider "our lost estate, and pity our infirmities and necessary frailty*." After he has told us of a threefold promulgation of this law of grace, under the patriarchs, by Moses and Christ, which he calls three editions of the same law; he subjoins, " Now I "say, that though the Heathen be not under (or have not) "this law of grace, in the third and last setting out, or in "the state under the gospel; yet they are under it (or have "it) in the state of the ancients, or as they had it in the first "promulgation; and upon supposition that any of them do, "according to the light they have, live up in sincerity to this "law, I dare not be the man that shall deny, that through "the grace of our Lord Jesus Christ (procuring this law or co- "venant for them, as for us and all the world) they shall be "saved even as we." And a little before he says, "These "characters thus engraven in the heart of man, is the same "law of grace in its practical contents, which is more large- "ly paraphrased upon in the scriptures."

Surely the apostle Paul had a very different notion of the state of the Heathen world from this gentleman, when he tells us
emphatically

* Peace. Disquis. Chap. 4. pag. 56, 57.

emphatically, *that they are strangers from the covenants of promise,* that *they are without God,* that is, without the saving knowledge of God; for another sense the word will scarce bear; that they are *without Christ, without hope, afar off,* &c. But it is not my design to offer scripture arguments against this anti-scriptural divinity. I leave this to others, and proceed to his proof: nor shall I in the confideration of them take notice of every thing that might be justly quarrelled; but only hint at the main faults.

1. He reasons to this effect: If there is no connatural law of grace written in the heart of man, then none of those who lived before Moses could be saved, in as much as there was then no other law by which they could be saved*. This argument he borrows from Suarez, and concludes it triumphantly thus, " Which is a truth so evident, as makes the proof of that law " by that reason alone to be good."

But for all this commendation, I think this argument has a double fault. 1. It proves not the point, viz. that there is a law of grace written in the hearts of all men by nature; but only that there was such a law written in their hearts that were saved. This argument is built upon a supposition that is plainly false, viz. that there was no other way that they could be saved but by the law of grace written in their hearts. This, I say, is false; for they were saved by the gospel discovery of Christ in the promise revealed to them by God, and wherein the generality of the Lord's people were more fully instructed by the patriarchs, who were preachers of righteousness. And this revelation and preaching was to them instead of the written word. Thus we see this mighty argument proves just nothing.

2. He reasons from Abraham's pleading with God on behalf of the righteous men in Sodom. Here he thinks it evident, that there were righteous men. He proves, that there were none righteous then, according to the tenor of the covenant of works, and therefore concludes, that these righteous persons did belong to, and were dealt with according to the covenant of grace†. But now what does all this prove? Does it prove that these men were under the covenant of grace, and that they were dealt with according to the tenor of it? Well, I grant it. But what will he infer from this, that therefore all the world

* Peace. Disquif. pag. 56.
† Ibid, pag. 60.

world were under the covenant of grace, or shall be dealt with according to its tenor? I would have thought that one who has read Suarez, might know that this conclusion will not follow. If there had been any righteous men in Sodom, it is true they were under the covenant of grace; and I add, if there be any such in the world, they are under it; therefore all the world are so? Who sees not that this will not follow? Again, supposing that there were righteous men in Sodom, how will Mr. Humfrey prove, that they had no other rule of their life, or ground of their hope, but his connatural law of grace? Why might they not have revelation? Was not Abraham, to whom God revealed himself, and made so many gracious promises, well known to some in Sodom? Might not the fame of such a person so near easily reach them? Was not he the deliverer of Sodom some eighteen years before, and did not Lot his friend, who was well acquainted with the revelations made to Abraham, live in Sodom?

3. Mr. Humfrey tells us, that the law of grace was in Adam's and Noah's time published to all the world, and that it never was repealed, and therefore all the world are still under it, and so in a capacity of salvation*.

But 1. This, were it granted, will not prove Mr. Humfrey's connatural law of grace. The gospel is revealed to all the inhabitants of England; therefore the law of grace is written in their hearts: he must know very little of many people in England, who will admit the consequence. 2. Nor will it prove, that all the world are under the gospel revelation, even in its first edition, to use Mr. Humfrey's words. Suppose God once revealed to the world, when it was comprised in the family of Noah, the covenant of grace, and so all this little world had the external revelation: will Mr. Humfrey hence infer, that all the descendants of Noah, after so long a tract of time, in so many different nations, have still the same revelation? If he do, the consequence is nought. It is as sure as any thing can be, that very quickly most of the descendants of Noah lost in so far that revelation, or at least, corrupted it with their vain additions to that degree, that it could be of advantage to no man. 3. Nor will what Mr. Humfrey talks of his repeal help out his argument. To deprive a people of the advantage of an external revelation, there is no need of a formal repeal by a published statute; it is
enough

* Peace. Disquis. pag. 62.

enough that men by their wickedness lose all remembrance of it, and suffer it to fall into desuetude, and God sees not meet to renew the revelation to them or their posterity.

4. Mr. Humfrey will prove his point by a syllogism, and it runs thus, *The doers of the law are justified*, Rom. ii. ver. 13. but the Gentiles are doers of the law; ergo, some of the Gentiles are justified before God.

The conclusion of this argument is the direct antithesis of that position, which the apostle makes it his business in that whole context to prove, as is evident from the account already given of that context. This is pretty bold. But let us see how he proves his minor. This he pretends to do from Rom. xiv. where it is said, that *the Gentiles do by nature the things contained in the law*, and so are doers of the law, and consequently shall be justified.

Well, is this the way this gentleman interprets scripture upon other occasions? I hope not. He has no regard to the scope or design of the apostle's discourse. All that the apostle says here, is, that the Gentiles are in so far doers of the law, that their doing is proof that they have some knowledge of it. The persons who here are said to be doers of the law, are the very same persons of whom the apostle says, ver. 12. that they *shall perish without the law*. But we have fully cleared this context before, and thither I refer the reader.

But Mr. Humfrey reforms his argument, and makes it run thus, He who sincerely keeps the law, shall be justified according to that of our Lord, *keep the commandments if thou wilt enter into eternal life*; and that of the apostle, *God will render eternal life to every one that patiently continues in well-doing* ; but, argues he, some Gentiles keep the law sincerely : and therefore it is according to the gospel, which requires not the rigour, but accepts of sincere obedience.

As to our author's major, if the meaning of it be, that we shall be justified before God for, or upon our sincere obedience, according to the gospel, I crave leave to differ from him ; nor will the scripture's adduced by him prove it in this sense. The first is a reference of a young man to the covenant of works, who was not seeking salvation, but *eternal life* by doing, in order to discover to him his own inability and his need of Christ. But as to this commentators may be consulted. The other text I have cleared above.

His

* Peace. Disquis. pag. 61.

His minor I flatly deny: well, but our author will prove it by a new syllogism, which runs thus, He who yields such obedience as the Jews, who are circumcised in heart, do, yields that sincere obedience, upon which the gospel accepts and justifies men; but the Gentiles, or some of them yield such obedience.

I have already entered my dissent against the last clause of the major, viz. That the gospel justifies men on sincere obedience; but it is not my design to debate the point of justification with our author at this time, and so I let this proposition pass: yet I again deny the minor, which our author essays to prove thus, That some of the Gentiles do obey in that sense, in which the Jews, who are circumcised inwardly or in heart, do obey: this he pretends to demonstrate from the apostle's words, Rom. ii. 26, 27. *Therefore if the uncircumcision keep the righteousness of the law, &c. and shall not uncircumcision, which is my nature, if it fulfil the law.*

But where will our author find the proof of his minor in these words? There is nothing like it, unless he take the antecedent of a hypothetic proposition, for a plain assertion. But this antecedent needs not be allowed possible, and yet the apostle's words and his assertion would hold good, and all that he aims at be reached: Every one knows, that in such propositions, it is only the connexion that is asserted. As for the meaning of the text, I have shewed before that it is not for our author's purpose.

5. But our author has another argument, which he thinks is clearer than all the rest, and professes himself perfectly stricken with the evidence of it, as with a beam of light never to be withstood, or any more to be doubted. Well this mighty argument runs thus, " If this was the chief advantage the " Jew had over the Gentile, that one had the oracles of God, " and the other had not, then was there not this difference " between them, that one is only in a state of nature, and " the other in a state of grace; or that one was in a capacity, " and the other under an impossibility of salvation. For this " were an advantage of a far greater nature. But this was the " advantage, Rom iii. 2. *Chiefly because to them were committed the oracles of God* *;" ergo.

I must confess, that I am not stricken with so much evidence upon the proposal of this argument, as it seems our author was.

To

* Peace Disquis. pag. 63, 64.

To me this argument appears a plain fophifm. That the Jews had the oracles of God, was a greater advantage, than our author feems to think it. And while the apoflle calls it the chief advantage of the Jews above the Gentiles, that they had the *oracles of God*, how will our author infer from this, that they were upon an equal footing as to the means abfolutely neceffary for falvation; or which is the fame, as to a capacity of falvation ; for certainly he that wants the means abfolutely neceffary to falvation is not capable of falvation, in that fenfe that belongs to our purpofe? For my part I would draw the quite contrary conclufion from it ; thus, The Jews had this privilege above the Gentiles, that they had the oracles of God entrufted with them, wherein the only way of falvation is revealed, *being witneffed to by the law and the prophets*, Rom. iii. 21. and therefore had accefs to falvation: whereas on the other hand, the Gentiles wanting divine revelation, which alone can difcover that righteoufnefs, whereby a finner can be juftified, did want the means abfolutely neceffary to falvation, and fo were not in a capacity of falvation. Now where is our author's boafted of demonftration ? The occafion of his miftake is this, he once inadvertently fuppofed, that thefe two advantages, divine revelation, and accefs of falvation, were quite different, and that the one was not included in the other. But of this enough.

Mr. Humfrey, I know, may fay, they had the law of grace in their hearts. But that is the queftion. Our author afferts this; but he does fo without proof. We have all this while been feeking proof of this: hitherto we have met with none. We have met with fome fcriptures interpreted or wrefted into a fenfe plainly inconfiftent with their fcope and intention, without any regard had to the context and drift of the difcourfe, which is no fafe way of managing fcriptures.

Next, he infifts upon the ftory of the Ninevites' repentance. They were without the church; it was a law of grace which led them to repent. But had not the Ninevites divine revelation? Did they not repent at the preaching of Jonah ? How will our author prove that Jonah never dropped a word, that there was a poffibility of ftopping the progrefs of the controverfy by their turning from their evil courfes? Did not Jonah apprehend, that the event would be a further forbearance ? But may be fome may fay, Jonah had no mind they fhould be fpared, and therefore would not drop any encouragement: but we know that it was not of choice that he went there; and as he went there in obebience to God, so no doubt, he who had been so sharply disciplined for disobedience, would speak what the Lord commanded him. Again, had they assurance of pardon or eternal salvation upon their repentance? Was it gospel-repentance? Or did it reach farther than a forbearance of temporal jugdments?

Well but the instance of Cornelius seems more pat to his purpose. He was a Gentile, was accepted with God; and Peter tells us, that *in every nation he that fears God and works righteousness, is accepted.* But who will assure me that Cornelius was a stranger to the scriptures? Did he not know them? Did he not believe them? How could that be? It is plain he was a proselyte and embraced the Jewish religion as to its substance, and that he did believe, since he *pleased God* and was *accepted.* Now we know, that *without faith it is impossible to please God.* What wanted he then? Why, he wanted to be informed that the Messiah promised was *come,* and that *Christ Jesus* was *he.* As to what the apostle says of God's *acceptance of persons of all nations,* any one that will give himself the trouble of considering his scope, and the circumstances of the place, will see, that it is nothing else but a comment upon the design of the vision he got to instruct him, that now God was to admit persons of all nations, Gentiles as well as Jews, to a participation of the covenant blessings.

DIGRESSION.

A short Digression concerning God's Government of the Heathen World, occasioned by the foregoing Objections, wherein an attempt is made to account for the Occurrences that have the most favourable Aspect to them, without supposing any Intention or Design of their Salvation, which is adjected as an Appendix to the Answers given to Mr. Humfrey's Objections, wherein it is made evident, That there is no need to suppose the Heathens under a Law or Government of Grace.

IF I should here stop, the persons with I whom have to do, might possibly allege, that the main strength of their cause remains untouched, and the most straitening difficulty that presses ours is not noticed. The short of the matter is, they inquire, What government are the Heathen world under? They conceive it must be be allowed a government of grace, fince they are not dealt by according to the demerit of their fins. Poffibly we might propofe fome queftions that would be no lefs hard to fatisfy, by thofe who talk of an univerfal law of grace: but this would not remove the difficulty, though it might embarrafs the oppofers of our fentiments. I fhall therefore open my mind in this matter, and offer what occurs on this head. If I miftake, it will plead fomewhat for me, that the fubject, fo far as I know, is not ufually fpoken of by others, and I have not of choice meddled with it, but was led to it by my fubject, that requires fome confideration of it. If we ftate right thoughts in this matter, it will give light to many things, that otherwife are dark. What I have to fay, I fhall propofe in the fubfequent gradation.

1. Man was originally made under a law that is holy, good, righteous, equal and juft; this law required of all fubjected to it exact, punctual and perfect obedience; and for its prefervation it was armed with a penal fanction, anfwerable to the high and tender regard, which the infinitely holy, wife and great God had for the honour of that law, that was the declaration of his will, bore the imprefs of his authority and reprefentation of all his moral excellencies. And befides all this, he alfo propofed a reward, fuitable to his wifdom and goodnefs, for which his faithfulnefs became pledged. It is not needful to launch out in proof of the feveral branches of this affertion. That man was made under a law, is queftioned by none, but athiefts; and they have their mouths fufficiently ftopped of old and late by many perfons of worth and learning. That this law is holy, juft and good, cannot without notable injury to the Deity be denied. That it exacted perfect obedience, is fo evident, that no perfon, who thinks what he fays, can deny it. A law not requiring perfect obedience, to its own precepts, is a law not requiring what it requires, which is plain nonfenfe. A pofterior law may not require perfect obedience to a prior: but every law requires perfect obedience to itfelf. That this law was armed with a penal fanction is evident from the wifdom of the lawgiver, who could not enact fuch laws, which he knew men would tranfgrefs, without providing for the honour of his own authority. Befides, if there is no penal fanction, it is not to be expected that laws could ever reach their end, efpecially as things have always ftood with man. But were all thofe proofs given up, the effects of vindictive juftice in the world, with the fears

that

that sinners are under, lest all these are only the beginning of sorrows, sufficiently confirm this truth, and moreover assure us, that it is such a penalty as suits every way the offence in its nature and aggravations. But I know none of those things will be questioned by those, whom we have mainly under view at present.

2. All the children of men, in all ages and in all places of the world, have been and are guilty of violations of this law. We have heard the deists owning this before; and Christians will not deny it. Deists would have thought it their interest to deny it: but since, it is unquestionable that the generality offend, in instances past reckoning. If they had affirmed, that any one did, in no instance offend, they might have been required to make good their assertion: but this they could not do. They durst not condescend. And therefore it must be owned that the best, not in one instance, but in many, violate this law.

3. Upon account of these violations of his holy and righteous law, all mankind, every individual, and every generation of men, that have lived in the world, are obnoxious to justice. By those sins they have forfeited any claim they might have laid to the reward of perfect obedience, and are liable to the penalty in the sanction of the law. And God might, at any time, have righteously inflicted it, either upon any individual or any whole race of men. I determine not now what that punishment was. They who talk that our offences are small, and extenuates them, seem scarcely impressed with suitable notions of God, and I doubt will not be sustained judges competent of the qualities of offences and injuries done to his honour. But whatever the punishment is, eternal, or not, which I dispute not now, because we agree about it with those, whom we now have under consideration, it is certain none can prove that it is all confined to time, or that any temporal punishment is sufficient for the least offence that is committed against God. And it is also clear, that, upon one's sinning, the penalty might be presently inflicted, without any injustice, provided the penal sanction were suitable and just in its constitution, as of necessity it must be, where God made the law and constituted the punishment.

4. Although God righteously might have cut off any generation of men, and swept the earth clean; yet has he seen meet to spare sinners, even multitudes of them, for a long time.

A piece of conduct truly aftonishing! Efpecially it would appear fo, if we underftood how much God hates fin. The only reafon why the Heathen world hath not admired it more, and been more extenfive in their inquiries into the reafons of it, is becaufe they had but very fhort and imperfect notions of God's holinefs, and the evil of fin. They took notice of God's forbearence of fome notorious offenders. Some of them were ftumbled at it, and fome of them endeavoured to account for it. But the wonder of God's fparing a world full of finners, was little noticed, and though they had obferved it, they would have quickly found themfelves as much at a lofs here, as any where elfe. The fcriptures have not gratified the curiofity of men with fuch a full account, as our minds would have defired, that are too forward to queftion him particularly about his ways, who gives an account of none of his matters : yet fome reafons of this conduct are dropped that may fatisfy the humble. 1. God made a covenant with Adam, wherein his pofterity, as well as himfelf were concerned and included. They were to be gainers or lofers as he acquitted himfelf well or ill. This tranfaction, I know, is denied by fome Chriftians. I fhall not difpute the matter with them : others have done it. I now take it for granted. And if they will not fuppofe it, it is but the lofs of this reafon. And let them if they can put a better in its room. Upon fuppofition, that there was fuch a tranfaction, and that it was juft, as we muft allow all to be, whereof God is the author, it was not only equal, but in point of wifdom, apparently neceffary, or at leaft, highly fuitable, that all concerned in this tranfaction fhould be brought into being, to reap the fruits of it. But this was impoffible if the world had not been fpared. 2. God, in fparing the world, had a defign of mercy upon fome. And many of them were to proceed from fome of the worft finners. He defigned to fave fome in all ages, and in moft places. Their progenitors muft therefore, of neceffity, be kept alive. He bears with the provoking carriage of evil men ; becaufe out of their loins he intends to extract others, whom he will form for the *glory of his grace*. 3. God is patient toward finners, to manifeft the equity of his future juftice upon them. When men are fpared and continue in fin, the pleas of infirmity and miftake are cut off, and they are convicted of malice. They are filenced, and onlookers fatisfied, that feverity is juftly exercifed on them.

Quanto

Quanto Dei magis judicium tardum est, tanto magis justum.*
As patience, while it is exercised, is the silence of his justice; so when it is abused, it silences men's complaints against his justice. Other reasons of this conduct we might glean from the scriptures: but my design allows me not to insist. Nor indeed do they descend so low as to satisfy curious wits. *Lo these are parts of his ways* and aims, *but how little a portion is heard*, that is, even by revelation, *known of him?* says Job, chap. xxvi. 14.

5. The world, or sinners in it, are spared, not by a proper reprieve, that is, a delay of punishment, after the offenders are taken up, questioned, tried, convicted, and solemnly condemned; the way, manner and time of their punishment fixed, by a judicial application of the general threatening of the law in this particular case, by the judge competent, and the sentence plainly intimated; a delay of the execution after this, if it is of the judge's proper motion, if the offender is not imprisoned, if he is employed, and if favours are conferred upon him, and obedience required of him, gives hopes of impunity and escape; and if the persons commit not new offences, without, at least, an appearance of insincerity, they are very seldom condemned upon the first sentence: but sinners are spared by a forbearance, or wise and just connivance, if the word would not offend. The Governor of the world knows and sees the carriage of sinners, is aware of their sins, and keeps silence for a time; but yet keeps an eye upon them, calls them not into question, puts off the trial, takes them not up, as it were, and winks at them. Now all this may be justly done for a time; the sinners may be employed, and acts of bounty, for holy and wise ends, may be conferred on them, and exercised towards them, and that without the least injustice, without any design of pardoning; as the sequel of this discourse will more fully clear.

6. This forbearance of God is wise, just and holy: for 1. He is the only competent judge, as to the time of punishing offenders. It cannot be made appear, that he may not thus delay, even where he has no thought of pardoning. 2. It implies no approbation of the faults formerly committed, or those they may commit, during this interval of time, since he has sufficiently testified against them by the laws he has made, which forbid them by the penalty annexed to those laws, and by examples of his severity upon

* "The flower that the judgment of God is, it is the more just."

upon others, which have not been wanting in any generation. Thefe may fufficiently acquit him, however for a time he keeps filent, and conceal, as it were, his knowledge of the offences of fome, or his refentments againft them, on account of them. 3. He accomplifhes purpofes worthy of him; which are fufficient to juftify him in this conduct, while he keeps filence, and carries to them as if there were no offence, or he knew none, and they go on in their rebellion, or fecret practices againft his law and government. Impudent offenders have no place left, either for denial or excufe of their crimes, or complaints againft the feverity of his refentments. Spectators are made to fee that it is not infirmity or miftake, but fixed alienation or enmity that is fo fharply punifhed. He ferves himfelf of them, and makes them, though they mean not fo, carry on the defigns of his glory, either in helping or trying, or bringing into being perfons, whom he has defigns of mercy upon. And fure he may juftly do this, fince not only he has the beft title to their obedience; but he has all the reafon and right in the world to ufe that life, while he fpares it, for what purpofes he pleafes, which they have forfeited to juftice. Who can blame him, if fometimes he fpares fecret plotters, and lets them go on till their plots are fufficiently ripened for their conviction, and others' fatisfaction. Nor is there any ground to quarrel, if he deal even with the worft, as equal judges do with the mother, guilty of fome manifeft crime; they not only fpare and delay the execution, till the child whom they defign mercy to, is brought forth; but do not take notice of her, or intimate even a purpofe of punifhment, till afterwards, left the child fhould fuffer by the mother's defpair and grief. 4. This is yet more remarkably juft in God, who can on the one hand fecure the criminal, fo that juftice fhall not fuffer by the delay, and on the other, that the criminal fhall not run out into thofe impieties, that would crofs the ends, endanger the fafety, or wrong the reputation of his government, with thofe who are capable of making an equal eftimate of things.

7. It was every way fuitable and neceffary that the perfons thus fpared, fhould be continued under a moral government. They were not to be ruled by mere force; 1. Becaufe they are, while under fuch a forbearance, capable of fome fort of a moral government. When a prince deals with perfons, whom he knows to be on treafonable plots againft his government, and conceals his refentment, he ftill manages them as fubjects, and continues them under

under a government; nor is he faulty in doing so. 2. They are not, while under such a forbearance, capable of any other government; for if once the Ruler of the world begin to deal in a way of force and justice with them, then this forbearance is at an end. 3. It were a manifest reproach to the Governor of the world, if they were supposed under no government at all. besides, on this supposition, the ends of his forbearance could not be reached. And moreover, the moral dependence of creatures on their Creator, which can only be maintained either in this way, or by putting them under the penal sanction of the law, would be dissolved, which cannot be admitted.

8. Sinners under this dispesation are still under the law of creation: it is true this law can no longer be the means of conveying a title to the great and principal reward; but that is their own fault, and not the governor's nor the law's. But notwithstanding of this, they are still under it, and it continues the instrument of God's government over them. For 1. The ground of obedience still continues, although some of the motives, yea, the principal encouragement, I mean, eternal rewards, are forfeited. The obligation to obedience can never otherwise be dissolved, than by the inflicting of a capital punishment, which puts out of all possibility of yielding any obedience. Some, I know make the power and right of obliging, to consist merely in a power of rewarding and punishing: but this is easily convicted of falshood: and although the learned Mr. *Gastrel* has advanced this, in his sermons at Boyle's Lecture, yet we have no reason to receive it, as *Beconsal* in his treatise of the *Law of Nature*, and others have sufficiently cleared. 2. This law is sufficient to answer the designs of this forbearance, and God's rule over them who live under it and by it. It has not lost its directive power; but it is able sufficiently to instruct, at least in these duties, either as to God, ourselves or others, that are of absolute necessity to keep some order and decorum in the world, carry on regularly the propagation of mankind, and the like. It is manifestly sufficient to be a test to try men's willingness to obey, and convince men of wilfulness in their rebellion; and to be a standing monument of God's holiness; yea, it continues to have that force upon the consciences of the generality, as to be a check to keep them from running into enormities subversive of all order and society, and destructive to the other ends of God's patience. 2. Experience fully clears, that men still pay

regard

regard to this law, and this is the only law that men deſtitute of a revelation own.

9. While God ſaw meet to continue this forbearance, it was not neceſſary nor ſuitable, that he ſhould plainly, particularly and ſolemnly intimate all the length he deſigned to carry his reſentments againſt offenders. 1. There was no neceſſity of this towards the clearing of God's holineſs; this being ſufficiently done by the promulgation of the law, its penalty, and many particular examples. 2. This would have undone the diſpenſation whereof we have been ſpeaking. 3. This is utterly inconſiſtent with all the deſigns of it. Men had been driven into deſpair, and ſo all moral government had been diſſolved.

10. Yea, it was conſiſtent with his holineſs, and ſuitable to his wiſdom, to permit men to fall into ſin, very great ſins, and for a time to go on in them. God can neither do any thing that is unworthy, nor omit any thing that is worthy of him, of a moral kind. And it is certain in faƈt, that ſuch ſins and enormities he has permitted: and therefore, however ſtrange it appears to us, that a holy God, who could have reſtrained, ſhould permit thoſe things; yet ſince he, who can do no evil, has done it, we muſt conclude this altogether conſiſtent with his holineſs. And it is manifeſtly ſo with his wiſdom, ſince no injury is done to his holineſs. For 1. By this means ſinners give full proof, what a height their enmity againſt God is come to. 2. They are the fitter to exerciſe his own people. And 3. They are riper for the ſtrokes he deſigns to inflict on them.

11. Notwithſtanding of all this, it was meet and neceſſary that ſome offenders ſhould be remarkably puniſhed, and ſome bounds ſet to offences; and more eſpecially thoſe offences which croſs the deſigns of God's forbearance, and tend to diſſolve the government and order, which it was neceſſary God ſhould maintain in the world. And hence it has come to paſs, that not the greateſt ſins, ſuch as theſe certainly are, which immediately ſtrike againſt God, but theſe which ſtrike againſt order and government, have been moſt remarkably puniſhed in all ages, as might be made appear by innumerable inſtances of the remarkable puniſhment of murders, treaſons, and undutifulneſs to parents. This is congruous to juſtice, not only on the above-mentioned account, but on this, that the notices concerning theſe laſt ſort of evils are much more clear in moſt inſtances, than thoſe which reſpect the former.

12. It

12. It is every way suitable to the wisdom, sincerity and holiness of God; yea, and of absolute necessity to the design of this forbearance, that he exercise bounty in lesser things; such as the good things of this life are: and that he vouchsafe those mental endowments to some of the spared sinners, which are necessary toward the maintenance of that government, which God was to keep up among them; such are civil wisdom, invention, courage, &c. These he may give without the least intimation of any design of special mercy. For what relation have these things to special mercy, which are heaped in abundance on the worst of men. However, that it was fit these things would be bestowed upon some in this case, is evident; because, 1. Eternal rewards are now forfeited, and there would have been nothing to induce to obedience if this had not been. 2. Hereby he gives a witness to his own goodness, which aggravates offences committed against him. 3. Hereby he draws on men to obedience, or rather to do those pieces of service, which are in their own nature, such as he allows and requires, although they design not his service, but their own pleasure and profit. 4. Hereby he clears scores with sinners, while he suffers not what is even but pretended service, to pass without a reward, which is sufficient to shew what a kind rewarder he would have been, if they had indeed obeyed. 5. Hereby he cuts off all excuse for their continuance in disobedience. 6. This conduct gives them an innocent occasion of discovering latent wickedness, which otherwise they would have had no access to shew, and keeps from that utter despair which would have marred the design of God's forbearance.

13. These vouchsafements of divine bounty lead to a sort of repentance; not that to which the promise of pardon is joined in the gospel. For 1. They give eminent discoveries of the goodness of that God whom we have offended, and consequently of the folly of offending him, which naturally leads to sorrow or regret. 2. They strengthen, as all benefits do, the orignal obligation to obedience. 3. They let us see, that obedience is not altogether fruitless, since they may expect less severe resentments if they return; yea, may expect some share in this bounty, and are not under an impossibility of mercy, for any thing they can know.

14. After all, I do yet see no reason to think, that they, who are merely under such a dispensation as this, which I take to be the case of the Heathen world, are under a law of grace; which
assures,

allures, that upon a return to former obedience, fins shall be entirely pardoned, and they have accefs to eternal rewards. I grant it highly probable, that if God had not intended grace to fome, fuch a difpenfation had never been. I admit, that this difpenfation is fubfervient to a defign of grace upon fome. I further allow, that there is no abfolute impoffibility of the falvation of perfons, however deeply guilty, who are not yet under the penalty: but if they are faved, it muft be by fome means or way revealed by God, and fuperadded to all the former, which I can never fee to amount to any law of grace, fince it is manifeft, 1. That all this may be exercifed toward them whom God in the end defigns everlaftingly to punifh. He exercifes *much long-fuffering to the veffels of wrath fitted to deftruction*. 2. There is nothing in this whole difpenfation, that in the leaft intimates any purpofe of God to pafs by former offences, either abfolutely or upon condition. 3. In fact it has never been found, that ever this difpenfation has led any one to that fincere repentance, which muft be allowed neceffary, in order to pardon. And I dare not fay, that God ever did appoint means for fuch an end, which after fo long a trial fhould never anfwer it. 4. All whom God has pardoned, or of whom we may fay, that he has brought them to repentance, have been brought by other means. So that upon the whole, I fee no ground for afferting an univerfal law of grace.

As what has been above faid takes off the principal pretence for fuch an univerfal law of grace, which fome feem fo fond of; fo if any fuch is afferted, it muft be owned to be a law of a very univerfal tenor, as being that wherein all mankind are concerned. It muft be allowed a law defigned to take off the force of the original law, concreated with our nature, that neceffarily refults from the nature of God and man, and their natural relation, at leaft as to one inftance, I mean the penal fanction, in cafe of fin. It muft be allowed to be a law not merely directive as to duty, but defigned to tender undeferved favours to finful man. Now he that can think a few, (or call them many) dubious actions, that is, actions capable of another, yea, contrary conftruction, a fufficient promulgation of fuch a law, as is of fo univerfal extent, as derogates, at leaft in one inftance, of fo great moment, from a law fo firmly and folemnly eftablifhed, without any known provifion for its honour, injured by fo many fins, and finally that tenders fuch great favours to the tranfgreffors of it, may believe what he pleases. I must own, this one consideration is with me enough to sink that notion.

But to conclude this whole matter, upon which we have dwelt so long. Upon the nicest survey of occurrences in the Heathen world, I can discern nothing that favours of any acquaintance with that forgiveness that is with God; unless it is that generally entertained notion of the *placability* of their deities. This notion, I make no doubt, had its rise from *revelation*, and was continued by *tradition*. And several things did concur to the preservation of this, while other notices that had the same rise were lost; the apparent necessity of it to man in his present sinful condition; the suitableness of it to lay a foundation for that worship, to which the remaining natural notices of a Deity urged them, and which was of indispensible necessity toward the support of human government; the darkness and blindness of men as to the exceeding sinfulness of sin; the holiness of God's nature, and the strong inclination all men have to be favourable, even to their faults, did contribute not a little toward its support. Finally, this placability did not so much respect the one true God, of whom they had very little knowledge, as their own fictitious deities, which they put in the room of the true God. And it is obvious, that when men took upon them to set up gods, they would be sure to frame such as might agree with their own apprehensions, and pass by their faults with as little difficulty as they committed them. Whatever there is to as this, we have no reason to think that this is a natural notice, it being neither self-evident, nor certainly deducible from principles that are such.

C H A P. XI.

Proving the Insufficiency of Natural Religion to eradicate our Inclinations to Sin, or subdue its Power.

I Think we have said enough to demonstrate the *insufficiency of natural religion*, to satisfy us as to the way how we may obtain the *removal of guilt* or the *pardon of sin*. Let us now see whether it is able to remove the *corruption of nature*, and subdue or eradicate our inclinations to sin.

Before we enter directly on this, it will not be impertinent, if it is not plainly necessary, that we say somewhat concerning

ing the *nature of this corruption.* We shall therefore offer the few following hints concerning it.

1. It is most certain, that man has corrupt inclinations. I think this will scarce be denied; since it is beyond contradiction evident, that the bulk of mankind in all ages, have run headlong into those courses which reason condemns as contrary to the law, under which we are made. The law condemns, reason justifies the law, and proclaims those courses unworthy of us; conscience checks and sometimes torments, and yet sinners run on. Can all this be without corrupt inclinations swaying, yea, as it were, forcibly driving that way? No sure.

2. It is certain, that not only there are such inclinations in man, but that they are exceedingly strong and forcible. Our own reason condemns those actions, and cries shame on the sinner's conscience, presages the resentments of the righteous God, the evil effects of them are visible, and they are felt to be destructive to our health, ruining to our reputation and estates, inconsistent with our inward peace; yea, in a few instances, human law provides terrible punishments: and yet, in spite of all these strong barriers, we are carried down with the stream: nor can the most rational considerations, from interest, honour or prudence stop our career. Certainly the force of inclination, that carries over all these, must be great.

3. It seems plainly natural and congenial to us. I shall not nicely inquire in what sense it is so. I am far from thinking, that our natures as at first made, were created with it. I have said enough before to prove this impossible: but I mean, that as our natures now are, however they came to be so, it is an inseparable appendage of them, cleaves to them, and proceeds not merely from custom, and is not acquired, though it is often improved by custom. Now this seems evident from many things,

1. The universality of it. All men, in all ages, in all places, and in all circumstances, have such vitious inclinations. I do not say that every individual is proud, ambitious, covetous, revengeful, passionate and lustful. No, but every one has some one or other of these, or the like, breaking out; which says, the spring is within, and is strong; though the constitution of our bodies, the climates we live under, our education and circumstances of life, have dammed in some of them, and cut out channels for others of them. Now it is plainly unaccountable how all men should be thus corrupt, if not naturally so. No parallel instance,

in any sort, can be given, where any thing not natural and congenial, at least as to its principle and inclination, has obtained such an universal sway. 2. It waits not till we are grown and framed by education, custom, engagement and inventions; but makes strong, discernible, and sensible eruptions in infancy and child-hood. As soon as we are capable, and very oft, while one would think us scarcely so, by reason of age, we are proud, revengeful, covetous, &c. which says this is congenial 3. It is often seen, that those corruptions break out in our young years, which neither education, example, circumstances, nor any thing else but a corrupted nature, can give any encouragement to. 4. Yea more, how strong are these inclinations, and that very early, which are discouraged, opposed, borne down, and have all outward occasions cut off from them. One is passionate among calm people, though he is punished for it and sees it not. Another is ambitious and proud among sober people, in mean circumstances, where there is no example to excite ambition, no theatre to act it upon, and the beginnings are curbed by precept, instruction, reproof, chastisements and example. 5. Those things are evidently interwoven with, and strengthened by the very constitutions of our bodies, and climates under which we live. Hence there are domestic and national vices, which cleave to some families and nations. 6. The best, the most sober, and freest from discernible eruptions of corruption, yet do own they find the inclinations strong, and driving them into indiscernible acts correspondent to them. 7. They who deny the force and being of these inclinations, and who pretend that the will of man is able to master all these, yet cannot but own, that there are such inclinations; and as for the pretended ability of the will to conquer them, they give the least proof of it who pretend most to it: for if the will is thus able, and if, as they pretend, they have sufficient moral arguments which persuade to it, why is it not done? What stops it? 8. I shall only further offer the testimonies of some few among the Heathens. *Timus* the *Locrian*, who lived before Plato, tells us in his discourses, " That vitiosity comes " from our parents and first principles, rather than from ne- " gligence and disorder of public manners; because we never " part from those actions which lead us to imitate the primitive " sins of our parents*." Plato tells us, that, " In times past " the

---

* Gale's Court of the Gentiles, Part 4. Lib. 1. Cap. 4. Par. 2.

"the divine nature flourished in men; but at length it mixed
"with mortal, and ἀνθρώπινον ἦθος, human customs prevailed to the
"ruin of mankind: and from this source there followed an in-
"undation of evils on men. Hence he calls corruption νοσ⊙ τ̄
"κατὰ φυσιν, the natural disease, or disease of nature, because the
"nature of mankind is greatly degenerated and depraved, and
"all manner of disorders infest human nature: and men being
"impotent, are torn in pieces by their own lusts, as by so ma-
"ny wild horses. Hence Democritus is said to affirm the dif-
"eases of the soul to be so great, that if it were opened, it
"would appear to be a sepulchre of all manner of evils."
Aristotle tells us, "That there is in us somewhat naturally
"repugnant to right reason, πεφυκ⊙ ἀδιβατον τος λογ.*" Seneca, Epist. 50. gives us a very remarkable account of his thoughts
in this matter. The whole were worthy to be transcribed, but
it is too long. I shall translate a part of it. "Why do we
"deceive ourselves? Our evil is not from without; it is fixed
"in our very bowels. *Alibi* † All sins are in all men, but all
"do not appear in each man: he that hath one sin hath all.
"We say, that all men are intemperate, avaricious, luxuri-
"ous, malignant; not that these sins appear in all; but be-
"cause they may be, yea, are in all, although latent. A
"man may be guilty, though he do no hurt. Sins are per-
"fect before they break forth into effect." It is worthy of our
observation, what Mr. Gale tells us, after he has quoted these
words, viz. that *Janfenius* breaks forth into a rapture upon
hearing these philosophers philosophize more truly about the
corruption of man's nature, than Pelagians and others of late.

But the *Oracles of Reason* tell us, that it is denied " that
" the lapse of nature is universal, because some through the
" course of their lives, have proved more inclinable or prone to
" virtue than to vice." I have spoke to this before, but I add,
1. This is not enough, that they are more prone to virtue than
to vice: for the question is, Whether they have inclinations to
vice? and not, Whether the contrary are stronger? 2. This
cannot be pretended to be the case with many. Now, since the
question is about a religion sufficient for all mankind, if any of
them have such a distemper, and natural religion provide no
cure, it is insufficient. 3. It is not, Whether there are men
that have been prone to some virtues, and averse from some vices,

* Arist. Ethick, Lib. 1. Cap. 13.   † " Elsewhere."

ces, possibly scandalous sins? But, Whether there have been men inclined to no sin, prone to all virtue? If they assert such a one, shew us the man. We cannot believe any such, since all we know are otherwise, till we see a condescension. 4. It is not the business whether men have done virtuous acts ordinarily, that is, the material acts of virtue: for corruption may run freely out in this hidden channel. A man may be ambitious, proud, and live among persons, with whom vice is decried, open vice I mean, and therefore affects a great exactness as to morality. This is good: but this is all but a sacrifice to ambition. One lust is the principal idol, all the rest are sacrificed to it. Corruption turns not troublesome, and is pleased, if it get vent any way. A strong spring, if it can get a vent under ground, may press for a vent above; yet it will easily be restrained there.

Now this being the case plainly with man, it is impossible for him to reach happiness, while this corruption remains; nor can he be sure of acceptance with God. While things are thus, nature is imperfect, man is out of order, reason, the nobler part, is at under, and passions, the brutal part, bear the the sway. This is more unseemly, than to see *servants on horses, while princes walk on foot.* There is continual occasion for remorse, checks, challenges of conscience, and fears of the resentment of a holy God. There can be no firm confidence of access to God, or near fellowship with him, while we entertain his enemies in our bosom; nay, have them interwoven, as it were, with our natures.

The deists I know make a horrible outcry against Christians, for asserting this corruption of nature. Herbert in his book *de Veritate,* has many bitter invectives against the asserters of it; and yet, overcome with the evidence of truth, he is obliged frequently to acknowledge it plainly: yea, not only does he acknowledge it, but he pleads this directly, in excuse of the most abominable wickedness. After he has told us, that the temperament or constitution of our bodies have a powerful influence to sway us to some sins, he subjoins, " *Quo pacto haud*
" *ita levi negotio damnandos existimo, qui ex ὑποτυπώσει aliqua*
" *prævaricantur. Quemadmodum igitur flagitii haud juste ar-*
" *gueris lethargum desidem, aut hydropicum bibacem; ita for-*
" *tasse neque veneris, aut martis astro percitum modo in peccan-*
" *tium humorum redundantiam, potius quam pravum aliquem*
" *habitum, delictum commode rijici possit. Neque tamen me hic*
" *conscelerati*

"*conscelerati cujusvis patronum sisto ; sed in id solummodo con-*
"*tendo, ut mitiori sententia de iis statuamus, qui corporea,*
"*brutali, & tantum non necessaria propensione in peccata pro-*
"*labuntur*.*" Well, here is a handsome excuse for vice. We muſt be as far from condemning him, who, prompted by paſſion, ſlays and murders, or hurried on by luſt, commits rapes and adulteries ; as of cenſuring him who is ſick of a lethargy, for his lazineſs and indiſpoſition to act ; or one that is hydropic, for his immoderate thirſt. This divinity will highly pleaſe profane men. The ſalvo he ſubjoins is very frivolous, and deſerves rather contempt than an anſwer. But to leave this, it is plain there are ſuch inclinations, and that if they are not rooted out we are undone. What though men might have hopes, if they but erred once, that they might eaſily obtain remiſſion ; yet ſure it muſt confound them, when they ſtill ſin on, and that out of inclination. Unleſs therefore natural religion is able to cure this diſeaſe, and eradicate thoſe inclinations, it ſerves to no valuable purpoſe, at leaſt it is inſufficient as to the great ends of religion, our own happineſs or acceptance with God. And that really it cannot do ſo, will be clear by the following conſiderations.

1. If this corruption is congenial to our natures, as the above-mentioned arguments go near to demonſtrate, and the Chriſtian religion fully proves, it is evident, that there muſt be ſome change wrought upon our natures. Now this is more than natural religion can pretend to, which knows nothing of regeneration, and the ſanctifying work of the ſpirit of grace. I know Plato and ſome others have talked of *inſpiration*, and ſome *aids* of God : but this was all but chat, amuſement, and a few tinkling words, which might pleaſe the ears ; but what evidence could they give, that any ſuch thing was attained, or attainable !

2. Though

* "Therefore I think that thoſe are not ſo eaſily to be condem-
" ned who ſin from any peculiarity of bodily conſtitution. As, there-
" fore, one could not juſtly blame a lethargic perſon for being lazy,
" or a dropſical perſon for being deſirous of drink ; ſo, perhaps, we
" ought not to blame any one that is prompted to ſin by the ſting of
" luſt or anger, provided that his ſin may be conveniently charged
" to the redundancy of peccant humours, rather than to any perverſe
" habit. And here I do not ſet myſelf up as the advocate of every
" wicked man, but only contend for this, that we ſhould judge more
" mildly of thoſe who fall into ſins, from a corporeal, brutal, and
" almoſt neceſſary inclination."

2. Though this were given up; yet of whatever nature this corruption and impotency is, call it natural or moral, it is certain, that it is ſtrong; natural religion cannot give ſufficient ſecurity that it is practicable to eradicate it. We know that ſome ſtreams of this corruption may be dammed in, ſome of the top branches lopped off, and ſome of the fruits of it may be plucked. This, in ſo far as it is done, is good for mankind, and uſeful in ſociety. Some of the philoſophers have gone a great way in it, and thereby have ſhamed moſt who are called Chriſtans. But what is all this to the eradicating of corruption, purifying the minds of men, and univerſal conformity in heart to the rule of duty? The attainments of philoſophers need not here be talked of: their virtues were but ſhows, and the ſhadows of them. Search to the bottom, and you will find, that what they called ſelf-denial, was only a piece of delicate intereſt in order to reach ſelf-ends: it was but a parting with one thing pleaſant to ourſelves, to gain a greater, which is ſelfiſhneſs to the height. As for that ſelf-denial, which Chriſtianity teaches, it was not heard of, or known in the leaſt. Liberality was but a mere trade of pride, which values no gifts, provided it have the glory of being liberal; modeſty was the art of concealing our vanity; civility, but an affected preference of other men before ourſelves, to conceal how much we value ourſelves above all the world; baſhfulneſs, but an affected ſilence in thoſe things, which luſts make men think of with pleaſure; benevolence or the deſire of obliging other men, but a ſecret deſire of ſerving ourſelves, by getting them to befriend us at other times; gratitude, but an impatience to acquit ourſelves of an obligation, with a ſhamefacedneſs for having been too long beholden to others, for ſome favour received. So that all theſe pretended virtues, in general, have only been ſo many guards made uſe of by ſelf-love, to prevent our darling and ſecret vices from appearing outwardly. All theſe are no evidences, what may be done towards the removal of corrupt inclinations. Nor indeed can nature's light ſatisfy us that it is practicable. Can it ſhew us the man that has done it? This were ſomewhat to the purpoſe, could he be named. But this cannot be. Will it tell us that we have a power to do it? But this is ſomewhat that we ſee and find by experience, the ſtrongeſt and moſt convincing of all arguments, not to be true. We find we may reſtrain or forbear ſome outward actions, but we have no experience of a power to lay aſide or diveſt ourſelves of inclinations

ſo

so deeply rooted. Besides, they, who talk of this power, whereof others have no experience, are liable to be questioned upon several things which they cannot fairly or satisfyingly answer. Why do not they more than others who find it not, but complain of the want of this power, shew that those inclinations are eradicated which they own should be laid aside, which they assert they have a power to lay aside, and which they say they have been long trying to overcome? The world will be forward to judge, at least, the thinking part of mankind will be so, that they are rather misled by some fond speculations to judge they have a power that they really want, than that this practical proof should fail, which seems scarce capable of an answer.

Now will men be effectually engaged in a work so difficult, which they are never like to bring to an issue? Will they not rather choose to yield to the conqueror than engage in a war that must last while they last, and that without prospect of conquest and being masters in the end? Yea, have they not done so? Who will be induced to such an undertaking without encouragement?

3. If this is practicable, yet it must be owned extremely difficult, and what men will not easily be engaged in. Inclinations are deeply rooted, strengthened by custom, and in most heightened by temptations, whereof the world is full. Now if natural religion is supposed able to persuade to such an undertaking, it must be well furnished with strong motives and inducements. Whence shall those be fetched? From the rewards of virtue, and the punishment of vice on the other side time? We heard how short the accounts of nature's light of these are. The impressions of these were always more deeply rooted in the vulgar, than the philosophers; yet they had no such effect. It is plain, outward encouragements do not attend the practice of virtue. There remains only then the beauty of virtue itself. Of this the philosophers have talked wonderful things. But the mischief of it is, it was but talk. When they missed other things, they could, even with their dying breath, as Brutus, one of the *adepti**, is said to have done, call virtue but an empty name. They lived otherwise than they talked, the best of them not excepted. It is excellently said by the ingenious Claudian,

Ipse

---

* " Perfect."

Ipsa quidem virtus pretium sibi solaque late
Fortunæ secura nitet, nec fascibus ullis
Erigitur, plausuve petit clarescere vulgi.
Nil opis externi cupiens, nil indigna laudis,
Divitiis animosa suis, immotaque cunctis
Casibus, ex alta mortalia despicit arce*.

This is indeed very prettily said; but this is all. Men may please themselves with refined speculations of the excellency of virtue: but it is not this alone that can sway corrupt man. It is not the question, what virtue really is? but what men think of it, and can be made to see in it? And it is certain, all the philosophers could never persuade the world of it; and no wonder, for they could not persuade themselves. Mankind have had other thoughts, and it must be other views than nature can give, that will beat them out of this. Another poet plainly opens the case,

Turpe quidem dictu (sed si modo vera fatemur)
Vulgus amicitias utilitate probat:
Cura quid expediat prior est, quam quid sit honestum,
Et cum fortuna statque caditque fides.
Nec facile invenies multis in millibus unum,
Virtutem pretium qui putat esse sui.
Ipse decor recti, facti si præmia desint,
Non movet, & gratis penitet esse probum †.

Here is the true state of the case. But to come closely up to the point; this beauty of virtue is not discernible till we have made some progress in it. While corrupt inclinations are in their vigour in the heart, such a beauty is not easily seen.

2. It

---

* De Consulatu Mallii Theodoriab Initio.—" Virtue indeed is its
" own reward, and it alone shines far and wide, regardless of for-
" tune; nor is it elevated by any power, or desires to become fa-
" mous by the applause of the croud, having no desire of outward
" help, nor any need of praise. Bold in its own riches, and immove-
" able by all accidents, it looks down on mortal things from a high
" eminence."

† Ovid. de Panto, Lib. 2. Eleg. 3.—" It is indeed scandalous to
" relate, but if we will only confess the truth, the multitude approves of
" friendship only for interest; the case of what is profitable is prior to
" the case of what is honourable, and their fidelity stands and falls with
" fortune; nor will you easily find one among many thousands, who
" thinks that virtue is its own reward. The beauty of virtue by itself
" does not move them, if rewards are wanting, and they grudge
" to be honest for nothing."

2. It is a beauty too fine to be perceived by vulgar eyes, or indeed by any, without deeper and nicer confideration, than moſt of men can go to the charge of. 3. Alone it is not fufficient to fupport and carry on in fo hazardous an undertaking. 4. This advantage is not to be felt till the virtue be obtained. It is a queſtion whether it will be attained. So that it is plain, natural religion wants motives to engage effectually to this.

4. It is ftill further confiderable to this purpoſe, that thefe vitious inclinations are ſtrong, if not ſtrongeſt, in thoſe who have neither capacity to dive into thofe few refined confiderations, which enforce the practice of virtue, and the fubduing of corruption, nor indeed to underſtand them when propofed, nor have they time or leifure to attend to the difcourfes of the philofophers when they are taught, or money to purchafe them. And natural religion provides no teachers, at leaſt if we take it according to the accounts that we get from the deiſts, who bear fuch a terrible grudge to a *ſtanding miniſtry*, and have fo oft in their mouths that reflection of Dryden, " Prieſts of all religions are the fame." Now what a fad cafe are poor men in, who are folicited by outward temptations and puſhed on by ſtrong inclinations, and have fo fmall affiſtance given them by natural religion.

5. As motives are wanting, fo the work is not eafily carried on, the way of management is difficult, and the directions given us by the philofophers or others, are exceedingly unfatisfactory. Some of them are impoffible, fuch as the entire laying afide of our affections; others of them ridiculous, fuch as that direction above-mentioned out of Plato, for the purification of our fouls by mufic and mathematics, &c. Others, and indeed moſt of them, only tell us what we are to do, bid us do the thing, but tell us not how to fet about it; fome of them only tell us how to conceal inward corruption, or divert it. And, perhaps, I ſhould not fay amifs, if I ſhould fay, that what the beſt moral philofophers either aimed at or attained, was only to dam in corruption on one fide, to let it run out at another; or to make that run in a fecret channel, which run open before. It were long to examine their feveral directions. The learned Herbert gives us a fummary of them, which I ſhall here prefent the reader with. 1. *We ſhould fuppreſs all our vitious affections.* This is but to advife the thing, without telling us how it is to be done. 2. *That we expiate our ſins by deep repentance, and by the inſtituted facrifices or rites.* This is only

a remedy for guilt, and an ill one too, as has been cleared above. 3. *That we avoid the society of evil men.* But then we *must go out of the world*, or at least out of the heathen world. 4. *That we use the company of good men.* But where shall we find them amongst those, who have no more but natural religion? 5. *That we inquire carefully what is to be done, and what is not to be done*; but the question is, when we know it, How shall we get the one avoided and the other followed, considering we have a strong aversion to good, and inclination to evil? 6. *That our sins, which arise from human frailty, should be corrected or laid aside.* But still the question occurs, How is this to be done? 7. *That we should use supplications and prayers to the gods, as the priests prescribe.* But for what, and upon what grounds? And what will this help the matter?

6. To conclude this argument, the universal experience of mankind bears testimony to the weakness of natural religion. Nothing in this matter was ever done, or done to purpose, save where revelation prevailed. Should we narrowly scan the lives, not of the vulgar, but of the Heathen philosophers, as Plato, Aristotle, Seneca, Plutarch, Cato and Brutus, we might easily pull off the mask, and discover how little it was that they attained in this matter, or rather nothing at all. Yea even a Socrates himself would not be able to stand before an impartial inquirer. I believe he could not give a good account of his amours, and those practical instructions, which he is said to have given his scholar Alcibiades. He repressed well the vanity and pride of other philosophers: but perhaps, nay I need not say perhaps, with greater pride; yea even his death, the most applauded part of his whole conduct, might be unmasked, and deprived of the unjust eulogies, which some have made on it, who, it may be, never read the accounts we have of it, or seriously considered his carriage on that occasion. It is true, he was unjustly put to death, and behaved very resolutely, but whether he fell not a sacrifice to his own pride, as much as to the malice of his enemies, may be questioned. This I say not to detract from those great men, whom I admire, considering their state; but to shew, that they went not so high as some would have us believe.

In fine, till revealed religion appeared, nothing was seen in the world, of true piety or religion, of mortification of sin, or holiness of life. The natural notices could never make one pious, or indeed moral. Whereas Christianity, upon its first appearance, in a moment, as it were, made millions fo. And they who have rejected it, and fet up for Heathenifm again, under the new, but injurious name of Deifm, are no friends to holinefs of life, piety towards God, fobriety in their own way, nor righteoufnefs among men. How mighty faints do Blount, Hobbs, Spinoza, Uriel, Accofta and others make?

I defigned to have proceeded further, to demonftrate the infufficiency of natural religion to anfwer the *ends of religion*, by the confideration of its infufficiency to fupport under the *troubles of life*, or amongft the *terrors of death*; but upon fecond thoughts I judged, after what has been faid, it was not needful. Befides, if any look but at it, they may eafily fee it utterly infufficient to this purpofe, as it is indeed to the other great ends of religion.

If the well-founded profpect of future rewards, and a clear knowledge of the nature and excellency of *things eternal* and *not feen*, the prefent intimations of divine love, in crofs difpenfations, the fupports of divine powerful grace under them, the ufefulnefs of thofe calamities, by virtue of divine ordination and concurrent influence of the divine Spirit, verified in the experience of the fufferers, are laid afide, as natural religion does, which knows nothing of thefe, all that men can fay to comfort under affliction, or arm againft the horrors of death, is but an unprofitable amufement, or at leaft, like rattles and other toys we give to children, that do not in the leaft eafe them of the pain they are under; but do for a little, divert the mind, while they are looked at; but as foon as the firft impreffion is over, which thefe new toys make on the mind, the fenfe of pain recurs again, with that redoubled force, which it always has, when it immediately fucceeds either eafe or want of fenfe. And if it is really violent, thefe things will not avail, no not to divert trouble for a little. It is but a forry comfort to tell me, that others are troubled as well as I, or worfe; that death, which I fear, will end it; that I muft bear it; that I have other enjoyments, which yet prefent pain will not allow me to relifh. Yet fuch are the beft confolations that *natural religion* affords.

CHAP.

CHAP. XII.

Wherein the Proof of the Insufficiency of Natural Religion is concluded from a general View of the Experience of the World.

AS a conclusion to, and illustration of what has hitherto been discoursed, for demonstrating the *insufficiency* of *natural religion*, I shall here offer a *six-fold* view of the *experience* of the world in general, without descending to particular instances, which have in part been touched at, and offered before, and are every where to be met with.

1. Let us view man as a creature made for this end, to *glorify God and enjoy him*, abstracting from the consideration of his corruption, which the deists sometimes deny, and sometimes with difficulty, do but in part admit. And let us consider him as left to pursue this noble end, in the use of his rational faculties, under the conduct of the mere light of nature: If we consider him thus, and inquire into the experience of the world, how far he has reached this end, we shall find such an account, as will much confirm the truth we have hitherto asserted, and weaken the credit of the deists' imaginary sufficiency of nature's light to conduct man to the end for which he was made.

If we look to the generality of mankind, we shall find them in a posture much like that wherein the prophet saw the princes in the vision, with *their backs* to the chief end, never once thinking for what they were made, pursuing other things; every one as lust led him, following his own humour, walking in a direct and open contradiction to that law, which was originally designed for the guide of our life, and the directory to bliss, that happiness, which all would have, though they know not where to find it.

If we look at the philosophers, we may see them *sitting up late, rising early, eating the bread of carefulness*, wearying themselves in the search of happiness, running into hundreds of different notions about it, and yet not one of them hitting, or at least understanding the true one; and as little agreed about the way to it. We may hear them talk of virtue, but never levelling it at its proper end, *the glory of God*. We may hear them urging its practice, but not upon the proper grounds. Rarely any regard to the authority of God, the only formal ground of obedience. Instead

stead of plain rules useful to mankind, they obtrude cryptic and dark sentences, rather designed to make others admire them, than to be useful to any. They every where tack their own fancies to the divine law, a weight sufficient to sink it as to its truth, in the apprehensions of men, or at least, as to its usefulness. They offer a rule defective in most things of moment, corrupt in many, ruining in not a few instances, destitute of any other authority than their own say, or *ipse dixit*, unintelligible to the generality, and naked as to inducements to obey it.

2. Let us consider man as made for this end, but barred from its attainment, by the interposition of those great hinderances and rubs which now are certainly in its way; I mean darkness, guilt and corruption. These are stones in the way. How has nature's light acquitted itself as to the rolling them away? Truly they have been like Sysiphus's stone, as fast as they have rolled them up, as fast they have recoiled and fallen back on them.

As to that darkness that has overspread the minds of men, if we look at the generalty, we find them like blind men, content to jog on in the dark, mired every where, stumbling frequently, and falling sometimes dangerously; yet satisfied with their case, not looking after light: not so much because they want it not, as because they have no notion of it, or its usefulness; like blind men that never saw the sun, and therefore suffer the loss of it with less regret, than they who once saw, but now have lost their eyes. They follow as they are led; are ready to take hold of any hand, though of one as blind as themselves, and are never sensible of the mistake, till sunk where they cannot get out again. The philosophers indeed seem a little more sensible of their case, and fancying truth to be hid in Democritus's well, dive for it, but lose their breath before they come at it, and fall into dangerous eddies or whirlpools, where they lose themselves instead of finding truth; or trying to fetch it up, but with a line too short, they fetch up some weeds that are nourished by their nearness to the waters, and please themselves with those. After all their painful endeavours we find them groping in the dark, as to all useful and necessary knowledge of God, or the way of worshipping him; of ourselves, our happiness, our sins, the way of obtaining pardon, our duty or our corruption.

As to guilt, if we look at the case of mankind, and their endeavours for the removal of it, we find the most part drowned in endless despair or fatal security; like men at their wit's end,

end, trying all ways that fear, superstition, or racked imagination can supply, and still unsatisfied with their own inventions, they are ready to try all ways that self-designing men, or even the devil can suggest to them, sparing no cost, no travel, no pain. They stand not to give *the fruit of their body for the sin of their soul.* The philosophers either think, through their pride, they have no sin, because they are not quite so bad as the vulgar; or, if they still retain some sense of sin, they are driven into the utmost perplexity, being convinced of the wickedness of the measures taken by the vulgar, or at least of their uselessness and impertinency, and yet unable to find out better; they try to divert their thoughts from a sore they know no plaister for.

As to corruption, we find all confessing it, crying out of the disease; and indeed it is rather because it cannot be hid, the sore runs, than because it is painful to many. The generality despair of stemming the tide, and finding it easiest to swim with the stream, are willingly carried headlong. The body of philosophers are indeed like weak water-men on a strong stream, they look one way but are carried another. Though they pretend they aim at the ruining of vice, yet really they do it no hurt, save that they speak against it. A few of the best of them being ashamed to be found amongst the rest, swimming, or rather carried down the stream on the surface, that is, in open vice, have dived to the bottom; but really made as much way under water as the others above.

3. Let us view mankind under the goodness and forbearance of God, these helps which some think sufficient. These words are used, or rather abused, as a blind in a matter of very great importance; and men who use them will scarce tell, if they can, even in the subject of the present discourse, in what sense they use them. But let it be as it will, some pretend the works of providence, particularly God's goodness and forbearance sufficient. Well, let us see the experience of the world in this.

If we view mankind under this consideration, we may see them so far from being led to repentance, that most part never once took notice of this conduct of God. Others, and they not a few, have abused it to the worst purposes. *Because judgment against an evil work,* has not been *speedily executed,* therefore their *hearts* were *wholly set in them to do evil.* The more inquisitive have raised a charge against God as encouraging wickedness.

wickednefs. And as for the favours they enjoyed themfelves, they looked on them, not as calls to repentance, but as rewards for their pretended virtues, and fcanty ones too, below the worth of them. Not a few of them have gone near to arraign God of injuftice for leffer afflictions they were vifited with; while others have been entangled and toffed to and fro by crofs appearances. So that none have by this *goodnefs of God*, been led *to repentance.*

4. Let us view man living in the place where revelation obtains, or where the Chriftian religion is profeffed and taught, but renouncing and rejecting it, and in profeffion owning only natural religion: Such are the deifts among us. If we confider their words, they talk indeed that natural religion is fufficient; and to make it indeed appear fo, fome of them have adorned it with jewels borrowed from the temple of God, afcribing to nature's light difcoveries in religion, which originally were owing to revelation, and were never dreamed of where it did not obtain; though being once difcovered, they have gained the confent of fober reafon. But now we are not confidering the *fpeech*, but the *power* of thefe men; not what they *fay* of the fufficiency of natural religion, but what *real experience* they have of it, and what evidence they give of this in their practice.

If we thus confider them, we find, that although when they have a mind to impofe their notion of the fufficiency of natural religion upon others, they pretend, that it is clear, as to a great many points or principles, that are confeffedly of the greateft moment in religion; yet when they begin to fpeak more plainly and freely their own inward fentiments, they fhew that they are not fixed, no not about the very principles themfelves, even thefe of them which are of the greateft confequence. Mr. Gildon, publifher of the *Oracles of Reafon*, is not far from afferting two anti-gods, the one *good*, the other *evil*; and fo falls in with the Perfians*. Blount favours the opinion of Ocellus Lucanus, about the *world's eternity*, and confequently denies, or at leaft hefitates about *creation*†. The *immateriality of the foul* feems to be flatly rejected by them all. Nor do they feem very firm as to its *immortality.* In fhort, after they have been at fo much pains to trim up natural religion, and make it look fufficient-like, they yet exprefs a hefitation about its *fufficiency to eternal life* ‡. We have heard Herbert to this
purpofe

---

* Oracles of Reafon, pag. 194, 212, -22?. † Ibid, 154, 187.
‡ Ibid, 117, 127.

purpose already. Blount, in a letter to Dr. Sydenham, prefixed to the *Deist's Reasons*, says plainly, that it is not safe to trust deism alone, without Christianity joined to it. And the Deist's hope is summed up in this, in the 4th chap. of the *Summary of the Deist's Reasons*, That " there is more probability of his salvation, than of the credulous and ill-living Papist*;"— and that is just none at all.

Nor does their practice give one jot of a better proof of the sufficiency of that religion which they profess: yea, it affords convincing evidence of its weakness, uselessness, and utter insufficiency. Their lives shew that they are not in earnest about any thing in religion. They are Latitudinarians in practice. Their words, their actions, have no favour of a regard to a Deity; but they go on in all manner of impieties in practice, and perhaps in the end, put a period to a wretched life by their own hands, as Blount, Uriel, Acosta and others have done, and the survivers justify the deed, upon trifling and childish reasonings; as not knowing but they may one day be put to use the same shift. I am not in the least deterred from asserting this, by the commendations that the publisher of the *Oracles of Reason* gives to Mr. Blount, as a person remarkable for virtue*. If a profane, jocular, and unbecoming treatment of the gravest and most important truths that belong, even by his own acknowledgment, to natural religion; yea, and are the principal props of it; and if gross and palpable disingenuity be instances of that virtue that he ascribes to him, and evidences of those *just and adequate notions of the Deity*, in which he says Mr. Blount was *bred up*, I could give instances enough from the book itself of such virtues: But I love not to *rake in the ashes of the dead*. Again, others of the Deists, having wearied themselves in chace of a phantom to no purpose, and having neither the grace nor ingenuity to return to the religion they abandoned, either land in downright atheism in principle and practice, or they throw themselves into the arms of the pretended infallible guide; and thereby give evidence how well-founded the Jesuitical maxim is, *Make a man once an atheist, he will soon turn Papist*.

5. Let us view men living under the gospel, embracing it in profession, but unacquainted with that Spirit that gives *life* and *power* to its doctrines, precepts, promises, threats and ordinances.

* Oracles of Reason, at the beginning, account of Blount's life.

dinances. They, besides that they are possessed of all the advantages of nature's light, have moreover the superadded advantages of revelation, and its institutions. They have ministers and parents instructing them, and discipline to restrain them, they are trained up in the faith of future rewards, and instructed in the nature and excellency of them, for their encouragement; they have punishments proposed to them to deter them from sin, which they profess to believe; yet if we consider the practice of the generality of such persons, it gives a sufficient evidence, that all this is not enough. Who but a man blind or foolish can then dote so far, as to pretend nature's light alone sufficient, when it is not so, even when helped by so many accessory improvements?

If we consider the experience of them who have received the gospel in truth, and felt its power, we find they have indeed reached the ends of religion in part, and have a fair prospect as to further success. Well, what is their sense of the sufficiency of nature's light? Why, if you observe them in their public devotions, you shall hear heavy out-cries of their own darkness, weakness and wickedness; you may hear serious prayers for divine light, and life to quicken them, strengthen and incline them to follow duty, and support them in it, against the power of temptations, which they own themselves unable to master, without the powerful aids of divine grace. If you follow them into their retirements, where the matter is managed betwixt God and them alone, where they are under none of these temptations, to maintain the credit of any received notions, and therefore must be presumed to speak out the practical sense of the state of their case, without any disguise; there you shall find nothing but deep confessions of guilt, darkness, and inability, with earnest cries, prayers, and tears, for supplies of grace: and what they attain in matters of religion, you shall find them freely owning, that it was not *they*, but the *grace of God* in them that brought them to this. And the more that any is concerned about religion, or know and has attained in it, still you will find him the more sensible of this state of things.

This is but a hint of what might have been said: but I have rather chosen to offer a general scheme of the argument from *experience*, which every one, from his own private reading and observation, may illustrate with observations and particular instances, than to insist upon it at large, which would have required a volume.

K k CHAP.

CHAP. XIII.

Wherein we make a transition to the Deists' Pleas for their Opinion, and take particular Notice of the Articles to which they reduce their Catholic Religion, give some Account of Baron Herbert, the first Inventer of this Catholic Religion, his Books, and particularly of that which is inscribed De Religione Gentilium, *as to the Matter and Scope of it, and the Importance of what is therein attempted to the Deists' Cause.*

WE have now proposed and confirmed our own opinion; our next business is to inquire more particularly into that of the Deists, and consider what they offer for it.

The first set of Deists, so far as I can learn, did satisfy themselves with the rejection of all supernatural revelation, and a general pretence, that natural religion was sufficient, without telling the world of what *articles* it did consist, what belonged thereto, or how far it went. The learned lord *Herbert* was the first who did cultivate this notion, and dressed Deism, and brought it to something of a form. This honour he assumes to himself, glories in it, and we see no ground to dispute this with him. I have met with nothing in any of the modern Deists that makes towards this subject, which is not advanced by him, and probably borrowed from his writings. It will not therefore be impertinent to give the reader some account of him.

This *Edward Herbert* was a descendant from a younger brother of the family of Pembroke. He was brother to the famous George Herbert the divine poet. His education was at Oxford, where he was for some time a fellow Commoner in University-College there. After he left the university, he improved himself by travels into foreign nations, and obtained the reputation of a scholar, a statesman and soldier. He was made *Knight of the Bath* at the coronation of king James I. in England, who afterwards sent him as ambassador to Lewis XIII. on behalf of the French Protestants: and upon his return he was created *Baron of Castle-Island,* in Ireland; and by king Charles I. anno 1629, he was created a baron of England, by the title of *Lord Herbert of Cherbury,* and died in 1648 [*].

This

---

[*] See Geograph. Diction. articles *Herbert* and *Deism*. See also the Life of Mr. George Herbert.

This learned person having once unhappily apoftatifed from the religion wherein he was bred, into *deifm*, though, as other Deifts likewife do, he did ftill feem to own the Church of England; yet he fet himfelf for the maintenance of deifm in his writings. And to this purpofe he publifhed fome time after the year 1640, (for I have not the firft edition of it) his book *de Veritate*, and fhortly after another, *de Caufis Errorum*. Thefe two books are for the moft part philofophical, and written with fome fingularity of notion. What is truth in them is rather delivered in a *new way*, than *new*; and by the ufe of vulgar words in new and uncommon acceptations, and his obfcure way of management of his notions, is fcarcely intelligible to any but metaphyfical readers, nor to fuch, without greater application, than perhaps the matter is worth. I fhould not think myfelf concerned in either of thefe two books, their fubject being philofophical, were it not that it is his avowed defign in them, to lay a foundation for his peculiar notions in religion.

There are two things at which Herbert, in thefe and his other writings, plainly aims at—to *overthrow revelation*, and to *eftablifh natural religion* in its room. It is not my defign or province at prefent, to defend revelation againft the efforts of this or any other author, though I think it were a bufinefs of no great difficulty to remove what Herbert has faid againft it; yet fince I have mentioned his attempt upon it, I cannot pafs it without fome fhort, but juft remarks upon his unfair, if not difingenuous way of treating revelation.

1. On many occafions, with what candor and ingenuity himfelf knew, he profeffeth a great refpect to revelation, and particularly to the fcriptures, and pretends he defigns nothing in prejudice of the *eftablifhed religion:* but any one that perufes the books will foon fee, that this is only like *Joab's kifs*, a blind to make his reader fecure, and fear no danger from the *fword* that he has under his garment: For notwithftanding of this, he every where infinuates prejudices againft all revelation, as *uncertain, unneceffary*, and of *little* or *no ufe* to any, fave thofe to whom it was originally, or rather immediately given.

2. Upon all occafions, and fometimes without any occafion given him from his fubject, he makes fallies upon truths of the greateft importance in the Chriftian religion; fuch as the doctrines of the *corruption of our nature, fatisfaction of Chrift*, and the *decrees of God*, &c. And having reprefented them difingenuoufly, or elfe ignorantly, (which I lefs fufpect in a man of
his

his learning) not in that way they are propofed in fcripture, or taught by thofe who maintain them, but under the difguife of grofs mifreprefentations, miftaken notions, and ftrained confequences: and having thus put them in beaft's fkins, as the primitive perfecutors did the Chriftians, he fets his dogs upon them to worry them; and this without any regard had unto the foundation they have in the fcriptures, or the evidence of the proofs that may be advanced for the fcriptures in general, or thefe doctrines in particular, and without all confideration of the inconfiftency of this way of treating truths plainly taught, and inculcated as of the greateft importance in the fcriptures, with that refpect, which upon other occafions he pretends to that divine book.

3. He ftates wrong notions of the grounds whereupon revelation is received, and overthrows thofe imaginary ones he has fet up, as the reafons of our belief of the fcriptures, and then triumphs in his fuccefs. How eafy is it to fet up a *man of ftraw* and beat him down with the finger!

4. The Deifts generally, and Herbert in particular, do grant, that the Chriftian revelation has manifeftly the advantage of all other pretenders to revelation, as in refpect of the intrinfic excellency of the matter, fo likewife in refpect of the reafons that may be pleaded for its truth.* And fo certain and evident is this, that one of their number owns, that Chriftianity has " the " faireft pretenfions of any religion now in the world," and exhorts to " make a diligent inquiry into it;" arguing, " that " if the pretences of Chriftianity be well grounded, it cannot " be a frivolous and indifferent matter;" and he grants further, that " the truth of the matters of fact which confirm it, is hard-" ly poffible to be denied †." Now notwithftanding of this manifeft and acknowledged difference betwixt the fcriptures and other pretenders to revelation, when Herbert fpeaks of revelation, he jumbles all pretenders together without diftinction, and urges the faults of the moft ridiculous and obvioufly fpurious pretenders, againft revelation, in general, as if every particular one, and efpecially Chriftianity, were chargeable with thefe faults: Is this candid and fair dealing, to infinuate to the unwary reader that thefe palpable evidences of impofture are to be found in all revelations alike, while, even they themfelves being judges, the fcriptures are not concerned in them?

Yet

* Religio Laici, pag. 9, 10. † Letter to the Deifts, pag. 139.

Yet this is the way that Christianity is treated by this learned author; and his steps have been closely traced in this piece of scandalous disingenuity, (for I can give it no milder name), by Blount and the other writers of the party, as I could make appear by many instances, if need required.

5. Our author makes high pretences to accuracy in searching after truth, and treats all other authors with the greatest scorn and contempt imaginable, as short in that point: yet he seldom states a question fairly, but huddles all up in the dark, especially, when he speaks about revelation, and heaps together difficulties about all the concernments of revealed religion, without any regard to the distinct heads to which they belong. This is a ready way to shake the faith of his reader about all truths, but establish him in none.

Other reflections I forbear, though he has given fair occasion for many: but this is not my subject. This part of his discourse has been animadverted on by a learned author, though the book is not come to my hand.*

The other branch of our author's design, *viz.* His attempt to establish the *sufficiency of natural religion,* is that wherein I am directly concerned. This he only proposes in his book *de Veritate* at the close, with a short explication of his famed *five Articles,* of which more anon. And in a small treatise entitled *Religio Laici,* subjoined to his book *de Causis Errorum,* he further explains them. The design of this last mentioned treatise is to shew, that the vulgar can never come to certainty about the truth of any *particular revelation,* or the preferableness of its pretences unto others, and that therefore of necessity they must sit down satisfied with the religion he offers them, consisting of five articles, agreed to, if we believe him, by all religions.

The religion, consisting of five articles, which we shall exhibit immediately, he attempts to prove *sufficient* by some arguments in that last mentioned treatise. But the principal proof, on which our author lays the whole stress of his cause, is at large exhibited in another treatise of our author, *de Religione Gentilium,* published at Amsterdam, anno 1663, by *J. Vossius,* son to the great *Ger. Joan. Vossius.* His pleadings in these and his other writings we shall call to an account by and bye.

Herbert,

* Baxter's More Reasons for the Christian Religion, and no Reason against it, in the Appendix.

Herbert, in his treatife *de Religione Gentilium*, pretends, Whatever miftakes the Gentile world was under in matters of religion; yet there was as much agreed to by all nations, as was neceffary to their eternal happinefs. Particularly, he tells us, that they were agreed about *five Articles*, of *natural religion*, which he thinks are *fufficient*, viz. 1. That is there one fupreme God. 2. That he is to be worfhipped. 3. That virtue is the principal part of his worfhip. 4. That we muft repent of our fins. 5. That there are rewards and punifhments both in this life and that which is to come.*

Charles Blount, who fet himfelf at the head of the Deifts fome few years ago, in a fmall treatife entitled *Religio Laici*, printed 1683, which in effect is only a tranflation of Herbert's book of the fame name, inverting a little the order, but without the addition of any one thought of moment; in this treatife, I fay, he reckons up the articles of natural religion much after the fame manner. 1. That there is one only fupreme God. 2. That he chiefly is to be worfhipped. 3. That virtue, goodnefs and piety, accompanied with faith in, and love to God, are the beft ways of worfhipping him. 4. That we fhould repent of our fins from the bottom of our hearts, and turn to the right way. 5. That there is a reward and punifhment after this life.†

Another, in a letter directed to Mr. Blount, fubfcribed A. W. has given us an account of them fomewhat different from both the former, in feven articles. 1. That there is one infinite, and eternal God, creator of all things. 2. That he governs the world by providence. 3. That it is our duty to worfhip and obey him as our Creator and Governor. 4. That our worfhip confifts in prayer to him, and praife of him. 5. That our obedience confifts in the rules of right reafon, the practice whereof is moral virtue. 6. That we are to expect rewards and punifhments hereafter according to our actions in this life; which includes the foul's immortality, and is proved by our admitting providence. 7. That, when we err from the rules of our duty, we ought to repent and truft in God's mercy for pardon.‡ To the fame purpofe, without any alteration of moment from what we have above quoted, Herbert reckons up and repeats the fame articles in his other treatifes.

Thefe

---

* De Relig. Gentil. pag. 186, 210, &c. † Ibid, 49, 50.
‡ Oracles of Reafon, pag. 197.

These other authors do but copy after Herbert. To him the honour of this invention belongs, and he values himself not a little upon it. Let us hear himself. " *Atque ita (fed non fine* " *multiplici accurataque religionum tum diffectione, tum infpec-* " *tione) quinque illos articulos fæpius jam adductos deprehendi.* " *Quibus etiam inventis me feliciorem Archimede quovis exifti-* " *mavi**." He acquaints us, that he confulted divines and writers of all parties, but in vain, for to find the univerfal religion he fought after; it is not therefore likely, if any had moulded this univerfal religion, or put it into a form meet for the Deifts' purpofe before him, that it could have efcaped his obfervation and diligence.

Now we have had a fufficient view of the articles, to which the Deifts reduce their religion. Let us next inquire after the proof of this religion; the burden whereof muft lean upon Herbert. The Deifts fince his time have added nothing that has a fhew of proof that I can yet fee. Well, after he has in his other treatifes, as has been faid, propofed and explained his religion, he at length comes to the proof of it in his treatife *de Religione Gentilium.* Here the main ftrength of his caufe lies, and with this we fhall mainly deal; yet fo as not to overlook any thing that has a fhew of proof elfewhere in his writings.

In this treatife *de Religione Gentilium,* he makes it his work to illuftrate and prove, " That the above-mentioned five arti-" cles were univerfally believed by people of all religions." This is the propofition at which that whole book aims. In the management of this fubject our author gives great proof of diligence, vaft reading, and much philological learning. He gives large accounts of the idolatry of the Heathens and their pleas for it, or rather of the pleas, which our author thought might be made for it; which has given occafion to feveral conjectures, as to our author's defign in that book, and his other writings.

I find a learned author, who has beftowed a few fhort animadverfions on this book, inclined to think it not unlikely, that Herbert's principal defign was, if not to juftify, yet to excufe

---

* De Relig. Gent. pag. 218.—" And thus, though not without a " manifold and accurate diffection and infpection of religion, I have " found thofe five articles, that have already been often quoted, on " finding which I thought myfelf more happy than any Archimedes."

cuſe the idolatry of the church of Rome†. And if one conſiders how many pleas Herbert makes for the Gentiles' idolatry, and that they are generally ſuch as may ſerve for the Romaniſts' purpoſe; and if it is further conſidered, that Herbert elſewhere ſeems, upon many occaſions, to found the whole certainty of revelation upon the authority of the church, and that alone, and the vaſt power he gives to the church as to the appointment of *rites*, yea, and all the *ordinances* of *worſhip*; if it is further conſidered how concerned ſome perſons were for an accommodation with the church of Rome at that time, when our author wrote, and how far Herbert was concerned in that party, who were ſtriving for this reconciliation; if I ſay, all theſe things are laid together, this conjecture will not appear deſtitute of probability. I might add to this, that Herbert makes uſe of pleas not much unlike thoſe which are uſed by the church of Rome to ſhake Proteſtants out of their faith, that they may at length fall in with the *infallible guide*. In fine, I dare be bold to undertake the maintenance of this againſt any oppoſer, that Herbert's method followed out, will inevitably make the vulgar atheiſts; whether he deſigned by this to make them Papiſts, I know not, nor ſhall I judge. How far this conjecture will hold, I leave to others to judge. I ſhall only add this one thing more, that the ſeeming oppoſition of Herbert's deſign unto Popiſh principles, and his thruſts at the Romiſh clergy, will not be ſufficient to clear him of all ſuſpicion in this matter, with thoſe who have ſeriouſly peruſed the books written by Papiſts in diſguiſe, on deſign to ſhake the faith of the vulgar ſort of Proteſtants, in ſome of which, there is as great appearance at firſt view of a deſigned overthrow of Popery, and as hard things ſaid againſt the Romiſh clergy. Good water-men can look one way and row another. What there was of this, will one day be manifeſt.

The Deiſts maintain, that " their religion, conſiſting of the " above-named five articles, is ſufficient." It is the avowed deſign of Herbert in his book, to aſſert this and prove it; and yet he ſpends it wholly in proving this propoſition, " That theſe " five articles did univerſally obtain." Now it ſeems of importance to inquire, why Herbert ſhould be at ſo much pains to prove this. How does univerſal reception of theſe articles eſtabliſh his religion, and of what conſequence is it to the Deiſts' cauſe?
For

† Abrah. Heidanus de Origine Erroris, Lib. VI. Cap. XI. pag. 370.

For clearing this, it muſt be obſerved, that it is a common religion that Herbert is inquiring after, which may be equally uſeful to all mankind ; and nothing can agree to this, which is not commonly received. And Herbert has before laid down this for a principle, that the only way to diſtinguiſh common notices from theſe which are not ſo, is *univerſal reception.* This according to him is the only ſure criterion. " *Religio eſt* " *notitia communis———Videndum igitur eſt, quænam in re-* " *ligione ex conſenſu univerſali ſunt agnita: univerſa conferan-* " *tur: Quæ antem ab omnibus tanquam vera in religione agnoſ-* " *cuntur, communes notitiæ habendæ ſunt. Sed dices eſſe laboris* " *improbi: at alia ad veritates notitiarum communium non ſu-* " *pereſt via; quas tamen ita magni facimus, ut in illis ſolis ſa-* " *pientiæ divinæ univerſalis arcana deprehendi poſſint.**"

But to ſet this matter in a full light, I ſhall make appear, That a failure in this attempt, to prove that theſe were univerſally a- greed to, is inevitably ruinous to the Deiſts' cauſe and plea for a common religion ; though the proof of this point will be very far from inferring that there is a common religion, as ſhall be cleared afterwards. And this will give further light into the reaſons of Herbert's undertaking.

To this purpoſe then it is to be obſerved, That the Deiſts being agreed about the rejection of the Chriſtian religion, and that revelation whereon it is founded, they are for ever barred from the acceptance of any other revelation as the meaſure of religion, that the world knows: For they own no revelation ever had ſo fair a plea, and ſuch probable grounds to ſupport its pretenſions, as the Chriſtian revelation has. However there- fore, the generality of the Deiſts were ſatisfied to lay aſide the Chriſtian religion, which will not allow them that liberty in following the courſes that they are reſolved upon, without put- ting any thing into its place ; yet the more ſober ſort ſaw, that to reject this religion and put none in its place, would, by the

---

* De Veritate, pag. 55.——" Religion is a common notice, we " ought to ſee therefore what things in religion are acknowledged by " univerſal conſent. Let all be gathered together, and thoſe things in " religion which are acknowledged by all to be true are to be reckon- " ed common notices. But you will ſay that this is a taſk of immenſe " labour. But no other way remains for arriving at thoſe truths that " may be reckoned common notices. Which however we value ſo " highly, that in theſe alone the ſecrets of divine univerſal wiſdom can " be found."

world, be counted plain atheifm, which defervedly is odious in the world. Therefore they faw there was a neceffity of fubftituting one in its place.

Now fince revelation was rejected, nothing remained, but to pretend, that reafon was able to fupply the defect and afford a fufficient religion, a religion that is able to anfwer all the purpofes for which others pretend revealed religion neceffary.

When once they were come this length, it was eafy to fee that it might be inquired, Whether this rational religion lay within the reach of every man's reafon, or was only to be found out by perfons of learning?

If it is pretended, that only perfons of learning, application and uncommon abilities, could attain the difcovery of this religion, the difficulties whereon the pretenders are caft, are obvious.

What fhall then become of their argument againft revealed religion, " that it is not univerfal, that it is not received by all mankind, that therefore it is not attended with fufficient evidence." Upon this fuppofition there is a fair ground for retorting the argument, with no lefs, if not more force, againft natural religion.

Again, what fhall become of that plea, which they make for natural religion, " that God muft provide all his creatures in the means neceffary for attaining that happinefs they are capable of?" May they not, on this fuppofition, be urged, that, according to it, the generality are not provided with fuch means?

Nor will it avail to pretend, that thofe who are capable of this difcovery, are obliged to teach others the *laws of nature*. For, it may be inquired, Muft the people take all on truft from them, or fee with their own eyes? If they muft take all on truft, then is there not here a fair occafion for charging prieft-craft upon them, who blame it fo much in others? Will not this oblige our wits, men of reafon and learning, to turn *creed* and *fyftem-makers?* Further, what will they fay of their own neglect, and the neglect of the learned world in this matter? How will they reconcile this to the notion of God's goodnefs, of which they talk fo much, to fufpend the happinefs of the greater part of mankind on their care and diligence, who quite neglect them, but keep up their knowledge, and thereby expofe the poor vulgar to inevitable ruin? Moreover, if they fet up for teachers, they muft fhew their credentials. Finally, there is no place, upon this fuppofition, left for the ftrongeft pleas for a fufficient

ent religion, that is common to mankind, which are taken from the nature of God and man, and their mutual relation ; becaufe all thefe arguments conclude equally for all mankind, and fo are not adapted to affert fome peculiar prerogative in one above another. Nor are any able to juftify a claim to any further ability this way, than he can fatisfy the world of, by the effects of it. When a man pretends to no other abilities, than fuch as are due to human nature, that *he is a man* is fufficient to juftify his claim; but if he pretends to fome eminency in natural or acquired endowments above others, he muft give fuch proofs of it, as the nature of the thing requires; that is, he muft make it appear, that he has that ability, by actings proportionable to the nature and degree of the power that he claims; and further than this is done, no wife man will believe him. It will not help them out here, to fay, that they only of better capacities, and who have more leifure, are able to difcover this natural religion ; but the vulgar are capable of judging and feeing with their own eyes when it is propofed : For, befides that all the former difficulties, or moft of them recur here, ftill it may be inquired, Is this made appear? The difficulties on this fide are unfurmountable.

Wherefore, of neceffity, they muft maintain, "that every man is able to find out and difcover what is fufficient for himfelf in matters of religion." But now when this is afferted, if the experience of the world lie againft them, and it be found, as is commonly fuppofed, that many nations, nay, the far greater part of mankind, had no fuch religion, this will much prejudge their opinion, about every man's having this ability of finding out a religion, or as much in religion as was neceffary to his own happinefs.

How will they perfuade the world of fuch an ability, if experience is not made appear to favour them? It is commonly thought, and we have made it appear, that the wifeft men, when they effayed what power they had of this fort, foully blundered, and fell fhort of fatisfying either themfelves or others ; and that the world generally acknowledged the want of any experience of this ability, and therefore looked after revelations with that greedinefs, that laid them open to be impofed on, by every vain pretender to fupernatural revelation.

Now if things are allowed to be thus, how fhall they prove man poffeffed of this power, if they are cut off from the advantage of the ufual fountain of conviction, in matters of this nature?

What

What is the way we come to know, that all men have a power of understanding, or that such a power is due to his nature? Is it not hence, that wherever we meet with men, we find them exerting the acts of understanding? And the like may be said of his other powers. Now if it is once admitted, that there are single persons, nay, whole nations, yea more, many nations that have no experience of this pretended ability, in reference to matters of religion, how will they ever be able to persuade the world that all men have it? More especially, if it be admitted, that the learned themselves were here defective, as to that which persons of the meanest abilities and least leisure are supposed able for: this will look very ill, if a man who toils all his days at the plough and harrow, could make this discovery, how could a man of learning and application find it hard.

In a word, if things are thus stated, as is generally supposed, and has been already proven, and shall be further cleared anon, then there is little left them to pretend for this natural and universal ability of mankind in matters of religion, if not perhaps, to tell us a story of God's being obliged, in point of *goodness*, to endow all mankind with a capacity, whereof there is no evidence in experience; yea, which the experience of the world plainly declares them to want. But this will not easily take with men of sobriety and sense: For it is not more evident, that *there is a God*, than, that *this God must do whatever is proper and suitable for him to do:* And on the contrary, that *it was not necessary or proper for him to do any thing that really he has not done.* If then, any shall pretend it becoming or necessary for God to do any thing, which experience shews he has not done, he will be so far from obtaining credit with the world, that on the contrary he will justly fall under the suspicion of atheism, and an evil design against God. For to say, that God in point of goodness, was obliged to do this, which experience shews he has not done is plainly to say, God acted not as became him. There was therefore a plain necessity of undertaking to prove experience on their side, if Deism was to be supported.

If the common apprehensions of men, who enjoy the light of Christianity, with respect to the state of the Heathen world, are well grounded, all the pretences of Deists as to the sufficiency of natural religion are for ever ruined, and quite subverted.

It was but necessary therefore, that the learned Herbert, who undertook to maintain the cause, should attempt to shew, that experience was on their side, and that in fact a religion in it-

self

self sufficient did universally obtain. And he had the more reason to be concerned in this matter, because he avows it as his opinion, that without a supposition of such an universal religion as the Deists do plead for, Providence cannot be maintained. "*Et quidem*, says he, *quum media ad victum vestitumque heic accommodata suppeditarit cunctis natura sive providentia rerum communis, suspicari non potui, eundem Deum, sive ex natura, sive ex gratia in suppeditandis ad beatiorem hoc nostro statum mediis, ulli hominum deesse posse, vel velle, adeo ut licet mediis illis parum recte vel feliciter usi sint Gentiles, haud ita tamen per Deum optimum maximum steterit, quo minus salvi fierent**." And as it is clear that this author thinks, that Providence is not to be maintained without an universal religion; so it is sufficiently evident, that this universal religion is not to be maintained, if experience lies against it.

Here then was a plain necessity for undertaking this argument, and proving, or at least pretending to prove, that all mankind had a sufficient religion, or were able to know all that was necessary. For we see the whole frame of Deism falls to the ground, if this is overthrown. This therefore was an undertaking worthy of our noble author's great parts, long experience, great charity to mankind, and the great concern he professes to find in himself for the vindication of Providence.

And sure if such a man, after so much pains, has failed in the proof of this point, any that may succeed him, may justly despair of success. He read all the Heathen authors to find this universal religion, and he was as willing and desirous to find it as any man. And he has given in this learned book evidence enough of his reading.

But since no religion was to be admitted, save that whereon all men were agreed, it was wisely done by our author, that he reduced this universal creed to a *few articles*. For one who knew so much of the state of the world, could not but see, that they were not very many wherein they were agreed.

Well,

* De Relig. Gentil. Cap. 1. pag. 4.—" And indeed as the common " nature or providence of things here, has furnished all men with full " means of food and cloathing, I could not suspect that the same God, " either from his nature or from grace, could or would be wanting to " any of mankind in supplying him with the means of attaining a more " happy state than the present; so that although the Heathens used those " means unskilfully or unhappily, yet the best and greatest God was " not to be blamed for their not being saved."

Well, he undertakes and goes through with the work, and concludes with that memorable triumph above mentioned; "*At-que ita (sed non sine multiplici, accurataque religionum tum dissectione, tum inspectione) quinque illos articulos, sæpius jam adductos deprehendi. Quibus etiam inventis me feliciorem quovis Archimede existimavi.*"

But one might possibly ask, How it could cost our author so much labour and pains to find out this religion, and to sever the articles belonging to it from others, with which they were intermixed, when every illiterate man must be supposed able to do this?

However, if our author is not belied by common fame, he repented, that he had spent his time so ill in contributing so far to the advancement of irreligion; though others contradict this and tell us, that dying he left this advice to his children,— "They talk of trusting in Christ for salvation; but I would have you be virtuous, and trust to your virtue, to make you happy."

Whatever there is as to this, I shall now proceed to examine our author's arguments.

CHAP. XIV.

Wherein it is inquired, Whether Herbert has proved that his five Articles did universally obtain?

WE have heard our author's five articles above; he pretends to make it appear, that they were every where received; we shall now inquire, Whether the arguments adduced by him do evince this? And then in the next place, we shall see whether it is indeed true. And for method's sake, we shall speak of every article apart, and dissect and inspect his book, to find all that he offers, which has the least appearance of proof.

ARTICLE I.

There is One Supreme God.

THAT which our author pretends to prove as to this article is, that it was generally owned by all nations, that there is one *Supreme Being*, and that this Supreme Being, whom they owned,

owned, was the fame whom we adore. We are not now to difpute, whether this article may be known by the light of nature; nor whether fome particular perfons went not a great way in the acknowledgment of it. This we have before granted: But the queftion is, Whether all nations agreed in this, *that there is one Supreme God*, and he the very fame whom we adore? Let us hear our author, " *Quamvis enim de aliquibus alijs Dei,* " *five attributis, five muneribus difceptatio inter veteres effet, uti* " *fuo loco monftrabimus; fummum tamen aliquem extare, and* " *femper extitiffe Deum, neque apud fapientes, neque apud infipi-* " *entes dubium (puto) fuit.**" And afterwards, when he thinks the firft part of his article fufficiently cleared, he proceeds to the fecond part of it, " *Reliquum eft, ut Deum fummum Gentilium, eundum ac noftrum effe probemus.*† Thus we fee what our author pretends. Whether he has proved this, we are now to inquire. He has not digefted his arguments, nor caft them into any fuch mould, as might make it obvious wherein the force of them lies, and therefore we muft be at pains to fcrape together, whatever is any where through his book dropped, that may contribute in the leaft toward the ftrengthening of his caufe; and we fhall not omit any thing willingly, that has the leaft appearance of force.

The firft obfervation our author infifts on to this purpofe is, " That the Gentiles did not intend the fame by the name *God*, that we now do. We by that name defign the Supreme, Eternal, Independent Being; whereas they intend no more than any virtue or power fuperior to man, on which man did any way depend." *Id omne Deum vocitarunt quod vim aliquam eximiam in inferiora, fed in homines præcipue ederet.*‡ This he frequently inculcates, and tells us in the firft page of his book, that the obfervation of this, was that which inclined him to think, or prefume

---

* De Relig. Gent. pag. 158.—" For although there may have been " difputes among the ancients about certain other attributes or offices of " God, as we fhall fhew in its own place, yet it was never doubted, I " think either among the wife or the unwife, that fome Supreme God " exifted, and had always exifted. "

† Ibid. 166.—" It remains to prove that the Supreme God of the " Heathen's was the fame as ours."

* De Relig. Gent. pag. 13.—" They called all that God, which " produced any confiderable effect on inferior things, but efpecially " upon men."

presume the Gentiles not chargeable with that gross Polytheism, with which most do, and he himself had, upon an slight view of their religion, well nigh once concluded them chargeable.

If the Gentiles meant the same by the word God, which we do, no doubt they stand chargeable with the most gross, unaccountable, absurd and ridiculous Polytheism imaginable: For scarce is there any thing animate or inanimate, but by some way or other became deified. *Quicquid humus, pelagus, cælum mirabile gignunt, id dexére deos, colles, freta, flumina, flammas.**

But our athor is not willing to admit that they were so absurd; and to induce us to favourable sentiments, he has blessed us with this observation, That when they called those creatures *animate* and *inanimate gods*, they meant no such thing as we do by that name. Well, if we should grant that the wiser sort, at least, or perhaps even the vulgar too, did sometimes so understand the word, as he alleges, will that serve his purpose, and satisfy him? Nay, by no means, unless we grant him, that they always so understood the word, save when they spoke of the *One true God*. But this is too much to be granted, unless he prove it; especially if we are able to evince, that not a few, both wise and unwise, believed that there were more than One Eternal, Independent Being: and possibly this may be made appear afterward. A learned author, in reproach of the Grecian and Roman learning, says, " That setting aside what they " learned out of Egypt, they could never by themselves de- " termine whether there were *many* Gods or but *one*†."

The next thing our author insists on to this purpose, is, " That different names do not always point out different gods, but different virtues of the same God." " *Tot Dei appel- " lationes, quot munera, adeoq; si triginta milia Deûm no- " mina quod ab Œnomao & Hesiodo in* Θεογονια *perhibetur, " supponat quispiam, & tot ejus munera dari, fatendum est,*" says Seneca, quoted by our author‡. And consequentially to
 this,

---

* Aurel. contr. Sym. Lib. I.—" Whatever wonderful thing the " earth, the sea, or sky produced, that they called gods—hills, seas, " rivers, fire."

† Wolsely's Scripture Belief, pag. 110.

‡ Seneca Lib. 5. Cap. 17. Herbert de Relig. Gent. pag. 13.—" We " must confess that there is as many names of God, as there are offices, " so that if any one suppose that there are thirty thousand different names " of gods, as is related by Oenomaus and Hesiod in his Theogony, we " must acknowledge that there are likewise as many offices of the Deity."

this, the fame Seneca tells us, " Sapientes nequaquam Jovem
" eum intellexiffe, qui in Capitolio aut alijs templis fulmino
" armatus cerneretur, fed potius mentem animumque exifti-
" maffe omnium cuftodem, univerfiq ; adminiftratorem, qui
" hanc rerum univerfalitatem condiderit, ac eandem nutu fuo
" gubernet, ac propteria divina quæq ; nomina ei convenire.
" Itaq ; optimo jure fatum appellari poffe, ut a quo ordo feri-
" efve caufarum inter fe aptarum dependeat. Ita is Providenti-
" am dicit, quum ipfe provideat ut omnia perpetuo ac peren-
" ni quodam curfu, ad finem ad quem diftinata funt, currunt:
" Naturam quoque nuncupari, ex eo enim cuncta nafcuntur,
" per eum quicquid vitæ eft particeps, vivet: Mundi quin etiam
" nomen illi congruere. Quicqoud fub afpectum cadit, ipfe eft,
" qui feipfo nititur, & omnia ambitu fuo complectitur, univer-
" faque numine fuo complet.*" To the fame purpofe fpeaks
Servius of all the Stoicks, quoted likewife by our author.† The
plain Englifh of all is, he would perfuade us that by thefe teftimonies he has proved, that the Gentiles, when they attributed
the name of GOD to fo many things, intended no more, but to
fet out fo many *different virtues,* which all refided in the *fame
God.*

As to this, we may grant, that our author has indeed proved,
That different names do not always point out different gods ; for
he has told us that each of their gods had many different names.
But this will do him no fervice, if we grant not, that different
names *never* point out different gods. But how fhall we do this,
when our author has fhewed us, that many nations worfhipped

* Herb. De. Rel. Gent. pag.47.—" Wife men did not mean by Jupi-
" ter, that ftatue that is feen in the Capitol and other temples, armed
" with thunderbolts; but rather thought that that Mind and Soul was Ju-
" piter, which was the Guardian and Governor of the Univerfe, who for-
" med this whole world, and governs it by his nod, and that all divine
" names agree to him. He may therefore be very juftly called Fate, as
" on him the order and feries of connected caufes depends. Thus too he
" may be called Providence, as he provides that all things fhould tend
" to the end for which they were deftined, in a conftant and perpetual
" courfe. He may likewife be called Nature, for all things arife from
" him, and he gives life to all that lives. Nay even the name of
" World may agree to him, for whatever is vifible is himfelf, who de-
" pends on himfelf, furrounds all things with his circumference, and
" fills all things with his divine prefence."

† De Relig. Gentil. pag. 37.

the sun, moon, and stars; and thought them gods, yea, distinct ones too, different in their *natures* as well as *names*. Each of them indeed had different names, nay each of them had many names, titles or elogies heaped on them by their fond worshippers, who no doubt fancied, that their gods were smitten with that same vanity, wherewith they themselves were tainted; which yet as learned Rivet observes, had a dangerous effect upon the vulgar in process of time: for they were not so quick in their observations as our author. *"Coacervatis enim elogiis, titulisque conges-*
" tis, capi numen putabant, maximoque inde affici honore; ita ut
" tandem quæ diversa tantum nomina superstitionis fuerant, gras-
" sante errore, diversa numina haberentur."*

Further, we know full well that some of the more wise and learned men, especially after the light of the gospel began to shine through the world, began to be ashamed of their religion, and especially the number of their gods, and to use the same shifts, to palliate the foolish and wild Polytheism, which the gospel so fully exposed: and particularly Seneca, who was contemporary with Paul, (and by some, upon what ground I now inquire not, is said to have conversed with him) and others of the Stoicks steered this course, to vindicate their religion against the assaults of the Christians. But it is as true, this was a foolish attempt, and its success I cannot better express, than in the words of the learned and excellent Dr. Owen, " Postquum au-
" tem severius paulo inter nonnullos philosophari cœptum est,
" atque limatiores de naturâ divinâ opiniones inter plurimos ob-
" tinuerant, sapientes pudere cœpit eorum deorum, quos pro-
" tulerant ferrea sæcula, ignorantiâ & tenebris tota devoluta.
" Omnia ideo, quæ de dijs fictitijs, Jove scil: totoque sacro he-
" lenismi choragio, vulgo celebrata erant, res naturales adum-
" brasse apud antiqous Μυθολογους contenderunt. Theologiam hanc
" Μυθικην vocant, quam nihil aliud fuisse aiunt, quam naturæ
" doctrinam allegoricam.†" And some passages after, he shews
the

---

* Ad Hos. 2. 8. Referente Owen Theolog. pag. 189.—" For
" they thought that the Deity was charmed with encomiums and ti-
" tles heaped one above another, and received great honour from thence,
" so that at length those different names, devised by superstition, by
" the progress of error, came to be reckoned different deities.

† Uni supra pag. 196.—" But after philosophy began to be more
" seriously cultivated, and more correct opinions concerning the divine
" nature had taken place among the generality, the wise men began to
" be

the vanity of this attempt. "Poſtquam enim evangelii lumen
"uſque adeo radiis ſuis terrarum orbem perculiſſet, ut erube-
"ſcenda veteris ſuperſtitionis inſania apud ipſum vulgus in con-
"temptum venerit, acutiores ſophiſtæ, qoud dixi, quo ſtultitiam
"iſtam colore novo fucatam, amabilem redderent, figmento
"huic (N. B.) cui adverſatur omnis hiſtoriæ fides, pertinacif-
"ſimé adhæſerunt. Imo, ut obiter dicam innovata eſt primis
"eccleſiæ temporibus apud ipſos Gentiles, tota philoſophandi
"ratio.*" Any one that would defire to ſee the folly of this
obſervation expoſed, on which our author lays ſo much ſtreſs,
may peruſe that chapter, whence theſe words are quoted†. Nor
is this more than what Velleius ſpeaks of Zeno a Stoick and o-
thers," Cum Heſiodi Θεογονιαν interpretatur, tollit omnino,(N. B.)
"uſitatas perceptaſque, cognitiones deorum.‡" &c.

But were this true, which thoſe quotations pretend, it will
not yet come up to our author's purpoſe; for theſe quotations
tell us not that all the world were of this mind, but only the
wiſe men; and I fear that this too needs a reſtriction. Now
this comes not near to the point. When our author has occaſion
to notice ſome abſurd practices or opinions that are againſt him,
he rejects them with this, "*Quod a paucis ſolummodo ſuperſtiti-*
"*oſe factum, non ſatis in religionem aſſeritur. Nos autem haud*
alia

"be aſhamed of thoſe gods, which had been invented in the iron ages,
"that were entirely involved in ignorance and darkneſs, and therefore
"they maintained that all thoſe things that had been commonly report-
"ed of the fictitious gods, viz. Jupiter and all the hierarchy of Greece,
"ſignified only certain natural things in the ſenſe of the ancient Mytho-
"logiſts. And they called this Mythological Divinity, which they
"ſaid was nothing elſe than the knowledge of nature, veiled by alle-
"gory."
* Ubi ſupra. pag, 198.—"For after the light of the goſpel had ſo
"far enlightened the world with its rays, that the ſhameful madneſs
"of the ancient ſuperſtition had fallen into contempt, even among the
"vulgar, the more acute ſophiſts, as I ſaid before, in order to render
"that foolery amiable, by giving it a new colour, adhered moſt obſti-
"nately to this fiction, though oppoſite to all the faith of hiſtory, nay,
"we may obſerve in paſſing, that in the firſt ages of the church, the
"manner of. philoſophiſing among the Heathens underwent a total
"change."
† Owen ubi ſupra. Lib 3. Cap. 6.
‡ Cicero de Nat. Door. Lib. 1.—"When he interprets the Theo-
"gony of Heſiod, he entirely overturns altogether the uſual and re-
"ceived traditions concerning the gods."

"*alia quam quæ omnes, vel plerique faltem coluére, fub religionis*
"*titulo ponimus.**" Now let this be, as it is, the ftate of the
queftion, and what fome of the wifer did, is nothing at all to the
purpofe; and this indeed is the point. In fine, we doubt not
before we have done, from our author's own book, to demonftrate, that what he aims at in this obfervation, and confequently all the ftory of the *myftick theology* of the Heathens, is utterly inconfiftent with all faith of hiftory, which makes us as fure
of this, as they can of any thing, that many nations, nay moft
nations, nay moft wife men held a plurality of gods, even in the
fenfe our author would deny. The next obfervation he makes, is
a-kin to the former. He, following Voffius, as he tells us, divides
all the Gentiles' worfhip into *proper, fymbolical* and *mixt*.†
Proper is, when the true God, or the fun, or the moon is worfhipped as the true God, and the worfhip is defigned ultimately
to terminate in their honour: Symbolic is, when the true God
is worfhipped in the fun, as an image, reprefentation or fym-
bol of him; then the worfhip is not defigned only, nor mainly
to terminate on the fun, but on the true God. As for the
mixt, we are not concerned to fpeak of it. He would every
where have us to believe, that all their worfhip was fymbolical,
and as fuch he frequently feems to juftify and avouch it as reafonable, which the Papifts will readily thank him for; and he
exprefly afferts this, that all " their worfhip, fave what was directly addreffed to the true God," which I believe was very little, " was fymbolic." *Atque cultum proprium nullum fuiffe
olim preterquam fummi Dei, videtur.*‡ It is well that he expreffes
this pofition modeftly, as being confcious how great ground o-
thers will fee to judge otherwife. And the reafon that follows,
drawn from the alleged evidences of the thing, we fhall have
under confideration anon. But toward the clofe of his book, he
calls them *ignorants*, or *fcioli*, that believes not as he believes
in this matter.

But

* De Relig. Gent. pag. 12.—" What was done fuperftitioufly by a
" few only, cannot be faid to be a part of the general religion, but
" we place under the title of religion no other things than thofe which
" all, or at leaft the moft patt practifed."

† Ibid. pag. 183.

‡ Ibid. pag. 226.—" And there feems to have been no proper wor-
" fhip of old, except that of the Supreme God."

But it would be expected, that when he advances such a bold position, and is so hard on them that dissent from him, he would give good proof of it; but if any expect that, he will find himself deceived. I find indeed a passage quoted with a high commendation to this purpose. " *Atque hic de cultu dei symbolico preclarum locum ex Maximo Tyrio, Dissert. 38. quem adducit Vossius, supprimere non possum. Barbari omnes pariter Deum esse intelligunt; constituere interim sibi alia atque alia signa: Ignem Persæ imaginem qnæ unum duret diem, vorax quid & insatiabile, sic Maximi verba vertit Vossius.**" But what is all this to the purpose? Doth this quotation from a Platonic philosopher, who lived an hundred and fifty years after Christ, when the gospel had overspread the whole world, and chased the Pagan darkness away, and made them ashamed of their old opinions, and improven reason, prove any thing? To spend time on this, after what has been said above, were to trifle with a witness. The Deists have not, nor can they ever prove the truth of this bold assertion; the falshood of which we may detect before we have done. But hitherto our author has only used his *shield*; we must next see whether his *sword* be not of better metal. All that has been hitherto said, is only a defensative for the Heathen's opinions and practice: We must now see by what arguments he proves that his first article did universally obtain.

His first argument leans upon a few quotations from some Heathens, who assert, that there is one Supreme Being, such as Hierocles, Zoroaster, and others, some of old and some of late.

But all this is nothing to the purpose: For were there twenty times more who said so, this will not prove the point he is obliged to make good. He has undertaken to shew that it was not doubted among wise or unwise, *that there was one supreme God, and he the same whom we adore.* Now what is this to the purpose, to bring the opinions of a few learned men, without telling what were the opinions of the nations or times where they lived, or of the world at large? It is not the question, What Seneca,

---

* De Rel. Gent. pag. 70.—" And here I cannot suppress a famous
" place in Maximus Tyrius, Diss. 38. which is quoted by Vossius.
" All the barbarians believe equally that there is a God, but set up
" different signs or representations of him. For example, the Persians
" chuse fire, an image that lasts but one day, something voracious and
" insatiable. Thus does Vossius render the words of Maximus."

neca, Zoroafter, Plato, and twenty more, thought, nay what whole nations befides thought? but, What the whole world thought in this matter? This the argument touches not.

His next argument is drawn from the confeffion of feveral divines. With this he begins his fifteenth chapter, and frequently fpeaks of it. But this fays no more for him, than other, and perhaps more confiderable teftimonies, do againft him. Befides, fince he has not condefcended on the perfons who fall in with him here, nor their words, we muft leave them; as we are not concerned in them, nor obliged to follow them further, than they do the truth.

But that which he lays the moft ftrefs on, is the fuppofed evidence of the thing*. This he frequently infifts on, as to all his articles; and its force amounts to this—It is fo clear that there is *one only Supreme Being*, and that the fun nor no other is he, that it could not efcape the moft dull and unthinking.

But here our author puts me in mind of the companions of Chriftopher Columbus, who firft difcovered America, about the year 1592; they were one day at table with him, and began to depreciate and undervalue the diifcovery he had made, telling him how eafily others might have done it. Well, fays he, I hold you a wager, I do what none of you fhall do, and prefently calling for an egg, fays he, none of you can make that egg ftand ftraight on the table; which when they had effayed to no purpofe, he takes it, and crufhes the end of it a little, and then it ftood eafily; which, when they all faid it was eafy to do: Well, fays he, it is very true, ye can do it after I have done it. It is eafy to fee things after they are difcovered to our hand, which we would otherwife never have thought of. All the world was not fo difcerning as our author was, and his followers pretended to be, and he has given us fufficient proof of that in his book, and I truly wonder with what face any man could make ufe of this argument after he had read, much more after he had writ fuch a book, wherein it is made clear as the day, that many nations believed no other God but the fun, moon and ftars, as we fhall fhew afterwards. And I muft take the freedom to fay, that our noble and learned author, with the reft of the Deifts, and all the philofophers, who lived fince the gofpel obtained in the world, owe more to the *Chriftian religion*, than they have the ingenuity to own. What they think fo

clear

---

* De Relig. Gent. pag. 182, 166.

clear, when *revelation* has not only taught them the truths, but the grounds of them, was dark not only to the vulgar, but to the wifest of old. I cannot better conclude this, than by tranfcribing a paffage of the ingenious Mr. Lock's *Effay on Human Under-ftanding*—" Had you or I,(fays he, fpeaking about *innate ideas*)
" been born at the bay of Seldania, poffibly our thoughts and no-
" tions had not exceeded thefe brutifh ones of the Hotentots that
" inhabit there ; and had the *Virginian king, Apochancana*
" been educated in England, he had, perhaps, been as know-
" ing a divine, and as good a mathematician as any in it. The
" difference between him and a more improved Englifhman,
" lying barely in this, that the exercife of his faculties was
" bounded within the ways, and modes and notions of his own
" country, and was never directed to any other or farther in-
" quiries : And if he had not any idea of a God as we have,
" it was only becaufe he purfued not thofe thoughts, that would
" certainly have led him to it." Thus far Mr. Lock. If fome men had been born where the gofpel light has not come, they would have learned to talk more foberly of the *fufficiency* of the *light of nature*.

The only thing that remains for him to prove as to this firft article is, That this One Supreme God, whom he thinks the Gentiles all centered in, was the *fame God* with him whom we worfhip. For this he refers us to three fcriptures—Rom i. 19. Acts x. throughout, and Acts xvii. 28, &c.

Our author has not drawn any argument from thofe paffages, but barely refers to them. He was particularly unlucky in quoting the laft of them : For it obliged him to take notice of an argument arifing obvioufly from the paffage, againft the pur- pofe he adduced it for the proof of ; and indeed that paffage af- fords feveral arguments againft our author's opinion in this mat- ter, which are not eafy to be folved, if they who follow him, were to be determined by fcripture arguments. But our noble author has fcarce fairly laid the objection, which he ftarted to himfelf from the *altar to the unknown God*. But to fpeak home to the purpofe—There are only two things that can be drawn from thefe or the like paffages. 1. That fome of the Gentiles *knew* the *true God*. 2. That all of them had fome notions of truth concerning God, or which were only rightly applicable to the *true God*. The actings of confcience within, and the works of God without them, enforced on them the impreffion of fome Power, fuperior to themfelves, on which they depended; and
this

this was indeed a notion of truth concerning God ; for this was only juſtly applicable to the true God : But yet they, through their darkneſs and wickedneſs, when they came to inquire more particularly after the true God, applied theſe notions to creatures, and took them for this true God.

Now this is indeed all, beſides bare and repeated aſſertions, that I can find in our author, to prove that his firſt article obtained univerſally : And how far it is from proving this, is evident from what has been ſaid.

ARTICLE II.

This One Supreme God is to be worſhipped.

THE ſecond article our author has not attempted a ſufficient, nay nor any ſeparate proof of : Wherefore we go on to the next.

ARTICLE III.

That Virtue and Piety are the principal parts of the worſhip of this one true God.

THIS he alſo pretends to have univerſally obtained, and that the Gentiles expected not Heaven for their worſhip, or their ſacred performances, but for their *moral* worſhip, that is, their virtues. To prove this, is the deſign of our author's 15th chapter, at leaſt till pag. 195.

The firſt thing he inſiſts on to this purpoſe is, the high reſpect which the Heathens put on thoſe things, while they ranked, *mens, ratio, pietas, fides, pudicitia, ſpes* and *felicitas*†, amongſt the number of their gods, and erected temples to them. This he proves at large. But what all this makes to his purpoſe, I am not yet ſatisfied.

This indeed proves that they had a reſpect to all thoſe things. Very true, ſo they had, and that becauſe of their uſefulneſs in human ſociety. Yea this proves that they had an undue reſpect to them, ſo as to perform acts of worſhip to them. But that they deſigned to worſhip God by thoſe virtues, which they would not allow they had from him, as we ſhall hear afterwards,

is

* Mind, Reaſon, Piety, Faith, Hope, and Happineſs.

is not so easily proven. Besides, this was only at Rome that these altars were erected, and so is far from concluding as to the rest of the world, where virtue, hope, &c. had no such temples.

The next thing our author mentions for proof of the universal reception of this article, is the *custom of the Heathens in deifying their heroes on account of their virtues and piety*. But our author knew too much of the Gentiles' religion to believe that this proves any more, than the fulsome flattery of the blinded world that deified even devils, and, as our author elsewhere well observes, men that were no better than devils; or if there was any more in this custom, when at first invented, it was only some ill applied piece of gratitude to persons, who had been their benefactors, or the benefactors of mankind. And all this respect, that was put on them, was not because their virtues reflected any glory on God, but because they had been useful to men. Besides, religion was old in the world before this novel Grecian invention took place. As the Roman poet and satyrist observed,

———— *nec turba deorum*
Talis, ut est hodie, contentaque sydera paucis
Numinibus, miserum urgebant Atlanta minore
Pondere.*

Nor did this universally obtain. So that the argument concludes just nothing. It neither proves that all the world were agreed that virtue and piety are the principal parts of the worship of God, nor that on account of these, men get eternal happiness. What their immortality was, of which they talked, we may see under the fifth article.

Some few quotations from Cicero, Seneca, Plato, and one or two more compose our author's last argument. Seneca speaking somewhere of Scipio Affricanus says, " Animam quidem ejus " in cœlum, ex quo erat, rediisse persuadeo, non quod magnos " exercitus duxit (hos enim Cambyses furiosus, & furore felici- " ter usus habuit) sed ob egregiam moderationem, pietatemque. " Cicero Lib. de Offic. Deos placatos facit pietas & sanctitas." And elsewhere he says, " Nec est ulla erga deos pietas, nisi " honesta

---

* " Nor was there such a multitude of gods, as there is now, and " the stars being content with a few deities, pressed the poor Atlas " with less weight."

" honefta de numine eorum ac mente opinio : Quum expeti ni-
" hil ab iis quod fit injuftum, ac in honeftum arbitrere *" Some
others he adduces from Plato and others, wherein they fay, that
happinefs and likenefs to God are obtained by virtue.

But to what purpofe are all thefe brought ? 1. There is word
here of gods, and their worfhip and piety as refpecting them;
but not one word of the One true God, of whom alone we
fpeak. 2. It is certain that this piety and fanctity according to
thofe authors, comprehended the worfhip of their gods, as our
author exprefly confeffes, "*Atque ad pietatem confummatum plu-*
"*rima infuper* (that is, befides virtue of which he fpeaks before)
"*poftulari aiebant, fed ea prefertim qu? grati in fuperos animi*
"*indicia effent, puta facrificia, ritu. & ceremon as & hujufmo-*
"*di alia quorum farrago ingens fuit : C terum fine prædictis*
"*divis five deabus, animum regentibus, aditum in cælum non*
"*dari.*†" This laft part is only our author's fay, and is not reconcileable with what he tells us of their deif;ing fome, who
we e fo far from being gods, that they were, fays he, *Ne viri
quidem probi.*‡ 3. As for what Cicero fays, " That for virtue
and piety we are advanced to heaven ;" I do not know well how
to reconcile it with what he fays elfewhere in his book *de Amicitia*, "*Vult plane virtus honorem : nec virtutis eft ulla alia merces*," otherwife than by thinking that by heaven, (his *cælum*,)
he meant, that which many of them meant by their *immortality*,
that is, an immortal fame, a good reputation after they are
gone, amongft the furvivers. As for Seneca, Chriftianity had
taught

* De Relig. Gentil. pag. 187.—" I am perfuaded that his foul re-
" turned to that heaven from whence it came, not becaufe he had great
" armies (for Cambyfis who was a madman, and fortunate in his madnefs,
" had thefe too) but on account of his remarkable moderation and pi-
" ety. . . . . Piety and holinefs appeafe the gods. . . . . Nor is
" there any piety towards the gods, except an honourable opinion of
" their deity and mind, when one thinks that nothing unjuft and dif-
" honourable fhould be afked of them."

† Ibid. pag. 185.—" And they faid, that many other things befides
" were requifite in order to conftitute perfect piety, but efpecially fuch
" things as were indications of a mind grateful to the gods, viz. facri-
" fices, rites, and ceremonies, and other things of this fort, of which
" there was a great number, but that there was no accefs to heaven
" without the aforefaid gods and goddeffes, who directed the foul."

‡ Ibid, pag. 195.—" Not even good men."

taught him a little more, and his testimony is not much to be regarded. 4. Were there twenty more of them, they never come near to a proof of the point: it is the sentiments of the world that we are inquiring after, and not what were the thoughts of some of the more improved philosophers. The question is not, Whether men by the light of nature saw an excellency in virtue, and that it was to be followed? but, Whether they looked on it as a part, a principal part of the worship, not of their deities, but of the *one true God;* and that for which heaven, not that imaginary heaven which men had at their disposal; but an *eternity of happiness in communion with God,* is to be obtained? Now our author advances nothing to prove this point.

ARTICLE IV.

We must repent when we do amiss.

AS to this article our author confesses several things, which it will be meet to notice in the entry. 1. He owns that the ancients, the wiser sort of them, thought not repentance a sufficient atonement for the grosser sort of sins;* and quotes Cicero, saying, *Expiatio scelerum in homines nulla est.*† Where God was offended they sought sanctuary in repentance, and thought it sufficient, but not where men were wronged. "*Cæterum licet* " *in remedium peccati, ubi Dei summi majestas læderetur, pœniten-* " *tiam sive dolorem efficacem esse crederent: Non ita tamen ubi ho-* " *mines injuria vel contumeliis afficerentur, de pœnitentia illa* " *statuebant Gentiles.*‡" 2. He confesses that they thought not, "Repentance alone a sufficient atonement.‖" He tells us, that they had *Expiationes lustrationesque, sine quibus neque crimine neque pœnā solutos semetipsos arbitrabantur.* Again, 3. He confesses that the word *repentance,* or *penitence,* was rarely used among the ancients, in that sense we use it. "*Neque mihi dubi-*
"*um*

* De Rel. Gent. pag. 197.

† Cicero de Leg. Lib. 1.—" There is no expiation of crimes " against men."

‡ De Rel. Gent. pag. 198.—" But although they thought that pen-
" itence or sorrow was an effectual mean of taking away sin,
" whereby the majesty of the Supreme God was injured, yet they had
" not the same opinion of penitence, in regard to those sins whereby
" men were injured and insulted."

‖ Ibid. pag. 195.

" um quin eorum (scil. peccatorum) pænituerit Gentiles, quæ
" tot mala, accercerunt; licet rarius quidem pænitentiæ verbum
" inter autores, eo quo jam usurpatur sensu reperiatur.*" Since
then he makes all these concessions, there remains no more save
this, that he pretends all the "world were agreed upon repen-
" tance, as that which was of use to expiate, at least, some les-
" ser faults committed against God, and that we should, when
" we sin, be grieved for it."

To prove this, he quotes some passages from Ovid, Seneca
and some others. The only considerable testimony is from Periander, who was one of the seven wise men of Greece: One of
whose sentences, he says it was Ἁμαρτων Μεταϐολευε, Te mali
pæniteat, ubi peccaveris. Seneca says, Quem pœnitet peccasse
pene est innocens. And Ovid,

> Sæpe levant pœnas, ereptaque lumina reddunt
> Quem bene peccati pœnituisse videst†.

But all these are alleged to no purpose. They do not prove
that repentance was looked on as an expiation by the Gentiles.
Ovid and Seneca lived too late in the world, and had too great
access to learn from others, to be much regarded in this matter;
but they only speak their own mind, and we have here no argument of the agreement of the world as to any thing about repentance. The opinions of the wise are no just measure of the
knowledge or apprehensions of the vulgar.

But that whereon our author seems to lay more stress, is their
sacrifices, which he pretends are an evidence of their grief for
sin, or repentance. Quorsum enim nisi interno dolore perciti, tot
ritus sacraque ad deos placandos excogitassent ‡ ?

But, 1. If the Gentiles had been as much agreed about repentance as our author pretends, they would indeed have spared all this pains and cost. 2. They were indeed *grieved*, but this
grief they did not willingly entertain, nor allow themselves in
as

---

* De Rel. Gent. pag. 198.—" Nor is it a doubt with me that the
" Gentiles repented of those crimes which brought so many evils upon
" them, although the word repentance, in that sense in which it is now
" used seldom occurs in their authors."

† " You see that he who duly repents of his offence often allevi-
" ates his punishment, and restores his lost light."

‡ " For to what purpose, unless they had been prompted by inward
" sorrow, would they have contrived so many rites and sacrifices for
" appeasing the gods?"

as their *duty*; but looked upon it as their *torment*, and fought sanctuary in means proper for appeasing their gods, as they thought. 3. This grief, which sacrifices prove them to have had, is no more but that uneasy sense of sin in the conscience, which is a part of its punishment, and no duty performed for their deliverance; and this forced them upon all ways that they could imagine to get rid of it; so that sacrifices were what they betook themselves to, to save themselves, or procure a deliverance from our author's *penitence*. 4. Further, our author, when it is for his purpose, can put another construction on their sacrifices; while we have heard above, he makes them only absurd enough testimonies of gratitude to the gods, and to have no respect to sin at all. It is indeed true, that sometimes they were in this way used; so Pythagoras is said to have used them when he offered hecatombe to the gods, for a proposition which he found out; but for ordinary they were designed as expiatory. 5. Do their sacrifices, which they offered to so many gods, prove that they were troubled for offending the *one true God*? I believe not. Ay, but this was what our author should have proved. 6. Does our author tell us that they were so little agreed about this purgative, that no less a person than Plato discarded repentance, and put philosophy in its room, as that whereby only we could be purged? And this leads me to a 7th thing, that shews of how little signification this pretended proof is, That it is known that the more discerning philosophers made most light of those sacrifices, yea, of sin, and consequently of our author's catholic remedy, *repentance*. As to the sufficiency of repentance for the place he assigns it, we have spoken to it above. Our author, I think, has badly proven that it universally obtained. And indeed had there been as much weight laid on it as is pretended, we could not have missed a more large account of it in the writings of the Gentiles. Further, 8. Our author pretends, that repentance is of no avail, as to the *grosser evils*, but only washes away *lesser sins*, and we fear our author would find some difficulty to prove that generally the Gentiles were so concerned for lesser sins, as he pretends. 9. Had they been so well agreed, as he pretends, about repentance, and had this been the design of their sacrifices, I do not well understand why our author should make such opposition betwixt sacrifices and repentance, as elsewhere he does; when he is speaking of several faults of the Heathen priests, he subjoins—
" Sed & hoc pejus, quod quum ex vera veritute, vel hinc ubi ex-
" ciderint

" *ciderint ex pænitentia verâ, pacem internam comparare debu-*
" *issent, ad ritus & sacra, quæ ipsi (Scil. Sacerdotes) peragerent*
" *res perducta est, &c.* *" Here it would seem plain, that the
people came at length, if not of their own accord, yet by the
persuasion of priests, to overlook repentance, and reject it,
substituting other things in its room ; and when once this obtained in one generation, it is like it might spread and obtain
in after ages, being transmitted from father to son, and the
priests carrying on the cheat ; and so at least the world in all
ages hath not made any account of repentance as the only expiation.   Again, it would seem from our author, that sacrifices
did not import, and were not evidences of repentance , but on
the contrary, means invented to make people neglect it.† I do
not well understand how they, who, if we may believe our author,
were all so fully agreed about repentance, and were so prone
and inclined to it, that their minds run into it without any
persuasion, should need so much the priests' persuasion, and be
easily drawn off from what they accounted so available.   Let us
hear our author. Speaking of man's recovery from sin, says
he, " *Atque instaurationem hanc fieri debere ex pœnitentia,*
" *docuére tum philosophi, tum sacerdotes, ita ut hanc agendam*
" *animamque purificandum, sed non sine eorum ministerio, sæ-*
" *pius inculcarent. Bene quidem si pœnitentiam satis populo*
" *persuasissent, quod neutiquam tamen ab illis factum fuit ; licet*
" *adeo pronâ in eam sit anima humana, ut etiam nullo suadente,*
" *in foro interno ex gratia divina, conscientiæque dictamine de-*
" *cernatur.*‡"   Our author tells us, that the people's sacrifices
were an argument of their repentance, as we heard above, and
that the priests persuaded them to it, and that they were all
                                                                                    agreed

* De Rel. Gent. pag. 10.—" But this too is worse, that when they
" ought to have sought inward peace by true virtue, or when they had
" fallen from it, by true penitence, the matter was reduced to rites and
" sacrifices performed by the priests."
‡ Ibid. pag. 107.
† " And both the philosophers and the priests taught that this re-
" covery must be brought about by repentance, so that they often in-
" culcated that this ought to be done and the soul purified, but not
" without their ministry. It would have been well indeed if they had
" sufficiently persuaded the people to penitence, which however was
" not done by them, although the human mind is so prone to it, that
" even without any adviser it is determined in the inward court by the
" divine grace and the dictate of conscience."

agreed, that repentance was the only atonement, and that the mind of man needs no admonisher to persuade it to repentance; and yet he tells us likewise in the passages adduced, That repentance was quite laid by, sacrifices and rites put in its place, the people so ignorant of the worth of it as to let it go, and so backward as not to look after it, unless the priests had pressed it more, (and yet we are told they inculcated it oft) and in fine, the priests so negligent that they quite neglected their duty. How to knit all this together I know not. I do think it were easier to make these words overthrow our author's argument, than to reconcile them with themselves, with truth, reason, or experience; but I spare reflections that offer themselves. Before our author, or the Deists, make any thing of this argument, they must prove, " That sacrifices universally obtained—That sacrifices were every where offered to the One True GOD— That those sacrifices were symbolical of repentance," as another Deist has it, and several other things taken notice of above.

ARTICLE V.

That there are rewards and punishments after this life.

WE are now come to our author's last article. He is not very constant in expressing himself about this article, and how far it was agreed to. Sometimes he pretends, that these rewards were *eternal happiness*, and that this was agreed; sometimes only it was agreed that there were rewards and punishments after this life; and sometimes he words it yet more modestly, that they *expected* rewards and punishments, either in *this life*, or *after it*. So pag. 203, when he enters expresly to treat of this article, *Et quidem præmium bonis & supplicium malis, (N. B.) vel in hac vita, vel post hanc vitam dari, statuebant Gentiles*.*"

And indeed when he comes to tell us how far is determinable in this matter by the light of nature, he makes this article of very little signification. " Non imperitè quidem, bonos " bona, malos mala, vel in eternum manere affirmabant vete- " res. At quis locum præmii, vel poenæ ostenderit? Quis " supplicii

* " And indeed the Heathens were of opinion, that there would be " a reward to the good, and a punishment to the wicked, either in this " life or after this life."

" fupplicii genus conjectaverit?" (And the fame is perfectly the cafe as to rewards, though our author waves that, for what caufe it is not hard to conjecture.) " Quis tandem durationis " terminum pofuerit * ?"

All that he pretends to have been received, was barely this, " That there are rewards and punifhments after this life." Let us hear himfelf, " Et quidem præter folennem illam notitiam " communem, nempe, deum bonum juftumq; effe, adeoq; " præmium vel pœnam tum in hac vita, tum poft hanc vitam, " pro actionibus, imo & cogitationibus fuis unicuique remetiri, " nihil quod verifimile magis effet ab illis ftatui poffe decerni-" mus †." But he tells us, that by the additions they made to this, and proceeding to determine further than they knew, even this came to be called in queftion, (which, by the way, ruins our author's caufe as to this article) but let himfelf fpeak, " Dum hæc philofophi, illa facerdotes, alia demum poetæ " adjicerent, tota inclinata in cafumq; prona nutavit veritatis " fabrica. Si femet fatis coercuiffent Gentilium coriphæi, ne-" minem, puto, diffentientem habuiffent.‡

He afferts very little, we fee, to have univerfally obtained as to this article, and he feems to do more than infinuate, that even, as to *this little*, at leaft, in procefs of time there were fome, and even not a few diffenters: For I know not what meaning elfe to put upon the " whole fabric of truth nodding," and " inclining to fall:" And this is to quit the caufe. We fhall however notice his arguments, but the more fhortly, becaufe of what has been already obferved.

Firft,

* De Relig. Gent, pag. 210.—" The ancients indeed not unfkilfully " affirmed that good things awaited the good, and evil the wicked, " even for ever. But who could fhow the place of reward or pun-" ifhment? Who could guefs the kind of punifhment? . . . Who " at laft can fix the term of their duration?"

† " And indeed befides that folemn common notice, that there is a " God who is good and juft, and confequently will reward and punifh " every one, both in this life and after this life, according to his ac-" tions, and even to his thoughts, we think that nothing more pro-" bable could be determined by them."

‡ " While the philofophers added fome things, the priefts others, " and the poets others further, the whole fabric of truth was ruined " and fell to the ground. If the leaders of the Heathens could have " reftrained themfelves, I think that they would have had nobody " differing from them."

First then, he pretends, that the perfuasion of this is *innate**, that the reasons of it are so obvious, and the arguments leading to it are so evident, that they could not but agree as to this.†

But I have already shewn, that every thing that is evident, or was so to our author and his companions and followers, was not so to the ancient sages. I guess that he learned most of these arguments he insists on from some others than the Heathen philosophers, or if they managed them so well, he would have done right to have pointed us to the places where they have done so. But when he has done this it will not prove an *universal consent:* For we are concerned in some others besides philosophers. As for what he pretends of this perfuasion's being *innate,* I think he has said much to disprove it himself; or if it be, I think the presages of future misery in the mind of man, have been much more strong than of happiness. And in a word, he only says it was innate, but does not prove it. Yea, if this did not universally obtain, according to our author's own doctrine, it was not innate.

Next he insists on the custom of *deifying heroes,* and placing them among the number of the immortal gods. This he hints at frequently. But this did not universally obtain as to time or place, and so hit not the point in the least. All were not so dignified, nay, not all that were *good;* nor does it prove, that even all that people, among whom this custom prevailed, were of that opinion; but only the persons principally concerned. And indeed it were easy to shew that they were not all of this opinion, which may possibly be made appear in the next chapter.

His next argument is deduced from a few testimonies of poets and philosophers asserting a future state, which he has scattered up and down, here and there. But what is this to all the world? Do the poets' fancies of *Elysian fields, Styx* and the like, give us the true measure of the sentiments of the world?

Thus I have viewed our author's proofs of his five articles, and their reception in the world. I have not knowingly omitted any thing of moment, advanced by him for his opinion. I shall conclude this chapter with a few general reflections on our author's conduct in this affair.

I do not a little suspect a writer of controversy, when he huddles up, and endeavours to conceal the state of the question, and shifts it upon occasion. It is always a sign either that his judgment

---

* De Reg. Gent. pag. 211.   † Ibid. pag. 4.

ment is naught, or that his defigns are not fair and good. I do not believe that our noble author's abilities required any fuch mean fhifts, if the badnefs of the caufe he unhappily undertook, had not obliged him : But that this is the courfe he fteers, is evident. Now he feems to undertake to fhew us, what the moft univerfal apprehenfions of men were in matters of religion ; and anon, he pretends to tell us what the more difcerning perfons, among the Heathens thought; and thus fhifts the fcene, as it is for his purpofe.

It is further remarkable, that our author has crammed in a great deal of philofophical learning, which makes nothing at all to the main purpofe of the book. He has writ a book of 230 pages to prove that thefe five articles obtained : whereas all the arguments he adduces, fcarce take up ten of them. The reft is a collection of hiftorical and philological learning about the Heathen gods and worfhip. He only drops here and there the fhadow of an argument; and then when we are fome pages by it, he tells us he has demonftrated this already, and we are referred back to fome of the preceeding arguments ; and that is, we are bid *fearch for a needle amongft a heap of hay*. This looks exceeding fufpicious like.*

Again, I do not like frequent and repeated affertions in a difp nt without arguments. Fewer affertions and more arguments, if the caufe had permitted, would have done better. It is faid that fome by telling a lie often over, come at length to believe it to be true. I am apt to think that the oft afferting over and over again what he undertakes to prove, might go further toward his own conviction, than all the arguments that he has advanced.

Our author undertakes to give us an account what the Heathen's thoughts as to thofe articles were, and what led them to thefe apprehenfions; but after all, you fhall find nothing but an account of fome of their practices, with our author's gloffes put on them, and the reafon that, not they, but he thinks may be alleged in juftification of their practices and opinions. If he had dealt fairly he would have told us in their own words, what their fentiments were, and likewife, what were their inducements that led them into thofe opinions: but to obtrude, as every where he doth, his conjectures and ftrained interpretations, as their meaning, is perfectly intolerable.

It

* Read the conclufion of our author's 8. Cap. pag. 54. and compare it with the Cap.

It is indeed true, that our author affords us several quotations from the Heathens; but doth he, by this means, give us a fair reprefentation of the point in controverfy, and their fentiments about it? No. If his reader is fo fimple as to take this for granted, he deceives himfelf. I know it is the cuftom of fome others, as well as our author, though perhaps on better defigns, to quote fome paffages from Heathen authors, in order to fhew their agreement with Chriftianity, and to what a length the mere light of nature brought them: but hereby they do deceive the reader: So Cicero's teftimony to the immortality of the foul, is alleged by our author, pag. 192, " *Quemadmodum igitur haut* " *alius Deus, haut alia virtus, ab Gentilibus, quam ab noftris,* " *olim celebratur, ita certè communis utriufque fpes immortalita-* " *tis fuit. Difertim Cicero* 2 *de. Leg. ait, animi hominum* " *funt immortales: Sed fortium bonorum divini & alibi in Lib.* " *de Seneclute ait : Non eft lugenda mors, quum immortalitas* " *confequitur.**" Now if any body fhould think that this teftimony of Cicero gives a full account of his apprehenfions about immortality, they would be very far deceived: For in his firft book of *Tufculan Queftions*, where he difcuffes this point *ex profeffo*, he difcovers indeed an inclination to believe it, and a defire that it may be true; yet fuch a hefitation about it, that he knows not how to perfuade himfelf of it, as we fhall fhew perhaps in the next chapter. In like manner Plato is cited by him, and many others to the fame purpofe: But what a fad uncertainty both Socrates and Plato were in about this point, I fhall fully demonftrate in the next chapter. I fhall here fet down only one notable inftance of the unfairnefs of this way of procedure. Our author quotes Solon's teftimony for *future felicity*, pag. 194. Let us hear our author's own words, " *Pulchram* " *diftinctionem inter felicem five fortunatem & beatum affert ex* " *Solone Herodotus Lib* 1. *Ubi Crœfo refpondens, ait neminem* " *dignum effe qui vocetur beatus antequam* τελευτήσει τον Βιον ευ *hoc* " *eft, vitam fuam bene clauferit; adeoque* ιοτοχη *five fortunatum*
" *hac*

---

* " As therefore there was no other God, nor any other virtue for-
" merly celebrated among the Gentiles than by our writers, fo furely
" both of them had a common hope of immortality; for Cicero fays
" exprefsly, 2d de Legibus, that the fouls of men are immortal, and
" thofe of the brave and good are divine: and elfewhere in his book on
" Old Age he fays, that death which immediately follows, is not to
" be mourned for."

" hac in vita, nequaquam *ὄλβιον* five beatum ante obitum ejus ho-
" minum appellari poffe. Huic concinit Ovidius,

   Diciq; beatus
Ante obitum nemo, fupremaque funera, debet.

" Propriè quippe loquendo, nemo beatus ante mortem: Ita ut
" beati inter Gentiles vocarentur, qui in Elyfus campis fempiterno
" ævo fruerentur*."

Now here we have a proof to the full of our author's conduct in his quotations, and the improvement of them. Was not Solon clear that there was a ftate of happinefs after this life? Who can doubt it, after our author has thus proved it? But what if Solon for all this, confined happinefs to *this life*, defining the happy man, " One who is competently furnifhed " with outward things, acts honeftly, and lives temperately †;" which definition no lefs a perfon than Ariftotle approves. And in all Solon's fpeech to Crefus, there is not one word, if it were not difingenuoufly or ignorantly quoted, that gives us the leaft ground to believe that Solon once fo much as dreamed of *happinefs after this life*. Stanley in his Life of Solon recites from Herodotes this whole fpeech, and the ftory to which it relates ‡. Crefus king of Lydia in Afia the Lefs, fends for Solon upon the fame of his wifdom. Solon comes. The vain king, dazzled with the luftre of his own greatnefs, afked the wife Solon, Whether ever he faw any man happier than himfelf, who was poffeffed of fo great riches and power? Solon named feverals, particularly Tellus the Athenian citizen, Cleobis and Bito, two brothers; the ftory of whom he relates to Crefus, and gives the reafons why he looked on them as happy, without ever a hint of their enjoying any happinefs after this life. At which

---

* " Herodotus from Solon quotes a fine diftinction betwixt a lucky
" or fortunate and a happy man, in his firft book, when Solon anfwer-
" ing Crefus, fays that nobody deferves to be called happy, till he has
" ended his life well, and confequently that although a man may be
" called lucky or fortunate in this life, but that he ought not to be cal-
" led happy before his death. And Ovid agrees with him, " Nor ought
" any to be called happy before his death, and the laft ceremony of
" his funeral." For properly fpeaking none is happy before his death.
" So that thofe were called happy among the Gentiles who enjoyed an
" eternal life in the Elyfian fields."

† Stanley's Life of Solon. pag. 26.   ‡ Ibid. pag. 28, 29.

which Crefus was angry, thinking himfelf undervalued ;
whereupon Solon thus addreffes him—"Do you inquire, Crefus,
" concerning human affairs of me, who know, that divine
" providence is fevere, and full of alteration? In procefs of
" time, we fee many things we would not ; we fuffer many
" things we would not. Let us propofe feventy years as the
" term of man's life, which years confift of 25200 days, be-
" fides the additional month ; if we make one year longer than
" another by that month, to make the time accord, the additional
" months belonging to thofe years will be thirty-five, and the
" days 1050,—whereof one is not in all things like another. So
" that every man, O Crefus, is miferable ! You appear to me
" very rich, and is king over many ; but the queftion you de-
" mand I cannot refolve, until I heard you have ended your days
" happily ; he that hath much wealth is not happier than he
" who gets his living from day to day, unlefs fortune continuing
" all thofe good things to him, grant that he die well. There
" are many men very rich, yet unfortunate; many of mode-
" rate eftates, fortunate ; of whom he who abounds in wealth,
" and is not happy, exceeds the fortunate only in two things,
" the other him in many ; the rich is more able to fatisfy his
" defires, and to overcome great injuries ; yet the fortunate
" excels him. He cannot indeed inflict hurt on others, and fa-
" tisfy his own defires; his good fortune debars him of thofe :
" But he is free from evils, healthful, happy in his children,
" and beautiful ; if to this, a man dies well, that is, he whom
" you feek, who deferves to be called happy ; before death
" he cannot be ftiled happy, but fortunate ; yet for one man
" to obtain all this is impoffible, as one country cannot fur-
" nifh itfelf with all things: Some it hath, others it wants ;
" that which hath moft is beft, fo in men not one is perfect ;
" what one hath the other wants. He who hath conftantly
" moft, and at laft quietly departs this life, in my opinion, O
" king, deferves to bear that name. In every thing we muft
" have regard to the end, whither it tends ; for many to whom
" God difpenfeth all good fortunes, he at laft utterly fubverts."
Thus we fee the whole paffage, in which it is evident that Solon meant only, that to make a man happy, it is requifite he
continue in the enjoyment of a competency till death, and that
then he die well, that is, quietly and in good refpect or credit
with men. That this is the meaning of *dying well* according
to Solon, is not only evident from the ftrain of the difcourfe,

but from the ſtories of Tellus, Cleobis and Bito, whom he inſtances as happy men, becauſe of their creditable deaths. The firſt he tells us died in defence of his country, after he had put his enemies to flight, " he died nobly, and the Athenians buried him in the place where he fell, with much honour." The two brothers, Cleobis and Bito, drew their mother's chariot forty-five ſtadia, and with the ſtreſs died next morning in the temple, and ſo died honourably. And any that will give himſelf the trouble to read Ovid's ſtory of Acteon, in his third book of his Metamorph. will ſee it clear as the day, that he meant juſt the ſame. He repreſents how happy one might have thought Cadmus, conſidering how many things he had that were deſirable in his lot, a kingdom, relations, and children, had not Acteon his grand-child's fate interrupted the ſeries of his joys, and made him miſerable. Whereupon the poet concludes, " Till death a man cannot be called happy ;" that is, till a man has without interruption, enjoyed a tract of proſperity, and dies creditably, without any mixture of ill fortune.

Jam ſtabant Thebæ: Poteras jam Cadme, videri
Exilio felix: Soreceri tibi Marſque Venuſque
Contigerant: Huc adde genus de conjuge tanta,
Tot natos, nataſque, & pignera cara nepotes.
Hos quoque jam juvenes: ſed ſcilicet ultima ſemper
Expectanda dies homini eſt, dicique beatus
Ante obitum nemo, ſupremaque funera debet.
Prima nepos inter res tot tibi Cadme, ſecundas
Cauſa fuit luctus, &c. *

And thus he proceeds to tell the ſtory of Acteon's being transformed into a hart. Thus we ſee with what candor our author quotes the Heathens. Here he has firſt broke off ſome words from their context, whereby the unwary reader is tempted

* Ovid. Metamorph. Lib. 3.—" And now Thebes was built ; now
" O Cadmus, you might ſeem to be happy in your baniſhment. Mars,
" and Venus was your father and mother in law ; add to this, a race
" from ſo illuſtrious a conſort, ſo many ſons and daughters, and grand-
" children, dear pledges, and theſe too already youths; but truly a
" man muſt always look for his laſt day, and nobody can be called
" happy before his death, and laſt funeral rites. Amidſt ſo much proſ-
" perity, O Cadmus, a grandſon was the firſt cauſe of mourning to you."

ted to believe, that the speaker meant quite another thing than really he did ; and then obtrudes this false sense of one or two men's words, who were wise men, and in their thoughts far above the vulgar, as the harmonious meaning of the Gentile world.

Nor do I think it strange that our author should serve us so, seeing he was prepossessed in favour of the Heathen's religion before he began to read their books. For he tells us in the entry of his book, the very first sentence of it, and more fully in the rest of the first chapter, That he was at once very concerned for the *divine providence*, and withal fully convinced that it could not not be maintained without there were a *religion common to all men*; or, as his words formerly quoted by us express it, " Unless every man was provided with the means that " were needful for attaining future happiness ;" so he went to the books of the Heathens under a persuasion that there was a *common religion* there, could he be so lucky as to light on it, and therefore no doubt he drew and strained things to his purpose, both rites and words. Thus he begins his discourse about expiation : " Quosdam Gentilium ritus, qui in sensum sani-" orem trahi possunt, jam tractaturus*," &c. And indeed he draws them to a sounder sense than ever they put on them. But, after all, *forced prayers are not good for the soul*, says the Scots proverb. And from one thus prepossessed, we can expect no fair account of the Gentile's sentiments.

Which, by the way, gives me occasion to remark, that if any one desires to understand the mind of the Heathen philosophers and sages, they should read them themselves, or Heathen's accounts of their lives and actions, rather than those done by Christians ; because very often when Christians write their lives, they have some design, and they strain every thing in the philosophers to a compliance either with their designs or apprehensions. The Heathen writers being under no influence from the scripture light, do plainly narrate things as they are, (not being so sensible of what things may reflect really upon the persons concerning whom they write ; the light of nature not representing clearly that wickedness which is in many of their actions and opinions) and scruple not to tell them out plainly :
whereas

---

* De Rel. Gent. pag. 195.—" Being now about to treat of some " rites of the Heathens, which may be drawn into a sound sense."

whereas Chriſtians, being aware how odious ſuch and ſuch
practices or principles are, dare ſcarce tell ſuch things of thoſe
famous men, as they were really guilty of; becauſe they know
how deep a ſtain it will leave on them, by thoſe who are taught
the evil of them by the ſcriptures.

I ſhall add this reflection more : If any one would conclude
from our author's confidence in ſome places of his book, where
he talks of many reaſons that he has advanced, and that he has
demonſtrated this and that ; if, I ſay, from this they would infer, that he was fully perſuaded in his own mind, about theſe
five articles, that they *univerſally obtained*, and are *ſufficient*,
he would very far miſtake our author, who, throughout his
book, ſufficiently betrays his *uncertainty* about them, and that
he wanted not a *fear* left it ſhould not be true, as ſome things
afterwards to be pleaded will ſhow. But leaſt this ſhould ſeem
to be ſaid altogether without ground, I ſhall ſingle out one in-
ſtance of our author's wavering in this matter, reſerving others
to another occaſion. It is pag. 19, where, after our author has
diſcourſed of the *more famous names* of the *true God*, and ſhewed that the Gentiles applied them all, ſave one, to the *ſun*, he
concludes thus, " Hæc ſaltem fuere ſolenniora ſummi Dei no-
" mina inter Hebræos extantia, quæ etiam ad ſolem, Sabazio
" excepto, a Gentilibus reducta fuiſſe, ex ſupra-allatis conjec-
" turam facere licet. Adeo ut quamvis ſuperius ſole numen
" ſub hiſce præcertim vocabulis coluerunt Hebræi, ſolem ne-
" que aliud numen intellexerunt Gentiles, niſi fortaſſe in ſole,
" tanquem præclaro Dei ſummi ſpecimme, & ſenſibili ejus,
" ut Plato vocat, ſimulacro, Deum ſummum ab illis cultum
" fuiſſe cenſeas : Quod non facile abnuerim, præſertim
" cum ſymbolica fuerit omnis feré religio veterum *." But
perhaps

---

* De Rel. Gent. pag. 19.—" Thoſe at leaſt were the more ſolemn
" names of the Supreme God, that we find among the Hebrews; all
" which except Sabazino, we may conjecture from what has been quo-
" ted above, was applied by the Gentiles to the ſun. So that although
" the Hebrews worſhipped a deity ſuperior to the ſun, eſpecially un-
" der theſe names, yet the Gentiles underſtood by them the ſun, and
" no other deity, unleſs perhaps in the ſun, as an illuſtrious repreſen-
" tation and ſenſible image, of the Supreme God, as Plato calls him,
" under which figure we may ſuppoſe that the Supreme God was wor-
" ſhipped by them. Which I would not eaſily contradict, eſpecially
" as almoſt all the religion of the ancients was ſymbolical."

perhaps though our author was not well confirmed in his opinion, when he began his book, yet he came to some more fixedness before he got to the end of it. Well, let us hear him, in his censure of the Gentile's religion in the last chapter of his book, where speaking of the worshipping the heavens, the sun, &c. he gives his judgment thus: " De hoc quidem dog-
" mate, idem ac de priore censeo: Nempe, nisi symbolicus
" fuerit, erroneum mihi prorsus videri cultum illum. Cæte-
" rum quod symbolici fuerunt olum hujusmodi cultus, multæ,
" quas supra adduximus, suadere videntur rationes: Sed suo·
" judicio heic quoque utatur lector *." What more uncertainty could any betray, than our author doth in these words? And indeed here we have enough to overthrow his whole book: for if this first article fall all will fall with it, as we may see afterwards.

But it is now time that we draw to a conclusion of this chapter, having sufficiently enervated our author's arguments, so far as we could discern them. If any of them seem to be omitted, I presume they will be found to be of no great consideration, and of an easy dispatch to any that is acquainted with this controversy. Our author's way of writing made it somewhat difficult to find his arguments. And indeed upon serious reflection, I can scarce understand at what our author aimed in this way of writing. He could never rationally expect that this would clear the subject he had undertaken. I had almost concluded that his design behooved to be an ostentation of knowledge of the Heathen's religion, in order to make his authority have the more weight, and to scare people from entertaining a different opinion concerning the religion of the Heathen world, from that which one who had so industriously searched into their writings, owned. But if this was it, our author has missed it. And I think instead of doing the Deists' cause any service this way, he has rather hurt it: for every one that shall peruse this work with attention, and find how

great

---

* De Relig. Gent. pag. 223.—" Concerning this doctrine indeed,
" I' am of the same opinion as concerning the former, to wit, that
" unless that worship was symbolical, it seems to me to have been
" quite erroneous. But the many reasons which we have addu-
" ced above, seem to persuade us to believe that worship of this kind
" of old was symbolical. But let the reader use his own judgment in
" this case likewise."

great our author's learning, diligence and induſtry have been, and yet how little he has been able to do, they will infer the weakneſs of the cauſe he has undertaken, and conclude, that the cauſe could bear no better defence, and that therefore a weak and indefencible cauſe has baffled our author's great abilities and application. For

——————— *ſi Pergama dextrâ
Defendi poſſent, etiam hac defenſa fuiſſent.**

C. Blount and they who have come after our author, as has been ſaid before, do but copy after him, and take his notions upon truſt, but others will be ſomewhat more wiſe, and will look whom they truſt in a matter of this importance.

CHAP. XV.

Wherein it is made appear that Herbert's Five Articles did not univerſally obtain.

WE have in the preceding chapter ſufficiently ſhewed how weak our noble author's proofs are of his *univerſal religion.* It now remains that we prove that what he pretends is indeed falſe. Our work here is far more eaſy, than what our author undertook. He aſſerts that *providence* cannot be maintained, unleſs all mankind are provided in the means needful for attaining future happineſs, and he is likewiſe clear, that leſs cannot be allowed ſufficient for this end than the five articles mentioned, wherefore he pretends that all the world agreed in owning theſe. Now to have made this laſt appear, it was needful it ſhould be proven by induction of all particular nations, that they thus agreed, and that as to all times; but this would have been ſomewhat too laborious. We maintain that all did not agree in the acknowledgment of thoſe five articles; And this is evinced, if we can ſhew only one nation diſſenting from any one of them. But we ſhall not be ſo nice upon the point, as only to mention *one nation*, or diſprove *one article.* Let us take a ſeparate view of each article, and ſee what the judgment of ſome nations were concerning them.

ARTICLE

* " ————If Troy could have been defended by any right hand, it
" would have been defended by this one."

ARTICLE I.

All the World did not agree in owning the One True Supreme GOD.

I MIGHT for proof of this, only defire any perfon to read our author's book, and there he would find this fufficiently clear. But I fhall fhortly co 1firm it to the conviction of any, who has not a mind to fhut his eyes, by the few following obfervations as to the fentiments of the world in this cafe.

1. It is moft evident to any one, who will give himfelf the trouble to read never fo little of the writings of the Gentiles, that many nations, I had almoft faid moft nations, did hold *a plurality of eternal and independent beings*, on whom they depended, and which they called gods in the propereft fenfe of the word. Herodotus quoted by our author tells us, " That all " the Africans worfhip the fun and moon only"—" Soli & " lunæ folummodo facrificant, & quidem Afri univerfi *." And Plato quoted likewife by our author, a few pages after, in his dialogue, which he calls Cratylus, tells us, " Qui Græciam " primi incoluêre, ii videntur mihi illos f lum deos exiftimafie, " quos nunc etiam barbari multi, pro diis habent, folem, lu- " nam, terram, aftra, cœlum †." Of this alfo the ancient infcriptions mentioned by our author‡, and more particularly by Hornbeck in his treatife *de Converfione Gentilium*, is a proof.— " Soli invicto & lunæ æternæ deo foli invicto Mythræ & om- " nipotenti deo Mythræ ||." Mythras was a name given to the fun by the Perfians, as our author proves. And if we may believe Maimonides, the Sabeans owned no God fave the ftars. " Notum eft Abrahamum patrem noftrum educatum effe in fide " Sabæorum, qui ftatuerunt nullum effe Deum, præter ftellas§.

Nor

* De Rel. Gent. pag. 36.

† Ibid. pag. 39.—" Thofe who firft inhabited Greece, appear to " me to have thought that thefe alone were gods, which many barba- " rians ftill hold to be gods, to wit, the fun, the moon, the earth, " the ftars, the heaven."

‡ Ibid. pag 26. || Hornbeck, pag. 19.

§ More Nevochim, referente. Hornbec ubi fupra. pag. 17.—" It " is well known that our father Abraham was educated in the faith of " the Sabeans, who thought that there was no God except the ftars."

Nor were the Egyptians of another mind. Diodorus's testimony is worth our notice to this purpose,—" Igitur primi illi homires " olim in Ægypto geniti, hinc mundi ornatum conspicientes, " admiranteique universorum naturam, duos esse deos, & eos " æternos arbitratri sunt, solem & lunam: Et illum quidem " Osiridem, hanc Isidim certa nominis ratione appellarunt *."

Thus we see what the apprehensions of several nations were, and how harmonious they are in dissenting from our author's assertion. It had been easy to have alleged many more testimonies even from our author against himself: But we aim at brevity.

2. It is not improbable, that some nations, though they might allow some priority of one of their gods to the rest yet did not think that there was any such great inequality, at least amongst their more notable deities, as could infer the supremacy of one to the rest, and their dependence on, and subordination to him. We find every where equal honours paid, equal or very little different titles of respect given to the sun or moon. So that it is very likely, though they might give the sun the preference in point of order, yet they did not apprehend any such great inequality, as seems needful betwixt one *supreme being* and his *dependents*. The people of Mexico in America, though they worship many gods, yet look on their two principal ones, whom they call *Vitzilopuchtli* and *Tezcatlipuca*, as two brothers. " *Mexicani primo colere soliti fuerunt immanem deorum turbam,* " *bis mille referunt, inter quos duo præcipui Vitzilopuchtli & Tez-* " *catlipuca duo fratres, quorum alter rerum providentiæ, alter* " *bellis præerat*†." And the inhabitants of Darien, St. Martha and other places thereabout, own only the sun, and the moon as his wife. Further, it is owned by our author several times,

that

---

* Owen Theolog. Lib. 3. Cap. 5. Herbert pag. 39.—" Therefore " those first men that were produced in Egypt, observing from thence " the beauty of the world, and admiring the nature of the universe, " concluded that there were two gods, the sun and the moon, and " they called the one Osiri, and the other Isis, giving certain reasons " for those names."

† Hornbeck, pag. 70.—" The Mexicans at first used to worship an " immense number of gods, to wit, two thousand, the chief among " which were Vitzilopuchtli and Tezcatlipuca, two brothers, the one " of whom had the care of the world, and the other presided over " wars."

that many nations hold two firſt beings, one *good* and another *evil*, whom they called *Ve-Jupiter*, and by the Perſian Magi he was called *Arimanius*. Though our author thinks a ſofter conſtruction is to be put on their meaning, than to charge them with making their Ve-Jupiter equal with the good God*: But we know our author muſt not be allowed to interpret, unleſs he can give good grounds for his opinion about the meaning of the Gentiles, which in this caſe he doth not once attempt, and we know that ſome looked on this *wicked principle* as the *ſupreme*, as we ſhall ſhow anon; and I think it will be hard to clear ſome of them, yea even no leſs a perſon than Plutarch, from making them *equal* and both *infinite;* if we may believe a late author, who tells us, " That as for Plutarch, one of the ſobereſt of the " philoſophers, he was the horrideſt Polytheiſt of them all; for " he aſſerts two Supreme Anti-gods; one infinitely good, and " the oth r infinitely evil.†" Moreover, ſome of the Deiſts do not think this opinion deſtitute of probability, as we have noted before‡. But whatever there is as to this, yet,

3. It is certain that many of them, notwithſtanding the huge number of gods they maintained, were utterly ignorant of the *true God*. This is ſo evident, that I cannot but wonder at our author's impudence in denying it, eſpecially, after the teſtimonies we have already quoted from him. We have heard already that the Egyptians and Grecians of old owned no other gods beſides the ſun, moon and ſtars. And we have heard the fame of the Sabeans, ſeveral Americans and inhabitants of Africa; and Ceſar tells us the fame of the Germans—" *Deo-* " *rum numero eos ſolum ducunt, quos cernunt, & quorum opi-* " *bus aperte juvamur, ſolem & vulcanum & lunam; reliquos ne* " *fama quidem acceperunt.*§" Yea, our author is forced to make a fair confeſſion, and contradict himſelf in the entry of his fourth chapter, where ſpeaking of the Gentiles and their worſhipping of the ſun, he delivers himſelf thus: " *Incongru-* " *um demum exiſtimaverant, ut qui cultum ab omnibus flagitaret,*
" *a cul-*

---

* De Relig. Gent. pag. 163. † Nichol's Confer. Part 2. pag. 57.
‡ Oracles of Reaſon. pag. 194.
§ De Bello Gallico, Lib. 6.—" They reckon in the number of the " gods only thoſe whom they ſee, and by whoſe power they are evi- " dently aſſiſted, that is, the ſun, the fire, and the moon. They have " not ſo much as heard of the other gods."

" *a cultoribus suis sese absconderet Deus. Solem igitur Deum*
" *fere omnes Gentiles statuebant, non summum quidem, sed sum-*
" *mo proximum, ejusque preclarissimam iconem, licet alii mun-*
" *dum totum, tanquam Deo plenum, summi numinis imaginem*
" *speciosam apprime præ se ferre contenderent***.*" Here you see
our author positive, that they put not the sun in the room of the
One true God: None of them did it; but we shall hear him
in the very next sentence tell us, that they did discard the true
God, and very absurdly put another in his place. " *Certe uti*
" *olim dictum* (says our author) *qui solem vice summi Dei colue-*
" *runt, perinde fecere, ac illi qui ad aulam potentissimi princi-*
" *pis accedentes, quem primum amictu splendido indutum cer-*
" *nerent, regium illi cultum deferendum existimaverant*†." And
our author knows full well that at Athens there was an altar erected to *the unknown God*; and Paul expressly tells them, that this
unknown God, was the *true God. Whom therefore ye ignorantly worship, him declare I unto you.* What says our author
to this? He directly contradicts the apostle, and then makes
him a compliment, that is well nigh to nonsense. " Cœte-
" rum, (says he) duriusculè Deus ignotus Atheniensium ad De-
" um Judæorum refertur: Ut ita priora S. S. loca Deum Gen-
" tilium eundum ac communem omnium Deum evincant. Nam
" Deus ille ignotus Atheniensium alius certè fuit, (this is a
" plain contradiction to the apostle's assertion) atque ideo puto
" arâ donatus, ne aliquis forsan incultus apud illos esset Deus:
" Ut bellè tamen hinc instruendi Gentiles occasionem captarit
" apostolus. Neque dubium mihi est, quin e libro naturæ
" edocti Deum summum tum agnoverint, tum coluerint Gen-
" tiles.

* De Relig. Gent. pag. 20.—" In fine, they reckoned it incon-
" gruous to suppose, that God, who required worship from all men,
" should hide himself from his worshippers. Therefore almost all the
" Heathens thought that the sun was a god; not indeed the supreme
" one, but next to the supreme, and his most illustrious Image; al-
" though others maintained that the whole world, as being full of God,
" bore a distinct impression of his image."

† " Surely, as was said long ago, those who worshipped the sun in-
" stead of the Supreme Deity, acted in the same manner as those who
" going to the court of a most powerful prince, should think that the
" first person they saw splendidly dressed was the king, and to be re-
" verenced as such."

" tiles*." Thus we see *quam bellè*, how pleasantly our author proceeds. He tells us that it is hard to think, though the apostle expresly says so, that this *unknown God* was the God of the Jews. But if we will not stand to our author's word, then he tells us what some scriptures he had formerly cited prove; viz. Acts x. *passim* Acts xvii. 28, 29. Rom. i. 19. But we have above shewed, that these are not for our author's purpose. We.l, what then remains? Nothing, but only this, " I have no doubt," says he, " but they knew the true God." But our author's certainty will not satisfy another; and we just now shewed, that our author was not so fully sure as he pretends to be in this place. But yet our apostle, he tells us, took very handsomely occasion hence to instruct the Gentiles; that is, if we believe our author, he took occasion from a false suppofition to instruct them. But it is a kindness that he used any compliment, though a ridiculous one. But leaving this, I go on.

4. They among the nations, who owned One Supreme God, did frequently, if not for most part, put some others in the room of the true God. Some made the World God. This is what Balbus the Stoick sets up for with all his might in Cecero's second book *de Nat. Deor.* throughout. " Atqui certè nihil
" omnium rerum melius est, Mundo, nihil præstabilius, nihil
" pulchrius: Nec solum nihil est, sed ne cogitari quidem quic-
" quam melius potest: Et si ratione & sapientiâ nihil est meli-
" us, necesse est hæc inesse in eo, quod optimum esse conce-
" dimus †:" And therefore a little after he concludes the *world*
God

---

* " It was rather somewhat hard to refer the unknown God of the
" Athenians to the God of the Jews, as the former places of holy
" scripture prove that the God of the Gentiles was the same with that
" of the Jews, and the common God of all men. For this unknown
" God of the Athenians was certainly another one, and I suppose was
" honoured with an altar for this reason, that no god perhaps might
" be without worship among them. Yet how prettily does the apos-
" tle take an opportunity from hence of instructing the Gentiles. Nor
" is it doubtful with me, that the Gentiles, taught by the book of
" nature, both acknowledged and worshipped the supreme God."

† " And certainly none of all things is better than the World, no-
" thing is more excellent, nothing is more beautiful; and not only
" nothing exists, but nothing can be imagined that is better than the
" World. And if nothing is better than Reason and Wisdom, these
" qualities must necessarily be conceived to belong to that which we
" acknowledge to be the best of all things."

God. Cicero himself was of the same mind: For, when Velleius the Epicurean had been heard and refuted by Cotta the academick; and Epicurus's wild opinions about the gods, had been fully exposed, which is the subject of the first book; Balbus the Stoick proposes and defends the Stoicks' opinion about the nature, being, and number of the gods, and their providence, and defends it after the best manner he can, (where, by the way, there is not one word of the *true God*, but a full discovery of the grossest ignorance of him, and the greatest wickedness and folly in asserting a plurality of gods, and parting all the excellencies of the true God among them). This makes up the second book. In the third book Cotta the academick, disputes against, and exposes the Stoicks' opinions, as defended by Balbus; and in the last sentence of the book, Cicero gives his ἐπίκρισις or censure of the whole in these words, " Hæc cum essent dicta, ita discessimus, ut Velleio Cottæ dispu-" tatio verior, mihi Balbi ad veritatis similitudinem videretur " esse propensior *." Velleius the Epicurean favours Cotta, who disproved the whole opinions about the gods, and put no better in their place. And Cicero was pleased with Balbus, who maintaned the Stoicks' sentiments. What they were we have just now noted. And whether Plato, Aristotle, yea and Socrates were not of this opinion, is not so very clear. Certain it is, that they paid a little too great respect to the *world*, if they were not. Let us hear our author. *Plato in timæo et legibus dicit & mundum deum esse & cœlum & astra, &c.*† But whatever were their sentiments, it is not of so great consequence to the question under consideration, to spend time in inquiring, since it is evident that many were of this opinion. Others thought that the *heaven* was God, and this is owned by Ennius the poet, quoted by our author, in that noted verse so frequently mentioned by Cicero, *Aspice hoc sublime candens, quem omnes invocant Jovem* ‡. And there also he tells us of an old inscription found at Rome, *Optimus Maximus cælus æternus*. Thus we see the heavens dignified with those very epithets, which our author pretends to have been peculiar to the Supreme God. And he tells us, that some are of opinion, that

---

* " When those things had been said, we parted, but so that the " discourse of Cotta seemed to Velleius to be truer, but that of Bal-" bus seemed to me to approach more nearly to the likeness of truth."
† De Relig. Gent. pag. 39.   ‡ Ibid, pag. 54.

that Pythagoras inclined this way: and our author leaves it in doubt. If Ariſtotle and Plato were not of this mind, that the heavens were the Supreme God, as we ſee ſome others were; yet they did own heaven for God, and to be worſhipped as ſuch. " *Sed non ſolummodi cælum divino honore colendum decreverant ſacerdotes, ſed et ipſi philoſophi celebriores, adeo ut non Stagirita tantum, ſed Emiuus ejus præceptor ita ſtatuerint* *.*" But the moſt prevalent opinion was, *that the ſun was the one true and Supreme God*.—That many, and perhaps moſt nations thought ſo, the teſtimonies above alleged fully prove, and we have heard our author confeſſing it as to ſome. I ſhall only add a few remarks more to this purpoſe. There is a qoutation of Macrobius, which I find in our author, that is worth noticing, " Aſſyrii (inquit Macr.) quem Deum ſummum maximumq; " venerantur, Adad nomen dederunt, ejus nominis interpæta- " tio ſignificat unus. Hunc ergo ut potentiſſimum adorant De- " um, ſed ſubjungunt deam nomine Atergatin; omnemque po- " teſtatem hiſce duobus attribuunt, ſolem teramque intelligen- " tes †." And our author further acquaints us as to the Perſians, " Quod Perſæ duo principia ſtatuebant, Oromazen ſcil. tanquem " boni fontem: Et Arimanium, mali.—Inter quos medium & " quaſi arbitrum poſuere ſolem ‡." I have in the cloſe of our former chapter, quoted a notable paſſage from our author to the ſame purpoſe, wherein he tells us, that all the names of the true God, were aſcribed to the ſun. Of the ſame opinion were the Phenicians, Britains of old, and their famed Druides, and perhaps moſt nations. Yea, ſo deeply did this fix its roots in the minds of moſt, that the greateſt among the Heathen philoſophers

---

* De Rel. Gent. pag. 19.—" But not only were the prieſts of opin-
" ion that the heaven ought to be worſhipped with divine honours,
" but alſo the moſt famous philoſophers, ſo that not only the Stagyrite
" but his maſter before him, was of that opinion."

† Ibid. pag. 24.—" The Aſſyrians, ſays Macrobius, gave the name
" Adad, which ſignifies *one*, to that Being whom they held to be the
" ſupreme and greateſt God. Therefore they adore him as the moſt
" powerful God, but they add to him a goddeſs named Atergatis, and
" aſcribe all power to theſe two, meaning the ſun and the earth."

‡ Ibid. pag. 28.—" That the Perſians hold two firſt principles, to
" wit, Aromazes as the fountain of good, and Arimanius of evil, be-
" twixt whom they placed the ſun in the middle, and as it were an
" arbiter."

sophers can scarce be freed from an inclination this way *. Plato tells us, how devout Socrates was in the worship of the sun, and that several times he fell into an extasy, while thus employed.† Nor are the famous Indian philosophers one whit more wise. "Not only the Brachmans, but all the Indians, "yea and the famed Appollonius (whom the Heathens compar- "ed to our blessed Lord, most blasphemously and groundlesly) "worshipped the sun ‡." And we have Appollonius's prayer to the sun, recorded by Philostratus in his life, Lib. 1. *O summe sol, eó me terrarum mitte, quo me projecturum esse cognoscis, & concede, precor, ut viros bonos, agnoscam; improbos vero neq, agnoscam, neq; agnoscar ab illis* §. Yea after the light of the glorious gospel had cleared the philosopher's eyes, and made them ashamed of much of their religion, yet even the Platonick philosophers could not quit the thoughts of the sun's being God.‖"

But not only did some look on the sun as the Supreme God; but (if we may believe Hornbeck, who was at great pains to understand the religions of the world, and particularly of America) several nations in America, particularly the inhabitants of New-France, and they who inhabit about the river Sagadahoc, worship principally the devil or a malignant spirit.'*

Thus we have fully demonstrated what we undertook, and hereby quite spoiled the whole story of an universal religion: And our author has been so unhappy, as to lay to our hands many of the arguments, whereby we have disproved his own position. This step being once gained, we shall be more brief in the consideration of the remaining articles: For they all fall with this. If there is a mistake as to this, there can remain nothing sincere in religion. If the *true God* is not *known*, he cannot be *worshipped*, and *rewards* and *punishments* cannot be *expected* from him; nor can we be sensible of, or sorry for any

offence

* This is fully proven by Dr. Owen, Hornbeck and others, in their books formerly referred to.
† See Owen's Theolog. Lib. 3. Cap. 4. pag. 182.
‡ Hornbeck pag. 31.
§ "O supreme sun, send me to that part of the world, to which "you know I am going, and grant, I pray, that I may know good "men, but that I may neither know bad man, nor be known by them."
‖ Owen ubi supra. Lib. 3. Cap. 5. pag. 194.
** Hornbeck de Conver. Gentil. Lib. 1. Cap. 9. pag. 70, 71.

offence done againſt him. So that we might ſtop here, as having ruined wholly that cauſe our author undertook to defend: But we ſhall conſider the reſt alſo.

ARTICLE II.

It was not univerſally agreed that the One True God is to be worſhipp'd.

HOW could they agree as to the worſhipping him whom they did know to be? If it would not frighten the perſons concerned, I might here pertinently aſk them the queſtion the apoſtle puts, Rom. x. 14. *How ſhall they call on him, in whom they have not believed? And how ſhall they believe in him, of whom they have not heard?*

And further, even they who owned one ſupreme God, many of them entertained ſuch notions of him, as made him unworthy of any worſhip. He tells us that many of them locked him up in heaven, denying his providence; and one would almoſt think our author had been of their opinion, while he tells us, " *Rectè dictum eſt olim, quod æternum beatumque eſt nec* " *negotii quicquam habere, nec exhiberi alteri*[*]." But whatever our author's thoughts were, it is well known, that this opinion prevailed very far, and obtained amongſt many, if not moſt nations, who owned one ſupreme God beſides the ſun. And they were further of opinion, that God had committed the whole management of the world to deputies. Our author informs us, that the ancient Heathens divided their gods into *ſuper-celeſtial, celeſtial,* and *ſub-celeſtial*[†]; and he tells us, that the chief god, and his companions the ſuper-celeſtial gods, have not any ſuch concernment in, or regard to the things that are tranſacted in this world, as to make them take any notice of them; and that the Supreme God has withdrawn himſelf and the ſuper-celeſtial gods from the view of mortals, as being of too ſublime a nature to be known by them: and that he has deputed the ſun, moon, and ſtars to inſpect the world, as the only gods who can be enjoyed by men. " Deum ſummum vero ſeipſum
ſuper-

[*] De Relig. Gent. pag. 174.—" It was well ſaid of old, that a being " that is eternal and happy, neither has any trouble in itſelf, nor gives " any trouble to another."
[†] Ibid, pag. 170.

"supercœleſteſq; Deos a conſpectu mortalium removiſſe, quod "ſublimis adeo eſſent naturæ, ut nulla eos acies fatis portinge- "ret, ejus loco non in conſpectum ſolùm, ſed in fruitionem "quandam produxiſſe deos illos cœleſtes, qui a nobis ſol, lu- "na, cœlum, &c. vocantur*." And the Indian Brachmins ſeem indeed to be of the ſame mind, as we know the whole followers of Epicurus were†. Yea, the inhabitants of Calecut, a kingdom in the Eaſt-Indies, are ſo abſurd as to imagine that the devil is God's deputy, to whom the government of the world is committed. And hence they worſhip the devil principally, (as likewiſe do the kingdoms of Decum and Narſinga) and "their king has in his oratory the image of the devil with "a crown on his head, ſo very frightful, that the moſt reſo- "lute tremble at the ſight of it: the wall is all painted "with leſſer devils; and in each corner ſtands one of braſs, "ſo well done, that it ſeems all in flames‡." Now if ſuch notions are entertained of God, it is no wonder though he be by many thought not worth the worſhipping. The conſequences of thoſe apprehenſions I cannot better expreſs, than Cicero has done in the very beginning of his firſt book *de Nat. Deorum.* "Sunt enim philoſophi, & fuerunt, qui omnino nul- "lam habere cenſerent humanarum rerum procurationem deos: "Quorum ſi vera ſententia eſt, quæ poteſt eſſe pietas? Quæ "ſanctitas? Quæ religio? ſi deii neque poſſunt nos juvare, "nec volunt, nec curant omnino, nec quid agamus animad- "vertant; nec eſt quod ab his ad hominum vitam permanare "poſſit: Quod eſt, quod ullos diis immortalibus cultus, hono- "res, preces adhibeamus §?" And much more to the ſame purpoſe.

* De Relig. Gent. pag. 171.—"But that the ſupreme God had "withdrawn himſelf and the other ſuper-celeſtial gods from the ſight "of mortals, becauſe they were of ſo ſublime a nature that no human "eye could ſufficiently reach them; but that he had ſet up in his place, "not only for our knowledge, but fruition, thoſe celeſtial gods, which "are called by us the ſun, the moon, the heaven, &c."

† Hornbeck, pag. 40.

‡ See *Calecut*, in Great. Geograph. Diction.

§ "For there are and have been philoſophers, who think th t the "gods take no care at all of human affairs, and if their opinion be "true, what piety can there be? or what ſanctity? what religion? "if the gods neither can, nor will help us, nor obſerve what we do; "nor is there any thing that can come from them into human life. "What reaſon is there then, why we ſhould offer any worſhip, ho- "nours or prayers to the immortal gods?"

purpose. Though he speaks of a plurality of gods, yet what he says holds true as to the case in hand: for if we entertain, or if the Gentiles did entertain, as we see some of them did, such notions of their supreme God, as he here speaks of, the same consequences must follow; and it is not credible that any, who thought so, could judge the supreme God worthy of worship. And indeed we find them no way concerned about it.

In fine, not a few of the wiser, who entertained the most just thoughts of God of any, yet being in the dark as to the way of worshipping God, have declared against any worship, at least in practice, till it should by himself be condescended on. Thus it is as to the wiser sort among the Chinese—"De Deo " eoque colendo non sunt soliciti. Unum quidem agnoscunt " summum numen, a quo omnia conservari & regi credunt : " Sed, quia quomodo coli velit, ignorare se profitentur ; sa- " tius autumant cultum ejus omittere, quam in eo designando " errare*." And perhaps the best philosophers in other nations were not of a different mind. Thus we see how far they were from being agreed about this article.

ARTICLE III.

The Gentile World were not agreed in judging that Virtue and Piety are the principal parts of the worship of God.

HOW it should come into our author's head to think that they were agreed, is a little strange, considering how little is to be found among their writers that looks this way. But I suppose the case was this, he had concluded that they were agreed about the *being* of *one true God*, and to make his religion complete he behoved to have them some way agreed about his *worship* too. But he found them endlessly divided about their solemn worship, and none of it directed to the one true God, but all expressly aimed at other things: wherefore there was no other thing left that could be to his purpose; and therefore he

finding

* Hornbeck ubi supra, pag. 47.—" They have no anxiety about " God or his worship. They acknowledge indeed one Supreme Dei- " ty, by whom they think that all things are preserved and governed ; " but as they profess that they do not know in what manner he chuses " to be worshipped, they think it better to let alone his worship al- " together, than to err in determining it."

finding that there was somewhat that all the world agreed in, paying some respect to, at least, in words, under the name of *virtue*; he would needs appropriate this to the true God for his worship, though he has no warrant from the Gentiles to do so. And truly after all, if this was the worship of the true God, or designed as such, whatever agreement there might be in opinion about the worship of the one true God, I think there was none in *practice*, if not in a total neglect of it: For how few were there, who can have the least pretence to challenge that name amongst all those, whose names have been transmitted to us! How true was the poet Juvenal's observation,

> *Rari quippe boni, numero vix sunt totidem quot*
> *Thebarum portæ, divitis vel ostia Nili* *.

But to leave this, and come to the point in hand somewhat more closely,

1. It is evident that the world was very far from being agreed, that there is *one God*: Far more were they divided about the acknowledgment of the true God, and whom they should own as such. It was therefore utterly impossible that they should condescend on this, as a principal part of the worship of God, whom they did not know to have any being.

2. So far were they from looking on virtue as the principal part of the worship of the gods, whom they owned, that the worship of many of their gods, was thought to consist in things that were cross to the plainest dictates of nature's light. Our author acquaints us frequently with the obscenities, the cruelties, and other extravagancies of their worship. The obscenities are too fulsome to be repeated. The furious extravagancies, religious, or rather superstitious fury and madness used in the worship of Bacchus, are known to every one. And for their cruelty, who knows not that human sacrifices were almost universally used? Some offered captives, some offered strangers, some sacrificed their dearest relations and children, and that in the most cruel manner †.

3. We need go no further than our author's book, to learn, that most nations were so far from looking on virtue as any part
of

---

* " For good men are rare, and scarcely as numerous as the gates
" of Thebes, or the mouths of the feeble Nile."

† See this fully proven in the learned and excellent Dr. Owen's treatise *de Justitia vindicatrice*, from pag. 66 to 100, by authentic testimonies, with such remarks as may be worth the reading.

of the worſhip due to any of thoſe gods they owned, that they placed it wholly in ſuch other things, as our author, amongſt others, has given us a large account of.

4. They, who were moſt zealous for virtue, were very far from looking on it as a part of the worſhip of God, or directing it to his glory. I believe our author, were he alive, for all his reading would find it difficult to find one fair teſtimony to this purpoſe. They looked not on themſelves as debtors to God for their virtue. Hence Cotta, after he has acknowledged that we are indebted to God for our riches and eternal enjoyments, adds; "Virtutem autem nemo unquam acceptam Deo " retulit, nimirum recté: Propter virtutem enim laudantur, & " in virtute recté gloriamur; quod non contingeret, ſi id donum " a Deo haberemus." Hence a little after, he adds, " Nam quis " quod bonus vir eſſet, gratias diis egit unquam *!" And much more to the ſame purpoſe. They thought that their virtue made them equal to their gods. " Hoc eſt quod philoſophia mi- " hi promittit, ut me parem Deo faciat.†" Yea not only ſo, but they pretended their virtues placed them above their gods. " Eſt " aliquid, quo ſapiens antecedat deum, ille naturæ beneficio, " non ſuo, ſapiens eſt‡." And again," Deus non vincit ſapientem " felicitate, etiamſi vincit ætate : Non enim eſt virtus major, " quæ longior §." Hence they will not have us ſo much as to pray to God, either as to virtue or felicity. It is a mean thing to weary the gods. " *Quid votis opus eſt? faſto felicem* ||." And much more to the ſame purpoſe.

ARTICLE

---

* Cic. de Nat. Deor. p. mihi. 187. Lib. 3.—" For nobody ever " confeſſed that he owed his virtue to God, for we are juſtly praiſed " on account of our virtue, and we juſtly boaſt of it, which would not " be the caſe if we had our virtue as a gift from God. . . . Nor did " any body ever give thanks to the gods becauſe he was a good man."

† Seneca, Epiſt. 48.—" This is what philoſophy promiſes me, to " make me equal to God."

‡ Idem, Epiſt. 53.—" There is ſomething in which a wiſe man " excels God, that the former is wiſe by his own benefit, but the lat- " ter by that of nature."

|| Epiſt. 73.—" God does not exceed a wiſe man in happineſs, though " he exceeds him in age, for virtue is not the greater in proportion as " it is older."

§ Epiſt. 51.—" What need has he of prayers who is actually hap- " py."

ARTICLE IV.

It did not univerfally obtain, that repentance is a fufficient expiation; or, that we muft repent for offences done againft the true God.

OUR author has acknowleged, that there is rarely mention of this amongft the ancients; and we have already, by quotations from him, cleared that the ancient Heathens did not think it a fufficient expiation, and indeed that it was of no great confideration among them, is fufficiently evident from their not taking any notice of it, even when the faireft occafions prefent themfelves. And finally, there can be nothing more certain, than that their repentance could not aim at the offence done to the true God, of whom many of them were utterly ignorant. But what has been faid is fufficient to fhew that it did not univerfally obtain in any fenfe, that can turn to any account to the Deifts.

ARTICLE V.

It was not univerfally agreed, that there are rewards and punifhments after this life.

1. HOWEVER many there were that maintained the immortality of the fouls of men, it is certain, that there were very many diffentients, who were of a different mind, and that of all forts of people.

The famed fects among the Indians, which they call *Schaerwaecha Pafenda* and *Tfcheclea*, if we may believe Hornbeck in his account of them, all deny a future ftate [*].

Nor are wife Chinefe, at leaft many of them, of a different mind. They are divided into three fects. The firft fect of their philofophers are the followers of the famed Confucius; their morals are as refined as perhaps thefe of the moft polite parts of the world, if not more. But as to the foul, they feem to make it a part of God, which at death returns to that firft Principle, whence it was broke off. Let as hear Poflevinus's account of them. As to this matter he fays, they maintain, " Hominis
" cor

---

[*] Hornbeck, pag. 31, ubi fupra.

PRINCIPLES OF THE MODERN DEISTS.

" cor effe unum & eandem rem cum illo primo rerum princi-
" pio; cumque homo moritur, cor perire prorfus & abfumi,
" fupereffe tamen ex eo primum principium, quod vitam ante
" conferebat." And further, they maintan, " Poffe hominem
" in hac vita fummam principii cognofcendi perfectionem ad-
" ipifci, & meditando pervenire ad maximam vitæ tranquil-
" litatem, & hoc effe fummum bonum, quod donec obtineat,
" continuo motu agatur, & de inferno uno in alium conjiciatur,
" ufque dum contemplando & meditando ad faftigium perven-
" erit tranquillitatis, quæ in principio illo primo eft*." Thefe
are the apprehenfions of their beft moralifts.

But there are other two fects, that plainly declare againft a
future ftate, are for the immortality of the foul, and have no
profpect beyond time†.

Of this fame opinion were not only fingle perfons, but many fects of the ancient philofophers, whom Cicero mentions,
and concludes his account of them thus—" His fententiis om-
" nibus nihil poft mortem pertinere ad quemquam poteft : Pari-
" ter enim cum vita fenfus amittitur ‡." And a little after,
fpeaking of the oppofition made to Plato's opinion about the
immortality of the foul, he fays, " Sed plurimi contra (Pla-
" tonis fcil. fententiam) nituntur, animofq; quafi capite dam-
" natos morte mulctant." And fome paffages after, fpeaking
of the fame opinion, he fays, " Catervæ veniunt contradicen-
" tium, non folum Epicureorum, quos equidem non defpicio,
" fed nefcio quomodo doctiffimus quifque contemnit. Acerri-
" mè autem deliciæ meæ dico Archias, contra hanc immor-
" talitatem differuit : Is enim tres libros fcripfit, qui Lefbiaci
                              " vocantur

* Hornbeck, pag. 47, 48.—" That the heart of man is one and the
" fame thing with that firft Principle of things, and that when a man
" dies, his heart quite perifhes and is confumed, yet that the firft Prin-
" ciple of it remains, which formerly gave him life. . . . That
" a man may in this life attain to the higheft perfection of the principle
" of knowledge, and arrive by meditation to the greateft tranquillity
" of life, and that until he obtain this, he is agitated by a perpetual
" motion, and thrown from one hell into a another, till by contempla-
" tion and meditation he arrive at the fummit of tranquillity which is
" in that firft Principle."

† Ibid, pag. 48, 49.

‡ Cicero, Tufc. Quæft. 1. pag. 329.—" From all thefe opinions,
" nothing after death can be interefting to any one, for fenfation is loft
" together with life."

"vocantur, quod Metylenis sermo habetur: In quibus vult effi-
"cere animos esse mortales: Stoici autem usuram nobis tan-
"quam cornicibus: Diu mansuros aiunt animos, semper ne-
"gant*."

Nor were they otherwise minded, many of them in Greece. When Socrates vents his opinion of the immortality of the soul that day before he died, Cebes, one of his disciples, who is the conferrer, or one of them at least that maintains the discourse with him, addresses him in these words: "Socrates, I "subscribe to the truth of all you have said. There is only "one thing that men look upon as incredible, viz. what you "advanced of the soul: for almost every body fancies, that "when the soul parts from the body it is no more, it dies along "with it; in the very minute of parting it evanishes like a "vapour or smoke, which flies off and disperses, and has no "existence †."

Yea, Pliny, Strabo, and many others, declare against the immortality of the soul; nay, Pliny on set purpose disputes against it ‡.

And the poets go the same way. It were easy to multiply proofs of this from them. Seneca speaks the mind of many of them, though perhaps not his own. *Trajæ Troa, A.* 1.

Post mortem nihil est, ipsaque mors nihil,
Velocis spatii meta novissima.
Quæris quo jaceas post obitum loco;
  Quo non mala jacent. Et
Tempus nos avidum devorat & chaos,
Mors individua est, noxia corpori,
Nec parcens animæ ‖.   Persius

* "Crowds of opposers come against me, not only of the Epicu-
"reans, whom indeed I do not despise, but I know not how
"every most learned man despises them. For my darling, I mean
"Archais, has disputed very eagerly against this immortality. He
"wrote three books, which are called Lesbian, because the dis-
"course is held at Mytelene, in which he endeavoured to prove that
"the souls of men are mortal. But the Stoicks only give them a long
"life like the crows,—they say that souls will live a long time, but
"they deny that they will live for ever."

† Plato's *Phædon* done into English from M. Dacier's Transl. vol. 2. pag. 100.

‡ Oweni Theolog. Lib 1. C. pag. 174.

‖ "There is nothing after death, and death itself is nothing, being "only the last stage of our swift course. Do you ask in what place
                                                              "you

Persius and all the poets made use of this as an encouragement to give way to themselves, in whatever lust prompted them to.

*Indulge genio, carpamus dulcia; nostrum est
Quod vivus, cinis, & manes, & fabula fies*.*

If it be said that this is an irony, and that he was not in earnest, it is easy to multiply quotations to this purpose from Horace, Catullus, and most of the poets, which are not capable of any such construction. But I forbear.

And although Cicero was for the immortality of the soul; yet in his first book of *Tusculan Questions*, he plainly derides the whole business of rewards and punishments after this life; as any one who will attentively peruse it may see. I forbear to transcribe the passage; because I behoved to transcribe much to shew the tendency of the discourse. He plainly tells us, that he could be eloquent, if he had a mind to speak against those things; *Disertus esse possem, si contra ista dicerem* †. The case is plainly this: That person to whom he discourses looks on death as an evil. Cicero tells him that perhaps it is because he fears those punishments after this life, which the vulgar believed; and after he has tartly ridiculed them, he concludes, That had he a mind, he could enlarge against those things, and plainly expose the whole tradition.

But because some talk so much of Plato, Socrates, Cicero, and we get so many quotations from them about the immortality of the soul and a future state; I shall here represent their own opinion somewhat more fully.

As for Socrates, he has not writ any thing that is come to our hands: all the accounts we have of him are from Plato, Xenophen and others, but especially Plato his scholar, who was with him at his death: From him then we shall learn at once, what both his master's opinion and his own were in this matter.

When

" you are to lie after your death, in which evils do not lie, and greedy
" time and chance devours us? Death is a divider, which hurts the
" body and does not spare the soul."

* " Indulge your inclination, let us enjoy pleasures; this span of life
" that we enjoy is ours, you will soon become ashes, a shade and a
" fable."

† Tuscul. Quest. Lib. 1. a little from the beginning. pag. mihi 312.

When Socrates is making his apology before his judges, he tells them, "That to fear death, is nothing else, but to believe one's self to be wise, when they are not; and to fancy that they know what they do not know. In effect, no body knows death; no body can tell, but it may be the greatest benefit of mankind; and yet men are afraid of it, as if they knew certainly that it was the greatest of evils *." And a little after speaking of death, "What! should I be afraid of the punishment adjudged by Melitus, a punishment that I cannot positively say whether it is good or evil †?" And thus he concludes his apology. "But now, it is true we should all retire to our respective offices, you to live, and I to die. But whether you or I are going upon the better expedition, it is known to none, but God alone.‡'

Again, in that famed discourse on this subject, before his death, after he has produced all the arguments he can for the immortality of the soul, he tells us pretty plainly, how things stood with him. "Convincing the audience of what I advance, is not only my aim; indeed I shall be infinitely glad that it come to pass; but my chief scope is to persuade myself of the truth of these things; for I argue thus, my dear Phedon, and you will find that this way of arguing is highly useful, (very true to folk that are not certain and can do no better, and only to these). If my propositions prove true, it is well done to believe them, and if after my death they be found false, I will reap that advantage in this life, that I have been less afflicted by the evils which commonly accompany it. But I shall not remain long under this ignorance §." And when he is near his close, and just about to take the poison, or a little before, having represented his thoughts about rewards and punishments after this life, which are little better than those of the poets, he concludes his account in these words; "No man of sense can pretend to assure you, that all these things are just as you have heard. But all thinking men will be positive, that the state of the soul, and the place of its abode, is absolutely such as I represent it to be, or at least very near it,"—provided the soul be immortal.

More might be alleged to the same purpose; but this is sufficient

* Dacier's Plato, Vol. 2. pag. 28. Socrates' Apology.
† Ibid. pag. 40. ‡ Ibid. pag. 47.
§ Plato's Phedon pag. 135, 136.

ficient to let us fee how wavering Plato and his mafter Socrates were. They talk confidently fometimes; but prefently they fink again. Let us next fee what Cicero's mind was. He treats this fubject on fet purpofe, in his firft book of *Tufculan Queftions*, which is wholly fpent on this fubject. He undertakes to fhew and prove againft the perfon whom he inftructs, that *death is not evil*, whether we are diffolved quite or not: and having, as he fancies, proven that death is not an evil, he proceeds and gives us this account of his undertaking—" I " fhall teach you, (fpeaking of death) if I can, *fi poffim*, that " it not only *not evil*, but *good* *." But a little after he tells us clearly what we may expect from him, when his hearer exhorts him to go on; fays he, *Geram tibi morem, & ea quæ vis, ut potero, explicabo: Nec tamen quafi Pythius Apollo, certa ut fint, & fixa quæ dixero: Sed ut homunculus unus e multis probabilia conjecturâ fequens, ultra enim quo progrediar, quam ut verifimilia videam, non habeo: Certa dicent ii qui & percipi ea poffe dicunt, & fe fapientes effe profitentur* †. And fpeaking about this opinion, his auditor tells him, how pleafant this is to him. It will be a little pleafant to hear them fpeak. *A. Me vero delectat: Idque primum ita effe (fcil. animos effe immortales:) Deinde etiamfi non fit, mihi tamen perfuaderi velim. M. Quid tibi ergo operâ noftrâ opus eft? Num eloquentiâ Platonem fuperare poffumus? Evolve diligenter ejus eum librum, qui eft de animo: Amplius quod defideres nihil erit. A. Feci meherculè. & quidem fæpius: Sed nefcio quomodo, dum lego, affentior: Cum pofui librum, & mecum ipfe de immortalitate animorum cæpi cogitare, affentio omnis illa elabitur* ‡. After he has inftructed his hearer, he profoffes his refolution to ftand by this

* Pag. 325.
† Pag. 326.—"*A.* I will obey you, and explain thefe things that you
" wifh, as I fhall be able. Yet what I am to fay will not be certain
" and fixed like the oracles of the Pythian Appollo, but I will proceed
" as one poor man of the many, following probabilities by conjecture,
" for I have no where that I can go further than I fee probability.
" Thofe will fay certain things who fay that certainty can be attained,
" and who profefs to be wife men."
‡ Pag. 329.—"*A.* But it pleafes me, and this firft, that fo is the cafe,
" (to wit, that the fouls of men are immortal) and then although it
" fhould not be fo, yet I wifh to be perfuaded of it. *M.* What need
" have you then of our fervice? Can we excel Plato in eloquence?
" Turn over diligently that book of his, which treats of the foul, you
" will

this opinion, but gets a caution from his inſtructor, that lets us ſee how things ſtand. *A. Nemo me de immortalitate depellet.* *M.* anſwers, *Laudo id quidem, et ſi nihil nimis oportet conſidere: Movemur enim ſæpe aliquo acutè concluſo: Labamus mutamuſque ſententiam clarioribus etiam in rebus: In his enim eſt aliqua obſcuritas**. And if ye would know what his reaſon was for inſiſting ſo long on the proof of this, he tells us near the cloſe, That it was to baniſh the contrary ſuſpicion, which was troubleſome. Much more might be adduced, but what has been ſaid ſufficiently demonſtrates how fluctuating and uncertain the beſt of them were, in reference to this important point.

If any ſhall ſay, that though theſe great men upon ſome occaſions, expreſſed themſelves with ſome heſitation, and did inſinuate ſome ſuſpicion that the oppoſite part of the queſtion might be true, yet upon other occaſions they are poſitive, and that this is as good an evidence of their being firmly perſuaded, as the other expreſſions are of their heſitation. I anſwer, the conſequence is naught. A ſeeming poſitiveneſs upon ſome occaſions, may be the reſult of the joint influence of a ſtrong deſire, that the thing ſhould be true, and ſome philoſophical quirk urged for its ſupport: For as Cicero well obſerves in the words laſt quoted, *Movemur ſæpe aliquo acutè concluſo;* and this eſpecially holds true, where there is a ſtrong inclination to believe the thing, as being of obvious advantage to us. Now this may be, where there is no certainty or firm perſuaſion. I readily own that theſe great men favoured the immortality of the ſoul: But I poſitively deny, that they received it with that firmneſs of aſſent, that is not only due, but unavoidable, to truths which carry their own evidence along with them. And I moreover aver, that the Deiſts, in quoting ſome of theſe aſſertions from them, wherein they ſeem poſitive, ſuppreſſing other expreſſions, wherein they diſcover a heſitation, do but abuſe the reader's credulity; and give neither a full nor fair account of the judgment of theſe men.

CHAP.

" will deſire nothing more on the ſubject. *A.* Indeed I have done ſo, " and oftener than once, but I know not how it is, I aſſent as long as " I am reading, but when I have laid down the book and begin to " think with myſelf of the immortality of ſouls, all that aſſent vaniſhes."

* "None ſhall drive me from my belief of immortality. *M.* I " commend that indeed, although we ought not to be too ſure of any " thing, for we are often determined by ſomething that is acutely concluded, yet afterwards we give way and change our opinions even " in things that are clearer, for there is ſome obſcurity in thoſe things."

CHAP. XVI.

Wherein some general considerations are laid down for proving that many of the best things, which are to be met with in the Heathens, were not the discoveries of Nature's Light, but came from Tradition.

NOTWITHSTANDING the grofs ignorance, which overfpread the Heathen world, was very great; yet it cannot be denied that there are very many furprifing hints of truth to be found, in many of their writings, in reference even to matters of religion.

The Deifts take up whatever they meet with of this fort, and confidently give it out, That all this they difcovered by the mere light of nature.

There are who, on the other hand, will fcarce allow them to have made any of thofe difcoveries by the *light of nature;* but afcribe whatever hints of truth are to be met with, to *tradition.* This is faid to be the opinion of Eufebius and Scaliger, by Dr. Owen*. And it is of late maintained by Mr. Nicolls, the ingenious author of the *Conference with a Theift* †. For which Mr. Becconfal, the author of a late treatife concerning the *Law of Nature*, is much difpleafed with him, and takes him to tafk ‡.

I defign not to make myfelf a party in this debate, I think that there is fomewhat of truth on both fides: But if either think to carry the matter to the utmoft, I think alfo there will be miftakes on both hands. It is too much to fay that they difcovered nothing in reference to religion by the mere light of nature: And on the other hand it favours of grofs ignorance to fay that all we meet with in the writings of the ancient fages, was difcovered by the light of nature. Nothing is more evident, than that many things have been handed from nation to nation, and from age to age, by tradition. This no modeft man will or can deny; it has been fo clearly made out by many.

What

---

* Theol. Lib. 1. C. 2. Parag. 4.
† Confer. Part 2. pag. 32, 33, &c.
‡ Beccon. of the Law of Nature, C. 4. pag. 54, 55, &c.

What I assert, and shall attempt to prove, is, "That many of the most notable things that we meet with in the Heathen writers, in matters of religion, are *not* to be looked on as *discoveries* made by the *light of nature*; but as *truths*, whereof they were informed by *tradition*. And moreover, that when we find them asserting some of those truths, which to us who enjoy the scriptures, and by the scriptures have our reason improven, appear to have a foundation in reason, we are not therefore to conclude, that *reason* led them to those truths; but rather, that in many cases they had even these from *tradition*."

In proving this point, I shall not proceed by single instances, but shall lay down these general considerations, which at once clear the truth of our assertion, and discover whence these traditions might come, and how easily they might be conveyed to them. Particular instances may be had in great abundance from those who have, of set purpose, largely insisted on this subject. Amongst others, Huetius, in his *Demonstratio Evangelica*, has largely discoursed of particular instances of this nature. I think the following observations taken together and duly considered, will put our assertion beyond question with the sober and judicious.

1. It is most certain, that the Jews, however in other regards inconsiderable, which makes it still the more observable, had more full, clear, and certain knowledge of the true God, religion, and matters of worship, than all the world besides. If the Deists please to controvert this proposition, we shall debate it with them when they please. And I dare be bold to say, that I shall prove, that there is more true and rational divinity in *one* of the *books of Moses*, than they shall be able to find in *all the Heathen writers*, when they put all that has been said by all of them together.

2. Their neighbours, and more especially the Egyptians, had many fair occasions of obtaining acquaintance with their opinions and practices in matters of relgion. Several persons at distant times, went out from the church and settled in distant nations. Ishmael went out from Abraham's family, and Esau from that of Isaac. Now it cannot be supposed, how wicked soever these persons were, but they would carry out with them some *true notions, opinions and practices*, in *matters of religion*. Nor can it reasonably be denied, that they founded their new government on some of these notices, though variously blended and mixt with corrupt additions and alterations,

both

both in matters of opinion and practice. And it is evident, that these hints, or remainders of truth, in matters of opinion and practice, as they were mixt with these corruptions, would obtain a general and great respect, as being found useful for maintaining order in societies, as being delivered to them by the first founders of their nations, as being commended by their practice, and perhaps established by laws and constitutions. Whence it is not possibly to be supposed that these notices or practices would in an age, or a few ages wear out.

Again, it is particularly observable in this case, that the church was, for a long tract of time, in a wandering and unsettled state; which obliged them to more of intimacy with the nations that lay near them, than afterwards was necessary, when they settled in a land by themselves apart, and were, by divine constitutions, barred from that familiarity.

Moreover, as to the Egyptians, they had much occasion of being particularly acquainted with the Jews' opinions and practices in the matters of God. The Israelites dwelt among them (besides what occasional converse they had before) about 217 years together. The correspondence was again renewed in Solomon's time, by his matching with the king of Egypt's daughter. Jeremiah, and a great company with him, staid a considerable time in Egypt, and prophesied there to the Jews, who had at that time no separate dwellings, and prophesied concerning Egypt; which, together with the reputation he had got at Jerusalem, by his predictions that were remarkably verified, the notice taken of him by the king of Babylon, and the contests he had with those of his own nation, could not but make him much regarded.

It is further considerable, that there were many things, which may reasonably be supposed to excite an uncommon curiosity in the Egyptians, to understand the religion of the Jews. It is known what a place Joseph long had in Egypt, and how he managed it. Afterwards the people, while under bondage, were scattered through the land, and the piety of some of them appearing in their sufferings, could not but be taken notice of, as their scattering through the land, gave occasion to the Egyptians to inquire, as to the principles that influenced it. The miraculous appearances of God on behalf of that people in Egypt and its neighbourhood, in the wilderness, would have excited the curiosity of a people, much less inquisitive than they were. The reputation of Solomon, his alliance with

the crown of Egypt, and his traffick with them, as they gave
a new occasion, so could not but spur them on to inquire further into matters of this sort. If to all this you add the general
character writers of all sorts give to the Egyptians, That they
were a people more than ordinarily fond about matters of religion, infomuch that our author Herbert observes, that they are
said to be the first that taught religion*; and if further it is considered, that the Gentiles, finding the unsatisfactoriness of their
own opinions and practices, were very much inclined to change,
and adopt the customs, practices, and way of every nation in
matters of religion, to try if they could find any thing more satisfying than their own ;—if, I say, all these are laid together,
it cannot be doubted that the neighbouring nations, and particularly the Egyptians, learned many things from the Jews in
matters of religion.

3. It is observable, that all these things fell out a considerable time before any of those great men appeared or flourished
in the world, whose writings are come to us, and contain those
truths, concerning the rise whereof we now discourse.

The seven sages, Thales, Solon, Pittacus, Bias, Chilo, Periander, and Cleobulus, who raised the reputation of Greece,
did not flourish till about the time of the Babylonish captivity,
and long after the dispersion of the Ten Tribes; some do reckon it 125 years †. Socrates and Plato flourished not for near
150 years after these again. Now these are among the first
who made any considerable figure for learning of this sort in
the Heathen world, whose writings are come to us.

4. All these great men did, for their own improvement, travel into foreign nations, and made it their business to learn their
opinions and practices. Particularly we are told of the most
considerable of them by Diogenes Laertius and others, That
they were very concerned to know the opinions of the Egyptian
priests in matters of religion, and most of what they knew in
these matters was taught them by those. This will be denied
by none, that is acquainted with the lives of those persons.

5. It is further observable, that in many instances there is
such a plain resemblance in their opinions to the scripture accounts of the *origin of the world*, the *deluge*, the *peopling of the
earth*, and most other things, as could not be casual; but shews
plainly that they were derived thence. This in particular instances

* De Relig. Gent. pag. 8.
† Le Clerk Comput. Hist. pag. 35, 40.

stances by many, particularly Huetius and others, to whom he refers, is so fully demonstrated, that it cannot, without manifest impudence, be denied.

6. What comes yet somewhat nearer to our purpose, it is very observable even as to those truths, which have some foundation in reason, such as these, about the immortality of the souls of men, and their state after death, and the like, that those great men of old proposed them commonly, without offering any proof of them, or any reasons for them. Now it is not credible that, if they had been led to those notices by reason, they would have offered those important truths, without offering reasons of them. This observation we find made, as to its substance, though not on such views, by no less a person than Cicero, who knew as well how matters then stood, to speak modestly, as any now can do. Speaking of the immortality of the soul, and the ancient philosophers' sentiments about it, he says, "*Sed redeo ad antiquos. Rationem illi sententiæ* "*sue non ferè reddebant nisi quid erat numeris aut descrip 10n-* "*ibus explicandum—Platonem ferunt primum de animorum* "*æternitate non solum sensisse idem, quod Pythagoras, sed ration-* "*em etiam attulisse* *."

7. Nor is it less considerable to prove, that the notions, which prevailed about the immortality of the soul, and a future state, (and the like may be said of many others) were not learned from *reason*, but from *tradition*; and that the impression and persuasion of these truths were more generally entertained, and more strongly riveted among the vulgar than among the philosophers. Whole shoals of them, or *Catervæ*, as Cicero above quoted speaks, denied and derided all these things, which the vulgar firmly believed. This observation I find made by the learned Dr. Owen, " † *Cum mundi conditu judicium post hanc vi-* " *tam exercendum, famam catholicam obtinuit. Eam etiam persua-* " *sionem comitata est immortalitatis animarum præsumptio, quæ* " *quamvis rationi etiam innitatur, tamen cum maxime semper* " *apud*

---

* " But I return to the ancients. They commonly did not give a
" reason for their opinion, unless when any thing was to be explain-
" ed by numbers or figures.——— They say that Plato was the first who
" not only was of the same opinion with Pythagoras concerning the
" immortality of the soul, but who likewise adduced a reason for it."

† " That with the end of the world there was to be a judgment after
" this life, had a general fame, and a presumption of the immortality
" of

" *apud vulgus, potius quam* 'σοφϋς *obtinuit, non nisi traditioni*
" *adscribenda est.*"

8. When these great men of old do give reasons of their opinions, they are such, as any one may see, never *led* them to these opinions: but having, by tradition *received* them, they were ashamed to hold them, without being capable to give any reason for what they held, and therefore, they set their wits on the rack to find out what to say for them. And it was but seldom they hit on the true ones. For most part their reasonings are plainly childish, trifling and sophistical. It were easy to demonstrate this. As to the arguments of Socrates and Plato for the immortality of the soul, they are plain sophisms: and upon what design they were urged, we have heard before, viz. to confirm themselves in an opinion, the belief whereof was accompanied with some advantage. A learned person says justly, "That Plato endeavours to prove the immortality of the soul by " such reasons, as, if they conclude any thing, would conclude it " to be a God*." And the same may be said of Cicero and others.

9. It is moreover remarkable, to this purpose, that not only are there are many things to be met with in the writings and practices of the ancient writers amonst the Heathens, whereof no colourable reason can be given, nor any account made, otherwise than by ascribing them to ancient and corrupted traditions; but further, that they knew not how to manage or improve those hints, which were this way handed to them. Most of them quite spoil these things in the telling. A few of the more wise, conscious of their own ignorance, yet wanting humility and ingenuity enough to acknowledge it, wrap themselves in clouds, and express themselves darkly, to conceal their own ignorance from the vulgar; and one that understands, would not know whether to laugh or be angry, to see their fond admirers, in later ages, sweating to fetch sublime meanings from words which the writers themselves really understood not.

10. In the last place, we find the ancients themselves, on some occasions, *owning*, that they owed the first discoveries of these things to tradition. Dacier in the life of Plato, tells us, "That he first instructs them in religion, about which he esta-
" blishes

" of souls accompanied this persuasion, which although it is supported
" by reason, yet as it has always prevailed most among the vulgar,
" rather than among philosophers, can only be ascribed to tradition."
* Dr. How's Living Temple, Part 1. pag. 122.

" blithes nothing, without having confulted God; that is, no-
" thing but what is conformable to *true tradition* and *ancient*
" *oracles **." To evince the truth of this, Plato's own words
are fubjoined, " God, (faith Plato) as we are taught by *an-*
" *cient tradition*, having in himfelf the beginning, the middle
" and end of all things, always goes on in his way, according
" to his nature, without ever ftepping afide; he is followed by
" *juftice*, which never fails to punifh the tranfgreffions committed
" againft his law †." And a little after fpeaking about the
punifhments of the wicked, he proceeds thus, " They are not
" limited to the miferies of this life, nor to death itfelf, from
" which even good men are not exempt; for thefe are penalties
" too light and fhort, but they are horrible torments." But
yet more remarkable to this purpofe are his words in his epif-
tles, " *Antiquis vero facrifq; fermonibus fides femper habenda,*
" *qui declarant animum nobis effe immortalem, et judices habere,*
" *quorum decretis, pro merito præmia et fupplicia maxima attri-*
" *buantur, ut primum quis e corpore decefferit* ‡."

Lay thefe things together, and as they are in themfelves evident enough: fo I think they amount to a full demonftration of
the affertion, we have above laid down, for the proof whereof
we adduced them; and they do abundantly fhew, how inconfi-
derately every thing met with in ancient writers is, put upon
the fcore of *nature's light.*

CHAP. XVII.

*Wherein we confider what Herbert's opinion was as to the fuffi-
ciency of his Articles, and offer fome reflections, fhewing how
foolifh, abfurd and ridiculous the Deifts' pretences to their
fufficiency are.*

WE have now demonftrated that thefe five articles *did
not* univerfally obtain in the world, and that confequently the Heathen world *had not the means neceffary to falvation.*

But

---

* Life of Plato, pag. 86. † Plato de Ligibus, Lib. 4.
‡ Plato, Epift. 7.—" But credit ought always to be given to ancient
" and facred fpeeches, which declare that our fouls are immortal, and
" that thefe are judges by whofe fentences great rewards and punifh-
" ments are to be diftributed according to merit, as foon as we fhall
" have left the body."

But should we grant what has been above proved to be false, viz. That these articles *did universally obtain*; yet all is not done, nor is the difficulty so got over; for we are not agreed, that these, though acknowledged, are *alone sufficient.*

We know our author would have us to believe, that they are sufficient. He tells us to this purpose, that when he had found them out, he saw that there was nothing wanting to make a complete religion *Quum hasce igitur eximias veritates seorsim perassem, disquisivi porro, quid hisce adjecerint, vel quidem adjicere possint sacerdot s, unde certior fidei cerca salutem æternam daretur norma, aut vit integritas sanctitasq; magis promoveretur, aut communis ubique stabiliretur concordia Videbam satis alia atque alia hic a idi posse, quin et addita fuisse; sed quæ veritates hasce obstruerent, enervarentque potius, quam vim roburque illis conciliarent*.* And indeed our author is so bold as to challenge all the world to shew what can be added to these five articles. *Ut viderent interea antistites, pr sulesq; per totum orbem diffusi, quid hisce quinq: Articulis, addere potuerint: Unde vera illa virtus, qua homines Deo similes, consortioque ejus dignos efficit; vel pietas, puritas sanctitasq vitæ magis promoveri possint* †. And growing still bolder by this imaginary success, he proceeds to inveigh, though more covertly, against the *satisfaction of Christ*, as destructive to *piety* Of which he gives a most disingenuous account, as commonly he does of all the articles of revealed religion, which he has occasion to mention.

But however co fident our author is, of the sufficiency of his five articles in this place; yet elsewhere he shews he had not over much certainty in his own mind, about this matter: For some pages after, he says, *Et quidem quinque hosce Articulos bonos, catholicosque esse unusquisq; Dubio procul fatebitur; id sa-*
lutem

---

* " When therefore I had got these excellent truths by themselves, I
" next inquired what priests had added, or could add to these, whereby
" they might be a surer guide of our faith concerning eternal salvation,
" or integrity and sanctity of life more promoted, or common concord
" established every where. I saw well enough that different things
" might be added, nay had been added to them, but such as rather obstructed and enervated these truths, than gave them any force or strength."

† " —That the priests and bishops, scattered over the whole world,
" might see in the mean time, what they could add to these five articles; or by what means that true virtue, which renders men like
" to God, and worthy of his fellowship, or by which piety, purity
" and sanctity of life, can be more promoted."

lutem tamen æternam comparandam non sufficere prohibebunt non nulli, cæterum, qui ita locutus fuerit, ne illo quidem audax ; nedum sævum temerariumq ; effatem (mea sententia) protulerit ; quum nulli satis explorata sint Judicia Divina ; quam etiam ob caufam, neque ea sufficere protexus dixerim : attamen magis probabilis mihi videtur eorum opinio, qui æqeu piè ac leniter de Dei Judiciis statuunt, dum homo, quod in se est, præstat ; neque enim in cujusve potestate est, ut fides sive traditiones quantumvis laxæ (præsertim ubi aliqua ex parte controvertuntur) ad se satis pertingant, neque tandem recta communiq ; ratione quinq ; Articulis nostris addi potest dogma, unde magis pii, sinceriqué evadunt homines ; aut pax, concordiaq ; publicà magis promoveatur*. Here our author is more modest.

Thus we have seen what his opinion is ; it now remains that we offer some reflections on it. Many offer themselves : I shall only touch at a few.

1. Though the Deists are as desirous as any, to confine religion to a narrow compass, and perhaps it is as much their interest, as it is of any sort of men, that it should consist of few articles ; yet, for shame, they cannot make it contain less, than those five articles. They own, and must own all those necessary to salvation, both in belief and practice. It is not possible, they themselves being judges, to reach the ends of religion, if any of them are cut off. Since then we have above proved that these did not universally obtain, it is plain, that all mankind had not *sufficient knowledge of religion*. Thus it is in fact.

But now where shall the blame of this be laid ? On themselves ? On the priests ? Or on God ? This last cannot be said.
Well

---

* " And indeed every one will doubtless confess, that these five arti-
" cles are good and catholic ; yet some will think they are not sufficient
" for attaining eternal life. But whoever would say so, would be guilty
" of uttering not only a bold, not to say a cruel and arbitrary sentence,
" in my opinion, as the Divine judgments are not sufficiently known
" to any one ; for which reason likewise, neither would I positively af-
" firm that they were sufficient. Yet the opinion of those seems to be
" the more probable, who judge equitably, piously and mildly of the
" Divine judgments, while a man does what depends on him ; for it is not
" in the power of every one, that Faiths or Traditions, however lax,
" (especially when they are any where controverted) should sufficiently
" extend to him ; nor in fine, can any doctrine be added to our five arti-
" cles by right and common reason, whereby men may become more
" pious and sincere, or peace and public concord may be more pro-
" moted."

Well then, muſt theſe villains of prieſts, with whom our author and all the ſucceeding Deiſts are ſo angry, bear the blame of it, in that they did not better teach and inſtruct the people, in the grounds of *ſincere religion*? But though our author, and all the Deiſts, would fain lodge the blame here; yet I am ſcarce ſatisfied of the juſtice of the charge; (though I am willing to own, that they were for the moſt part arch-villains) for how ſhall it be made appear that they themſelves knew the grounds of ſincere religion? I know our author blames them for not imparting the knowledge of ſincere religion to the people; and that he may be ſure to ſhut the door upon them that they may not eſcape, he adds by way of parentheſis, *licet illis ſatis cognitam* *. But how proves he this, that they knew that *chaſte* and *ſincere religion* well enough? Might not they be ſuppoſed ignorant of it, as well as moſt of the philoſophers, the greateſt moraliſts not excepted? Again, I do not well ſee what right they had to teach, or how they were obliged. Did the law of nature authoriſe them to be public teachers? I believe the Deiſts think not. Was not every man able to ſhift for himſelf, and find the way to bleſſedneſs? If he was, what need was there to truſt theſe villainous prieſts? Who was obliged to liſten to them? If every man was not able, without the help of ſome inſtructor, then if that inſtructor failed in his duty, as it certain they did almoſt perpetually, (nay our author will not allow, nor ſee I any need of that *almoſt*) what becomes of the poor vulgar, who, without inſtruction cannot reach competent knowledge? He is not able to reach it, his inſtructors fail of their duty; and for any thing I ſee, the poor man wants, and muſt always want a ſufficient religion, and that without any fault of his.

Well then, unavoidably, either every man is able to do and know for himſelf, in matters of religion; or a great many, even moſt of the poor vulgar, are loſt for good and all; and there is no help for it, and that without their fault. If the laſt be ſaid, our author has loſt his point quite; and if this be a fault, he will lay it at the door of Providence, that has not ſufficiently provided all men, in the means neceſſary for their future happineſs: If the firſt be ſaid, then the blame muſt lie at every man's own door. But methinks our author is not willing of this; for

he

---

* Pag. 180 *ſub finem*.—" Although it was ſufficiently known to " them."

he would always excuse the vulgar, and suppose them so rude and ignorant, that they had not either will, courage, nor ability to step otherwise, than they were led. But after all, the fault must be lodged at their doors, or the Deists' whole cause is lost. I confess, any one that was under such impressions of their stupid ignorance, as our author seems to have been, will even think it hard enough to say that every one of them had this ability, to find out a sufficient religion ; and I believe, not without ground ; though I still think, that they might have known, and done more than they did ; but this will do the Deists' cause no service.

2. But further, the Deists must own that natural religion, according to this mould of it at least, did never obtain in purity, without any additions, in any place of the world. Our author confesses, that on this foundation, there was every where a strange superstructure raised. After he has spoken of those articles, he subjoins "Hæc igitur sincerioris Gentilium religionis partes fu-
"ere ; reliquæ vel commentitiæ fabellæ vel archetypæ nugæ,
"vel scitamenta quædem prohiberi possunt : inter quæ (damno
"mortalium) nonnulla infana, nonnulla etiam impia viseban-
"tur*." Now, this being the case, I would gladly know, if our author's five articles are looked upon as of such virtue, that they could hallow all these additions made to them, or at least, so far antidote the poison of them, that persons, who embraced this complex frame of religion, consisting of these five articles, and such additions as in every nation were made to them, might yet reach happiness, or not.

It is pretended that these five articles of natural religion, though contaminated with these additions, (as our author speaks when he enters upon his discourse about those orthodox points of religion, " Ritibus, cæremoniæq ; contaminabantur, conspur-
"cabanturq†,") are sufficient to lead to happiness, then this is plainly to say, that the religion of every country was good and sufficient, and that every one might be saved by that religion he was bred in.‡ If the defence of this is undertaken, it will

* Pag. 212.—" These then were the parts of the more pure religi-
" on of the Heathens, the others were devised fables, or ancient trifles,
" or false ornaments, among which, to the loss of man, some mad and
" even impious things were likewise to be seen."
† Pag. 184. Cap. 4. at the close.
‡ Herbert de Veritate. pag. 272.

will be found a pretty hard province, and one will not eafily be able to defend, That the complex religion of every country was fufficient, or that the virtue of thofe articles was fuch, as to preferve from the hurt of the additions. What if, in the complex frame of moft religions of the world, fome of our author's fundamental articles are juftled out of their own place? Perhaps, while each religion fets up for fo many inferior gods, they rob the one fupreme God of much of his glory, to adorn thefe imaginary gods with. It may be, more ftrefs is laid on rites than on virtue, which our author makes the principal part of worfhip. Perhaps more ftrefs is laid on their rites for expiation, than on repentance. What if the additions made are fuch, as are utterly inconfiftent with a due regard to thefe articles, or a juft improvement of them? What if there are other things yoked in with them in moft religions, that are as derogatory to the honour of God, as thefe can be fuppofed conducive for its advancement? How can fuch a horrid medley of things, found and unfound, orthodox foundations and impious fuperftructures, be acceptable to God, or ufeful to man? One half, to wit, our author's *five catholic articles*, is defigned to lead men to blifs, pretend the Deifts: And the other, to wit, the *rites* and *ceremonies*, are defigned to the worft of purpofes, by thofe villains of priefts, who aim at cheating the world. Now, how fhall fuch crofs defigns agree or confift? Or, how can means adapted to fo very different, nay, quite oppofite ends, be united and hang together? Or, if they are united, how can that religion, which confifts of fuch jarring and incoherent materials, turn to any account? But this opinion is fo ridiculous, that I need not infift in difproving of it. No man of fobriety can ever pretend that thefe articles can be of any ufe, if each of them is not kept in its own place, and if care is not taken to guard againft all additions, which are inconfiftent with a due refpect to thofe articles. Some little additions, perhaps one might fuppofe would do no great hurt: but if there are any, that entrench on the foundations, and put them out of their place, the whole fabric falls, and all is ruined. Now I think it were no hard work to prove, that the additions were fuch, in every nation, as rendered the whole utterly ufelefs, and infufficient to any of the moft confiderable ends of religion, either with refpect to God or man.

But if it is pretended, that while thofe five articles are afferted fufficient, it is only meant, that if perfons would abandon

all

all thofe extravagant, deftructive and filthy additions, which every where are made to them, and only regard them, then in following thefe they might attain to life and eternal happinefs: if, I fay, this is alleged, then I would afk, how fhall we diftinguifh betwixt thofe articles and others that are interwoven with them, in each country? By what marks fhall the neceffaries be known from the not neceffaries? The fundamentals from the acceffaries? Is every man able, with our author, to diffect and infpect the feveral religions of the countries where they live, and feparate the neceffaries from thefe that are not fo? Our author found this a pretty hard tafk: What fhall poor mean people then think of it? Our author has fhown what fair pleas might be made for many of the moft pernicious parts of the religions of the nations. Would a poor countryman be able to rid his feet of fuch fetters? It is utterly impoffible that the one half of mankind could diftinguifh betwixt what was to be rejected, and what was to be retained. In a word, it is evident, that all the world over, things pernicious and deftructive were fo twifted in with things of another fort, and fuch fair pleas made for them, that it was utterly impoffible for the poor ignorant vulgar to divide the one from the other. Since then thefe five articles fignify nothing unlefs they were fevered from thefe other things, which were every where interwoven with them, and moft part of mankind were utterly unable to do this, which I doubt no man ever did before our author, it feems evident, that of whatever ufe they may be to our author, who was fo fharp-fighted, as to fpy them out and diftinguifh them from the other things with which they were mixt; yet they can be of no ufe to the far greater part of mankind, and confequently the far greater part of the human race ftill muft be owned deftitute of the means that may be juftly termed fufficient to lead them to future happinefs. Thefe five articles, as in fact they have always been interwoven with other things, were not fufficient to fave any; and whatever their force might be, if they had been fevered from other things, yet they not being fo, before our author did it, and moft part of men being utterly uncapable of making this diftinction, they muft be looked on as infufficient to many, at leaft of mankind, who therefore certainly were deftitute of means needful for future happinefs, and fo left to perifh. I know our author pretends that fome were able to diftinguifh, and did make a difference betwixt thefe articles and the additions: *Verum quinq; articulos fupra dictos*

(uti

(uti quæ in corde defcribuntur) fine ulla hæfitatione accipiebant olim Gentiles dubio procul; de reliquis puto, ambigebant, tum ii præfertim, qui inter illos faltem fapientiores exiſtimabantur*. How ill-grounded our author's confidence as to the univerſal acceptance of his five articles is, we have feen above. What he fubjoins about the Gentiles diftinguiſhing the additions that were made *to* them, *from* them, comes not up to the point: For the queſtion is not, Whether fome could thus diftinguiſh the one from the other? but, Whether all did, or could? And when he pretends that fome of the more difcerning did fo, what proof advances he? Nothing but his bold *puto*. This reflection might be further urged, but I fhall pafs it, and proceed to another.

2. How fhall one be fatisfied that thefe five articles are all that were neceſſary; or that they are fufficient? Are the Deifts all agreed about this? No, we have heard one above making *feven* neceffary. Nay our author is not too confident, as we have heard above, when he fays, *Quam nulli fatis explorata fint judicia divina; quam etiam ob caufam, neque eos fufficere protenus dixerint*†. We fee our author is not very fure about the fufficiency of thofe articles. But he feems pretty pofitive that there is no other article difcoverable by the common reafon of mankind, that can be of any great ufe, or that is neceſſary to anfwer the great ends of religion, the public peace and bettering of mankind. But we fee the Deifts are not all agreed here: fome think more needful. But I have two or three words to fay to all this—May no article be allowed neceffary that is controverted? So our author infinuates. And Blount in his *Religio Laici*, is pofitive oftener than once‡. Then I would know of the Deifts, Have never thefe articles, any or all of them, been controverted? Have not we already proven, that the *firſt* article has been controverted, about the *being of one*

---

* Pag. 211.—"But doubtlefs the Heathens formerly received without any hefitation, thofe five articles above mentioned (as being written in their hearts) of the reſt I think that they doubted, and efpecially thofe among them who were reckoned wifer than others."

† Vid. pag. 47. "—As the divine judgments are not fufficiently known to any one, for which reaſon likewife, neither would I pofitively affirm that they were fufficient."

‡ Compare pag. 3 and 4.

one supreme God? Is not our author's *third* article, viz. "That virtue (as it is discoverable by the light of nature) is the principal part of the worship of God," disputed by Christians? Do not the followers of Spinoza deny repentance to be a duty, and that in compliance with their master, who pretends to demonstrate in his *Ethicks*, "That he who repents is twice miserable*?" Has not the *fifth* been controverted by many of old? Let any who denies this read Cicero, Lib. 1. *Tusc. Quest.* or Plato's *Phedon*, and they will learn, that it has been controverted by more of the wise men than embraced it. And do not very many of our modern Deists call it in question? Again, have there not been some other articles as universally agreed, as little controverted, and perhaps less than some of these? To give but one instance, Has not the article about the *worship of God*, that he was to be worshipped with some solemn external worship, whom we owned as God, been as much agreed to as any of the rest? Doth it not arise from the common reason of mankind? But I shall wave this.

4. There is another thing that I would know of the Deists, concerning their five articles. Do they think them, as they are proposed, sufficient? or must they not be well explained? If as they are proposed, I would gladly see the man that can have the face to maintain, what is not only untrue, but ridiculous. Will, for instance, the owning *virtue* to be the principal part of the worship of God, signify any thing to the world, while they know not, and are not agreed what is virtue and what is vice? Is not this to mock the world, to propose general articles, and tell the world is agreed about them, while yet one half is not agreed what is the signification of these general words? Is not this a plain cheat? It is true, Blount, who has copied all from our author, as the present Deists do from him, tells us that these articles must be well explained. "Neither "can I, (says he) imagine so much as one article more in com-"mon reason, that could make man better, or more pious, "when the foresaid were rightly explicated and observed †." But now, are not these articles sufficient unless rightly explicated?

---

* Spin. Ethicks pag. 4. Prop. 54. *Pœnitentia virtus non est, sive ex ratione non oritur, quem facti pœnitet, his miser seu impotens est.*—"Penitence is not a virtue, nor arises from reason, for he who repents of "what he has done, is twice miserable, or weak."

† Religio Laici. pag. 73.

cated? No, he dares not say it. Well, was the world agreed about this right explication of them? Who ever did rightly explain them? Point us to the person who did it, either for himself or others? Was every body able to do it for himself? If not, then I fear the world wanted still a sufficient religion, after all the pains taken to provide them in one. And further, what is the meaning of our author's wording the third article, " That virtue is the principal part of the worship of God?" This may be true, though it be not the *only part*. Well, though it is the *principal part*, may there not be *another part necessary*? Tho' perhaps the head of a man is the principal part, yet there are some other parts necessary. Was not the world as much agreed that there should be another part, as that this *was* a part of the worship of God? I believe it is easy to prove the world was more agreed as to the *first* than the *last*. Why then must this be overlooked? I believe I could guess pretty near,—he was afraid to do it, because he saw that he would presently be confounded with the differences about the way of worship, and that he would never be able to maintain, that *reason* was sufficient to direct as to the *solemn worship of God*; and that, if he should assert it, he would have not only Christians to dispute the point with him, but Heathens. But lest it should be thought what is alleged of the Heathen's looking on reason as incompetent for this, is groundless, I shall only copy you a little of Socrates and Alcibiades's discourse about worship out of Plato, or rather remind the reader of what we quoted from him before. Socrates meets Alcibiades going to the temple to pray, and dissuades him from it, because he knew not how to do it, till one should come and teach him. Socrates says, " It is al-
" together necessary you should wait for some person to teach
" you how you ought to behave yourself, both towards the
" gods and men." Alcibiades replies, " And when will that
" time come, Socrates? And who is he that will instruct me?
" With what pleasure should I look on him!" Whereupon Socrates bids him hope " that God will do it, and will take the
" mist off his soul, and cure him of that darkness, that hinders
" him from distinguishing betwixt good and evil." Whereupon Alcibiades says, " I think I must defer my sacrifices to
" that time." To which Socrates returns, " You have rea-
" son: it is more safe to do so, than run so great a risk*"
And

* M. Dacier's Plato Englished, Vol. 1. pag. 249, 250. Second Alcibiad. Or, Of Prayer.

And the fame Plato elfewhere tells us, " That this inftructor " muft be a perfon fomewhat more than human." Nor was Jamblicus, a famous Platonick philofopher, who lived in the fourth century, otherwife minded, whofe words, as I find them tranflated by Mr. Fergufon, run thus: " It is not eafy to know " what God will be pleafed with, unlefs we be either immediate- " ly inftructed by God ourfelves, or taught by fome perfon " whom God hath converfed with, or arrive at the knowledge " of it by fome divine means or other *."

5. There is another thing that I would gladly be informed of, and that is, whether every fort of knowledge of them be fufficient? Or, is a clear, certain and firm perfuafion needful? If the firft, How can a dark, uncertain and wavering knowledge have that influence upon practice, and that vigour to excite to a compliance with them, which is abfolutely needful in order to attain the benefit of them? If the latter, How will our author prove, that it was any where to be met with, as to them all, in the Heathen world? Or, how will he make it appear, that it is attainable by mere reafon? Methinks our author's words above-noted, as to the fifth article, feem not to import any great certainty. This might be urged to that degree that it would be very hard, nay, I fear not to fay fo, impoffible, for the Deifts to rid their feet of it.

6. I would further know, Will thefe five articles be fufficient to this end, to lead to *eternal happinefs*, whether men direct to it or not? Is not the *intention* of fome confideration in moral actions? And what if I fhould deny that the religion of Heathens was directed to this end, the obtaining of future happinefs? If I fhould, I know fome very great men are of my mind. I fhall name two, the one a Chriftian, the other a Heathen. The *firft* is the famous Samuel Puffendorf, counfellor of ftate to the late king of Sweden. His words are worthy to be here tranfcribed, though fomewhat long. "Now to look back to " the firft beginnings of things, we find, that before the nativi- " ty of our Saviour, the inhabitants of the whole univerfe, ex- " cept the Jews, lived in grofs ignorance as to fpiritual affairs. " For what was commonly taught concerning the gods, was " for the moft part involved in fables, and moft extravagant abfurdities.

* Lib. 4. de Lege Civ. by Dr. Leflie againft the Jews. pag. 386. Ferg. Enquir. into moral virtue, &c. pag. 177. Jambli. de Vita. Pythag. Cap. 28.

"absurdities. It is true, some of the learned among them have
"pretended to give some rational account concerning the na-
"ture of the gods and the soul; but all this in so imperfect
"and dubious a manner, that they themselves remained very
"uncertain in the whole matter. They agreed almost all of
"them in this point, that mankind ought to apply themselves to
"the practice of virtue, but they did not propose any other fruits,
"but the honour and benefits, which thence did accrue to civil
"society. For what the poets did give out concerning the
"rewards of virtue and punishments of vice after death, was
"by these, who pretended to be the wisest among them, look-
"ed upon as fables, invented to terrify and keep in awe the
"common people. The rest of the people lived at random,
"and what the Heathens called religion, did not contain any
"doctrine or certain articles concerning the knowledge of di-
"vine matters. But the greatest part of their religious worship
"consisted in sacrifices and ceremonies, which tended more to
"sports and voluptuousness, than to the contemplation of di-
"vine things. Wherefore the Heathen religion did neither
"edify in this life, nor afford any hopes or comfort at the time
"of death*." Thus far he. Now methinks here is a quite different account of the Heathen world from that which our author
gives us, and that given by no churchman, but a statesman;
and one as learned as our author too, and that both in *history*
and the *law of nature*, as his works evince; and in my opinion
it is the juster of the two accounts. The *second* is Varro, quoted
by our author, who divides the religion of the Heathens into
three sorts, *Primum genus appellat* Mythicon, *secundum*, Civile
tertium, Phyficum †. The first is that of the poets, which is altogether *fabulous* The other which he calls *natural*, is that
of the philosophers, which is wholly employed about the nature
of the gods. And Varro expressly says, it was not meet for
for, nor of any use to the vulgar. The third sort was what
he calls *civil*, which was wholly calculated for human society,
and its support: and to this all the public worship belonged, if
we may believe Varro in the passage we now speak of. When
he has opened the nature of each of them, he concludes with
an account of the design of them. "*Prima theologia maxime*
"accom-

---

* Introduct. Hist. of Europe, pag. 357. Ch. 12. Par. 2.
† See it also in August. de Civit. Dei, Lib. 6. Cap. 5.

" *accommodata est ad theatrum: secunda scil. naturalis ad mun-*
" *dum: Tertia ad urbem* *." No word here of eternal life, as
the design of any of them. The passage itself fully excludes it,
and had it not been too long, had been worthy to be transcribed.

7. To draw to a conclusion, Was it enough to the Heathens
that these things were sufficient, although they did not know
them to be so? Or was it needful that they should know them
to be so? If the last be said, how could they be sure about that,
even the vulgar sort of them, which our author after all his application to this controversy, could not win to be sure of? If the
first be said, I would ask any Deist, Was not the end of natural
religion fixed, and were they not certain? Or might they not,
at least, be fixed and certain about it? If it was not, how could
they use or chuse means, or direct them to an end which was
not fixed, and they were not certain about? If it was, then with
what courage could they use means with respect to an end and
means, in the use of which they had so many difficulties to
grapple with; yet they could not be sure that they were sufficient by the least use of them to gain the end? Was it enough of
encouragement, that they might use them at all adventures, not
knowing whether they were, in themselves, sufficient to reach
the mark or not? Methinks our author is very defective as to
motives to excite to virtue.

C H A P. XVIII.

*Containing an answer to some of the Deists' principal arguments
for the sufficiency of Natural Religion.*

WE have now considered what the Deists plead from *universal consent;* and have sufficiently cleared that it is not
by them proven, that the world was *agreed* as to *these articles*;
that indeed the world did not agree about them; that even
they who owned them, were led to this acknowledgment, at
least of some of them, rather by *tradition* than *nature's light*;
and that though they had acknowledged them, they are not
sufficient. It now remains that we consider those arguments,
wherein they conceive the great strength of their cause to lie.

* " The first theology is fittest for the theatre, the second, to wit,
" the natural, for the world, and the third for the city."

The first argument, which indeed is the strongest the Deists can pretend unto, is thus proposed by their admired Herbert: "*Et quidem quum media ad victum, vestitumque heic commoda suppeditent cunctis natura sive Providentia rerum communis, suspicari non potui, eundem Deum, sive ex natura, sive ex gratia, in suppeditandis ad beatiorem hoc nostro statum, mediis, ulli hominum deesse posse vel velle, adeo ut licet mediis illis parum recte, vel feliciter usi sint Gentiles, haut ita tamen per Deum optimum maximum steterit, quo minus salvi fierent.*"*
To the same purpose speaks Blount in his *Religio Laici*, and *A. W.* in his letter to him in the *Oracles of Reason*, of whom afterwards. The force of all that is here pleaded will best appear, if it is put into a clear argument, and I shall be sure not to wrong it in the proposal. The argument runs thus:

The goodness of God makes it necessary that all men be provided in the means necessary for future bliss.

But all men are provided in no other means of attaining future bliss save nature's light.

Therefore no other means are necessary for all men save the light of nature.

The minor or second proposition needs not to be proven, since is it is owned by those who maintain revelation, that it is not given to all men, and therefore that many have indeed no other light to guide them, save that of nature, in matters of religion, or in any of their other concerns.

The first proposition, "That the goodness of God makes it necessary that all men be provided in the means of attaining future blessedness," is that which they are concerned to prove. And the strength of what they urge for proof of it amounts in short to this:

The goodness and wisdom of God seem to render it necessary that all creatures, but more especially the rational, be provided in all means necessary to obtain those ends they were made capable of, and obliged to pursue.

But men are made capable of, and obliged to pursue eternal happiness and felicity.

Therefore the goodness and wisdom of God make it necessary that all men should be provided in the means necessary to obtain future and eternal bliss.

Here we have the strength of their cause, and we shall therefore

---

* For the translation, see note at bottom of pag. 277 of this book.

fore confider this argument the more ferioufly, becaufe fome feem to be taken with it, and look upon it as having much force. Before I offer any direct anfwer, I fhall make fome general reflections on it. The firft procefs is only defigned to make way for this laft, which indeed is the argument, and contains the force of what is pleaded by the Deifts.

Now concerning this argument, we offer the few following reflections, which will not a little weaken its credit, and make it look fufpicious-like.

1. That propofition whereon its whole weight leans, viz. " That the goodnefs of God obliges him to provide his creatures in the means neceffary for attaining their ends," is one of that fort, about which we may, in particular cafes and applications of it, be as eafily miftaken, and are as little *in tuto**, to be pofitive in our determinations, as any where elfe. For, although we are furer of nothing than that *God is good*, and *muft act congruoufly to his goodnefs*, in general ; yet when we come to make particular inferences, and determine what, in point of goodnefs he is obliged to do, we are upon very flippery ground, efpecially if we have not, as in this cafe it is, the effects to guide us. For, befides that goodnefs is free in its effects, divine and not affixed to fuch ftated rules knowable by us, as juftice is, goodnefs, in its actings, is under the conduct and management of all-comprehending wifdom, which in every cafe wherein God is to act, confiders that a being not only infinitely good is to act, but alfo one who is infinitely wife, holy, juft and righteous ; and therefore all-comprehending wifdom takes under confideration, or rather has in its view the concernment of all thofe properties of the divine nature ; and withall, all the circumftances belonging to each particular cafe, and takes care that the cafe, in all its circumftances, be fo managed, that not one of the divine perfections fhine to the eclipfing of another ; but that all of them appear with a fuitable luftre. Now, it is certain that we, who are of fo narrow underftandings, and fo many other ways incapacited to judge of the ways of God, cannot reach either the different interefts of the divine properties, and judge, in a particular circumftanciated cafe, what befits a God, who is at once good, holy, wife and righteous ; nor can we reach all that infinite variety of circumftances, which lying open to the all-comprehending view of infinite and confummate wifdom, may make it appear quite otherwife to him than to us. Hence, in

---

* " In fafety."

in fact, we see that an almost infinite number of things fall out in the government of the world, which we know not how to reconcile to divine goodness: and as many are left undone, which we would be apt to think infinite goodness would make necessary to be done. This consideration, if well weighed, would make men very sparing in determining any thing necessary to be done, in respect of divine goodness, which either it is evident he has not done, or of which we are not sure that he has done, which perhaps we shall make appear, if it is not from what has been already said evident, to be the case.

2. I observe, as to what is advanced, " That man is made capable of, and obliged in duty to pursue eternal felicity," that although from revelation we know this to be true as to man in his original constitution, and by the remaining desires of it we may guess that possibly it was so; yet, if we set aside divine revelation, and consider man in his present state, concerning which the question betwixt us and the Deists proceeds, we cannot by the help of nature's light only, with any certainty conclude, " that man is capable of and obliged to pursue eternal felicity." We see the man dissolved by death. Nature's light knows nothing of a resurrection. Without a resurrection there is nothing can be said for man's eternal felicity. Though we grant his soul to have no principle of corruption in itself, and so to be in this sense immortal; yet this cannot secure us against the fears of annihilation. And the gusts and desires of felicity, from which we may be induced to suspect some such state designed for man, being apparently frustrated, by the dissolution of man, to which they have a respect, cannot but make men, who have no more save nature's light, hesitate mightily about this assertion; since it is plain, that the desires we find in ourselves of felicity, do respect the whole man; and the aversion we have to dissolution respects our natures in their present entire frame and constitution. Besides, it is of moment, that if man, now entire, is at a loss how to judge of the ends for which he was made, much more must he be supposed in a strait how to judge and determine for what ends any particular part belonging to his constitution was designed, after the dissolution of the whole in a separate state, that is, in all its concernments, so much hid from and unknown to us. Further, although undoubtedly as long as we are, it is our duty to make it our chief aim to please God, and seek for felicity only in him; yet since, not only our beings, but that felicity which may be supposed attainable

by

by us, are emanations from fovereign, free and undeferved bounty, without fome intimation from him, in way of promife, we can draw no fure conclufion as to its continuance, were we innocent, much lefs can we being guilty.

3. This argument concludes nothing in favour of the Deifts; whatever it may fay for the Heathens. For were it granted, that God is obliged to provide all men in the means neceffary to future felicity; and that he has not given all men any other means: yet it cannot be hence inferred, that he has given no other means to fome. In this cafe, if all this were granted, which yet we have not done, it would follow, that they, who have no other means, muft look on thefe as fufficient, and that they really are fo: But ftill God is left at liberty to prefcribe other duties to any particular perfons, or nations, by *revelation*; and if this revelation come, they are obliged, to whom it comes, to attend, receive and obey it. Now if the *fcriptures* be a *divine revelation*, attended with fufficient evidence, which the Deifts muft either allow, or overthrow what it pleads for itfelf; they are everlaftingly undone, unlefs they receive it, and comply with it.

4. I obferve, that the conclufion of this argument, which it aims at the eftablifhment of, viz. *That God in point of goodnefs, muft provide all men in the means neceffary to future felicity, and confequently has done it*, is exceedingly prejudiced, by its lying crofs to the plain fenfe and experience of the world in all ages, as has been plainly made appear. Now in this cafe, where the principles or premiffes are dark, and fuch whereabout we may eafily be miftaken, which is the cafe here, as appears by the two firft reflections; and the conclufion carries a manifeft contradiction to what we muft certainly know, and have experience of; in this cafe we have reafon to conclude, that there lies certainly a fallacy or miftake in one or other of the principles, though we cannot difcover prefently were it precifely is. And therefore, although men could not eafily except againft the premiffes or principles, whence it is deduced; yet they would think themfelves fufficiently warranted, if not plainly to reject, yet to be fhy in admitting the conclufion: forafmuch as the admitting the conclufion will oblige them to deny what their own fenfe and experience, as well as that of the world, affures them about: Whereas, it is much more reafonable to think and determine that there lies fome fallacy in the principles, though it may be they are not in cafe to detect it. No man,

man, by the arguments againſt motion, can be brought to queſtion its being, much leſs its poſſibility; yet there are thouſands, even no mean ſcholars, who cannot anſwer the arguments that conclude againſt it. But in very deed, this argument is not ſo ſtrong, as to need ſo much nicety.

Having thus far weakened it by theſe general reflections, I ſhall next lay down and clear ſome propoſitions that will lay a foundation for a cloſe anſwer to it.

1. All men, at preſent, are involved in guilt, have corrupt inclinations, and are under an inability to yield perfect obedience to the law, they are ſubjected to. That all in more or leſs, are guilty of ſin, cannot be well denied, and we have heard the *Oracles of Reaſon* owning, "That all do err ſometimes, " even the beſt, in their actions." That men are corrupt, or have corrupt inclinations, has been above ſufficiently evinced. That all are under ſome ſort of inability to yield perfect obedience, is atteſted by the experience of all, and beſides, is an inevitable conſequent of the former: for it is not poſſible to ſuppoſe one poſſeſt of corrupt inclinations, and yet able to yield perfect obedience. Nor need we ſtand to prove what the Deiſts own. For A. W. in his Letter to Charles Blount, ſpeaking of the law of nature, ſays, " I do not ſay that we are able perfectly to obey it." I diſpute not now of what ſort this inability is, whether only moral, ſuch as ariſes from the will's inclination to evil; or natural, which imports ſuch an inability as ſuppoſes the nature of the faculties vitiated, though the faculties are not wanting. The condemnings of our own hearts, and the nature of the moral government we are under, ſufficiently aſſures us, it is ſuch as does not excuſe from fault; and further we are not concerned: though, after all, I do not underſtand how the will can be fixed in an inclination to evil, or averſation from good, unleſs the nature of the will be ſuppoſed affected with ſome indiſpoſition, though the faculty is not removed. But of this only by the bye. It is enough to our preſent purpoſe, that man is guilty, corrupt, and thence unable. He that will deny this, muſt ſuppoſe us blind and ſenſeleſs.

2. If reaſon can aſcertain us of any thing, it does of this, that things were not originally thus with man, or that man, when he was firſt made, was not thus guilty, corrupt or impotent. None will any dare to ſay, that at firſt he was guilty. And to aſſert him either corrupt or impotent, overthrows all the juſt notions we have of the Deity. How can it be ſuppoſed, that infinite

wiſdom

wisdom could enact laws, which were not only not likely to take effect, but really could not possibly be obeyed by men subjected to them! How can we suppose infinite goodness to establish laws under a penalty, and deny the powers, which were indispensably requisite to obey them, and without which it was not possible to evite the penalty! How can we suppose infinite righteousness and holiness to consent to a constitution of this kind! How is it conceivable, that a God, wise, just and good, should originally have implanted in our natures inclinations contrary to those laws, that were the transcript of, and bore the impress of all these perfections! Or, how can we once dream that he implanted inclinations, which it was criminal to satisfy or comply with! For my part, I see not what can be reasonably said in answer to this.

3. It is further evident, that man could not have fallen into this state he now is in, or from that wherein he was made, but by his own default. If this is denied, I inquire, were shall the blame be laid? Will they lay it at God's door? Besides, that this is blasphemy, it is further evident, that all the former absurdities will recur: For it is to no purpose to give powers, and take them away again without any default in the person who loses them, the obligation to obedience or suffering upon disobedience still continuing. Nor can it be laid upon any other, because if man is without his own fault, robbed of the powers necessary to obey, the obligation to obedience cannot be righteously continued. Nor was it consistent with the divine wisdom, to have obliged men to obedience, under a penalty, while there was a possibility of man's losing the power to obey, without a fault on his own part. It remains then, that man has by his own fault forfeited what he has in this part lost. And to this our own conscience, and the consciences of all sinners, who are sensible of sin, consent, that God is free and we guilty.

4. Hereon it inevitably follows, that man is at present in a corrupt, sinful, and impotent state, into which by his own default, he has fallen. Nor see I how it is possible to evite this, which only sums up the three preceding assertions. The first whereof is undeniable with sober and ingenuous persons, being attested by the plainest and clearest experience, and the other two stand firm upon the clearest deductions that our reason can make. If any Deist shall say, How can this be that we are fallen into such a state? I answer, 1. The question is not, How can it be? but, Is it so? I think I have said enough to shew that it is so. 2. Hereby

by we may see natural religion has its mysteries too, as well as revealed. And I think I have told more than one of them. 3. If this will not satisfy, then get as much faith and humility as will teach you to subject yourself to supernatural instruction, and you may come to understand how it came to be so. If you will not, you must remain in the dark, and there is no help for it.

Now I have laid a plain foundation for an answer to this argument, whereon the Deists value themselves so much. It was not because I thought so long an answer needful for the argument, but to make the matter a little more plain, that we have discoursed it at this length.

The argument then runs thus, *The wisdom and goodness of God make it necessary that all his creatures should be provided in the means necessary for attaining the end of their being, and this holds especially as to the rational: But man was made capable of eternal felicity; or this is the end of his being.*

I need say nothing more to what has been advanced, than has been said above. I answer to the first proposition,—Be it allowed that God's wisdom and goodness required that the rational creature should be provided in the means necessary for the attainment of the end of his being, in his first make and original state: Yet neither God's goodness, nor his wisdom, obliges him to restore man, if by his own fault, he has fallen from that state, wherein at first he was made. Now this is the case with man in his present state, as we have told above.

If it is said, that this is but our assertion, That man is in a lapsed state: I answer, 1. I think it is more than an assertion, and must do so till I see what I have offered for proof of the foregoing propositions fairly answered. Nay, till I see the whole arguments that have heretofore been offered against the sufficiency of natural religion, answered. For, I think they all prove that man is at present in a lapsed state. But, 2. I add, that the Deists must mind, we are upon the defensive, and it is their province to prove, that man in his present condition is not so situated, as we say. It was *ex abundanti* for clearing of truth, that I condescend to prove this. It was enough to me to have denied that man is now in his original state, and put the proof upon them; in regard they affirm, and the whole stress and force of their argument leans upon that supposition which we deny.

The

PRINCIPLES OF THE MODERN DEISTS.

The second argument, on which the Deists lay much stress, is drawn from the supposed ill-consequences attending our opinion. They pretend, that it is horribly cruel to imagine, that all the Heathen world were lost. This they inculcate upon all occasions, rather to expose their adversaries, I am afraid, than to confirm the truth. The sum of this argument we see proposed by Herbert in his words above quoted. Where he tells us, that all will own his articles to be good ; *Ad salutem tamen æternam comparandam, non sufficere prohibebunt nonnulli. Cæterum, qui ita locutus fuerit, næ ille quidem audax ; nedum sævum temerariumq ; effatum mea sententiâ protulerit**. The short of the matter is this, " If natural religion is not sufficient, we must give all the Heathen world for lost ; but this is a cruel and harsh assertion, injurious to God, and cruel to such a vast number of men." And here they raise a horrible outcry. With this they begin, and with this they end.

This argument, although it has no force, as we shall evince, yet makes such a noise at a distance, that a great many ingenuous spirits seem to be mightily affected with it: I conceive therefore that it will not be improper to lay open the causes of this, and the rather because they discover where the fallacy of the argument lies, and whence it is that men are so easily prepossessed in this matter. To this purpose then it is to be observed,

1. That there are some things which in themselves are not desirable ; to which therefore no uncorrupted rational nature, much less that of God, could incline merely upon their own account: which yet, in some circumstantiate cases, may be every way congruous to justice and righteousness; yea, and worthy of the wise and good God. The torment of any rational creature is not in, or for itself desirable : God has no pleasure in it. The nature of man, if not deeply corrupted, yea, and divested of humanity, recoils at it; yet there is none, who will not allow that in many circumstantiate cases, it is not only worthy of, but plainly necessary in point of wisdom and justice, for the most merciful of men, to inflict upon their fellow creatures such punishments, as their own natures do shrink at the apprehensions of. Nor can it be denied that the holy God, notwithstanding

---

* De Rel. Gentil. pag. 217. "—Yet some will think they are not " sufficient for attaining eternal life. But whoever would say so, would " be guilty of uttering not only a bold, not to say a cruel and arbitrary " sentence in my opinion."

standing of, and without prejudice to his infinite goodnefs, may, nay in fome cafes muft, likewife thus punifh his own creatures. Now, if fuch things are reprefented as they are, in their own natures, without a due confideration of circumftances and ends inducing to them, it is eafy to make them appear not only hard, but odious.

2. However juft, righteous and congruous fuch actions are; yet he who undertakes to expofe them as cruel, barbarous and hard, efpecially, if he has to do with perfons, weak, ignorant, partial in favour of the fufferer, and averfe from the author of the torment, has a far more eafy tafk, even though he is of weaker abilities, and employed in defence of the worft caufe, than he who undertakes to defend fuch actions. The reafon of this is obvious; all that makes to his purpofe, who defigns to expofe the action as cruel, lies open in its nature and horror to the thoughts of the moft inconfiderate; and if to this he only fets off the reprefentation with a little art, fo as to touch the affections, which in this cafe is eafily done, he has carried his point; the judgment is not only deceived, but the affections are fo deeply engaged in the quarrel, as to preclude the light of the moft nervous and valid defence imaginable. Whereas on the other hand, all things are quite otherwife. The circumftances inducing to fuch actions, are ufually deep, and not fo eafily difcernible, and therefore not to be found out, without much confideration; and when they are found out, they are not eafily collected, laid together, and ranged in that order, which is neceffary to fet the atrocity of the crime in a due light, efpecially where the perfons who are to judge are weak and biaffed. Befides, the evil of thofe crimes, being for moft part more fpiritual, makes not fo ftrong an impreffion on the affections. And this confideration holds more efpecially true, where the queftion is concerning the judgments of God, which proceed upon that comprehenfive view, which infinite wifdom has of all circumftances, that accent the evil, aggravate the fault, and enhance the guilt of fins committed againft him; many of which circumftances no mortal penetration can reach. And further, this more particularly holds true, where it is not God himfelf, but man that pleads on behalf of the actings of God. It is very obfervable to this purpofe, that hiftorians of all nations almoft condefcend upon inftances, wherein the fight of fevere, but juft punifhment of atrocious offenders has not only excited the compaffion of the populace to the fufferers, but enraged

them

them againſt the judge. Even they who would have been ready to reclaim againſt the partiality and negligence of the judge, if the crimes had been paſſed without juſt puniſhment, when they ſee the puniſhment inflicted, through a fond ſort of compaſſion to the ſufferers, complain of the cruelty of the judge, laying aſide all thoughts of the atrocity of the crime.

3. Where they, who make it their buſineſs to traduce ſuch actions, as hard and cruel, and they alſo, whom they labour to perſuade of this, are connected by alliance, or common intereſt with the ſufferers, are themſelves in the ſame condemnation, or, upon the ſame and ſuch like accounts, obnoxious to that juſtice, which adjudges thoſe ſufferers to theſe torments, which they ſtudy to repreſent as cruel and barbarous, it is no wonder to ſee the repreſentation make ſuch deep impreſſions, and rivet ſuch a perſuaſion, that the puniſhments are cruel and hard, as may not only bias a little againſt any defence that can be made for the judge, but may even make them refuſe to admit of any apology, or condeſcend ſo far as to give any that can be made a fair hearing. But all unbiaſſed perſons muſt allow, that ſuch can never be admitted judges competent, as to what is juſt or unjuſt, hard or otherwiſe; the caſe being, in effect, their own, and they by this means being made both judge and party.

4. However great, terrible and heavy any puniſhment that God is ſuppoſed to inflict, may in its own nature appear, or how great ſoever the number of the ſufferers may be, yet we can never, from the ſeverity of the puniſhment, or the number of the ſufferers, diſprove its juſtice, unleſs we can make it appear, that no circumſtances, which can poſſibly fall under the reach of infinite wiſdom, can render ſuch ſeverity towards ſo many perſons, worthy of him. Now, however eaſy this undertaking may appear to perſons leſs conſiderate, it will have a far other aſpect to ſuch as impartially ponder, that all men are manifeſtly partial in favour of thoſe of their own race, and in a caſe which is, or may be their own, and have no ſuitable apprehenſions of the concernments of the divine glory in it, or no due regard for them: Beſides ſuch is their ſhallowneſs, that they can neither have under view many important circumſtances, that are fully expoſed to all-comprehending wiſdom, nor can they fully underſtand the weight, even of theſe circumſtances, that they either do, or may, in ſome meaſure know.

5. Every

5. Every man, who is wife and juft, when either he hears of, or fees any punifhment that appears very fevere and terrible, muft fufpend his judgment as to the hardfhip of it, till the author of it is fully heard as to the inducements, and neither ought he to deny what his eyes fee, his ears hear, or he is otherwife informed of, upon fufficient evidences. He is neither to queftion the matter of fact, nor condemn the judge of cruelty, becaufe of the feeming feverity of the punifhment. This is a piece of common juftice, which every judge, even amongft men, may reafonably claim from his fellow creatures, although his actions and the reafons of them, cannnot be fuppofed to lie fo far out of their ken, as thofe of the divine judgments: Much more is it reafonable for men to pay this deference to God, confidering how unable the moft elevated capacities are to penetrate into all the reafons, which an infinitely wife God may have under view; and there is the more reafon for this, fince man alfo is naturally fo very apt to be partial in his own favour, and to fail of giving a due regard in his thoughts unto the concernments of divine glory.

Thefe obfervations, as they are in themfelves unqueftionably true, fo they do fully lay open the caufes of that general acceptance, which this plea of the Deifts has obtained with lefs attentive minds; and how little weight is to be laid upon them. In a word, if they are well confidered, they are fufficient to enervate the force of this whole plea.

But leaft the Deifts fhould think their argument flighted, or that confcioufnefs of our own weaknefs, makes us choofe long weapons to fight with, I fhall clofely confider the argument. Perhaps what makes a noife, at a diftance, will be lefs frightful if we take a nearer view of it. We deny that the Heathen world had means fufficient for obtaining eternal happinefs. The Deifts fays, this is *cruel* and *rafh*. Let us now fee whence this may be proven.

1. Doth our cruelty lie in this, That we have laid down an affertion, upon which it follows, that in fact *all the Heathen world are loft?* But now, do not the Deifts own, that in very deed, all impenitent finnners muft perifh? No doubt they do, who talk fo much of the *neceffity of repentance*. Well, are not all who want revelation, guilty of grofs fins? Is not idolatry a grofs fin? are they not all plunged in the *guilt* of it? Socrates, the moft confiderable perfon for his virtue, that lived before Chrift, cannot be excufed. He denied his difowning the gods of Athens. He joined in their worfhip. If this was againft his

his confcience, the more was his fault. And, even with his dying breath, he ordered a cock to be facrificed to Efculapius. Epictetus, the beft perhaps among the philofophers who lived after Chrift, in his *Enchiridion*, enjoins to worfhip after the mode of the country where we live ; and no doubt practifed as he taught. Gentlemen, condefcend, if ye can, upon one, who was not guilty of grofs fins. Did they repent? What evidence bring you of it? That the multitude lived and died impenitent, none dare queftion. That there was *one* penitent none can prove. That the beft of them were guilty of grofs fins cannot be denied, and there is no evidence of their penitence. Yea, there is no reafon to think that they looked upon repentance as a virtue ; but much to the contrary. Well, gentlemen, do not your *own principles* conclude, that the bulk of the Heathen world are, in fact inevitably loft? And that there is but little ground of hope, and great reafon to fear, that it fared not much better with the few *virtuofi* ?

2. But doth the cruelty lie in the number of the perfons fuppofed to be loft? No. This cannot be faid. For if the caufe be fufficient, the number of the condemned makes not the condemnation the more cruel. Befides, let them go as narrowly to work as they can, they are few, very few, for whom they can plead exemption : and their pleas for that handful will be very lame. So that for any thing I fee, the Deifts, in this refpect, are not like to be much more merciful than we.

3. But perhaps the cruelty lies in this, That we fuppofe them condemned without a caufe, or without one that is fufficient. But this we do not, we fuppofe none to be condemned, who are not finners againft God, and tranfgreffors of a law ftamped with his authority, which they had accefs to know. And were not the beft of them guilty of grofs fins? What evidence have we of their repentance? Is it not juft, even according to the Deifts' principles, to condemn impenitent finners? Thus we fuppofe none condemned, but for their fins.

4. But perhaps the cruelty lies in this, That we fuppofe them all equally miferable; Socrates to be in no better cafe than Nero. But this follows not upon our affertion. None are fuppofed miferable beyond the juft demerit of their fins.

5. Well, perhaps the cruelty lies in this, That we fuppofe their torments after this life to be intenfe in degree, or of a longer continuance than their fins deferve. This we are fure of, that their fins being offences againft God, deferve a deeper punifhment

punishment, than some men can well think of; and that God is just, and will proportion punishments exactly to offences, and have a just regard, as well to the real alleviations as aggravations of every sin. And if God has, in his word, determined that every sin committed against him, deserves eternal punishment, no doubt his *judgment is according to truth.* We are not judges in the case.

6. Well, but the rashness and cruelty perhaps lies here, That by our assertion we are obliged to pass a positive and peremptory judgment about the eternal state of all the Heathen world, that they are gone to hell, and laid under everlasting punishments, leaving no room for the mercy of God. But to this we say, revelation has taught us, even where there is the justest ground of fear, to speak modestly of the eternal condition of others, and to leave the judgment concerning this to the righteous God, to whom alone it belongs, and who will *do no iniquity.* That all the Heathen world deserve punishment, cannot, without impudence, be denied. That God will pass any of them without inflicting the punishment they deserve, neither revelation nor reason give us any ground to think. That none of them shall be punished beyond their deservings, scripture and reason demonstrate. But in these things our assertion of the insufficiency of natural religion is not concerned. It obliges us to pass no judgment further than this, " That the Heathens, and all who " want revelation, had no means sufficient to bring them to e-" ternal happiness, and that consequently they had no reason " to expect it; and we have no reason to conclude them pos-" sessed of it." And in this case we leave them to be disposed of, as to their state, after this life, by the wisdom and justice of God.

7. But perhaps the cruelty lies in this, That they are supposed to want the means necessary to attain eternal happiness, while yet they are capable of, and exposed to eternal misery for their sins. But, 1. How will the Deists' prove, That God, without a promise, is obliged to give man eternal happiness for his obedience? 2. Since none of them are to be punished beyond the just demerit of their sins, may not God righteously inflict that punishment, whatever it is, that their sins, in strict justice, deserve, though he had never proposed a reward, which reason can never prove our best actions worthy of, even though we had continued innocent? But, 3. That man, in his present case, has lost the knowledge of eternal felicity, and the means of attaining
it,

it, and is unable to attain it, is owing not to any defect of bounty and goodnefs of God, much lefs of juftice; but only unto the fin of man, as has been demonftrated in our anfwer to the foregoing argument, by reafons drawn from nature's light. Notwithftanding of which, it muft ftill be owned, that nature's light cannot acquaint us, how man fell into his prefent lamentable condition, as we have above made appear.

8. But is it not fafer and more modeft, may fome fay, to fuppofe, that God of his great mercy did, by revelation, communicate to fome of the beft of the Heathens, who improved nature's light to the greateft advantage, what was further neceffary to their falvation, or, at leaft to bring them into a ftate of happinefs, of fomewhat inferior degree to that which is prepared for Chriftians. I know many Chriftian writers of old and of late have multiplied hypothefis of this kind: Some have fuppofed apparitions of angels, faints, nay damned fouls and devils; of which ftories I am told that Collius difcourfes at large in the fecond book of his treatife *De Animabus Paganorum**. Some tell us, " That to fuch of them as lived virtuoufly, God always at fome time or other fent fome man or angel favingly to illuminate them †." So the Areopagites. Some tell us of Chrift's preaching to them in purgatory, fo Clemens Alexandrinus; fome will have them inftructed by the Sibylls, as the fame author fays elfewhere; fome talk of their commerce with the Jews, in which way no doubt fome of them came to faving acquaintance with God; others fay, that upon their worthy improvement of their *naturals*, God might and did reveal Chrift to them and *fpirituals*, becaufe *habenti dabiter* ‡. So Arminius. And of this Herbert frequently intimates his approbation, but with an evident contradiction to, and fubverfion of his whole ftory about the fufficiency of natural religion. Befides, the bottom of this is a rotten Pelagian fuppofition of a merit in their good works: and that *habenti dabiter*, fpoken of in another cafe, after all the pains fome are to ftretch it, will not reach this cafe: and after all we are left in the dark, as to the way wherein they will have fupernaturals communicated to them. The late ingenious author of the *Conference with a Theift*, fuppofes a place provided for the fober Pagans in another world, wherein they fhall enjoy a confiderable happinefs §, and wrefts what

our

---

* De cœlefti Hierar. Ch. 9.   † Strom. Lib. 6.
‡ " To him that hath fhall be given."
§ Nicol. Confer. Part 2, pag. 80.

our Lord says to his disciples, John xiv. 3. of the *many mansions that are in his Father's house*, to favour his notion. But now as to all these suppositions and others of the same alloy, however their authors may please themselves in them, I think they are to be rejected. Nor is this from any defect of charity to the Heathens, but because they are supported by no foundation, either in scripture or reason. However some of them are possible, yet generally speaking, none of them have the countenance so much as of a probable argument. The scripture proof, adduced by that last mentioned ingenious author, has no weight in it. There is no countenance given to it from the context, nor any other place of scripture, and I cannot approve of his boldness in stretching our Lord's words beyond what his scope requires. But these things have been considered at length by others, whom the reader may consult*. All these suppositions are at best but ingenious fancies, wherewith their authors may please themselves, but can never satisfy others. Nor can they be of any advantage to the Heathens. I think I have made it sufficiently appear in the foregoing discourse, that they wanted *means sufficient* to lead them to *salvation*, and so had no ground to support a reasonable hope of it. It is granted even by those, whose peculiar hypothesis in divinity lead them to be most favourable to the Heathens, that *they had no federal certainty of salvation*; and for any *uncovenanted mercy*, of which some talk, I know nothing about it. Scripture is silent. Reason can determine nothing in it; and therefore disputes about it are to be waved. It is unwarantable curiosity for men to pry into the secrets of God; *things that are revealed do belong to us*. Where revelation stops we are to stop. Even Herbert himself dare carry the matter no further than a *may be*; and what may be, may not be.

CHAP.

---

* See Anth. Tuckney, Appendix to his Sermon on Acts iv. 12.

CHAP. XIX.

Wherein Herbert's Reasons for publishing his Books in Defence of Deism are examined and found weak.

THE learned Herbert, toward the close of his book *De Religione Laici*, to justify the publication of his thoughts, as to a *catholic religion*, common to all mankind, mentions seven supposed advantages of this opinion, or so many pleas for Deism. What weight there is in them, we shall now consider.

He introduces himself with a protestation that he published not his book with any ill design against Christianity, which he honours with the title of *optima religio:* But on the contrary says, That he aimed at establishing it, and intended to strengthen true faith, " *Denique me animo adeo non optimæ religioni in-* " *senso, aut a vera fide alieno tractatum hunc edidisse testor; ut* " *utramque statuminare in animo habuerim*, &c.

I shall not dive into his designs; for which he has long ago accounted unto the only competent Judge. But of the design, or rather tendency of his books, we may safely judge. And as to this I say, that if it is granted, that the scriptures are the only standard of the Christian religion, which cannot modestly be denied; I shall upon this supposition undertake to maintain against any who will defend him, That his books aim at the utter subversion of the Christian religion, that his principles overthrow entirely the authority of the scriptures, and are not only inconsistent with, but destructive to the essentials of Christianity. And I further add, that this is every where so obvious in his writings, that it will require a strange stretch of charity, to believe our author could be ignorant of it.

Our author having told us what was not his design, proceeds next to condescend upon the reasons inducing him to assert this common religion. And

1. He tells us that he maintains this common religion, " *Quod* " *providentiam divinam*, &c. Because it " vindicates the univer- " sal

---

* Herbert Relig. Laici, pag. 28.—" In fine, I profess that I have
" published this treatise with a mind so far from being hostile to the
" best religion, or averse to the true faith, that I intended to establish
" both."

"sal Providence of God, God's principal attribute, whose dignity
"can never be sufficiently supported. Neither do any particu-
"lar religion, or faith (to give you our author's own words,
"*Fides quantumvis laxa)* maintain this, so as to represent
"God's care of all mankind, in providing for them such com-
"mon principles as those contained in our catholick truths."

Here our author teaches two things, and I think them both false. (1.) He tells us, "That his catholick religion vindicates "the universal providence of God, or serves to maintain its "honour." This I think false. The foundation of it we have proved to be not only precarious, but false. For we have cleared, that his five articles did not universally obtain; and further, that if they had, they were not sufficient to happiness. Yea, our author himself, after he has told us, that the universal providence of God cannot be maintained, unless we suppose him to have provided all his creatures, in the means necessary for obtaining their happiness, next informs us that he has provided man in no other means, save these five articles*. And he further tells us in his words above quoted, that he dare not positively say they are sufficient, nor can we be sure of it, since it depends upon God's secret judgments, which we cannot certainly know.† And we have heard Blount above own, That Deism is not safe, unless it be pieced out by some help from Christianity ‡. Well, is this the way our author asserts the honour of divine universal Providence, first to tell us, that its honour cannot be maintained without supposing a *sufficient religion universally to have obtained*, and then to tell us that he is *not sure*, that ever there was such a religion? Is not this the plain way to bring the universal Providence of God in question?

Again, 2dly, Our author teaches, "That no particular reli-"gion can support the honour of universal Providence." This I take to be also false. The Christian religion asserts and proves, that God, who has created all things, preserves them, and governs them in a way suitable to their nature and circumstances, and in so far clears the equity of God's proceedings with the Heathen world, in particular, as may satisfy sober men. It acquaints us, that God did, at first, provide man in a covenant-security for eternal happiness, and in means sufficient for obtaining

* De Rel. Laici, pag. 1, 4. † De Rel. Gentil. pag. 217.
‡ Oracles of Reason pag. 87.

ing of it; that man, by his own fault, incapacitated himself for the use of these means, and forfeited the advantage of the covenant-security; that God, in justice hath left the Heathen world under the disadvantage of that forfeiture; that during the time he sees meet to spare them, he governs them, in such a way as is suitable to their lapsed state, of which we have spoke before. We confess we are not able to explain all the hard chapters in the book of Providence, and solve every difficulty relating thereto; but this affords no ground for the denial either of God's general or special providence. As the difficulties about God's omniscience, omnipresence, eternity, &c. will not justify a denial of these attributes, or the existence of a Deity vested with them; so neither will the difficulties about Providence justify a refusal of it; and if this vindication of Providence fail of giving satisfaction, I am sure Herbert's will never satisfy.

What our author adds about his *fides quantumvis laxa*, which he supposes some to stand up for, and maintain as a sufficient religion, I do not well understand. But yet since this expression is very often used in the writings of this author, in reproach of particular religions, especially the Christian, which lays the greatest stress upon faith, it cannot be passed without some remark. That which our author seems to intend by this *fides quantumvis laxa*, or " faith how lax soever it may be," is a faith that consists in a general assent to the truth of the doctrines, without any correspondent influence upon practice. And he would have us to believe that the Christian religion, or, at least, Christians, do reckon this sufficient to salvation. This is a base and disingenuous calumny. And our author could not but know it to be such, if he was acquainted either with the scriptures, or the writings and lives of that set of Christians against whom this calumny is particularly levelled, who unanimously teach, that the faith that is available, is that which *works by love*, and is to be found only in them who are *created in Christ Jesus to good works*. If Herbert was a stranger to the one or the other, he was the unmeetest person in the world to set up for a judge and censurer of them.

2. The next advantage that Herbert condescends on, of his catholick religion, is, *Quod probam facultatem homini insitarum conformationem, usumque doceat. Nulla enim datur veritas catholica, quæ non in foro interno describitur, vel non illuc saltem necessario reducitur**. That is, " This alone teaches man the due use

---

* Herbert Rel. l aici, pag. 28.

"use and application of his faculties." But this is only our author's assertion. Christianity is no less consistent with the due use of our faculties and their application to their proper objects, than our author's religion. It destroys none of them, lays none of them aside, and does violence to none of them; but restores, improves and elevates them to their most noble and proper use.

Our author adds, for a confirmation of his assertion, that there is no catholick verity, but what either is inscribed in the mind, or what may be reduced to some innate truth. Whether there is any verity inscribed in the mind in our author's sense, I question. Mr. Locke has proven, that there is none such, and in particular has evinced that our author's five articles are not innate truths, no not according to the description he himself gives of such notices. He examines the characters of innate truth given by our author, and undertakes to shew them not applicable to his five articles*.

3. Our author tells us, he embraced this catholick religion, *quod incontroversa a controversis distinguat*†, &c. It is needless to repeat all our author's words here. What he says is in short this, That "*particular religion* (and here he must be understood to speak particularly of Christianity) *contains austere and frightful doctrines that prejudge some men of squeamish stomachs at all religion* (and is it to be wondered at, that men who have no heart to any religion, are easily disgusted?) But our author has provided them with one that will not offend the most nice and delicate palate, as consisting of *principles universally agreed to*; which he supposes such persons will readily close with, and so retain some religion, whereas otherwise they would have none.

Here our author evidently designs a thrust at the Christian religion, and insinuates that it is stuffed with *austere and horrid doctrines*. I know full well what are the doctrines he particularly aims at: the doctrines concerning *the corruption of man's nature, the decrees of God, the satisfaction of Christ*, are particularly intended. But if these doctrines are considered as delivered in the scriptures, or taught by Christians according to the scriptures, what is there offensive in them? What horrid or frightful?

I do

* Locke's Essay on Human. Under. Book 1. Ch. . § 15, 16, 17, 18, 19.
† "Because it distinguishes uncontroverted points from those which "are controverted."

PRINCIPLES OF THE MODERN DEISTS.

I do indeed grant, that some Christians, through their weakness, without any ill-design, have to represented, or rather misrepresented some of these points, particularly concerning *the decrees of God,* as to give offence to sober persons of all persuasions. But as to this, they, and they only, are to bear the blame. As for the doctrines, What have they done? Must the fault of the professors be cast on the religion they profess? This no reasonable man will allow to be just.

I do likewise acknowledge, that whereas there are different sentiments among Christians concerning some of these points; and some of the contending parties have so unfairly stated, and foully misrepresented the opinions of their opposers, in the disguise of imaginary consequences, or consequences, at least, denied and abhorred by the maintainers of the opinions they oppose, as to give some umbrage to this, startle weak men, and prejudge them against religion. This they do to expose their adversaries, and frighten others from the reception of their sentiments. For such I can make no excuse. The practice itself is scandalously disingenuous, and can admit of no reasonable vindication, and so fair an occasion being given, I cannot pass it without a remark. A notable instance of this sort I meet with in a book just now come to hand. The ingenious author of *the short Method with the Deists,* in a letter directed to Charles Gildon, newly recovered from Deism, cautions him against the Dissenters, and to enforce his caution, presents him with such an account of their opinions, as is indeed suited to frighten the reader. He tells him, that they maintain, " That God sees no " sin in the elect, let them live never so wickedly. They " damn the far greater part of the world, by irreversible de- " crees of reprobation, and say, that their good works are hate- " ful to God; and that it is not possibly in their power to be " saved, let them believe as they will, and live never so religi- " ously: They take away free will in man, and make him a " perfect machine. They make God the author of sin, to " create men on purpose to damn them;——they make his " promises and threatenings to be of no effect, nay, to be a " sort of burlesquing, and insulting those whom he has made " miserable, which is an hideous blasphemy *." But to what purpose is all this said? 1. Did not the writer know, That this is not a representation at all of the opinions maintained by the Dissenters, but of the consequences tacked to them by their adversaries?

* Letter subjoined to the Deist's Manuel, pag. 22, 33.

versaries? Does he not know, that they detest and abhor these positions as much as he does, that they refuse these to be consequences of them? Is it then candid to offer that as their opinions, which they abhor, and which they will not allow to follow upon their opinion? Again, 2. Doth not this gentleman know that the principles to which he has tacked these consequences, are the very doctrines taught in the *articles of the Church of England*, unanimously maintained by all the great men of that church, till Bishop Laud's days; which were preached by them in the pulpit, taught in the schools, and upon all occasions avouched as the doctrine of the Church of England; and, as such, to this very day are owned by no inconsiderable number of that church? With what justice then, or ingenuity, can he call this the doctrine of the Dissenters? 3. From whom does he expect credit to this disingenuous account of the Dissenter's opinion? Such as know them, will believe nothing upon the reading of this passage; but that the writer either understood not the opinions he undertook to represent, or that against his light, he misrepresented them, and so is never to be credited again, without good proof, in any thing he says of them. 4. Was it the author's design to gain a proselyte to the opposite opinions? This I believe it was. But this is the most unlucky way of management in the world; for if his disciple is a man of sense, he will be shy of believing that such monstrous opinions can be received by a body of men, among whom, there must be owned by their worst enemies, to be not a few learned and sober. And if he find himself abused, upon search, may he not be tempted, not only to reject this account, but all that he received upon the same authority? When persons of sense, who have been abused, are undeceived, they are wont ever after to incline to favourable thoughts of the persons and principles they were prejudged against; and to suspect that cause of weakness, which cannot be supported, but by such mean and unmanly shifts, as this of representing the opposite opinion. 5. If the adverse party shall take the same course, what a fine work shall we have? And to speak modestly, they want not a colourable pretence for a retortion. But who shall be the gainers? Neither of the contending parties surely: For men will never be beaten from their opinions by calumnies that they know to be unjust. None will gain, save they, who are lying at the catch, for pretences to countenance them in the rejection of the Christian religion. It is none of my business to debate this controversy with this author.

If he has any thing new to advance upon thefe heads, let him advance it, he will find antagonifts in the Church of England, able perhaps to cope with him, though the Diffenters fhould fail. This gentleman had managed his oppofition with more modefty and ingenuity, if he had attentively perufed the learned Bifhop of Sarum's difcourfe on the 17th article of the Church of England. But I hope this author, upon fecond thoughts, when his paffion is over, will be afhamed of what he has written.

But now to return to Herbert and the Deifts. If we abftract from thefe two abufes, and confider the doctrines of Chriftianity as reprefented in the fcriptures, or according to them, there is no ground to charge them with any thing frightful, or of ill confequence to religion. Yea, I dare be fo bold as to fay, That if practical religion, confifting in godlinefs, righteoufnefs and fobriety, is any where to be found in the world, it is to be found amongft thofe, as readily as any where elfe, and in as eminent a degree, who have been trained up in the belief, and under the influence of thofe very doctrines, which fome, and particularly Herbert, would perfuade us to be fo horrid, as to frighten men at once out of their wits and religion. If it be faid, that this is not owing to the influence of thefe principles. I anfwer, This, at leaft, proves thofe principles not inconfiftent with practical religion, in as much as they, who believe them, are eminent in it; and, if we inquire of them, what has influenced their walk, they are ready to atteft, that the belief of thefe very truths has had the principal influence upon that effect; and to offer a rational account of the tendency of thefe doctrines to promote practical religion.

Now we have wiped off the infinuated reproach, defigned by our author, againft the Chriftian religion. Let us next confider what there is in this plea. He tells us, His religion confifts of incontroverted articles, and fo will frighten no body. But, 1. This is not true in fact, as we have demonftrated above. His articles have been controverted. The fufficiency of them has been believed by very few. Again, 2. Will our author fay, That nothing is neceffary, to religion, which is controverted? Will the Deifts undertake this point? If fo, their religion is loft, as is evident from what has been demonftrated above. 3. This no more proves our author's five articles to be a fufficient religion, than it proves one of them alone to be fuch. He who owns no more in religion, but this only, *there is a God*, may as well plead, that religion retains only what is incontrovertible. But the Deifts' will fay, there are other points neceffary.

ry. Well does not this give me an anfwer to their argument, when I fay, there are other points neceffary befides their five articles.
4. Whereas he would perfuade us, that no man will fcruple his his religion: Is not this enough to make any reafonable man fhy of admitting it, that its author and inventer dare not fay pofitively, that it is fufficient to anfwer the purpofe, for which it is defigned, and that others undertake to demonftrate, that if it is trufted to, it will prove a foul-ruining cheat? In a word, it is not worth the while to calculate a religion for thofe, who will admit nothing in religion, but what is incontroverted: for, in fhort, they are for *no religion.* And I think we have in particular evinced, that our author's five articles will be too hard in digeftion for fuch delicate ftomachs.

4. Our author tells us, that he embraced this catholick religion, *Quod concordiæ communis fubftructionem agat, &c.** That is, in fhort, let all the world agree to the fufficiency of our author's five articles, and leave all other things to be rejected or received as trifles, not neceffary to be difputed about, and then there is an end of all the contefts, then there is a foundation laid for everlafting peace, and the golden age will be retrieved, *Jam redit et virgo, redeunt Saturnia regna* †.

This trifle deferves rather pity than an anfwer. What! will all the world agree that this religion is fufficient, while its inventer durft not fay fo?

5. He embraced it, "*Quod authoritatem majeftatemq; indu-*" *biam religioni, et hierarchiæ inde politiæque conciliat,*" *&c.* That is, "becaufe it conciliates refpect to religion, to the ec-" clefiaftical hierarchy, and civil government." Religion will be refpected, when it requires nothing but what is neceffary. Church and ftate will be refpected when it punifhes nothing but tranfgreffions againft incontroverted atticles.

But is not this to trifle with a witnefs? The weaknefs of this plea is fo obvious, that I may well fpare my pains in expofing it. Will it maintain the dignity of religion to confine it to a number of articles, which for any thing we know, or the Deifts know, may cheat us of our reward in the end, fince they cannot poffitively affure us of its fufficiency, and we are pofitively fure it is not fufficient? Will it maintain the honour of church officers, to admit a religion, which fubverts the very foundation of all

refpect

* "Becaufe it lays a foundation for common concord."
† "Now Aftra returns, the reign of Saturn returns."

respect to them, *viz.* The divine institution of their order? As for the advantage of it to the civil government, the Deists may offer it to the consideration of the next parliament, and they will consider whether it is proper to conciliate respect to the civil government.

6. Our author embraced his religion, *Quod adeo non moliat religionem, ut ejus severitatem stimulum addat.* That is, "It is "so far from favouring liberty in sin, that it urges harder to vir-"tue, (severe virtue) than revealed religion." There is no hope of pardon here upon the satisfaction of another. Men must work for their life, and when they fail, they must satisfy by their repentance.

Well, but do they, who teach the necessity of satisfaction, exclude repentance? And if they make both satisfaction and repentance absolutely necessary, though each in its own order and place, to forgiveness, methinks they will yet have the advantage in point of severity. Again, but what if repentance will not satisfy? If this is so, and our author seclude all other satisfaction, will not his religion lead men rather to despair than virtue.

7. Our author's last inducement was, *Quod sacrarum literarum fini ultimo intentioniq quadret,* &c. That is, "because this "catholick religion answers the ultimate design of the scrip-"tures. All the doctrines taught there level at the esta-"blishment of these five catholick verities, as we have often "hinted; there is neither sacrament, rite or ceremony, there "enjoined, but what aims (or seems to aim) at the establish-"ment of these five articles."

8. But is not this a notable jest. Our author would persuade us, That his religion answers the great end of the scriptures, better than that religion, which the scriptures themselves teach. If our author says not this, he says nothing. If the end of the scriptures is not good, it is not for the honour of our author's religion that it agrees with it: If it is good, and the religion taught in the scriptures themselves, answer their own design best, why then, I would chuse that religion, and leave our author to enjoy his own: If he says, *his* answers it better, then I would desire to know where the compliment lies, that he designed to the scriptures. But I desire to know further of the Deists, Whether do the scriptures teach any thing besides these articles, to be necessary? Where do the scriptures tell that these are sufficient? Are divine institutions, sacraments, &c. necessary

toward the compassing of the ends of religion? If they are not, how does it commend our author's religion, that it quadrates with the design of these institutions? If they are necessary and useful, this catholick religion is at a loss that wants them. I am sensible our author has cautioned against this, when he tells us, That they either do, or seem to aim at this. I see *old birds are not caught with chaff.* Now I have found it. This catholick religion, will really serve the purpose, that revealed truths and institutions do only seem to aim at. But after all, this is but *say* and not *proof.* And I will undertake to shew against all the Deists under heaven, that the confinement of religion to these five articles, as taught by the light of nature, is not only not agreeable to the principal design of the scriptures, but inconsistent with it.

Thus I have considered the inducements which led Herbert to embrace this catholick religion, and found them wanting. And I must say, if this noble author had not been straitened by a bad cause, that is not capable of a rational defence, his learning, which was very considerable, could not but have afforded him better pleas. Charles Blount, in the close of his Religio Laici, tells us, It was for the same reasons he embraced Deism, and copies after Herbert, with some little variety. What he has, that our author has taken notice of in this place, will occur in the next chapter, where they are again repeated under another form. *Men that have little to say have need to husband it well, and make all the improvement of it that they can.*

CHAP. XX.

Wherein the Queries offered by Herbert and Blount, for proving the sufficiency of their five Articles are examined.

THE learned Herbert in an appendix to his *Religio Laici*, moves some objections against himself, but fearing after he has said all he can, some may remain unsatisfied still, he betakes himself to another course, and essays to dispute his opposers into a compliance with his sentiments by Queries. Of this sort he proposes seven. Charles Blount concludes his *Religio Laici* in the same method, with this difference, that he has added other seven queries, making in all fourteen, and prefixed this title, *Queries proving the validity of the five Articles.* The

The arguments couched in these queries, in so far as they tend to prove the sufficiency of this catholick religion, are not new, but materially the same, which we have formerly considered. The method is indeed different, more subtile, and better suited to their great design. Direct proofs are less deceiving, and their weakness is more easy discoverable by vulgar capacities. Queries conceal the weakness of arguments, intangle, perplex and amuse less attentive minds, and by them, the subtile asserters of a bad cause ease themselves of the trouble of proving their ill grounded assertions, (which yet, by all rules of disputing, belongs to them only) and turn it over upon the defender. This is enough as to the method, to let us see how suitable it was to their purpose.

The Queries proposed by Blount are the same with Herbert's, and he adds others which Herbert wants. Wherefore we shall consider them as proposed by Mr. Blount. But whereas some of them are to more advantage urged by Herbert, we shall offer these in Herbert's words, that we may overlook nothing, which has the least appearance of force in this cause.

Query I. " Whether there can be any other true God, or
" whether any other can justly be called *optimus maximus*, the
" greatest and best God, and common father of mankind, save
" He who exercises universal providence, and looks so far to
" the good of all men, as to provide them in common and suffi-
" cient or effectual means for obtaining the state of eternal hap-
" piness after this life, whereof he has implanted a desire in
" their minds? If the laity or vulgar worship any other God,
" who does not exercise this universal providence, are they not
" guilty of false worship, or idolatry? And if any one deny this
" common providence, is he not guilty of treason against the
" divine Majesty, and of a contempt of his goodness, yea, and
" of atheism itself?" Thus Herbert*. Blount proposes the same query, but more shortly, thus, " Whether there be any
" true God, but he that useth universal providence concerning
" the means of coming to him †."

The design of this query is to prove the necessity of a catholick religion, or a sufficient religion common to all mankind, and to fix the black note of atheism upon all who deny it. The argument whereby this is evinced is the very same, which we have examined above, as the Deists' first and great argument.

What

* Herbert's Relig. Laici, Appendix. pag. 1, 2.
† Blount Rel. Laici, pag. 90.

What is added concerning univerfal Providence, we did confider in our anfwer to Herbert's firft inducement to Deifm. And fo we might entirely pafs this query as anfwered already, were it not for the feeming advantage given to it by this new drefs, wherein it appears.

This query has a direct tendency to drive men into atheifm, and tempt them to lay afide all worfhip for fear of falling into idolatry. It is in itfelf felf-evident, that if God has given all mankind, or to every man, means fufficient and effectual to lead them to eternal happinefs, they muft know of it, or, at leaft, there muft be eafy accefs for them to know it. With what propriety of fpeech can it be faid, That the means leading to eternal happinefs, are given to every man to be by him ufed for that end, if they know them not, or, at leaft, if the knowledge of them be not eafily acceffable to all, who will apply themfelves to an inquiry after them? Nor is it lefs evident, That the fuitablenefs, efficacy and fufficiency of thefe means, for reaching this end, muft be fufficiently intimated to them. If it is not fo, how can men rationally be obliged to ufe means which they do not know to be proper for compaffing the end? With what courage or confidence can any rational man, with great application, over many difficulties, ufe, and all his life continue in the ufe of means, concerning which he has no affurance, that they will put him in poffeffion of the end? After all his pains he may mifs the end he had in view. How can any reafonable foul pleafe itfelf in fuch a courfe? Can it be reafonably thought worthy of the wifdom and goodnefs of God, to give man the means of attaining eternal happinefs, and means fufficient, and yet leave men in the dark as to the knowledge of this, That they are defigned for, and fufficient to reach the end for which they were given? What can rationally induce men in this cafe, to give God the praife of his goodnefs, in affording them thefe means, or to ufe them for that end, for which they were given, if this is hid from them? It is then evident, That, if God has afforded all men fufficient means of reaching eternal happinefs, they muft know this, or, at leaft, have eafy accefs to know thefe means, what they are, and that they are defigned to, proper for, and will prove effectual to this end. And confequently, if men find not fuch means, after fearch, they have evidently reafon to conclude, that God has left them without them, at leaft, that they want them in their prefent circumftances; fince after all their inquires they cannot find them, nor can they difcover

cover that any means, they know of, will be effectual to reach this end.

This is evidently the condition of man at prefent, left to the mere light of nature. We have proved juft now, That if God had given thefe fufficient means, every men muft, at leaft, upon application, have had accefs to know them, and to know that they are fufficient.

But, upon application, they find no fuch matter, and therefore have reafon to fufpect, that God has not given them thefe means, if not pofitively to conclude that they are without them. Herbert himfelf glories that he was the firft who found out what thefe means were. They had efcaped the knowledge and induftry of the moft learned and diligent before his time. And if fo, certainly the vulgar behoved to be at a lofs about them. When he has found them, he dare not be pofitive about their fufficiency : *" Quam etiam ob caufam, neque ea fufficere (ad fa-* *" lutem, viz. æternam) protenus dixerim,"* fays he [*]. Yea, he more than infinuates, that we cannot come to be pofitively affured of their fufficiency, and fo muft remain in the dark, fince the determination of this depends upon the fentiments of God, which are known to none, as he fays. Now when a man fo learned, fo diligent, and fo evidently prepoffeffed with a ftrong inclination to favour any means that had a fhew of fufficiency, found fo much difficulty to hit upon any fuch, and did fo evidently hefitate about the fufficiency of thefe he had found ; muft not the laity, for whom, upon all occafions, he pretends fo much concern, hefitate more? Yea, have they not reafon evidently to conclude, that there are no fuch means provided for them ?

But Herbert here teaches them, that none is to be acknowledged as the true God, nor worfhipped as fuch, who has not provided every man in effectual and fufficient means for attaining eternal happinefs. Well may the layman fay, " I neither " know, nor can I ever be fatisfied, that I have fuch means; " yea, I have the greateft reafon to think that I want them ; if " the good God had given them, he would not have mocked " me, by concealing them, and fo precluding me from the ufe " of them ; he would have pointed me to them, and intimated " their fufficiency, fo as to make it knowable to me, upon ap-" plication, without which he could never expect that I fhould
" ufe

---

[*] Herbert de Rel. Gent. pag. 217.

"use them: I have therefore reason to conclude myself destitute of them, and so I will worship no God, since there is none that has provided me in the means necessary to eternal happiness: For if I should, I would be guilty of worshipping one, who is an idol, and not the true God." Here we see where this gentleman's principles must inevitably lead the poor man, either to direct atheism, or to worship one, whom he has reason vehemently to suspect to be merely an idol, and not the true God.

Having thus discovered the dangerous tendency of this query, I shall now give a direct answer to it. And to it I say, That *the God*, who makes man, implants in his child's mind a desire of eternal felicity, intimates to him that he is made for this end, obliges him in duty to pursue this end, under a penalty in case he fail of it, and yet denies or leaves his child without the means that are absolutely necessary for compassing it, antecedently to any fault upon the child's part, will scarce obtain the titles of *optimus maximus*, *great* and *good*, or of a *common Father*,

But the GOD who made man perfect, in his original state, and put him in the full possession of all the means that were necessary to obtain that end, whatever it was, for which he was made, and which he was in duty obliged to pursue, loses not his interest in, and unquestionable right to the title of *optimus maximus*, *great* and *good* ; nor does he cease to be a *common Father*, and to act the part of such an one, if, when his children contrary to their duty, have rebelled against him, by their own fault dropped the knowledge of the end, for which they were made, lost the knowledge of the means, whereby it is to be obtained, put themselves out of a capacity of using the means, or reaching the end ; if, I say, in this case, he leaves them to smart under the effects of their own sin, and treats them no more as children, but as rebels, who can blame him ? Does he not act every way as it becomes one, who by the best of titles is not merely a father, but the sovereign ruler and governor of all his creatures, to whom of right it belongs to *render a just recompence of reward* to every transgressor ?

Now, this is the case, as we have already proven. If the Deists will make their argument conclusive, they must prove that this is not the case with man. And when we see this done, we shall then know what to say. Till then we are not much concerned with their query. If they say, How can this be?

be? Can men by the light of nature know how this came to pafs? I anfwer, that it is not the queftion, How it came to be, fo? but, Whether, in fact, it be fo? That it really is thus, is before proven. The Heathens have confeffed it. And though we fhould never come to be fatisfied, how it came about, yet that it really is fo, is enough to acquit God.

Nor is God's univerfal Providence hereby everted, he ftill governs all mankind fuitably to their condition. He rules thofe, whom of his fovereign and undeferved grace, he has feen meet to deal with, in order to return to his family, in a way of infinite mercy and grace. He governs the reft of the world, whom in his fovereign and adorable juftice and wifdom, he hath left to lie under the difmal confequences of their own fin, in a way becoming their ftate. He provides them in all things, that do neceffarily belong to the ends, for which they are fpared. Further, he leaves himfelf *not without a witnefs* as to his goodnefs, *in that he does good, gives them rain from heaven, and fruitful feafons, filling their hearts with food and gladnefs*. Which is fufficient to fhew his fuperabundant goodnefs, that reaches even to the unthankful and evil, and gives them ground to conclude, That their want of what is further neceffary, flows not from any defect of goodnefs on his part; but from their own fins, of many of which their own confciences do admonifh them. If God vouchfafes the means of recovery to any, they have reafon to be thankful to fovereign grace. If God gives not, what he may juftly refufe, who can in juftice complain of him? They muft leave their complaint upon themfelves, and acquit God. And while man is continued in being, it will remain his indifpenfible duty to worfhip this God, who made him, fpares him, notwithftanding of his fins, for a time, punifhes him lefs that his iniquities deferve, and confers many other undeferved favours on him. Nor is he guilty of *worfhipping an idol* in doing fo.

Thus we have anfwered this query: And I might now propofe to the Deifts a counter query, "Whether they, who make *that* neceffary to the fupport of the univerfal providence of God, his goodnefs, and confequently his being, of which no man can be fure that it really is, which all men have reafon to believe is not, and which moft men, who have made it their bufinefs to confider the cafe ferioufly, do firmly believe not to be in being, may not reafonably be fufpected to defign the overthrow of thefe attributes of God, and confequently of his very being?"

Thus

Thus Vaninus endeavoured to establish atheism: he ascribes such attributes to God, and endeavoured to fix such notions of his perfections, as could not be admitted, without the overthrow of other perfections, unquestionably belonging to him, or owned in any consistency with reason and experience. For he well knew, that if once he could bring men to believe God to be such an one, if he was, they would be brought under a necessity of denying, that there was any God.

Query II. "Whether these means appear universally otherwise, than in our foresaid five catholic articles*?"

These gentlemen think they have, by their first query, sufficiently proved, that there must be a catholick religion: Now they will prove theirs to be it. But I have overthrown the foundation, and so the superstructure falls. I have evinced, that there is no such catholick sufficient religion, by reason and experience. I have proved that the pretence of its being necessary to support the notion of God's providence and goodness, can, never possibly persuade any considerate man, to believe against his reason and experience, against the sight of his eyes, and what he feels within himself, that he really is in possession of a sufficient religion, without revelation; and consequently that the urging of this pretence can serve for nothing, if not to make men question the goodness and providence of God, and so his very being, to the overthrow of all worship and religion. I have moreover made it appear, that these five articles are not catholick, and though they were so, yet are not sufficient.

Query III. "Whether any thing can be added to these five articles or principles, that may tend to make a man more honest, virtuous, or a better man?" So Blount †. To this query Herbert adjects a clause, viz. "Provided these articles be well explained in their full latitude ‡." And is not this the principal end of religion?

By the foregoing queries the Deists' think they have proved the necessity of a catholick religion; and that their five articles is this catholick religion. By this query they pretend to prove their religion sufficient.

To this purpose they tell us, That their five articles are sufficient to make a man virtuous, honest and good; that this is the principal end of religion; and that nothing can be added to them,

---

* Blount Rel. Laici. pag. 90.   Herb. Rel. Laici, Appendix.
† Ibid. pag. 91.   ‡ Herb. Ibid.

them, which can be any way helpful as to this end. If by making a man virtuous, honeſt and good, they mean no more, than the Heathens meant by theſe words, who took them to intend no more, but an abſtinence from the more groſs outward acts of vice, contrary to the light of nature, with ſome regard in their dealings among men, to the common and known rules of righteouſneſs, and uſefulneſs: If, I ſay, this is their meaning, which I conceive it muſt be, then I deny that this is the principal end of religion. No man that underſtands what religion means, will ſay it. The Heathens were influenced to this by other motives, than any thing of regard to the authority of the One true God. Their Ethicks, which enjoined this goodneſs, virtue and honeſty, preſſed it by conſiderations of a quite different nature. Of God, his legiſlature, his laws, as ſuch, they took little or no notice of, as we obſerved from Mr. Locke before ; and therefore, whatever uſefulneſs among men there was to be found in their virtues, they had nothing of religion, properly ſo called, in them.

But if by making a man honeſt, virtuous and good, they mean the making of him inwardly holy, and engaging him in the whole of his deportment, in both outward and inward acts, to carry as becomes him, toward God, his neighbour and himſelf, with a due eye to the glory of God as his end, and a juſt regard to the authority of God, as the formal reaſon of this performance of duty in outward and inward acts: If, I ſay, they take their words in this ſenſe, I do own this to be one of the principal ends of religion. But then I deny that ever any man, by their five articles, as taught by the light of nature, or by any other of the like kind, known only by the mere light of nature, was in this ſenſe, ſince the entrance of ſin, made virtuous and good. Nay, the moral Heathens were not led to that ſhadow of virtue and goodneſs, which they had in the ſenſe beforementioned, from any regard to theſe five articles, as they are articles of religion ; that is, as they are principles directive as to the duty, which man owes to the One only True and Supreme Being.

And taking virtue, goodneſs, and honeſty in this laſt ſenſe, which is that alone wherein we are concerned, I have above proven the light of nature, and particularly theſe five articles, as known by it, utterly inſufficient to make any man virtuous, honeſt and good. And I have demonſtrated not *one*, but *many things* beſide what is contained in theſe five articles, however explained to the utmost advantage that can be done by mere unassisted reason, to be *absolutely necessary* to the *ends of religion.* Nor will what Herbert has adjected mend the matter, viz. *That his articles must be well explained in their full latitude.* These words, if they have any sense, it is this, "It is not enough to believe and receive our articles, as in general proposed, this will make no man good. He must not only, for instance, agree to it, that there is one Supreme God, and that he is to be worshipped by a virtuous life, but he must be acquainted with all the attributes of this God, necessary to be known, in order to the direction of his practice, and he must understand and be fixed as to the nature, measure and all other necessary concerns of these virtues that belong to his duty." This is undeniably the meaning of this expression, and this inevitably overthrows all that our author has been building. Were these five articles, in this latitude, universally agreed to? Our author knew the contrary. If any man should assert it, it were enough to make him be hissed off the stage, as either brutishly ignorant of the world, or impudently disingenuous. Well then, our catholick religion is lost. Again, since the explications belong as much to our author's religion as the articles themselves, (for without them he confesses the articles not sufficient) how shall the poor layman ever be satisfied about them? Have there not been as many, and as intricate disputes about them, as about the articles of revealed religion? Where is now the boasted agreement? Where is the uncontroverted religion? What attribute of God has not been questioned, disputed and denied? Have not his creation of all things, his Providence, &c. which of all others have the most remarkable influence upon practice, by many been denied? Have not horrid notions of them been advanced by some? What will now become of men of squeamish stomachs, that can admit of no religion, but one that is smooth, and has no rugged controversies in it? Why, poor gentlemen, they must part with our author's religion, and so be, what they were before, *men of no religion.* Upon the whole, we see that this query, designed to prove the *Deists' religion sufficient,* has proven it a chimera.

Query IV. " Whether any things that are added to these five " principles from the doctrine of faith, be not uncertain in " their original?" So Blount *. Herbert to this adds, " That
though

* Blount Rel. Laici, pag. 91.

" though God be true, yet the laity can never be certain about
" revelation: For, (fays he) how do ye know that God fpake
" thefe words to the prophets? How do you know that they
" faithfully repeated or wrote what God fpoke to them, and no
" more? How do ye know that tranfcribers have performed
" their part faithfully? How do ye know, that that particular
" revelation made to a particular prieft, prophet or lawgiver,
" concerns not only all other priefts and lawgivers, but alfo the
" laity? Efpecially, how fhall ye know this, if the matter of
" revelation require you to recede from reafon? *" And here
we have a proof of the *fourth reflection*, of his unfair treatment
of the Chriftian revelation, which we made above, Chap. 13.
For either he infinuates, that the fcriptures teach things contrary to reafon; and if fo, where was our author's ingenuity when
he called it *optima religio*, and upon other occafions pretended
fo much refpect to it? Does not this juftify our charge of difingenuity againft him, in the *firft reflection* we have made, in
the place now referred to? If he owns, that this is not the fault
of the Chriftian religion, but of other pretended revelations;
then he juftifies our *fourth reflection*, wherein we charge him
with jumbling revelations, true and falfe together, that have,
at leaft, feemingly fair pretences, and thefe that have none; and
deceitfully charges upon all *in cumulo*, the faults peculiar to the
worft. If this is not enough to perfuade you to the truth of his
proteftation above-mentioned, *viz.* that he defigned no hurt
to the Chriftian religion, he has an obfervation, with which he
concludes this query, that will beat the perfuafion of it into
your brains, or elfe of fomewhat befide; and it is this, in his
own words, " I think it worthy of the layman's obfervation,
" that there is this difference betwixt the pretended revelations
" offered to us, by the lawgivers, and thofe offered to us by
" priefts, interpreters of the oracles God, (under which no-
" tion he takes in all prophets) whether they gave their re-
" velations or refponfes for hire, or merely to fet off their own
" conceits *(five venales five nugivendi;)* that the revelations,
" which the lawgivers pretended they had from heaven, and
" promulgated as fuch, did ufually make the people more juft
" and fociable, or agree better together; whereas the pretend-
" ed revelations of the priefts and prophets, of whatever fort,
" (or in his own words, *Oraculorum interpretibus five venalibus*
" *five*

* Herb. Rel. Laici, Appendix, pag. 3.

" *five nugivendis)* did usually make the people more unjust or
" impious, and did divide them among themselves *."

Here is a rare observation, worth gold to the layman. He may, with more safety, receive and use the laws which Lycurgus, Solon, and the other Heathen lawgivers pretended they had from heaven; and I would add Moses and his writings, but that I fear our author has cast him, because he set up for an interpreter of God's mind, and, upon some extraordinary occasions, acted the part of a priest: Our author, I say, would persuade him, that he may, with more advantage, read these writings, than those of the prophets and apostles, or any other of the sacred writers, who were not lawgivers. It is true, both are to be looked upon but as pretended revelations, and so in effect cheats: but the lawgivers beguiled the people to their advantage; whereas these rogues of priests, and others who joined with them, offered cheats that were hurtful to justice among men, and the peace of society.

If any say, I am wresting our author's words, and that certainly his comparison respects only the Heathen lawgivers, and Heathen priests; I answer, If this is the meaning, it is altogether impertinent to the design of the query, which avowedly aims at this, " That laymen, living among us, (for I do not believe our author designed to send his book to the Pagans) can never be satisfied as to the truth of any particular revelation," and all his subordinate queries do directly thrust at the scriptures; and then he closes with this observation, as of the greatest moment to the design of the query. And therefore I cannot own, that I have done any injury to our author, in the interpretation I have given of it; but I have spoke his meaning more plainly, than he thought convenient to do. The next query is to the same purpose, and therefore we shall propose it, and answer both.

Query V. " Supposing the originals true, whether yet they
" be not uncertain in their explications; " so that unless a
" man read all authors, speak with all learned men, and
" know all languages, it be not impossible to come to a clear
" solution of all doubts?" Thus Blount †. Herbert, in his fifth query, speaks to the same purpose, he makes a huge outcry about the schisms and sects that are among us, and tells us

plainly

---
* Herb. Rel. Laici, Appendix, pag. 3.
† Blount Rel. Laici, ubi supra, pag. 91.

plainly, that if we will adhere ſtiffly to revelation, we muſt of neceſſity get an *infallible judge*, to whoſe deciſions we muſt ſubmit in all things. He endeavours to prove that the ſcriptures will not decide the controverſy; and impertinently enough labours to diſprove what none ever aſſerted, That miracles wrought by the writers will not decide the differences about the meaning of their writings. For it is evident this query only reſpects the *meaning* of the revelation, as the former did its *original*. However, I know who will thank our author for aſſerting the neceſſity of a *living infallible judge*. If any think I have wronged our author as to this, let them inſpect his book, and they will find I have done him juſtice. But for the ſatisfaction of thoſe who have it not, I ſhall ſubjoin his own expreſs words; he informs the layman, that he can never be ſatisfied about the meaning of this revelation, about which there are ſo many controverſies, unleſs either he can " *Linguas cunctas ediſcere, ſcriptores cunctos celebriores perlegere, doctiores etiam, qui non ſcripſerunt, conſulere; aut aliquis ſaltem controverſiarum illarum ex conſenſu communi ſummus conſtitueretur judex* *." And then he goes on to prove, that there is no other poſſible way of deciding theſe differences, and coming to the meaning of revelation, but in theſe two ways pointed at in the words now quoted. The firſt is ridiculous, and therefore we muſt be Deiſts or Papiſts.

The deſign of theſe queries is obvious. They were afraid that their arguments might prove weak, which they had advanced for the ſufficiency of their catholick religion; and now in effect, they tell the laity, that if they have a mind to have a religion at all, they muſt cloſe with this which the Deiſts preſent them. And though we cannot ſatisfy you, may the Deiſts ſay, in all points, about our catholick religion, yet you muſt reſt ſatisfied with it: for you can never be ſure about revelation, either as to its original or meaning. Men brought to ſuch a ſtrait, ſince they cannot have ſuch a religion as they would wiſh, muſt take ſuch as they can get.

Theſe queries directly attack revelation; and ſo belong not to our ſubject. The learned defenders of revealed religion have

---

* " Learn all languages, read over all the moſt celebrated writers, " conſult the moſt learned men, who have not written, or at leaſt ſome " ſupreme judge of all controverſies muſt be appointed by common " conſent."

have confidered thofe trifles, and repelled the force of them. I fhall only confider them, in fo far as they belong to our fubject, and offer the few following animadverfions upon them.

1. I fay, if the layman muft, for the fake of thofe difficulties, quit revealed religion, he muft part with the Deifts' catholick religion upon the fame account. Herbert has told us, and it were indeed ridiculous to fay the contrary, that this catholick religion is comprehenfive not only of their five articles, but their explications. Now, are there not as many, and no lefs intricate debates about this religion, as about that which is revealed? Is not its fufficiency difputed? Muft not the layman read all books, converfe with all learned men, &c. before he can reft fatisfied in it? Are there not intricate and perplexed difputes about the authority, extent, ufe, matter, and manner of the promulgation of the law of nature? Where fhall the layman find the notices that belong to this religion? Shall he turn inward, and find them infcribed upon his own mind? So our author advifes. But learned men fay, and pretend to prove the contrary. And if moft men look into their own minds, they will either fay with the latter that they are not there; or complain that they are become fo dim that they cannot read them unlefs fome charitable Deift will afford them his fpectacles. But when they have got them, what fhall they do next for the explications? Are the explications written there too? The Deifts dare not fay it. But thefe likewife are necessary fay the Deifts, as we have heard from Blount and Herbert before. Shall the laity confult the Doctors about their meaning? But do not Doctors differ? Do not the Magi, and not a few learned Greeks, as Zeno and Cryfippus, &c. teach Sodomy to be lawful? Was it not the judgment of others, that a wife man ought καὶ κλέψειν τε καὶ μοιχεύειν, καὶ ἱεροσυλησειν ἐν καιρῷ, μηδὲν γὰρ τῶτων φυσει αἰσχρὸν ἔιναι; that is, *To fteal, and commit adultry and facrilege upon occafions, for none of thefe things are by nature evil.* So Theodorus, as Hefychius Illuftrius reports in his life [*]. Does not Ariftippus and Carneades, with many others, overthrow the whole law of nature, telling us, that nothing is naturally juft or unjuft, good or evil, but by virtue of fome arbitrary law? Has not the fame opinion been revived, broached and inculcated by Hobbs and others among ourfelves? Has not Plato long fince obferved in his
Phedon,

---

[*] See Dr. Owen on the Sabbath, Exercit. 3. §. 13.

Phedon, " That if any one name either filver or iron, prefent-
" ly all men agree what it is that is intended; but if they
" fpeak of that which is juft or good, prefently we are at vari-
" ance with others, and among ourfelves." In a word, he
that will caft at revelation, for its controverfies, is a fool to go
over to natural religion, in expectation to be free of contioverfy.
Thus we are at leaft upon a level with the Deifts.

2. If the layman, in defiance of the Deifts' queries, may
reach a fatisfying affurance of the divine authority of the fcriptures, where is then the neceffity for his quitting revelation? It
will quite evanifh. This, I fay, he may have, without trou-
bling his head about impertinent queries of this fort, if he duly
attend to that one, plain and rational direction given by our
LORD, John vii. 17. *If any man will do his will, he fhall
know of the doctrine, whether it be of God, or whether I fpeak
of myfelf.*

The fcriptures containing a full account of all the concerns
of the Chriftian religion, are exhibited to him, and put in his
hand by the church as a revelation from God, wherein all his
concerns for eternity are wrapped up. I do not plead, that
the teftimony of the church is a fufficient ground for bottoming
his faith. But this I fay, that the teftimony of the church is a
fufficient ground for any man to judge and conclude firmly,
that its pretenfions are not contemptible, and that it deferves
the moft ferious confideration imaginable. But when I fpeak
of the church, to whofe teftimony this regard is to be paid, we
fet afide, as of no confideration, a multitude of perfons, whether of the clergy or laity, who do, in their practice vifibly
contradict the confeffed rules of their religion. Such perfons
are fcarce to be reckoned of any religion, and their teftimony
is of no confideration, either for or againft religion. Nor do
we reftrict the notion of the church to the reprefentatives of it,
much lefs to the Church of Rome, that monopolize this name.
But I take it for that body of men, of whatever ftation or quality, who have received, and do act anfwerably to the Chriftian
religion they profefs, in fome good meafure at leaft. Now I
fay, the teftimony of this church, or body men, deferves great
regard in this matter. If we confider them, There are among
them perfons of untainted reputation, enemies themfelves being judges. Not a few of them are of unqueftionable judgment,
deep difcerning, folid learning, and ftrict inquiries after truth.
They are not a few but many. Nor are they confined to one
nation

nation or age; but such they have been in all ages, in all nations, where Christianity has obtained free access. Many of them are persons, whom envy itself cannot allege biassed, by external gain of one sort or of another. They are persons of different, nay cross civil interests, and of different outward conditions. Such are the persons who give this testimony. Again, if we consider their testimony, They bear witness to the Christian religion in all its concerns, its truth, sufficiency, usefulness to all the ends of religion, with respect to time or eternity, and its efficacy for beginning, carrying on, maintaining, reviving and consummating such as sincerely receive it, in godliness towards God, righteousness towards men, sobriety with respect to ourselves; and that both as to inward principles and outward acts. Further, if we consider in what way they give in their testimony, the weight of it will appear. They bear witness to all this, not only by their words, but by their deeds, living in a conformity to it, parting with all that is dearest to them for it, cheerfully undergoing the greatest hardships, patiently bearing the most cruel torments, to the loss of life itself; and this they do neither upon mere constraint, nor on the other hand, from a rash and inadvertent neglect of a due regard to the unquestionable advantages of peace, health, life, and the other good things they part with; but they venture upon doing and suffering freely and of choice, upon a sober, rational consideration of the advantage of cleaving to their religion, and of its being such, as will do more than compensate any loss they can sustain for it. Again, they bear witness to the concerns of this religion, as to a thing that they have not received upon bare hear-say, but upon narrow scrutiny, as that whereof they have the experience. They do not only give this testimony, when it is new to them, but after long trial, when they are most sedate and composed, and when they can expect nothing of advantage by it, and when they must lay their account with contempt, opposition and loss. They give this testimony in whatever place they are, where it is honoured, or where it is opposed. They give it with the greatest concern, and recommend this religion to those whom they would least deceive, even with their dying breath, when they dare not dissemble, and that after a long trial, in the course of their lives, in the greatest variety of outward conditions, sufficient to have discovered the weakness of their religion, if it had any. They have made choice of this religion, and adhered

to

to it, under the greateſt outward diſadvantages, who were not prepoſſeſſed in its favour by education, but prejudged againſt it; and they have embraced it, where they had a free choice to accept or reject it, and advantages to tempt them to a refuſal. They do not require an implicit belief as Mahometans do, but provoke to experience and trial. Now I dare boldly ſay, that this teſtimony is a better, more plain, obvious, and every way more juſtifiable ground of rational aſſent to the divine authority, truth, efficacy, and ſufficiency of the Chriſtian religion, than can be given for the like aſſent, to any other particular religion whatſoever. Nay, there is more in this one teſtimony, as it is, or at leaſt may be qualified with other circumſtances, diſcernible even by the moſt ordinary layman, here for brevity's ſake omitted, (the urging of this in its full ſtrength, not being my preſent deſign) than can be offered for all the other religions in the world, natural, or pretending to revelation, were all that can be ſaid for them altogether put in one argument. Any reaſonable man cannot but think his eternal concerns ſafer in following this ſociety, than any other whatſoever: There is not ſuch another company elſewhere to be met with, as might be demonſtrated to the conviction of the ſtiffeſt oppoſer. But this I plead not at preſent. I ſay not, that he ſhould build his perſuaſion of Chriſtianity upon this teſtimony. All that I make of it is this, That he has reaſon to conſider the ſcriptures, as thus atteſted, as a book that has, at leaſt, very plauſible pretences to divinity, a book that deſerves ſerious peruſal, a book that cannot poſſibly have any obvious and unqueſtionable arguments of impoſture, and conſequently, that it deſerves to be read through, and fully heard before it is caſt; and that though there occur in it ſome things that he cannot preſently underſtand, or whoſe uſe and value he cannot take up, he ought not therefore to be prejudged againſt the divine authority of the book upon the account of them, till, at leaſt, it is heard to an end. For, who knows not, that things which appear incredible, unreaſonable, yea ridiculous, before their cauſes, order and deſign are underſtood, may, upon acquaintance with theſe, appear convincingly credible, uſeful, and every way reaſonable? This is all I claim of the layman at preſent, and he deſerves not the name of a reaſonable man who will deny it upon ſuch a ground. And if the Deiſts had conſidered this, we had not been troubled with the many childiſh and trifling prejudices, wherewith their *Oracles of Reaſon* and other books are ſtuffed. Nor could they have been diverted from the serious consideration of the scriptures, by such pitiful exceptions.

Well, the scriptures being put into the layman's hand, thus attested, he sets himself to the perusal of them, and such a perusal as the case requires; looking to God for direction, he tries the means appointed by them, for satisfaction as to their divinity. While he is seeking light from God, in such a matter, he dare not expect it, if he continue in the neglect of known duty, or the commission of known sin, and therefore he studies to avoid them. He is resolved to follow truth, as it is discovered, and to subscribe to the scripture pretensions, if they give sufficient evidence of themselves. Nothing is here resolved, but what is reasonable beyond exception. In pursuance of this just resolution, he reads them, and upon his perusal, what passages he cannot understand, or reach the reason of, he passes at present and goes on, till he see further what may be the intention of them. And he finds in plain and convincing expressions, his own case, and the case of all men by nature, clearly discovered, and urged upon him by this book; the words pierce his soul, dive into his conscience, and make manifest the *secrets of his heart*, (known to none but God) manifest his sins, in their nature and tendency, and all their concernments. His conscience tells him, *all this is true* to a title, though he did not know it before, and none other save the heart-searching God, could know what was transacted within his heart, though overlooked by himself. The discovery not only carries with it an evidence of truth, which his conscience subscribes to; but the words wherein it is expressed, bear in themselves upon his soul with a light, authority and majesty formerly unknown, evidencing their meaning and truth, and filling the soul with unusual and awful impressions of the majesty and authority of the speaker. Thus being convinced and judged, and the *secrets of his heart made manifest*, he is forced to *fall down and acknowledge, that God is* in the word *of a truth*. And he is ready to say, *Come see a* book *that told me all that ever I did* in my life, *is not this* the book of God? Thus he stands trembling under the sense of the wrath of God, due to him for his sins. He reads on, and finds in the same book a discovery of *relief*, proposed frequently in plain passages. He is urged to an acceptance of it. The discovery carries along with it a full evidence of the *suitableness, excellency*, and *advantage* of the remedy: And by a gust of its goodness, or inward sense, he is drawn

to

to an approbation. Upon this approbation the promised effects follow. His fears are dissipated, his hopes revived, his soul is made acquainted with formerly unknown and God-becoming expressions of the nature and excellencies of God, and going still on every day, repeated experience occur of the justness of the discoveries the word makes of himself, the authority of its commands, faithfulness of its promises, the awfulness of its threatnings, none of which fall to the ground. He, in a word, has repeated experience of the unparalleled efficacy of the whole, for the cure of his darkness, his corruption, &c. which despised other applications; and towards his advancement to a sincere and conscientious regard to all his duties, outward and inward, toward God and man.

Let us now but suppose this to be the case with the man upon his perusal of the scriptures, though with respect to innumerable souls, it is more than a bare supposition: upon this supposition, I say, 1. The man has the highest security he can desire, that this book is, as to its substance, the very word of God, as certainly as if it were spoken to him immediately by a voice from heaven. This cannot well be denied by any that understands this supposition. 2. I say, the man thus convinced may laugh at all Herbert's queries as impertinent. He finds God speaking by the word, and owning it for his. He needs not therefore trouble himself who wrote it, or whether they were honest men who transcribed it, or whether they performed their part, whether it was designed for him; and the like may be said of all his other queries. He will find no occasion for that distinction betwixt *traditional* or *original revelation*, mentioned by Herbert, and insisted upon by Mr. Locke,* on what design I leave others to judge. In this case, as to the substance, it is all one to him, as if it had not come through another hand, nor has he reason to suspect, that God would permit to creep into, or stand in a book, which for the substance, he still owns and evinces to be from him, any thing of a coarser alloy, at least any such corruption as might make it unworthy of him to own it, or unsafe to use it to the design it was given for: Yea, he has the strongest security that the perfections and providence of God can afford, to rest fully assured of the contrary. He has no reason to be stumbled at passages that he cannot understand, or such as by others are reckoned ridiculous, but rather to say

with

* Locke's Essay on Hum. Understand. Book 4. Cap. 18. §. 6, 7, 8.

with Socrates, in another cafe. "What I underſtand I admire, and am fully convinced to be every way worthy of its author; and therefore I conclude what I underſtand not, to be equally excellent, and that it would appear ſo if I underſtood all its concerns." Finally, This ſuppoſition takes off all pretence of heſitation about the meaning of the ſcriptures, as to what the man is particularly concerned in. The ſtory of the neceſſity of an *infallible judge*, is built upon this ſuppoſition, That the ſcriptures are ſo obſcure in matters neceſſarily relating to the faith and practice of the vulgar, that they cannot be underſtood by them ſatisfyingly, in the uſe of appointed means. This ſuppoſition is palpably falſe, contrary to ſcripture, reaſon and experience, as is evinced by our writers againſt the Papiſts, who fully conſider their pleas, and particularly thoſe which Herbert and the Deiſts have borrowed from them, who may be conſulted by the reader.

3. Thus far I have made appear, that the layman has the juſteſt reaſon in the world to look upon it as his duty, or the will of God, that he ſhould give the ſcriptures ſuch a peruſal. 2. That in doing his will there is a way, at leaſt, ſuppoſable, wherein he may reach full ſatisfaction in his own mind, in defiance of the Deiſts' queries about the divinity of the ſcriptures, and reach the higheſt rational ſecurity, even that of faith, bottomed upon divine teſtimony, and inward ſenſe or experience; which Herbert himſelf, upon all occaſions, truly aſſerts to be the higheſt certainty. I ſhall now advance one ſtep further, and aſſert, that this is more than a mere ſuppoſition, that it is matter of fact, that they, who do receive the ſcriptures in a due manner, eſpecially among the laity or illiterate, do find and reſt upon this ground in their perſuaſion. Upon this ground it was alone, that multitudes did at firſt receive it, and for it reject the religions they were bred in; and not as the Deiſts imagine, upon a blind veneration to teachers, prieſts or preachers, whom, by education, they were taught to abhor: And upon this ground they ſtill do adhere to it, and receive it as written in the ſcriptures. The words of Mr. Baxter, as I find them quoted by Mr. Wilſon (for I have not ſeen Baxter's book in anſwer to Herbert *de Veritate*) are remarkable to this purpoſe, "I think, ſays he, That in the very hearing or reading, God's Spirit often ſo concurreth as that the will itſelf ſhould be touched with an internal guſt or favour of the goodneſs contained in the doctrine, and at the ſame time the underſtanding with an
"internal

" internal irradiation, which breeds fuch a fudden apprehen-
" fion of the verity of it, as nature gives men of natural prin-
" ciples. And I am perfuaded, that this increafed by more
" experience and love, and inward gufts, doth hold moft Chrif-
" tians fafter to Chrift, than naked reafonings could do. And
" were it not for this, unlearned ignorant perfons were ftill in
" danger of apoftafy, by every fubtle caviller that affaults
" them. And I believe that all true Chriftians have this kind
" of internal knowledge, from the fuitablenefs of the truth and
" goodnefs of the gofpel to their new-quickened, illuminated,
" fanctified fouls*." The apoftle tells us, *God who commanded
the light to fhine out of darknefs, hath fhined into our hearts, to
give the light of the knowledge of the glory of God in the face of
Jefus Chrift.*—If the Deift fay, How proves the layman this to
me? I anfwer, That is not the queftion. For the defign of
the Deifts in thefe queries, is to prove, that the layman cannot
be affured about the original and meaning of revelation in his
own mind, and fo muft clofe with their catholick religion. Now
in direct contradiction to this, I fay, here is a ground to ftand
upon. And if he has this ground, even a fober Deift muft allow
he has no reafon to be moved from it, but muft fully *know that
the doctrines are of God*. And fo I have overthrown the defign
of the query. As for the Deifts' queftion, How he proves it to
others? it is impertinent. It is not reafonable to expect, that
every common man can ftop the mouths of gain-fayers. It is
enough for him, if he can give a reafon, which is good, and muft
be owned fuch in itfelf. If the Deift queftions matters of fact,
that he finds matters fo and fo ; I anfwer, A blind man may
queftion whether I fee this paper now before me ; and yet I
have good reafon to believe it is there, though I fhould fail of
convincing him.

If the Deift fay, I have perufed the fcriptures, and found no
fuch effect; I anfwer, in matters of experience one affirmative
proves more than twenty negatives; unlefs the application is in
all refpects equal, and the effect depend upon a neceffary caufe:
For where a voluntary agent is the caufe of the effect, there it
does not neceffarily follow upon the like application. But to
wave this general, which would require more room to explain,
than I can allow it in this place, I fay further, to the complain-
er,

* Baxter's Animad. on Herbert de Verit. pag. 135. quoted by M.
J. Wilfon, Scriptures interpreter afferted, Appendix pag. 20.

er, Have you given the scriptures such a perusal, as I have proved in a way of duty you are obliged to do? Have you used the means, in so far, at least, as is possible for you? Have you sought, have you waited for God's guidance and preservation from mistake, and from unjust prejudices against him, his works his word, (if this be such) and his ways? Do you carefully study to avoid what may reasonably be thought, even by a considerate Heathen, to obstruct the grant of the assistance desired from God? Do you carefully avoid known sin? Do you endeavour the performance of what you know to be duty? Are you resolved to follow in practice where light leads? If you dare not frankly answer, you have no reason to complain. For my own part, I am persuaded, that in fact, none who have done his will even thus far, have reason to table a complaint against the word. Others who take a quite contrary course, are unreasonable in the complaint. Disputes about what might be the case, upon supposition of a person's doing all, that in his present circumstances he is able to do, and yet miss of satisfaction as to the divine authority of the word, until the subject of this question be found, I think not myself concerned in, at least in a controversy with the Deists. It is unreasonable to question the scripture's authority, or the evidence of it, upon suppositions that never were in being, and I am persuaded, never shall have a being.

But these things I leave. This dispute lies wholly out of our road. But I have been obliged to this digression, in pursuit of the Deists' impertinent queries. I say *impertinent*, because, were all granted that is aimed at in these queries, it will not avail one rush, towards the proof of the point the Deists are on, viz. *the validity of their religion:* For were revealed religion uncertain, is it a good consequence, that therefore the Deists' religion is certain? What I have said in defence of revealed religion, I would have to be looked upon only as a digression, and not as a full declaration of my opinion; much less would I have this understood as the substance of what can be pleaded on behalf of that blessed book that has *brought life and immortality to light.* This is not the hundredth part of what even I could say, were this my subject. And others have said, and can plead much more than I am able. However, this I owed to the truth of God. Such as would see all these pretences against revelation, repelled, are desired to consult those, who designedly treat of this subject.

There

There are other things in thefe queries now animadverted upon, that deferve rather contempt than an anfwer. In particular, it is fuppofed, as one of the principal foundations of thofe two queries, now under confideration, That a man cannot reach certainty in his own mind upon folid grounds, and rationally acquiefce in it as fuch, unlefs " he knows all that can be faid " againſt it, read all books, converfe with all learned men, " &c." than which there is not a more extravagant expreffion in *Bevis* and *Garagantua*. Admit it, and I fhall demonftrate againſt any that will undertake it, that *nothing is certain*. I cannot but admire that fo learned a perfon as Herbert could ufe fuch an extravagant fuppofition. But what will not a bad caufe drive a man upon? This confirms what is ordinarily obferved, that there is no opinion, however unreafonable, but has fome learned man for its patron, if not inventor.

We fhall now go on to the reft of the queries, which will be of more eafy difpatch. That I have dwelt fo long upon thefe two, is out of a regard to revelation and its honour, and not from any weight in the queries. As for them, this alone had been a fufficient anfwer, which I propofe in a way of a counter-query, and conclude with it—" If a layman that is illiterate cannot be " fatisfied as to the truth of revealed religion, how doth this " prove the Deifts' five articles to be a fufficient and good re- " ligion."

Query VI. " Suppofing all true in their originals, and in " their explications, whether yet they be fo good for the in- " ftructing of mankind, that bring pardon of fin upon fuch " eafy terms, as to believe the bufinefs is done to our hand?" And,

Query VII. " Whether this doctrine doth not derogate from " virtue and goodnefs, while our beft actions are reprefented as " imperfect and finful, and that it is impoffible to keep the ten " commandments, fo as God will accept of our actions, doing " the beft we can?" Thus Blount gives us Herbert's fixth query in two.* There is no material difference in Herbert, fave only that he harps upon the old ftring, and fpends himfelf in bitter invectives againſt the fcripture-doctrine about the decrees of God, of which we have faid enough before. And therefore I think it needlefs to burden this paper with his words.

The

---

* Blount Rel. Laici, pag. 91. 92.

The two former queries ſtruck at ſcripture-revelation itſelf, theſe two ſtrike at the matter contained in the ſcriptures. And here there is a double charge laid againſt the doctrine revealed in the ſcriptures, as black as hell can invent, and as falſe as it is black. The ſixth query charges it with favouring ſin, by bringing pardon upon too eaſy terms; and the ſeventh charges it with derogating from virtue.

For an anſwer to both, I might oppone experience. Sin is no where by any ſo oppoſed, virtue no where ſo ſincerely cultivated, as among thoſe who ſincerely receive the doctrine of *ſatisfaction*, and believe the utmoſt as to the *inability* of man in his preſent fallen caſe, without ſupernatural aſſiſtance, and gracious acceptance, to pleaſe God. Dare the Deiſts compare with them in this reſpect? If they ſhould, I know what would be the iſſue, if the judge had conſcience or honeſty. A Socrates, Seneca or Plato, deſerves not to be named in the ſame day with the meaneſt ſerious Chriſtian, that believes theſe doctrines, either with reſpect to *piety* toward God, or *duty* toward man.

But as to the firſt charge, I ſay the ground of it is falſe; the query is diſingenuous and deceitful. The ground of it is a ſuppoſition, that revelation excludes the neceſſity of repentance. This is manifeſtly falſe: both Herbert and Blount knew it to be falſe; and could not but do ſo, if ever they read the Bible. And the query comparing revelation upon this known miſrepreſentation, with natural religion, is ſhamefully diſingenuous. Let the query be, Whether it is more favourable to ſin, to ſay, it is not to be pardoned without a ſatisfaction to juſtice by Chriſt, and repentance upon our part, as revelation teaches; or, that upon our repentance merely, God is obliged to pardon it, as the Deiſts ſay? Now, I leave it to the Deiſts to anſwer this.

As to the ſecond charge, revelation derogates nothing from virtue. It teaches indeed that our beſt actions are imperfect, and he knows not what perfection means, or what is required thereto, that will deny it. It teaches that *they who are in the fleſh cannot pleaſe God*. It talks at another rate than Herbert, of the condition of ſinful man, as to acceptance with God. He gives him a direction, " *Cum bonum pro virili præſtas, merce-* " *dem a bonitate illa ſuprema pete, exige, habe; quo pacto re-* " *verá ſapies* *." That is, " Manfully perform your duty as " you can, and (whatever ſin remain) aſk, demand, and have
" your

---

* Herbert de Veritate, pag. 108.

" your reward. This is the way to be truly wife." This petulent advice the scripture does not juftify, and fober reafon reprobrates. Where fin interveens, whatever the finner does, in way of obedience, I conceive it will be as good wifdom as our author teaches him, to be very fober with his *demands*. But to return : Revelation, by teaching man's inability, doth not hinder him from virtue; but takes him off from his own ftrength, which would fail him in the performance, and leads him where he may get ftrength, and where innumerable perfons have got ftrength to perform duty acceptably ; and it points to the only ground, whereon finful and imperfect obedience can be accepted with, or expect a reward from God.

Query VIII. " Whether fpeaking good words, thinking " good thoughts, and doing good actions, be not the juft ex-" ercife of a man's life ? Or that without embracing the forefaid " five principles or fundamentals, it be impoffible to keep peace " among men, that God may be well ferved ?" Thus Blount*. This is Herbert's feventh and laft query, and he only adds one claufe to it, wanting here ; " Whether the layman may not " fpend his time better in thofe exercifes mentioned, than if he " employed it in deciding controverfies he does not under-" ftand.†"

The fuppofed neceffity for the layman perplexing himfelf with controverfies, at which Herbert here aims, in cafe he fee meet to embrace revelation, we have above weighed and caft. But as to the query itfelf, it is utterly impertinent. For this is the queftion they fhould have propofed, " Whether their religion " is fufficient to bring a man to thefe juft exercifes, and to " maintain peace in fociety?" And not as they propofe it, " Whether thefe exercifes be in themfelves good ?" which nobody denies: let this be the queftion, and we anfwer negatively. For this we have given fufficient reafons above.

Query IX. " Whether the forefaid five principles do not beft " agree with the precepts given in the ten commandments, and " with the two precepts of Jefus Chrift, *viz.* To love God above " all, and our neighbour as ourfelves? as well as with the " words of St. Peter, That in every nation he that feareth God, " and worketh righteoufnefs is accepted of God ‡?"

* Blount Rel. Laici, pag. 92. † Herb. Rel. Laici, Appen.
‡ Blount, ibid. pag. 92, 93.

This query is the same with Herbert's seventh and last persuasive to Deism, which we have answered above. It is falsely supposed that revelation teaches, that the knowledge of the ten commands, or Christ's summary of them, is sufficient to salvation. Yea, revelation teaches expressly, that no man can practise them without grace from Christ, and that there is no other way of salvation but by faith in him. Again, it is falsely supposed, that the agreement of these articles with (that is to say, their not contradicting) these commands, proves them a sufficient religion. This argument, if it proves any thing, it proves too much; for it will prove any one of them alone to be sufficient. If the Deists mean, that their five articles, not only are not inconsistent with, but sufficient to bring men the length required by the ten commands, our Lord's summary of them, or *to fear God and work righteousness*, as Cornelius did: I answer negatively to the question, they can bring no man to this. Cornelius, of whom Peter speaks, had embraced the Old Testament revelation. What Peter speaks of men *of all nation being accepted with God*, relates to the discovery God had made to him of his design to admit men of all nations promiscuously to acceptance with him through the gospel-revelation: And consequently, that the opinion hitherto received by Peter and other Jews, of the continued confinement of revealed religion and its privileges to Israel, was a mistake. So that this place helps not the Deists, if it is not cut off from its scope and cohesion, or interpreted without respect to it. This way of interpretation of scripture is not safe. I know not where Mr. Blount learned it; but I can tell him where there is a precedent of it—Matt. iv. And if the Deists have a mind to follow that precedent, they shall not be followed by me.

Query X. " Whether the doctrine of faith can by human rea-
" son be supposed or granted to be infallible, unless we are in-
" fallibly assured, that those who teach this doctrine do know
" the secret counsels of God?*"

To this I answer, That I am sufficiently secured as to the infallible certainty of the doctrine, if I have received the scriptures upon the ground above-mentioned, without supposing any who now teach it, to have any further acquaintance with the secret counsels of God, than the word gives them.

Query

* Blount Rel. Laici. pag. 93.

Query XI. " Whether all things in the scriptures, (besides the
" moral part, which agrees with our five principles) such as pro-
" phecy, miracles and revelations, depending on the history,
" may not be so far examined, as to be made appear by what
" authority they are or may be received *?"

I answer, Revelation, in all its parts, is capable to stand the
test of the strictest trial, provided it be just, and managed as
becomes it. But I must tell the Deists one thing in their ear,
That if the scriptures once evince themselves to be from God,
by sufficient evidence, they are obliged, upon their peril, to receive all that it teaches them, though they cannot prove it by
reason; nay, nor explain it. But what if any revealed doctrine
be contrary to reason? Upon the forgoing supposition, this query cannot be excused of blasphemy, but is highly impertinent
and unreasonable.

Query XII. " Whether in human reason any one may, or
" ought to be convinced by *one single testimony*, so far as to be-
" lieve things contrary to, or besides reason †?"

One single testimony is writ in a different character in the query, perhaps to give us to understand, that by it is meant the
testimony of the revealer, *God*. And it cannot reasonably be
understood of any other: for upon no other *single testimony* save
that of *God*, is an assent to revelation demanded, or pleaded
for, by those he opposes.

This being premised, I say this query consists, and is made
up of three as impious suppositions as can enter the thoughts of
any of the sons of men; besides that they are mutually destructive of one another. 1. It supposes that the one single testimony of God is not a sufficient warrant for believing whatever he
shall reveal. 2. It supposes that a revelation come from God
may contain things really contradictory to our reason. 3. It
supposes that the single testimony of God is not a sufficient ground
to believe things that are besides our reason, though they be not
contrary to it, that is, truths, which we cannot prove by reason,
or about which there are some difficulties that we cannot solve.
Take these three impious suppositions out of the query, and it
has no difficulty in it. If once we suppose a revelation to be
from God, we must lay aside the second supposition as impossible, *viz.* That it can contain *any thing really contrary to reason*.
Set aside this, which makes the query *selo de se*, destroy itself,

and

* Blount Rel. Laici, pag. 93.   † Ibid. pag. 94.

and let the question be proposed, Whether we may believe upon the *single testimony of God* whatever does not really contradict our reason, though it contains some difficulties, which we cannot solve? And then I say, it is impious to deny it.

Query XIII. And lastly, " Whether, if it were granted they
" had revelations, I am obliged to accept of another's revela-
" tion for the ground of my faith? Especially if it doth any
" way oppose these five articles, that are grounded upon the
" law of nature, which is God's universal *magna charta*, enact-
" ed by the All-wife and Supreme Being, from the beginning
" of the world, and therefore not to be destroyed or altered by
" every whiffling proclamation of an enthusiast*."

This query is of the same alloy with the former. To it we answer shortly, The Christian revelation, (in others we are not concerned) exhibits matters of universal concernment, upon evidence of their divinity, capable to satisfy those who now live, as well as those to whom they were originally made; and so are impertinently called *another's* revelation. And we are obliged to receive it as the ground of our faith, and rule of our practice as much as they. The supposition that is added, that it contains doctrines or precepts contrary to the law of nature, is impious and false. What he adds further about the "whiffling proclamations of enthusiasts," if it is not applied to the sacred writers, we are not concerned in it. If it is applied to them, *First*, It is false, that they taught any thing contrary to the law of nature. *Secondly*, It is impious to call them, in way of contempt, *enthusiasts*; or, at least, it is intolerably bold for any man to call them such, before he has proven it; which he never did, nor will all the Deists on earth ever be able to do. *Thirdly*, It was rude and unmannerly to treat them with so much contempt, especially without arguments proving the charge, whom the whole authority of the land, all the persons vested with it, and the body of the people, respect as men infallibly directed of God. *Fourthly*, It was disingenuous to treat them thus, after such pretensions as our author had made of respect to them, in this and his other books.

Finally, Mr. Blount, instead of a fourteenth query, concludes with the testimony of Justin Martyr, as probative of his point. His words run thus, "·Finally, submitting my discourse to my
" impartial and judicious reader, I shall conclude with the saying
"· of

---

* Blount Rel. Laici, pag. 94.

" cf Juſtin Martyr, *Apol. cont. Triphon*, pag. 83. " That all
" thoſe who lived according to the rule of reaſon, were Chriſ-
" tians, notwithſtanding that they might have been accounted
" as Atheiſts; ſuch as among the Greeks were Socrates, Hier-
" aclitus, and the like; and among the Barbarians, Abraham
" and Azarias: For all thoſe who lived, or do now live, ac-
" cording to the rule of reaſon, are Chriſtians, and in an aſſured
" quiet condition *."

As to this teſtimony of Juſtin Martyr, it is not probative with us; though we honour the fathers, yet we do not think ourſelves obliged to ſubmit to all their dictates. This is ſaid, but not proven by him, either by ſcripture or reaſon. And I fear not to ſay, It is more than he or any other can prove. Abraham is impertinently claſſed amongſt thoſe who wanted revelation; Socrates and Hieraclitus, in ſo far as they lived according to reaſon, are aſſuredly praiſe-worthy, and upon this account are not to be reckoned Atheiſts. That they were Chriſtians I flatly deny. Nor can it be proven from ſcripture or reaſon *that their condition is aſſuredly quiet.* And further than this I am not concerned to paſs any judgment about their ſtate at preſent: What it is *that day will manifeſt.*

Blount Rel. Laici, pag. 94, 95.

END of the INQUIRY.

AN ESSAY

CONCERNING THE

NATURE of FAITH;

O R,

THE *GROUND* UPON WHICH

Faith affents to the Scriptures:

WHEREIN

THE OPINION OF THE *RATIONALISTS* ABOUT IT, IS PROPOSED AND EXAMINED, ESPECIALLY AS IT IS STATED BY THE LEARNED MR. *LOCKE* IN HIS BOOK ON *HUMAN UNDERSTANDING.*

BY THE SAME AUTHOR.

AN ESSAY, &c.

CHAP. I.

Containing some general Remarks concerning Knowledge, Faith, and particularly divine Faith, and that both as to the faculty and actings thereof.

ALL knowledge is commonly, and that not unfitly, referred to the understanding or intellective power of the mind of man, which is conversant about truth. Our assent to, or persuasion of any truth is founded, either 1. Upon the immediate perception of the agreement or disagreement of our ideas, and so is called *intuitive knowledge*. Or 2. It results from a comparison of our ideas with some intermediate ones, which helps us to discern their agreement or disagreement; and this goes under the name of *rational knowledge*. Or 3. It leans upon the information of our senses, and this is *sensible knowledge*. Or 4. It depends upon the testimony of credible witnesses. And this is FAITH.

Faith again, if it is founded upon the testimony of angels, may be termed *angelical*; if on the testimony of men, *human*; and if it is founded on the testimony of God, it is called *divine faith:* It is of this last we design to discourse, as what particularly belongs to our present purpose.

When we speak of divine faith, we either mean the faculty or power whereby we assent unto divine testimony; or the assent given by that power. Both are signified by that name, and faith is promiscuously used for the one or other.

Faith, as it denotes the faculty, power or ability of our minds to perceive the evidence of, and assent to divine testimony, is again either *natural* or *supernatural*. That naturally we have a faculty capable of assenting in some sort to divine testimony, is denied by none, so far as I know. But that ability whereby we are at least habitually fitted, disposed and enabled to assent in a due manner to, and receive with a just regard, the testimony of God, no man by nature has. This is a supernatural gift.

Several questions I know are moved concerning this ability. It belongs not to my subject, neither doth my inclination lead me to dip much in them at present. I shall only suggest the few remarks ensuing.

1. It seems unquestionably clear, that man originally had a power, ability or faculty capable of perceiving, discerning and assenting to divine revelations upon their proper evidence: For it is plain, that God did reveal himself to man in innocency, and that he made man capable of converse with himself. But if such a faculty, as this we speak of, had been wanting, he had neither been capable of those revelations, nor fitted for converse with God.

2. It may most convincingly be made out, That all our faculties have suffered a dreadful shock, and are mightily impaired by the entrance of sin, and corruption of our natures thereon ensuing; and particularly our understandings are so far disabled, especially in things pertaining unto God, that we cannot in a due manner, perceive, discern or entertain divine revelations upon their proper evidence, unto the glory of God, and our own advantage, unless our natures are supernaturally renewed. But this notwithstanding, the faculty of assenting to divine testimony is not quite lost, though it is impaired and rendered unfit for performing its proper work in a due manner. I know none who asserts, that any of our faculties were entirely lost by the fall.* In renovation our faculties are renewed, but there is no word of implanting new ones. It is certain, unrenewed men, such as Balaam and others, have had revelations made to them; and did assent to those revelations. Nor is it less clear, *that the devils believe and tremble*.

3. Whether

---

* " We cannot conceive how reason should be prejudiced by the
" advancement of the rational faculties of our souls with respect unto
" their exercise toward their proper objects; which is all we assign
" unto the work of the Holy Spirit in this matter." *Dr. Owen on the Spirit*, *Preface*, pag. 9.

3. Whether men, in a state of nature, whose minds are not renewed, may not so far discern and be affected by the characters and evidences of God impress upon divine revelations, particularly the scriptures, where those evidences shine brightly, as thereby to be obliged, and actually drawn to give some sort of assent into the testimony of God, I shall not positively determine: though the affirmative seems probable to me. The impress of a Deity is no less evident on the scriptures than his other works. *He has magnified this word above all his name.* Besides, I do not see, how the very faculty itself can be thought to remain, if it is not capable of discerning any thing of God, where he gives the most full and convincing evidence of himself, as unquestionably he doth in the scriptures. Nor do I doubt but multitudes of sober persons, trained up within the church, and thereby drawn to a more attentive and less prejudicial perusal of the scripture-revelation, do, upon sundry occasions, find their minds affected with the evidence of God in them, and thereby are drawn to assent to them as his word, though not in a due manner, and that even where they remain strangers unto a work of renovation. And I am sure, if it is so, it will leave the rejecters of the scriptures remarkably without excuse.

4. Whether some transient act of the Spirit of God is always necessary upon the mind, to draw forth even such an assent, as that last mentioned, I shall not determine; that in some cases it is so, is not to be doubted. The faith of temporary believers undoubtedly requires such an action as its cause, and where any thing of this evidence affects the minds of persons, at present deeply prejudiced, as they were, who were sent to apprehend Christ, and went away under a conviction, *that never man spake as he did;* there such a transient work of the Spirit of God seems necessary to clear their minds of prejudices, and make them discern the evidences of a Deity: But whether it is so in other cases, I shall not conclude positively.

5. But were it granted, That faith, that is, the faculty or power of believing, which is nothing else save the mind of man considered as a subject capable of assenting to testimony, still remains; and that though wofully impaired, weakened and disabled, it yet continues in so far able for its proper office or work, that either by the assistance of some transient operation of God's Spirit, breaking in some measure the power of its prejudices, and fixing it to the consideration of its proper object, or

even

even without this, upon a more sedate, sober, less prejudiced observation, it may, though less perfectly, perceive the impress and evidences of God appearing in the revelations he makes of himself, and that thereon it may be actually so affected, as to give some sort of assent, and reach some conviction, that it is God who speaks: Were, I say, all this granted, it will amount to no great matter; since it is certain, that every sort of faith or assent to divine testimony, is not sufficient to answer our duty, obtain acceptance with God, and turn to our salvation. Nor is it so much of our concernment to inquire after that sort of faith which fails of answering these ends; and therefore I shall dip no further into any questions about any faith of this sort, or our ability for it.

6. It is more our interest to understand what that faith is, which God requires us to give to his *word*, which he will accept of, and which therefore will turn to our salvation; and whence we have the power and ability for this faith. Of these things therefore we shall discourse at more length in the next chapter designed to that end.

CHAP. II.

Wherein the Nature of that Faith, which in Duty we are obliged to give to the Word of God, our obligation to, and our ability for answering our Duty, are inquired into.

WE have above insinuated, and of itself it is plain, that every sort of faith or assent to divine testimony answers not our duty, nor will amount to that regard which we owe to the authority and truth of God, when he speaks, or writes his mind to us. We must therefore, in the first place, inquire into the nature of that faith which will do so. Nor is there any other way wherein this may better be cleared, than by attending to the plain scripture accounts of it.

Now if we look into the scriptures, we find, 1. The apostle Paul, 1 Thess. ii. 13. when he is commending the Thessalonians, and blessing God on their behalf, gives a clear description of that faith which is due unto the word of God. *For this cause also,* says he, *thank we God without ceasing, because when ye received the word of God which ye heard of us, ye received it not as the word of men; but (as it is truth) the word of God, which*

which effectually worketh also in you that believe. If we advert to this description, we cannot but see these things in it, *First*, That some special sort of assent is here intended. The Thessalonians did not think it enough to give such credit, or yield such an assent as is due to the word of men, even the best of men. *Secondly*, In particular it is plain, that such an assent is intended as some way answers the unquestionable firmness of the testimony of the God of truth, which is the ground whereon it leans. *Thirdly*, It is obvious, that somewhat more is intended than a mere assent, of whatsoever sort it is: The words plainly import such an assent, or receiving of the word of God, as is attended with that reverence, submission of soul, resignation of will and subjection of conscience, that is due to God. This the use of the word elsewhere in scripture strongly pleads for, and the manner wherein the apostle expresses himself here is sufficient to convince any man that no less is intended. 1. Less than this would scarce have been a ground for the apostle's *thanksgiving* to God, and for his doing this *without ceasing*. And indeed we find that this expression elsewhere used imports not only people's assent to, but their consent and approbation of the word of God; yea, and their embracing in practice the gospel, Acts viii. 14. and xi. 1. 2. We are told Heb. xi. 1. that it is *the evidence of things not seen*. ελεγχος, which we render, *evidence*, signifies properly a *convincing demonstration*, standing firm against, and repelling the force of contrary objections. Faith then is such an assent as this, It is a firm conviction leaning upon the strongest bottom, able to stand against, and withstand the strongest objections. 3. The apostle more particularly describes the ground whereon it rests, or what that demonstrative evidence is, whereon this conviction is founded, and that both negatively and positively, 1 Cor. ii. 5. It stands not in the *wisdom of men*, but in *the power of God*. That is, it neither leans upon the eloquence, nor reasonings of men, but upon the powerful evidence of the Spirit's demonstration, as it is in the verse before.

Having given this short and plain account of faith from the scripture, we must in the next place prove, that in duty we are bound to receive the word of God with a faith of this sort. Nor will this be found a matter of any difficulty: For,

1. The scriptures hold themselves forth to us as the Oracles of God, which *holy men of God spake as they were moved by the Spirit of God*, and wrote by divine inspiration, and *the Holy Ghost is said*

said *to speak to us by them*. Now the very light of nature teaches us, that when God utters oracles, speaks and writes his mind to us, we are in duty bound readily to assent, give entire credit to, and rely with the firmest confidence on the veracity of the speaker; and further, we are obliged to attend to what is spoken with the deepest veneration, reverence and subjection of soul, and yield an unreserved practical compliance with every intimation of his mind.

2. The scriptures *were written* for this very end, *That we might so believe* them as to *have life by them*, John xx. 30. 31. And again, Rom. xvi. 25, 26. *The scriptures of the prophets according to the commandment of the everlasting God, are said to be made known to all nations for the obedience of faith.* Certainly then we are in duty obliged to yield this *obedience of faith*.

3. The most dreadful judgments, yea eternal ruin, and that of the most intolerable sort, are threatened against those, who do not thus receive the words of God from his servants, whether by word or writ, is no matter. *Whosoever shall not receive you, nor hear your words, when ye depart out of that house or city, shake off the dust of your feet. Verily I say unto you, It shall be more tolerable for the land of Sodom and Gomorrah than for that city,* Matt. x. 14, 15. Accordingly we find the apostles preach the word at *Antioch* in *Pisidia*, Acts xiii. demand acceptance of it both of Jews and Gentiles, and upon their refusal, they testify against them in this way of the Lord's appointment, ver. 51. And all this severity they used without offering miracles, or any other proof for their doctrine, so far as we can learn, besides the authoritative proposal of it in the name of God.

4. We find the apostle, in the words above quoted, commending the Thessalonians for *receiving* the word in this manner, which is proof enough, that it was their duty to do so.

This much being clear, it remains yet to be inquired, Whence we have power or ability for yielding such an assent, whether it is natural or supernatural? Now if we consult the scripture upon this head, we find,

1. That this ability to believe and receive the things of God to our salvation and his glory, is expresly denied to unrenewed man, or man in his natural estate, 2 Thess. iii. 2. *All men have not faith:* 1 Cor. ii. 14. *The natural man receiveth not the things of the Spirit of God; for they are foolishness unto him: Neither can he know them, because they are spiritually discerned,* John viii.

viii. 47—*Ye therefore hear not God's words, becaufe ye are not of God.*
2. This is exprefsly denied to be of ourfelves, and afferted to be a fupernatural gift of God, Eph. ii. 8. *By grace are ye faved through faith; and that not of yourfelves, it is the gift of God.*
3. The production of it is exprefsly afcribed unto God. He it is that *fulfils* in his people *the work of faith with power*, 2 Thef. i. 11. He it is that gives them, that is, that enables them, *on the behalf of Chrift to believe and fuffer for his name*, Phil. i. 29. It is one of *the fruits of the Spirit*. Gal. v. 22. And of it Chrift is the *author*, Heb. xii. 2. The further proof and vindication of this truth I refer to polemical writers.

But here poffibly fome may inquire, How it can be our duty thus to believe the fcriptures, fince we are not of ourfelves able to do fo? In anfwer to this, I fhall only fay, 1. The very light of nature fhews, that it is our duty to yield perfect obedience, but yet certain it is we are unable to anfwer to our duty. 2. The fcriptures plainly require us to *ferve God acceptably with reverence and godly fear,* and with the fame breath tells us, we muft *have grace* to enable us to do it, Heb. xii. 28. 3. We have *deftroyed* ourfelves, and by our own fault impaired the powers God originally gave us, and brought ourfelves under innumerable prejudices and other evils, whereby the entrance of light is obftructed: But this cannot reafonably prejudge God's right to demand credit to his word, on which he has impreft fufficient objective evidence of himfelf, which any one that has not thus faultily loft his eyes, may upon attention difcern. 4. It is therefore our duty to juftify God, blame ourfelves, and wait in the way he has prefcribed, for that *grace* which is neceffary to *enable* us; and if thus we do his will, or at leaft aim at it, we have no reafon to defpair, but may expect in due time to be enabled to underftand and know, whether thefe truths are of God, or they who fpoke them did it of themfelves, John vii. 17. Though yet we cannot claim this as what is our due.

From what has hitherto been difcourfed, it is evident, that this faith, whereby we affent to the fcripture, is fupernatural, or may be fo called upon a twofold account: 1. Becaufe the power or ability for it, is fupernaturally given; and 2. The evidence whereon it refts is fupernatural.

In this chapter, we have directly concerned ourfelves only in the proof of the firft of thefe, viz, *That our ability thus to believe*

lieve is supernaturally given; and this has been the constant doctrine of the church of God, which we might confirm by testimonies of all sorts, did our designed brevity allow*.

But our modern Rationalists do resolutely oppose this. The author of a late atheistical pamphlet, that truly subverts all religion, may be allowed to speak for all the rest; for he says no more than what they do assent to: He tells us, "That when " once the mystery of Christ Jesus was revealed, even human " reason was able to behold and confess it; not that grace had " altered the eye-sight of reason, but that it had drawn the ob- " ject nearer to it †." To the same purpose speak the Socinians; Schlichtingius tells us, " Man endued with understanding " is no otherwise blind in divine mysteries, than as he who " hath eyes, but sits in the dark: remove the darkness, and " bring him a light and he will see. The eyes of a man are " his understanding, the light is Christ's doctrine." To the same purpose doth the paradoxical *Belgick Exercitator*, that sets up for philosophy as the interpreter of the scripture, express himself frequently. Nor is his pretended answerer *Volzogius* differently minded; though he is not so constant to his opinion as the other ‡.

But these gentlemen may talk as they please, we are not obliged to believe them in this matter. The scriptures plainly teaching us, that our minds are blind, our understandings impaired and obstructed in discerning the evidence of truth, by prejudices arising from the enmity of the will, and depravity of the affections. Nor were it difficult to demonstrate from scripture, that no man can believe, or understand the word of God aright, till, 1. The Spirit of God repair this defect of the faculty, or *gives us an understanding,* 1 John v. 20. 2. Break the power of that enmity that rises up against the truths of God as foolishness. 3. Cure the disorder of our affections, that blinds our minds. And 4. Fix our minds, otherwise vain and unstable, to attend to what God speaks, and the evidence he gives of

---

* See Mr. Wilson's Scripture's genuine Interpreter asserted. Appendix, pag. 4, 5. &c.

† Treatise on Human Reason, pag. 58. published 1674, and to the credit of the church of England, with an Imprimatur, quoted by Mr. Wilson, ubi supra, pag. 13.

‡ Wilson ibid. pag. 7. 11.

of himfelf. But this is not what we principally defign, and therefore we fhall infift no longer upon this head: Our prefent queftion is not about our ability or power to believe, but the *ground* whereon we do believe. What has been fpoken of the former hitherto, is only to prepare the way for the confideration of the latter, to which we now proceed.

CHAP. III.

The Ground, or the formal Reafon, whereon Faith affents to the Scriptures is inquired after; the Rationalift's Opinion about it, and particularly as ftated by Mr. Locke in his Book on Human Underftanding, is propofed and confidered.

THOUGH we have fpoken fomewhat concerning our ability to believe the word of God, and the fupernatural rife thereof, in the preceding chapter; wherein we have offered our thoughts of that which goes under the name of *fubjective light;* yet this is not the queftion mainly intended in thefe papers. That which we aim more particularly to inquire after, is the *ground* whereon the mind thus fubjectively enlightened, or by the Spirit of God difpofed, fitted and enabled to difcern and affent to divine revelations, *builds* its affent, and wherein it *refts fatisfied*, or acquiefces.

The queftion then before us is this, What is that *ground* whereon, or reafon which moves and determines us to receive the *fcriptures as the word of God?* What is the *formal reafon* whereon our faith refts? or what is the proper anfwer to that queftion, *Wherefore do ye believe the fcriptures to be the word of God, and receive truths therein propofed as the word of God, and not of man?*

It is in general owned by all, who believe the fcriptures to be a divine revelation, that the authority, truth and veracity of God, who is truth itfelf, and can neither deceive, nor be deceived, is the ground whereon we receive and affent to propofitions of truth therein revealed.

But this general anfwer fatisfies not the queftion: For, though it is of natural and unqueftionable evidence, that God's teftimony is true, cannot but be fo, and as fuch muft be received; yet certain it is, that divine teftimony abftractly confidered, cannot be the ground of our affent unto any truth in particular:

But that whereon we must rest, and whereon our faith must lean, is, "The testimony of God to it, evidencing itself, or as it gives evidence of itself unto the mind." The knot of the question then lies here, "What is that evidence of God's speaking or giving testimony to truths supernaturally revealed, whereby the mind is satisfied that God is the revealer? Or when God speaks, or intimates any truth to us, how, or in what way doth he evidence to us, that he is the revealer, what ground is it whereon we are satisfied as to this precise point?"

Now whereas there are persons of three sorts, who may be called to assent to divine revelations, the question proposed may be considered with respect to each of them.

1. The question may be moved concerning those persons to whom the scripture revelations were originally made; and as to them it may be inquired, When God did reveal his mind unto the prophets, what was that *evidence*, what were those τεκμηρια or *certain signs*, whereby they were infallibly assured, that the propositions they found impressed upon their minds, were from God?

2. As to the persons to whom they did immediately reveal these truths, it may be questioned, What *evidences* they had to move them to *assent*, and give *faith* to those truths which were proposed to them as divine revelations? On what *ground* did they rest satisfied, that really they were so?

3. Whereas we, who now live, neither had these revelations made to us *originally*, nor heard them from the persons to whom they were so given; but being comprised and put together in the Bible, they are offered to us as a *divine revelation*, and we are in duty, upon pain of God's displeasure in case of refusal, called and required to believe, and assent to whatever is therein revealed, *as the word of God and not of man*; hereon it may be moved, What is that evidence which *this book* gives of itself, that it is of God, whereon our minds may rest assured that really it is so?

As to this question, in so far as it concerns the first sort of persons mentioned, we shall not dip much into it; all I shall say is this, in the words of the judicious and learned Dr. Owen, "In the inspirations of the Holy Spirit, and his actings on the minds of holy men of old, he gave them infallible assurance that it was himself alone by whom they were acted, Jer. xiii. 28. If any shall ask by what τεκμηρια or infallible to-
"kens

"kens they might know assuredly the inspirations of the Holy
"Spirit, and be satisfied with such a persuasion as was not lia-
"ble to mistake, that they were not imposed upon? I must say
"plainly, That I cannot tell; for these are things whereof we
"have no experience*."

There is one thing dropt as to this matter by the ingenious Mr. Locke, that deserves some animadversion. Though he delivers nothing positively about those evidences which the prophets had, yet negatively he tells us, that the prophets' assurance did not at least solely arise from the revelations themselves, or the operation of the Spirit impressing them upon their minds, which he calls the *internal light of assurance:* But that beside this, to satisfy them fully that those impressions were from God, *external signs* were requisite †; and this he endeavours to prove from their desiring *confirmatory signs,* as Abraham and others did; and from God's giving such signs undesired. To this purpose his appearance to Moses in the bush, is by our author taken notice of. As to the opinion itself, I look on it as highly injurious to the honour of divine revelation, and I take the grounds whereon it is founded to be weak and inconcludent: For, 1. Mr. Locke, nor any for him, shall never be able to prove, that these divinely inspired persons always required or got such *confirmatory signs* extrinsical to the revelation or inspiration itself; yea, it is manifest, that for most part they neither sought them nor got them. 2. When they did seek or get them, Mr. Locke cannot prove, that either God or they found them necessary for the present assurance of the person's own minds; as if that internal light of assurance, to use Mr. Locke's words, had not of itself, while it abode, been sufficient to satisfy the mind fully, that it was God who was dealing with it, or revealing himself to it. It is plain, that other reasons of their desiring such signs may be assigned. When the matters revealed were things at a distance, which required some extraordinary out-goings of God's power to effectuate them, in that case they desired, and God condescended to grant to them some extraordinary signs, not to assure them that God was speaking unto them, but to strengthen their convictions of the sufficiency of

God's

---

* Dr. Owen on the Spirit, Book 2. Chap. 1. §. 10. pag. 104.

† Human Understanding, Book 4. Chap. 19. §. 15. pag. 593. Edition 5th, 1706.

God's power, for enabling to do what he required
was difficult, or accomplishing what he promised t
fiance of the greatest opposition. Sometimes divi
were promises of things at a distance, that were n
ally accomplished till after a long tract of time, a
intervenient obstructions; in this case they were
lieve these promises, and wait in the faith of then
that light, that first assured them, was gone, and f
or signs might be of use to enable them to adhere u
formerly given upon that supernatural evidence, t
companied the revelation. Such signs then migh
strengthen the remembrance of that first evidence
had when the revelations were first imparted to the
other reasons of a like nature might sufficiently acc
desiring these signs, and God's giving them : But as
we design not a determination or full decision of

We shall only consider the question with respec
last sort of persons. And as to those who heard,
revelations immediately from inspired persons, ou
vines seem positive, that the evidence whereon th
to what they delivered as the mind of God, co
did result from the miracles they wrought, and o
signs, or proofs, which they gave of their missio
Monsieur Le' Clerk in his Emendations and
Hammond on the New Testament, gives us this gl
ii. 5. "Paul, says he, would have the Corinthians
" not as a philosopher proposing probabilities to
" the messenger of God, who had received comma
" him, to deliver to them those truths which he pr
" that he thus received them, he did shew by
" which he wrought." And a little after he adds,
" faith leans upon miracles wrought by God's pow
" is grounded upon the divine power, the cause c
" cles." As to this opinion itself, I shall express
particularly just now : But as to Monsieur Le' Cler
from this text, he had no manner of ground for it.
look into the verse before, and there we find the a
the Corinthians, that in his preaching he avoided
words of man's wisdom, and delivered his messa
monstration of the Spirit, and of power. Upon th
in the 5th verse, he tells them, his design in doing
their *faith* might *not stand in the wisdom of men, bu*

of God, that is, on the powerful demonstration of the Spirit of God, mentioned in the foregoing verse. How Monsieur Le' Clark came to dream of miracles, and fetch them in here, while the scope and every circumstance of the text stood in the way of this exposition, I cannot divine; for nothing is more foreign and remote from the sense of this place. If the author had followed the old approved interpreter of scripture, I mean the scripture itself, and had looked into the foregoing verse and context, he had given us a more genuine account: But philosophy now set up for an interpreter, I had almost said a perverter, did certainly lead him into this violent and ridiculous gloss. But to come to the matter itself.

Miracles can be no otherwise the ground of any assent, than as they afford ground for, or may be made use of as the medium of an argument, whereby the divine mission of the worker is concluded and proven. This then must be the opinion of these gentlemen, That they who heard the apostles or prophets, could not be satisfied in their minds, that what they said was divinely revealed, until they were convinced of it by proofs drawn from miracles or signs, wrought by the preacher; and that this is not merely my conjecture, is evident from the accounts we have of their opinions and hypothesis, whereof this is reckoned as a principal one, that the mind of man being rational, cannot be moved but by a rational impression, that is, by the force of effectual reasons*. And to the same purpose we shall find Mr. Locke expressing himself by and by.

Upon this hypothesis, it is evident, 1. That if a Heathen came into a Christian assembly, and heard Paul preaching, or even Jesus Christ himself, if he had never seen them work any sign or miracle, he would not be obliged to believe their doctrine. 2. If the apostles preached to those among whom they wrought no miracles, gave no such outward signs, such persons could not be obliged to believe them, the evidence whereon such a belief is founded being denied. 3. They who heard them, and saw the miracles, could not be obliged to assent unto their doctrine, until by reasoning they would have time to satisfy themselves, how far natural causes might go towards the production of such effects, and how far these things, admitting them to be supernatural, could go toward the proof of this,—that what they delivered was from God. 4. If there was

---

* Spanhem. Elench. Controversiarum pag. 320. Edition 1694.

was any among them so dull, as not to be capable to judge of these nice points, I do not see how, upon these principles, they could be obliged to believe. These and the like are no strained consequences; for it is undeniable, that our obligation to believe arises from the proposal of due objective evidence; if this is wanting no man can be obliged to believe.

As to us who neither conversed with the inspired persons, to whom such revelations were originally given, nor saw the miracles they wrought, we are told by those Rationalists, That we have *historical proof*, that there were such persons, that they wrote these revelations which we now have, and that they wrought such miracles in confirmation of their mission and doctrine; and upon the evidence of these proofs we must rest, they will allow us no other bottom for our faith. Hence Monsieur Le' Clerk tells us. " That whatever faith is this day in the world " among Christians, depends upon the testimony of men."

Among many who have embraced this opinion, Mr. Locke in his *Essay on Human Understanding*, has delivered himself to this purpose, and upon several accounts he deserves to be taken special notice of: I shall therefore represent faithfully and shortly his opinion, and the grounds whereon it is founded, and make such animadversions upon them, as may be necessary for clearing our way. His opinion you may take in the ensuing propositions.

1. When he is speaking of the different grounds of assent, and degrees thereof, he says, " Besides those we have hitherto " mentioned, there is one sort of propositions that challenge " the highest degrees of our assent upon bare testimony, whe- " ther the thing proposed agree or disagree with common ex- " perience and the ordinary course of things, or not. The " reason whereof is, because the testimony is of such an one, " as cannot deceive or be deceived, and that is of God himself. " This carries with it assurance beyond doubt, evidence be- " yond exception. This is called by a peculiar name, *revela- " tion*, and our assent to it, *faith*: Which as absolutely deter- " mines our minds, and as perfectly excludes all wavering as " our knowledge itself *."

2. But notwithstanding, he tells us in the very same paragraph, " That our assurance of truths upon this testimony," or to give his own words, " Our assent can be rationally no high- " er

---

* Human Understand. Book 4. Cap. 18. §. 14. pag. 564, 565.

" er than the evidence of its being a revelation, and that this
" is the meaning of the expreſſions it is delivered in." That
is, as he himſelf explains it, " If the reaſons proving it to be a
" revelation are but probable, our aſſurance amounts but unto a
" probable conjecture."

3. He diſtinguiſhes betwixt *traditional* and *original revela-tion*. By the laſt of theſe, ſays he, " I mean that firſt impreſ-
" ſion which is made immediately by God on the mind of any
" man, to which we cannot ſet any bounds; and by the other,
" thoſe impreſſions delivered over to others in words, and the
" ordinary ways of conveying our conceptions one to another*."
And afterwards ſpeaking of *immediate* or *original revelation*, he
tells us, " That no evidence of our faculties by which we re-
" ceive ſuch revelations, can exceed, if equal, the certainty
" of our intuitive knowledge †." And in the preceeding paragraph, ſpeaking of *traditional revelation*, he tells us, " That
" whatſoever truth we come to the clear diſcovery of, from the
" the knowledge and contemplation of our own ideas, will al-
" ways be certainer to us, than thoſe, which are conveyed by
" traditional revelation ‡."

4. He tells us, " That true light in the mind can be no
" other but the evidence of the truth of any propoſition," and
hereon he proceeds to tell us, " That there can be no other e-
" vidence or light in the mind, about propoſitions that are not
" ſelf-evident, ſave what ariſes from the clearneſs and validity
" of thoſe proofs upon which it is received:" And he adds,
" That to talk of any other light is to put ourſelves in the dark,
" or in the power of the prince of darkneſs ‖."

5. In the next paragraph he tells us plainly, That there is
no way of knowing any revelation to be from God, but by
" rational proofs: or ſome marks in which reaſon cannot be
" miſtaken **."

6. In this next paragraph he tells what before we have taken notice of, That the internal light of aſſurance which the
prophets had, was not ſufficient to teſtify, that the truths im-
preſſed on their minds were from God, without other ſigns ††.

Thus far of Mr. Locke's opinion, which in ſum amounts to
this, " That that even the original revelations, had not in them,
intrinſick

---

* Human Underſtand. Book 4. Cap. 18. §. 3. pag. 582.
† Ibid. §. 5. pag. 583.   ‡ Ibid. Book 4. Cap. 18. §. 4. pag. 582.
‖ Ibid. Book 4. Cap. 19. §. 13.   ** Ibid. §. 14.   †† Ibid. §. 15.

intrinfick evidence, fufficient to affure them on whom fuch impreffions were made, that they were from God; that other figns were neceffary to fatisfy them; and that others who received fuch revelations at fecond hand, not from God immediately, but from infpired perfons, have no other evidence to ground their affent on, befides that which refults from arguments drawn from thofe figns, whereby they did confirm their miffion; and that we have no evidence who faw not thefe figns, befides that of the hiftorical proofs, whereby it is made out, that the perfons who wrote the traditional revelations we have, wrought fuch figns in confirmation of their miffion from God."

It is worth our while to dwell a little here, and more narrowly confider Mr. Locke's thoughts, and the grounds of his opinion; I fhall therefore offer a few obfervations on this doctrine.

I. Mr. Locke in his firft propofition, fpeaks very honourably of divine faith. As to the affent or act of faith, he fays, "That it is an affent of the higheft degree; affurance without doubt." As to the ground of it, he fays, "That it is fuch as challenges an affent of the higheft degree;" that it is "evidence beyond exception." Thefe are goodly words. *He has fpoken well in all that he has faid.* I wifh that his meaning and heart may be found as good as his words. *All is not gold that glifters.* Let us then look a little more narrowly into his meaning.

To find it out, we fhall fuppofe that God, as no doubt he did, does reveal immediately to Paul this propofition, *Jefus is the Son of God.* Here is a revelation: by Paul it is affented to. Well here is faith. Now in his believing this propofition, he may be faid to affent to three things,—That what God fays is true,—That Jefus is the Son of God,—and, That God fays this to Paul.

Now, I afk Mr. Locke, or any of our Rationalifts that are of his mind, To which of thefe three is it that Paul affents, with an affent " of the higheft degree," and of which he has " evidence beyond exception?"

1. Could Mr. Locke only mean, that we have the higheft affurance of this general verity, *That God's teftimony is infallibly true?* No fure. For the affent to this truth is not an act of faith, but of intuitive knowledge. The truth itfelf is not a truth here divinely revealed, but of natural evidence. This is not

not so much in this instance expressly assented to, as supposed known.

2. Doth Mr. Locke mean, that we assent to this proposition, *That Jesus is the Son of God?* Had Paul " assurance beyond doubt," and " evidence beyond exception," of this? But surely Mr. Locke knew that Paul, on this supposition, does not at all assent to the proposition, *Jesus is the Son of God absolutely*, but *as it is revealed.* Well then, all the evidence that Paul has to ground his assent upon, is the evidence of this, *That God says so to him.* If then the evidence of God's saying so to him is not such as " challenges an assent of the highest degree," Paul cannot have the " highest degree of assurance" of that proposition, the faith whereof leans entirely upon his assurance of this, *That God has revealed it.* For as Mr. Locke says very truly in that same paragraph, " Our " assurance of any particular truth, that is, the matter revealed, " can never rise higher in degree than our assurance of this, " that it is revealed." If then Paul has not " evidence beyond exception," that God reveals the proposition we speak of to him, he can never have such assurance of the truth of the proposition materially considered. Wherefore,

3. Did Mr. Locke think in this case, that Paul would have evidence beyond exception, challenging the highest degree of assent, and thereon assurance beyond doubt, or of the highest degree, of this, that God did in very deed say to Paul, *That Jesus is the Son of God;* or of this truth, *That Jesus is the Son of God as revealed.* It is the assent to this proposition that in proper speaking is faith. The assent to the general proposition above-mentioned, is not an act of faith at all. Nor is the assent to the proposition revealed, materially considered, an act of faith. Faith in this case, is only the assent to that proposition *as revealed,* or to the *revelation of it.* If then, Paul has not the highest evidence for, and thereon the highest assurance of this, *That God says this to him,* his faith can never be said to be the highest degree of assurance or assent. This then Mr. Locke must mean, or he means nothing. But yet I suppose he scarce thought so: For, 1. He tells us afterwards, that we can have no evidence for receiving any truth revealed, that can exceed, if equal, the evidence we have for our intuitive knowledge. If we have not then evidence, equal at least to that which we have for our intuitive knowledge, for our belief of God's being the revealer, or that he speaks to us,

we cannot have the higheſt degree of aſſurance. 2. He afterwards tells us, that we have no evidence for this, that this or that truth is revealed to us by God, but that which reſults from reaſons or arguments, drawn from marks, whereby we prove that God is the ſpeaker: but Mr. Locke owns, that the evidence of all our reaſonings, is ſtill ſhort of that which we have for our intuitive knowledge. Now methinks this quite overthrows Mr. Locke's goodly conceſſion. With what confiſtency with truth or himſelf, Mr. Locke wrote at this rate, is left to others to judge.

II. Whatever there is in this conceſſion yielded in favour of faith, Mr. Locke afterwards takes care that we who now live ſhall not be the better for it: For afterwards he tells us plainly, " That whatſoever truth we come to the clear diſcovery of, " from the knowledge and contemplation of our ideas, will al- " ways be certainer to us, than thoſe which are conveyed by " traditional revelation." We have no revelation at this day, but that which Mr. Locke calls traditional. And here it is plain, that Mr. Locke thinks that our certainty of any truth we have from this, is inferior in degree to any ſort of natural knowledge, whether intuitive, rational or ſenſible.

III. It is manifeſt, that the foundation of all is, what Mr. Locke teaches in the fourth poſition above-mentioned; wherein he tells us, " That to talk of any other light in the mind, beſide that of " ſelf-evidence, reaſon, and ſenſe, is to put ourſelves in the " dark." I have added this laſt, " the light of ſenſe," becauſe Mr. Locke, though he mentions it not here, yet elſewhere he admits it. That we may underſtand Mr. Locke's aſſertion exactly, it muſt be obſerved, that writers, when they treat of this ſubject, uſually take notice of a twofold light. There is *ſubjective light*, by which is meant either our ability to perceive, diſcern, know and judge of objects, or our actual knowledge, aſſent, &c. Again there is *objective light*, by which they mean that evidence whence our knowledge reſults, whereon it is founded, and which determines the mind to aſſent or diſſent. Now it is of this laſt that Mr. Locke is treating in his chapter of *Enthuſiaſm*, from whence this propoſition is taken. And his opinion is this, That there is a threefold objective light, which is a real and juſt ground for the mind to aſſent on. There is, *firſt, ſelf-evidence*, which is the ground of our intuitive knowledge, reſulting from the obvious agreement or diſagreement of our ideas, appearing upon firſt view or intuition, when they are

are compared. *Secondly*, There is *rational light*, or the evidence refulting from arguments, wherein the agreement or difagreement of our ideas is cleared by affuming intermediate ideas, by the help of which our mind is cleared, as to what judgment it is to pafs. *Thirdly*, There is the *light of fenfe*, or the evidence refulting from impreffions made on our minds by the intervention and means of our organs of fenfe.

But befides thefe, he admits of no other objective light or evidence, that may be a juft ground of affent; and adds, " That " to talk of any other, is to put ourfelves in the dark; yea, in " the power of the prince of darknefs, and turn enthufiafts."

This grape muft be preffed, that we may tafte its juice, how it relifhes. In the confideration of this doctrine delivered by Mr. Locke, we fhall not at prefent inquire whether it really does not preclude all place for faith, properly fo called. This in the iffue will be further cleared.

But whatever there is as to this, if Mr. Locke's doctrine hold, certain it is, that either faith, if there is fuch a thing, muft be founded on one of thofe three grounds of affent, or forts of objective light, or it is altogether irrational. For an affent not founded on, and to which we are not determined by real objective evidence, is brutifh, irrational, and really enthufiaftick, as being no reafon or ground: And befides thefe three forts of grounds, Mr. Locke admits of none. Faith therefore muft be founded either on one or other of them, or it muft want all reafon for it.

Further, it is to be obferved, That Mr. Locke's taking felf-evidence for that which is immediately perceptible without the intervention of any intermediate ideas, by the natural power of our intellectual faculties, not affifted, renewed, elevated and influenced by any fupernatural influence; and taking fenfible evidence for that which is conveyed by the intervention of bodily organs, from corporeal fubftances, cannot be thought to make either of thefe the ground of faith to the teftimony of God. And therefore it muft have no reafon fave that rational evidence, which makes the middle fort of objective light. But I need not fpend time in proving this, fince it is no more than what he has taught us in the fifth propofition above-mentioned.

This opinion thus far explained is indeed the fum, and contains the force of what is pleaded, or, for ought I know, can be pleaded for the judgment of our Rationalifts. We fhall therefore

fore weigh the matter more seriously, and proceed by some plain steps in the ensuing propositions.

1. "If good and solid reasons can be produced for proof of another sort of objective light or evidence, besides those three mentioned by Mr. Locke, it must be admitted, though we should not be able to give a satisfying account of its nature, and other concernments."

(1.) This I believe was never denied in the general as to other things, by any person of judgment, adverting to, and understanding what he said, and why it then should be refused in this case, I can see no ground.

(2.) If any has ever in general denied this in words, I am sure every man in fact admits it. Who is he that receives not many truths, that admits not the being of many things, upon good proof, from their causes, effects, inseparable adjuncts, &c. of the nature of which he can give no satisfying account? We all own the mutual influence of our souls and bodies upon one another, upon the proofs we have from the effects: But whoever understood the manner, how the soul operates on the body, or the body upon it? Instances of this sort are innumerable.

(3.) Sufficient proofs must always determine our assent; and if there are such in this case, it is unreasonable to refuse it.

(4.) If we have sufficient reasons to convince us, that there is a fourth sort of objective light distinct from those three admitted by Mr. Locke, and only deny it because we understand not, or cannot give a clear account of its nature, I cannot tell, but on this same ground we shall reject, and be obliged to refuse these three sorts admitted by him, for the very same reason. Mr. Locke perhaps has done as much as any man to explain them: but were he alive, I believe he would be as ready to own as any, that he has been far from satisfying himself, or offering what may fully clear others as to the nature of these things, Wherein evidence consists? What it is? What is self-evidence, or that evidence which is the ground of our sensible or rational knowledge? How they operate and influence the assent? All his accounts are only descriptions taken from causes, effects or the like. But what objective light or evidence is, wherein it really consists, (and the like may be said of the rest) is as much a mystery as it was before, when he tells us, That self-evidence *(ex. gr.)* is that which is immediately perceived without the intervention of intermediate ideas. Here I learn, that it is not rational evidence, that requires such intermediate ideas,

ideas. But this is all I can learn, unlefs it be, that it is perceptible by the mind, that is, it is evidence. But what evidence is, I am yet to learn. I think this propofition is plain.

2. "A fourth fort of objective evidence, different from thofe "three affigned by Mr. Locke, is not impoffible."

(1.) If any fay it is, it lies upon him to prove it. That Mr. Locke, or millions more, obferved no fuch light in their minds, found themfelves determined to affent by no other objective evidence or light, will not prove it impoffible; yea will not prove, that actually there is no fuch light; nay, will not prove, that there was no fuch light in their own minds. For Mr. Locke, though he obferved as accurately the manner of his mind, its actings, as moft men, yet might not obferve it fo, but that he poffibly overlooked fomewhat that paffed there. And if really Mr. Locke did not affent upon other evidence to fome things, though he obferved it not, I doubt not but by this time he is fenfible it was his lofs that it was fo. It cannot be pretended, that it is impoffible for want of a fufficient caufe, while that God is in being, who is author of the three forts of lights, that are admitted, and who is *the Father of lights*. Nor can it be pretended, that the members of this divifion ftand contradictorily oppofed to one another, as it is in this, Every being is *dependent* or *independent*.

(2.) If any will fay yet, It is impoffible there fhould be a fourth or a fifth fort of light or objective evidence, I fhall defire him only to ftay a while, and confider the *light of fenfe*. It is nothing elfe fave "that evidence that refults from impreffions "made on our minds by means of our organs of fenfe." Well, hereon I fhall afk two queftions,

Firft, Is it not poffible for him who made thofe conveyances or organs of fenfe, to frame more fuch, quite different from thofe we already have, and by means of them impart to us other preceptions, and determine as to affent on the evidence of the impreffions conveyed to our minds by thefe other fenfes? If it is poffible, as I fee not how rationally it can be queftioned, here is at leaft a fourth fort of objective light determining our minds to affent, admitted as *poffible*.

Secondly, Here I would inquire, Whether may not He, who, by thefe bodily organs we already have, impreffes ideas upon our minds, and determines our affent to their agreement or difagreement, *immediately without the intervention of fuch organs*, make impreffions on our minds, whereby our affent or judgment

ment may rationally be swayed? To deny this, will look very odd und irrational to sober men, that have due thoughts of God. If it is admitted, we have here at least the *possibility* of another ground of assent, or objective light, acknowledged, different from those condescended on by Mr. Locke.

(3.) We that have the benefit of sight, have in our minds a sort of objective evidence or light, different from all those which are born blind have. And why should it be then thought impossible that others may have in their minds an evidence that we have no experience of, and that it may be equally real, convincing, or more so than any that we have.

(4.) Mr. Locke grants, That there are *extraordinary ways* whereby the knowledge of truth may be imparted to men; that God sometimes illuminates by his Spirit the minds of men, with the knowledge of truths; that there is no bounds to be set to such divine impressions. Now if all this is so, why may there not be evidence of a different sort, resulting from such extraordinary impressions, illuminations, &c. allowed to be also possible?

(5.) Either God can reveal his mind so to man, as to give him the highest evidence or objective light that he speaks to him, who gets that revelation, or he cannot. If he can, then there is *possible* an objective evidence, and that of the highest sort, different from those three mentioned by Mr. Locke: for that it must be different is evident, because Mr. Locke in this case will allow no place for self-evidence, or that evidence we have in our intuitive knowledge, which he determines to be the highest degree of these three sorts he has admitted and owned. Speaking of immediate revelation, he says, " No evidence of our " faculties, by which we receive such revelations, can exceed, " if equal, the certainty of our intuitive knowledge, as we " heard above." Since then this evidence of the highest degree, is different from that which we have in our intuitive knowledge, (if it is at all) it must be of a different sort from any of those three: For by concession, it is not self-evidence; and rational or sensible it is not, because these sorts of evidence are of a degree inferior to intuitive evidence. If then it is evidence of the highest degree, since Mr. Locke will not admit it to be self-evidence, it must be none of the three: and so we have a fourth sort admitted possible. But if God cannot reveal his mind, so as to give the greatest objective evidence that he speaks, or is the revealer, then I say, it is plain, and follows

unavoid-

unavoidably, that God's teftimony can never have from man the *higheft degree of affent*, which Mr. Locke above exprefsly acknowledged to be its due. It is in vain to fay, that God's teftimony is infallible: for our affent to any truth upon God teftimony, as Mr. Locke truly fays, can never rife higher, than the affurance we have of this, that really we have God's teftimony, and take its meaning. If then God cannot give us the higheft evidence or objective light as to this, no truth he offers can have from us the higheft degree of affent. To me this looks like blafphemy, to imagine, that God has made a rational creature, to whom he cannot fo impart his mind as to give it fuch evidence as is abfolutely neceffary to lay a ground for entertaining his teftimony with that refpect, which is its unqueftionable due. That his teftimony is in itfelf infallible, will never make our affent of the higheft degree, unlefs the evidence of his giving teftimony is of the higheft degree.

3. " We affert, That *de facto* there really is a fort of objec-
" tive evidence or light, different from thofe condefcended on
" by Mr. Locke."

(1.) The prophets to whom immediate revelations were made, had objective evidence, or light fufficient to ground the higheft affurance, that the truths impreffed on their minds were from God. It is impious to deny it. But this Mr. Locke will not allow to be fuch evidence as we have in our intuitive knowledge; and all muft confefs, that it did not refult from their outward fenfes; and that it was not grounded on reafonings from evidences, marks or figns, extrinfical to the revelations themfelves, feems undeniable, or even from reafoning, and making inferences from what was intrinfical to the revelation. For, 1. We find not, that this perfuafion came to them by fuch argumentation or reafoning. We can fee no ground from any accounts we have in fcripture to think, that they took this way to affure their own minds. Yea, 2. The fcripture-accounts of the way of their being convinced, feem all to import, that as God impreffed the truths on their minds, fo that immediately by that very impreffion, he fixed an indelible and firm conviction of his being the revealer. Again, 3. We fee, that the evidence was fo convincing as to bear down in them the force of the ftrongeft reafonings and the cleareft arguments that ftood againft it, as we fee evidently in the cafe of Abraham; he is commanded to offer his fon Ifaac; if this command had not been impreffed on his mind with an evidence, that God was the revealer;

er, beyond what any reasoning upon signs and marks, and I know not what, could pretend to, the strong plain arguments, that lay against it, strengthened by a combination of the strongest natural affections, must have carried it. 4. If Abraham was convinced by such reasonings, that God revealed this, that this command was from God, is it not strange that he makes no mention of them, when, it was so obvious, that it was liable to be questioned whether God could give such a command? But the truth of it is, it is obvious to any one that thinks, that nothing could prevail in this case, but the incontrollable and irresistible evidence resulting from the very impression, whereby the command was revealed. But we wave any further consideration of this, which now we have no experience of.

(2.) Mr. Locke will admit, that the primitive Christians, who embraced the gospel, did it upon sufficient objective evidence. He is not a Christian who denies it. But he will not admit intuitive evidence in this case. And I shall, I hope, afterwards make it appear, that it was not on the evidence of such reasonings, as Mr. Locke talks of, that they embraced it.

(3.) The scriptures demand our assent, and offer no evidence but this of God's authority. And arguments are not insisted on to prove, that it is God that speaks; God calls us not to assent without objective evidence, and yet waves the use of such arguments as Mr. Locke would have to be the foundation of our faith. There must be therefore some objective light of a different sort supposed, that must be the ground of our assent. And that there really is so, the scriptures teach, as we shall see afterwards, when this proposition must be proven, and explained more fully.

(4.) Abstracting from what has been said, we have as good ground as can be desired, and as the nature of the thing admits, for believing there is really a light *distinct* from those mentioned by Mr. Locke. As to the persons who have it, this light evidences itself in the same way as the other sorts of intellectual light do. They are conscious of it, and find it has the same effect, determining the mind to assent, assuring it, and giving it rest in the full conviction of truth. As to others who want it, they have such evidence as a blind man has, that there is such a thing as visible evidence. They have the concurring suffrage of persons sober, judicious and rational, who have given evidence of the greatest cautiousness in guarding against delusion, enthusiasm, and groundless imaginations. Besides, the effects pecu-

peculiarly flowing from such a faith as leans on this foundation, gives evidence to it. But I cannot stay to prove this further at present.

4. "Though perhaps an account every way satisfying can-not be given of the nature of this light, nor can we so clear what it is, and wherein it consists, as to make those who are unacquainted with it, understand it, or have as exact a notion of it as they have, whose experience satisfies them as to its reality: Yet such an account may be given of it, as may secure it against the imputation of unreasonableness, and unintelligibility." To this purpose, I shall only observe the few things ensuing.

(1.) That light or objective evidence, whereon we are obliged to believe, and all that are subjectively enlightened to believe the scriptures, and ground their assent, is such, that a more intelligible account by far may be given of it to those, who have no experience of it, than can be given of the objective evidence of visible objects to persons who have no experience of sight. To clear this,

(2.) It is to be observed, that in the writings of men, especially of some, who have any peculiarity of genius, and excel in any kind, we find such characters, marks and peculiar evidences of them, not only in the matter, but in the manner of expression, and way of delivering their thoughts: there is such a spirit, and somewhat so peculiar to themselves to be observed, that such as have any notion of their writings, cannot thereon avoid a conviction, that this or that book, though it bears not the author's name, or those other marks, whereon we depend as to our opinion of the authors of books, of whom we have no particular acquaintance, is yet written by such an author, the vestiges of whose peculiar spirit and genius run through, and are discernible in the strain of the book. There are few men, who are acquainted with books, and read them with attention and judgment, who have not the experience of this. And hence we are frequently referred to this, as what may satisfy us, that books that bear such author's names are genuine and truly theirs.* And it is found more convincing than the attestation

* "Though you had not named the author, &c. I could have known and avouched him. There is a face of a style, by which we scholars know one another, no less than our persons by a visible countenance." *Bishop Hall's Preface to Dr. Twiss's doubting Conf. resolved,* pag. 2.

of no incredible witnesses in many cases. Yet it must be confessed, that persons of the best judgment, and most capable to express their thoughts, will find it difficult, if not impossible to express intelligibly wherein this objective evidence consists: But that really it is there, that there is such a thing, is impossible for them to question.

(3.) If poor men, who differ infinitely less from one another, than the most exalted created being can be supposed to do from God, do impart to the product of their own thoughts, and leave on their writings such peculiar and discernible characters of their own genius and spirit, as, at first view, upon the least serious attention, convinces the reader, that they are the authors, and enables him to distinguish their writings from others, is it not reasonable to suppose, that a book written by God, must carry on it a peculiar and distinguishing impress of its author; and that by so much the more certainly discernible, by any that has right notions of him, as the difference betwixt him and the most exalted human genius is infinitely greater, than that betwixt the most contemptible pamphlet-writer and the most elevated scholar? Nay, is it not impossible rationally to imagine the contrary? Can we think that he, who in all his works, even in the meanest insect, has left such objective evidence, and such impressions of himself, whereby he is certainly known to be the author, has not left impressions, more remarkable and distinguishing, on his *word*, which *he has magnified above all his name*, that is, all the means whereby he designs to make himself known, and which he designed to be the principal means of imparting the knowledge of himself to men, and that for the highest purposes,—their *salvation* and *his own glory*.

(4.) This impress, those characters, prints and vestiges of the infinite perfections of the Deity, that unavoidably must be allowed to be stamped on, and shine, not merely, or only, or principally, in the matter, but in that as spoken or written, and in the writings or words, in their stile, the spirit running through them, the scope, tendency, &c. This θεοπρεπεια or God-becoming impress of majesty, sovereignty, omniscience, independence, holiness, justice, goodness, wisdom and power, is not only a sufficient and real, but in very deed, the greatest objective light and evidence imaginable. And where one has an *understanding given to know him that is true*, and is made thereby to entertain any suitable notions of the Deity, upon intuition

tuition of this objective evidence, without waiting to reason on the matter, his assent will be carried, and unavoidably determined to rest on it as the highest ground of assurance. And this assent, founded on this impress of the Deity in his own word, is indeed an assent of the highest degree. And thus far faith resembles our intuitive knowledge, with this difference, not as to the manner of the mind's acting, but as to the ability whence it acts; that in our intuitive knowledge, as Mr. Locke, and those of his opinion, restricts it, the evidence or objective light is such as not only is immediately without reasoning discerned, but such as lies open to, and is discernible by our understandings, without any subjective light, any work of the Spirit of God, either repairing our disabled faculties, or elevating and guiding them to the due observation, or fixing their attention, or freeing their minds of the power and present influence of aversion of will, disorder of affections, and pejudices that obstruct the discerning power. Whereas this is really necessary in this case; and though the objective evidence is great, and still the same, yet according to the greater or lesser degree of this assistance, our assent must be stronger or weaker, more fixed or wavering.

(5.) When this objective evidence is actually observant to, and under the view of the mind thus enabled, disposed and assisted, there doth arise from it, and there is made by it, an impression on the whole soul corresponding thereto. The beaming of God's sovereign authority awes conscience. The piercing evidence of his omniscience increases that regard, the view of his goodness, mercy, love and grace, operates on the will, and leaves a relish on the affections, and this truly resembles sensible evidence, though it is of spiritual things, and of a spiritual nature; nor is it, as it is evidence, inferior to, but upon many accounts preferable to that which results from the impression made by sensible objects. And this, as was observed of the former, is also greater or less, according, and in proportion unto the view we have of that objective light above-mentioned. This self-evidencing power is a resultancy from, and in degree keeps pace with that self-evidencing light.

(6.) The effects wrought on the soul are such, many of them, as not only are most discernible in the time, but likewise do remain on the soul, some of them ever after, many of them for a long tract of time, and in their nature are such as evidently tend to the perfecting of our faculties, are suitable to them, and

for

for their improvement, even according to what unprejudiced and sober reason determines, as to that wherein the defects of our faculties, and their perfection consists. And the reality of those effects, whereof the mind is inwardly conscious, appears to the conviction of beholders, in their influence upon the person's deportment before the world. And,

(7.) Hence it is, that though our conviction neither needs, nor is founded on reasonings; yet from those effects ground is given, and matter offered for a rational and argumentative confirmation of our assent, and the grounds thereof, and the validity of it for our own confirmation, when that evidence which first gave ground for our faith, and wherein it rests, is not actually under view, as also for the conviction of others.

(8.) This evidence is such as indeed challenges, and is a sufficient bottom for an assent of the highest degree. And indeed the saints of God, and that even of the meanest condition, and who have been under the most manifest disadvantages, both as to capacity and education, with the like accasions of improvement, upon this bottom have reached faith, comprising assurance without doubt, even that *full assurance of faith*, yea *the riches of the full assurance of understanding*, as has been evident by the effects in death and life, of which we have notable instances not a few in Heb. xi. throughout, both in adversity and prosperity, life and death.

5. " I observe, That this light or objective evidence where-
" on faith is bottomed, has no affinity with, but is at the fur-
" thest remove from enthusiastick impulse, or imaginations."

(1.) This is not a persuasion without reason. Here is the strongest reason, and the assent hereon given leans upon the most pregnant evidence.

(2.) It carries no contradiction to our faculties, but influences them, each in a way suitable to its nature and condition.

(3.) Yea more, none of our faculties in their due use do contradict, or at least disprove it. Whereas enthusiastick impressions are irrational.

(4.) This is not a persuasion, nor a ground for it without, or contrary to the word, but it is the evidence of the word itself, that by it we are directed to attend to, and improve.

(5.) Yea it is what our other faculties in their due use will give a consequential confirmation to, as we have heard. Wherefore,

(6.) Mr. Locke shall be allowed to run down enthusiasm as much

much as he pleaseth, and " persuasions whereof no reason can " be given, but that we are strongly persuaded," or not to give credit to those that can say no more for themselves, " but " we see or feel," &c. But these things as delivered by Locke, need some cautions. As, 1. A persuasion whereof no reason can be given, is certainly not faith, but fancy: but a persuasion, whereof he that hath it, through weakness, cannot give an account, may be *solid*. 2. A persuasion may be solid, of which he that hath it, cannot give another evidence of the same kind as he hath himself. It is enough that proof of another sort, and sufficient in its kind, is offered. 3. If one says, he sees and he feels, this may be satisfying to him, though he cannot give any distinct account of the evidence he hath. And that he cannot thus account for the nature of things that are within him, concludes not against the reality and truth of what he has the experience: but his experience is not ground of conviction to others, unless other proofs are offered. A man of a shallow capacity, destitute of education, might be convicted of enthusiasm by a subtile blind man, to whom he cannot for his seeing give an evidence of the same kind, nor open the nature of visible evidence, nor give any other proof that he is not mistaken, but that he sees; and yet notwithstanding of this he is not mistaken, assents not without reason, and has no ground to call in question what he sees, but may and will securely laugh at all the blind man's quirks, and tell him, *he is blind*. The case is parallel. We must not by this atheistical scare-crow be frightened out of our faith and experience.

6. " That many read the scriptures, without discerning any " thing of this light, is no argument against it." For,

(1.) Many want that supernatural ability, that understanding whereby God is known, whereby Christ's *sheep know his voice from that of a stranger, and so not being of God, they cannot hear his words.*

(2.) Many want, and are utterly destitute of any tolerable notions of God: It is impossible such should discern what is suitable to him.

(3.) Many have perverse notions of God rivetted on their minds, and that both among the learned and unlearned; and finding the scripture not suited to, but contrary to those false pre-conceived impressions, they look on it as foolishness.

(4.) Many want that humble frame of spirit, which has the promise promife of divine teaching; *the meek he guides in the way.* It is they who are fools in their own eyes, who get wifdom.

(5.) Many are proud and conceited deeply, and no wonder then that they know nothing.

(6.) Many have the vanity of their minds uncured, and fo hunt after vain things, and fix not in obfervation of what is folid, and thereby *their foolifh hearts are hardened,* and their minds darkened and diverted.

(7.) Not a few are under the power of prevailing lufts, difordered affections, and out of favour to them they are fo far from defiring an increafe of knowledge, that on the contrary, *they like not to retain God in their knowledge.* What they already know, is uneafy to them, becaufe contrary to their lufts, and therefore they would be rid of it.

(8.) Many there are that defpife the Spirit of God, reject his operations, feek not after him, contemn him: And no wonder fuch as refufe the guide, lofe their way.

(9.) Many, for thofe and other fins, are judicially left of God to the *god of this world, who blinds the minds of them that believe not.*

(10.) Many never attempt to do his will, and fo no wonder they come not to a difcerning whether the word fpoken and written, is of God. And if all thefe things are confidered, we fhall be fo far from queftioning the truth, becaufe many fee not the evidence, that this very blindnefs will be an argument to prove the truth of it, and a ftrong evidence of the need of it, and of fupernatural power to believe it.

Finally, Perfons fober and attentive want not fome darker views of this evidence, which may and fhould draw on to wait for more. And I take the honourable confeffions, in favour of the fcriptures, made by adverfaries, to have proceeded from fome fainter views of this fort.

Thus I have confidered the force of what I find pleaded by Mr. Locke; ftated the queftion; cleared in fome meafure our opinion as it ftands oppofed to that of the Rationalifts; affigned an intelligible notion of the *reafon of faith*; and fhewed it to be fuch as the meaneft are capable of, and fuch as is propofed to all who are obliged to believe the fcriptures: whereas thefe hiftorical proofs are above the reach of thoufands, and were never heard of by innumerable multitudes, who, on pain of damnation, are obliged to receive the fcriptures as the word of God.

IV. Having

IV. Having in our third obfervation overthrown the ground of Mr. Locke's opinion, we are now to clear, that what Mr. Locke builds on, muft of courfe fall; particularly what he tells us, Lib. 4. Cap. 18. Par. 6. pag. 584. " That they, who make
" revelation alone the fole object of faith, cannot fay, that it
" is a matter of faith, and not of reafon, to beleive, that fuch
" or fuch a propofiiion, to be found in fuch or fuch a book,
" is of divine infpiration; unlefs it be revealed, That that
" propofition, or all in that book was communicated by di-
" vine infpiration." And he goes on telling us, That with-
" out fuch a particular revelation, affuring us of this, that this
" propofition is by divine infpiration, it can never be matter
" of faith, but matter of reafon, to affent to it."
What Mr. Locke defigns by this difcourfe, I know not; unlefs he meant to put us under a neceffity to prove every propofition of the fcripture to be of divine infpiration, before we believe what it exhibits. And if this is what he intends, he overthrows the Chriftian religion entirely, at leaft as to its ufe and advantage to the generality. But waving what further might be obferved, I fhall only animadvert a little upon that one affertion, " That our belief, that this or that propofition is from God, is " not an act of faith but of reafon." As to which I fay,

1. If Mr. Locke defigned no more but this, That the mentioned affent to the fcripture propofitions, is an act of, and fubjected in our rational, or intellective faculty, it might well be admitted. Or,

2. If Mr. Lock meant, that this affent is agreeable to the nature of our minds, that is, that it is not really contrary to the true principles of reafon, nor fuch as proceeds without fuch grounds as the nature of our underftandings require for founding an affent, we fhould admit, that in this fenfe it is an act of reafon, that is, a rational act, as not only being elicit by our underftandings, but depending on fuch a reafon or ground, as the nature of the intellectual power requires, and which muft always be confiftent with our certain knowledge. But,

3. Neither of thefe being intended, we cannot go along with Mr. Locke in what he means by this expreffion, That our belief of fcripture propofitions, is an act of reafon, that is, an affent not built upon divine teftimony, but on fuch other arguings and reafonings, as we can find out for proving that God revealed it. Becaufe we fay, and fhall afterwards prove, that the fcriptures do evidence themfelves to be from God, in that way a-

above-expressed, and afterwards to be explained and confirmed, which we hope shall be done in such sort, as may effectually repel the force of what Mr. Locke has pleaded in opposition to the scriptures, and shew, that there is no reason for ranking all the truths therein delivered amongst those conjectural things that lean only on probabilities and reasonings from them, which Mr. Locke evidently does, while he sinks traditional revelation as to the point of certainty below our intuitive, rational and sensible knowledge; and banishes all faith, properly so called, out of the world, leaving no room for it, and substituting in its place an act of reason, proceeding upon probabilities, that is, on historical proofs, which he reckons only among probabilities; nor do I blame him for this last, though perhaps some things he has offered on this head, might be excepted against; but this is not my business.

The question in short amounts to this, " Whereas the scrip-
" tures, wherever they come, oblige all to whom they are of-
" fered, to receive them not as the *word of man*, but, as in-
" deed they are, the *word of God*; upon what ground or for-
" mal reason is it, that we assent thus unto them, and receive
" them as the *word of God*, to his glory and our salvation, in
" compliance with our duty?"

In answer to this important query, I shall offer what, upon a review of former experience, consideration of the scriptures, and what others, especially that judicious and profound divine Dr. Owen, in his two treatises on this subject, have written on this head, appears satisfying to me: And this I shall do in the few following *Propositions*, which I shall, with as much brevity and perspicuity as I can, lay down, and shortly confirm with some few arguments.

PROP. I. " That faith whereby we assent unto, and receive
" the word of God, to his glory and our salvation, is faith di-
" vine and supernatural."

1. There are at this day, who teach, That whatever faith is at present to be found amongst men, is built upon, and resolved into the testimony of men[*]. And therefore it will be necessary to insist a little in confirming and explaining of this important truth.

2. To clear this we observe, that the understanding, or that faculty, power or ability of the soul of man, whereby we perceive,

[*] Le' Clerk in his Logicks.

aſſent unto truths upon their proper evidence, may
hed or branched into diverſe ſubordinate powers, in
he different truths to which it aſſents. 1. We have
f aſſenting unto the ſelf-evident maxims of reaſon,
, *The ſame thing, at the ſame time, cannot be and not*
eir own ſelf-evidence, without any other argument,
propoſal of them in terms we underſtand. 2. We
ility to aſſent unto other truths, upon conviction of
by arguments, drawn from the fore-mentioned ſelf-
ths, or any other acknowledged or owned by us.
an ability to aſſent unto truths, upon the evidence
nony of credible witneſſes, or perſons worthy to be
ad of deſerving credit. This ability, and the aſſent
to ſuch truths, upon ſuch teſtimony, are both called
common name, faith.
then is that power or ability of the mind of man,
is capable of receiving, and actually aſſents unto
the evidence of the teſtimony of perſons worthy of
know what they teſtify, and will not deceive us.
as the perſon giving this teſtimony, is either God,
gels, good or bad, faith may be conſidered as either
an or *angelical*. This laſt, as of no conſideration to
, we ſhall lay aſide. That faith, or ability, whereby
the teſtimony of men worthy of credit, is called *hu-*
And that whereby we aſſent to truths upon the evi-
e teſtimony of God, who cannot lie, is called *divine*

e faith is that power, or ability whereby we aſſent
receive truths propoſed to us upon evidence of the
limony of God, to our own ſalvation, in compliance
ity, to the glory of God.
s account of divine faith, we add, *in compliance with*
o the glory of God, and our own ſalvation, becauſe
nen may yield ſome aſſent unto truths, upon the evi-
iod's teſtimony, which neither anſwers their duty,
to the glory of God in their ſalvation, of which we
r deſign to ſpeak, and therefore by this clauſe have
nd laid it aſide, as not belonging to that faith where-
ſpeak, and whereby we conceive all, to whom the
ome, are obliged to receive them.
faith now deſcribed may be called divine, and ſuper-
d really is ſo on two accounts, 1. Becauſe this abili-

ty is wrought in them, in whom it is found, by the divine and supernatural power of God. 2. Because it builds not its persuasion of, yields not its assent unto the truths it receives upon any human authority or testimony; but upon the testimony of God, who can neither be ignorant of any truth, deceived, or deceive us.

7. It now remains, that we confirm this proposition that we have thus shortly explained. And this we shall do by its several parts. *First*, then we assert, " That this faith is wrought in " these, who have it, by the power of God." Now for clearing this, we shall only hint at the heads of a few arguments, leaving the further proof to polemic treatises. 1. This ability to believe and receive the things of God to our salvation and his glory, is in scripture expressly denied to natural or unrenewed men. 2 Thes. iii. 2. *All men have not faith.* 1 Cor. ii. 14.—*The natural man receiveth not the things of the Spirit of God: For they are foolishness unto him: Neither can he know them, because they are spiritually discerned.* Joh. viii. 47.—*Ye therefore hear not God's words, because ye are not of God.* 2. This is expressly denied to be of ourselves, and asserted a supernatural *gift of God.* Ephes. ii. 8.—*By grace ye are saved through faith, and that not of yourselves, it is the gift of God.* 3. The production of it is ascribed unto God. He it is that fulfils in his people *the work of faith with power,* 2 Thes. i. 11. He it is that gives them, that is, that enables them, *on the behalf of Christ, to believe and suffer for his name,* Phil. i. 29. It is one of the *fruits* produced by the *spirit,* Gal. v. 22. and of it Christ is the *author.* Heb. xii. 2.

Secondly, We are next shortly to prove, " that this faith " builds its persuasion on the testimony of God evidencing it- " self such unto the mind," and not on human testimony. 2. It is in scripture expressly said not to *stand in the wisdom of men,* 1 Cor. ii. 5, that is, it leans not on the word, authority, eloquence or reasonings of men. 2. It is expressly in that same verse, said to *stand in the power of God,* that is, as the foregoing words compared with ver. 13. explain it, *in the words which the Holy Ghost teacheth,* and which he demonstrates or evidences by his power, accompanying them, to be the *word of God.* 3. It is described in such a way as fully clears this; it is held forth as a *receiving of the word, not as the word of man, but as it is indeed the word of God, which effectually work-*
eth

eth in you that believe, 1. Thef. ii. 13. Many other proofs might be added, but this is fufficient to anfwer our purpofe.

Thirdly, We fhall next fhortly prove, " that we are obliged " in duty thus to believe the fcriptures, or to receive them as " the word of God, and not of men." 1. The fcriptures are indeed, and hold forth themfelves every where as the word of God. They are the oracles of God, which *holy men of God fpake by the motion of the Spirit of God*, and *wrote by divine infpiration*, and the *Holy Ghoft fpeaks to us by them*.* Now when God utters oracles, fpeaks, writes and utters his mind to us, we are in duty obliged and bound to affent to what he fays, and yield what obedience he requires. This the very light of nature teacheth. 2. The fcriptures were written for this very end, that we might believe, *and that believing we might have life*, John xx. 30, 31. *The fcriptures of the prophets* (which contain the *revelation of the myftery* of God's will, otherwife not known) *according to the commandment of the everlafting God, are made known unto all nations for the obedience of faith*, Rom. xvi. 25, 26. Again the fcriptures are termed *a more fure word of prophecy* than the voice from heaven, and men are faid to *do well, to take heed* to them, 2 Pet. i. toward the clofe. That is, it is their duty to take heed to them, or believe them. 3. The moft dreadful judgments are threatened againft thofe who receive not the word of God from the prophets or apoftles; whether by word or writ, is all one. *Whofoever fhall not receive you, nor hear your words, when ye depart out of that houfe or city, fhake off the duft of your feet. Verily I fay unto you, it fhall be more tolerable for the land of Sodom and Gomorrah, in the day of judgment, than for that city*, Matth. x. 14, 15. Accordingly we find the apoftles preach the word at Antioch in Pifidia, Acts xiii.; demand acceptance of it both of Jews and Gentiles; and upon their refufal they teftify againft them in the way of the Lord's appointment, ver. 51. Though fo far as we can learn, they there wrought no miracle to confirm their miffion. 4. We have above heard the apoftle commending the Theffalonians for *receiving the word as the word of God, and not of man*. 1 Theff. ii. 13. which fufficiently fhews that it was their duty.

Whereas fome may here fay, " How can it be our duty to believe the word of God, fince it has been above proved, that
we

---

* Heb. v. 12.—2 Pet. i. 20, 21.—2 Tim. iii. 16.—Mark xii. 36. Acts i. 16.—Acts xxviii. 25.---Heb. iii. 7.

we are not able of ourselves thus to do it." I answer briefly, 1. The very light of nature requires perfect obedience of us; and yet we are not able to yield to it. 2. The scriptures plainly require, *that we serve God acceptably, with reverence and godly fear,* Heb. xii. 28. and yet we must have grace whereby to do it. 3. We have *destroyed ourselves,* Hos. xiii. 9. and that through this, our faith or natural ability of believing truths upon testimony, is so impaired and weakened, and by prejudices so obstructed otherwise, that we are not able to discern the evidence of God's authority, in his word, nor assent thereon to his testimony in a due manner, yet this cannot reasonably prejudge God's right to demand credit to his word, whereon he has impressed such prints of his authority, as are sufficiently obvious to any one's faith, that is not thus faultily depraved. 4. We have therefore no reason to question God, who gave us eyes, which we have put out, but to blame ourselves, and aim *to do his will,* that is, wait on him in all the ways of his own appointment; and we have no reason to despair, but that in this way we may have graciously given us of God's sovereign grace, an understanding to know whether these truths are of God, or they who spoke them did it of themselves, (1 John v. 20. John vii. 17.) Though we cannot claim this as what is our due.

Thus we have in some measure cleared what that faith is, whereby the scriptures must be believed to the glory of God and our own salvation, and confirmed shortly our account of it from the scriptures of truth. We now proceed to

PROP. II. " The reason for which we are obliged in duty " to believe or receive the scriptures as the word of God, is " not, That God has by his Spirit wrought faith in us, or given " us this ability thus to receive them."

This proposition we have offered, because some do blame Protestants for saying so; whereas none of them really do it. Nor can any man reasonably say it. For clearing this observe,

1. It is indeed true, that we cannot believe them, unless God give us this gracious ability or faith to believe them, and by his Holy Spirit remove our natural darkness, and clear our minds of those prejudices against his word, wherewith naturally they are filled.

2. Yet this is not the reason wherefore we do assent unto, or receive the scriptures; for it were impertinent, if any should

ask

ask, Upon what account do ye believe the scriptures to be the word of God? to answer, I believe it because God has wrought the faith of it in me. This is not to tell wherefore we do believe, but to tell how we came to be furnished with power or ability to believe.

PROP. III. " We are not to believe the scriptures upon the
" authority of any man or church : or, The reason wherefore
" we are in duty bound thus to assent to, or receive the scrip-
" tures as the word of God, is not, that any man, or church,
" says so."

This is fully demonstrated by our writers against the Papists. For confirmation of it, it is sufficient for our purpose at present to observe,

1. That to believe, that the scriptures are the word of God, because such a man, or church says so, answers not our duty. Our duty is to believe God speaking to us, upon the account of his own veracity ; and not because men say, that this is his word. This is not to believe God and his prophets for the sake of their own testimony, but for the authority of men, (2 Chron. xx. 20.)

2. The faith that leans upon this testimony, is built not on the *truth of God*, but on the *testimony of men*, who may be deceived and deceive : *All men are liars.*

3. We have no where in the word this proposed as the ground whereon, in duty, we are obliged to believe the scriptures.

4. The church, and what she says, is to be tried by the word, and her testimony is so far only to be received as the word consents : and therefore we cannot make this the ground of our faith, without a scandalous circle, which the church of Rome can never clear herself of.

5. But I need insist no further on this head. That church which only claims this regard to her testimony, is long since become so well known, and so fully convicted of manifold falshoods, that her testimony rather prejudges than helps to confirm whatever it is engaged for.

PROP. IV. " The rational arguments whereby the truth of
" the Christian religion is evinced and demonstrated against
" atheists, though they are many ways useful, yet are not the
" ground or reason whereon, in a way of duty, all who have
" the

" the Scriptures propofed to them, are obliged to believe and
" receive them as the word of God."

These moral and rational confiderations are, and may be many ways ufeful to ftop the mouths of enemies, to beget in them, who yet are unacquainted with the true intrinfick worth of the word, fome value for it, and engage them to confider it; to relieve them that do believe againft objections, and ftrengthen their faith. This is allowed to them; and is fufficient in this loofe and atheiftical age, to engage perfons of all forts, who value the fcriptures, to ftudy them. But yet it is not upon them that the faith required of us, as to the divine authority of the fcriptures, is to be founded. For,

1. Thefe are indeed a proper foundation for a rational affent, fuch as is given upon moral proof or demonftration. And they are able to beget a ftrong moral perfuafion of this truth. But this affent which they beget, cannot, in any propriety of fpeech, be called faith, either divine or human. For faith is an affent upon teftimony.

2. The faith that is required of us, is required to be founded not on the *wifdom of men*, that is, the reafonings or arguings of men. Now this leans only and entirely on thefe.

3. This faith is, in way of duty, required of many. Many are in duty obliged to receive the fcriptures as the word of God, to whom thefe arguments were never offered. The apoftles never made ufe of them, and yet required their hearers to receive and believe their word.

4. This faith many are obliged to, who are not capable of underftanding or reaching the force of thefe arguments.

PROP. V. " The faith of the fcripture's divine authority is
" not founded in this, That they by whom they were written,
" did, by miracles, prove they were fent of God."

I need not fpend much time in clearing this. It will fufficiently confirm it to obferve,

1. That many are, and were in duty obliged to yield this affent to, and believe the fcriptures, who faw not thefe miracles.

2. We are no other way fure of thefe being wrought, than by the teftimony of the word.

3. This way is not countenanced by the word: for it no where teaches us to expect miracles as the ground of our affent, but upon the contrary declares, that the word of Mofes and the
prophets

prophets is sufficient to lay a foundation for faith, without any new miracle, (Luke x. 31.)

Prop. VI. " The reason whereon, in duty we are bound
" to receive the scriptures as the word of God, is not any pri-
" vate voice, whisper or suggestion from the Spirit of God,
" separate and distinct from the written word, saying in our
" ear, or suggesting to our mind, that the scriptures are the
" word of God."

There is no need to insist long in proof of this. For,

1. Many are bound to believe the word of God, to whom never any such testimony was given: but no man is bound to receive the scriptures, to whom the ground whereon he is bound to believe them, is not proposed.

2. There is no where in the word, any ground given for any such testimony. Nor doth the experience of any of the Lord's people witness, that they are acquainted with any such suggestion. And besides, the question might again be moved concerning this suggestion, Wherefore do ye believe this to be the testimony of God?

Prop. VII. " That whereon all, to whom the word of God
" comes, are bound to receive it with the faith above described,
" is not any particular word of the scripture bearing testimony
" to all the rest. As for instance, it is not merely or primarily
" upon this account, that I am bound to receive all the written
" word as the word of God, because the scripture says, 2 Tim.
" iii. 16. *That all scripture is given by inspiration of God.*"

This is very plain upon many accounts, some of which I shall shortly offer.

1. We had been obliged to believe the scriptures with faith supernatural, though these testimonies had been left out. Yea they who had them not, were obliged to believe the word of God.

2. These have no more evidence of their being from God, than other places of scriptures: and therefore we are not to believe the scriptures merely on their testimony; but have the same reason to receive with faith as the word of God, every part of the scripture as well as these testimonies.

Prop. VIII. " The reason why we are bound, with faith
" supernatural and divine, to receive the word of God, is not,
" that

"that the things therein revealed, or the matters of the scriptures, are suitable unto the apprehensions which men naturally have of God, themselves and other things, and congruous to the interests, necessities, desires and capacities of men."

I shall not spend time in overthrowing this, which some seem so fond of; only for confirming the proposition observe,

1. This suitableness of the matter unto the apprehensions, or natural notions of men concerning God, themselves and other things, &c. as discerned by men unrenewed, and made out by their reasonings, is not a ground for faith, or an assent to testimony, but for a persuasion of another sort.

2. There are many things revealed in the scripture, which are to any mere natural man no way capable of this character. No man receives, or can reasonably receive on this account, the doctrine of the Trinity, and the like. It is true, these are not contrary to our reason: but it is likewise true, they have no such evident congruity to the notions our reason suggests of God, as should engage us to receive the discovery as from God; yea on the contrary, there is a seeming inconsistency that has startled many.

Prop. IX. "When therefore it is inquired, Wherefore do ye believe, and by faith rest in the scriptures as the word of God, and not of man? We do not answer, It is because God has given us an ability so to do; because the church says, it is the word of God; because there are many strong moral arguments proving it so; because they who wrote it, wrought miracles; because God has by some voice whispered in our ear, or secretly suggested it to us, that this is the word of God; or because there are particular scriptures which bear witness to all the rest that they are of God; nor finally, because the matter therein revealed, seem worthy of God to our reason."

This is the sum of what has been hitherto cleared: and the reasons offered against all these, whether we take them separately or conjunctly. They prove, that not one of them, nor all taken together, are the formal reason whereon we are obliged to believe the word of God, or receive it with faith supernatural and divine.

Prop.

PROP. X. " The formal reason or ground whereon I assent
" to, or receive the whole scriptures, and every particular
" truth in them, and am obliged in duty so to do, is, the au-
" thority and truth of God speaking in them, and speaking eve-
" ry truth they contain, evidencing itself to my faith, when
" duly exercised about them, and attending to them, by their
" own divine and distinguishing light and power. Or when it
" is inquired, Wherefore do ye believe, receive, assent to,
" and rest in the scriptures as indeed the word of God, and
" not of man? I answer, I do believe them, because they car-
" ry in them, to my faith, an evidence of God, or do evidence
" themselves by their own light and power to my faith, duly
" exercised about them, that they are the word of God, and not
" of man."

Now for explaining this, which is the assertion that contains the truth principally intended, I shall offer the few following remarks:

1. However great the evidence of God in the word is, yet it cannot, nor is it requisite that it should, determine any to receive and assent to it, whose faith and ability of believing is not duly disposed. Though the sun shine never so clearly, yet he that has no eyes, or whose eyes are vitiate, and under any total darkening indisposition, sees it not. No wonder then, that they, who have not naturally, and to whom God has not yet, by supernatural grace, given eyes to see, ears to hear, or hearts to perceive, discern not the evidence of God's authority and truth in the word.

2. Although there really may be in any an ability, or faith capable of discerning this evidence; yet if that faith is not exercised, and duly applied to the consideration of the word, whereon this evidence is impressed, he cannot assent unto, or believe it in a due manner, to the glory of God, his own salvation, and according to his duty. There is evidence sufficient in many moral, metaphysical and mathematical truths; and yet abundance of persons, who are sufficiently capable of it, do not assent unto these truths, nor discern this evidence: not because it is wanting, but because they do not apply their minds to the observation of it in a due way. God has not imparted such an evidence to his word, as the light of the sun has, which forces an acknowledgement of itself upon any, whose eyes are not wilfully shut: but designing to put us to duty, he has imparted such evidence, as they, who have eyes to see, if accord-

ing to duty they apply their minds, may difcern, and be fatisfied by.

3. This light and power evidencing the divine authority of the fcriptures, is really impreffed upon every truth, or every word which God fpeaks to us, efpecially as it ftands in its own place, related to, and connected with the other parts of the fcripture, whereto it belongs. But of this more hereafter.

4. When to the queftion, Wherefore, or on what grounds do I affent to the fcriptures as indeed the word of God and not of man? it is anfwered, I do it, becaufe it evidences itfelf to be God's word by its own light or power, there is no place for that captious queftion, How know ye this light and power to be divine, or from God? For, it is of the nature of all light, external and fenfible, or internal and mental, (concerning which two it is hard to determine which of them is properly, and which only metaphorically, light) that it not only clears to the mind other things difcernible by it, but fatisfies the mind about itfelf, proportionably to the degree of its clearnefs. The light of the fun difcovers fenfible objects, and fatisfies us fo fully about itfelf, that we need have recourfe to no new arguments to convince us that we have this light, and that it is real. In like manner the evidence of any mathematical truth, not only quiets us about the truth, but makes the mind reft affured about itfelf. And fo the divine light and power of the word, not only fatisfies our minds, as to thofe truths they are defigned of God to difcover, but, in proportion to the degree of light in them, or conveyed by them, fatisfy the mind about this light or power, that it is *truth* and is *no lie*. Nor is there need for any other argument to convince a mind affected with this, of it. It is true, if a blind man fhould fay fo to me, How know ye that the fun fhines, and ye fee it? I would anfwer, I know it by the evidence of its own light affecting mine eyes: And if he fhould further fay, But how prove ye to me, that ye are not deluded, that really it is fo? Then I would be obliged to produce other arguments whereof he is capable: but then it muft be allowed that the evidence of thefe arguments is not fo great as the evidence I myfelf have of it by its own light; though they may be more convincing to him. And further, this is not to convince myfelf, but to fatisfy him, and free my mind from the difturbance of his objections. In like manner, if one, that denies the fcriptures, fhall fay, Wherefore do ye believe or reft in the fcriptures as the word of God? I anfwer, I do it, becaufe they

they evidence themselves to my mind, by their own light, or power, to be of God. If he shall say, I cannot discern this. I answer, It is because your mind is darkened, ye want eyes, or have them shut. If he shall further urge, That my light is not real, I will prove it by arguments, which may stop his mouth, and be more convincing to him than my assertion, which is all that hitherto he has; but yet these arguments are not that whereon my mind rests satisfied as to the truth; though they may be of great use, not only to convince him, but to relieve my mind against such subtile sophisms, as he might make use of, which though they could not persuade me out of the sight of my eyes, or the evidence shining into my mind, yet troubled me how to answer them, and at times, when, through my inadvertency, or indisposition of my eyes, or through clouds overspreading and interposing betwixt this light and me, these objections might shake me a little.

5. Considering we are but renewed in part, and our faith is imperfect, and liable to many defects, the ministry of the church is of manifold necessity and use, to awaken us to attend to this light, to cure the indispositions of our minds, to hold up this light to us, to point out and explain the truths it discovers, whereby our minds are made more sensible of the evidence of this light. And upon many other accounts of a like nature, are the ordinances necessary, and through the efficacy of the divine ordination and appointment, useful for establishing our minds, naturally sluggish, dark, weak and unstable, and which are exposed to manifold temptations, in the faith of the scriptures.

6. In order to our holding fast our faith, and being stable in it, besides this outward ministry, and the inward work of the Holy Ghost, giving us an understanding to discern this evidence, and besides the forementioned use of the moral arguments above-mentioned; besides all these, to our believing and persevering in a due manner, in the faith of the scriptures, we stand in need of the daily influences of the Spirit of God, to strengthen our faith or ability of discerning spiritual things, to clear our minds of prejudices, and incidental indispositions, to feel the truths on our minds, and give us refreshing tastes of them, and confirm us many ways against opposition.

7. This light, whereby the written word evidences itself unto the minds of those who have spiritual ears to hear, and apply them, is nothing else save the impress of the majesty, truth,

omniscience, wisdom, holiness, justice, grace, mercy, and authority of God, stamped upon the scriptures by the Holy Ghost, and beaming or shining into the minds of such persons upon their hearing or perusal, and affecting them with a sense of these perfections, both in what is spoken, and in the majestic and God-becoming way of speaking: they speak as *never man spake*; the matter spoken, and the manner of speaking, has a greatness discernible by a spiritual understanding, that fully satisfies it, that God is the speaker. And all the impressions of God's wisdom, faithfulness, omniscience and majesty, that are stamped upon the matter contained in the scriptures, being conveyed only by the word, do join the impressions that are upon the word, and strengthen the evidence they give of their divine original, since these impressions do not otherwise appear to our minds, or affect them, than by the word. The word, by a God-becoming manifestation of the truth, that scorns all these little and mean arts of insinuation, by fair and enticing words, and artificially dressed up argumentations, with other the like confessions of human weakness, that are in all human writings, commends itself to the conscience, dives into the souls of men, into all the secret recesses of their hearts, guides, teaches, directs, determines and judges in them, and upon them, in the name, majesty and authority of God. And when it enters thus into the soul, it fills it with the *light of the glory* of the beamings of those perfections upon it, whereby it is made to cry out, *The voice of God and not of man.*

8. This power, whereby the word evidences itself to be the word of God and not of man, is nothing else save that authority and awful efficacy, which he puts forth in and by it over the minds and consciences of men, working divinely, and leaving effects of his glorious and omnipotent power in them and on them. It enters into the conscience, a territory exempt from the authority of creatures, and subject only to the dominion of God, it challenges, convinces, threatens, awakens, sets it a roaring, and the creation cannot quiet it again. It commands a calm, and the sea, that was troubled before, is smooth, and devils and men are not able to disturb its repose. It enters into the mind, opens its eyes, fills it with a glorious, clear, pure and purifying light, and sets before it wonders before unknown, undiscerned in counsel and knowledge, concerning God, ourselves, our sin, our duty, our danger, and our relief, the works, the ways, the counsels and purposes of God. It speaks

to the will, converts it, and powerfully difengages it from what it was moſt engaged to, what it embraced, and was even glued to before, ſo that no art or force of eloquence, argument, fear or hope, could make it quit its hold; it makes it haſtily quit its embraces, and turn its bent another way, the quite oppoſite, and with open arms embrace what nothing could make it look to before, takes away its averſion, makes it willingly not only go, but run after what it bore the greateſt averſion to before, and obſtinately refuſe to cloſe with any other thing. It enters the affections, makes them riſe from the ground, gives them ſuch a divine touch, that, though they may through their fickle nature, be carried at a time by force another way, yet they never reſt, but point heaven-ward. It comes to the ſoul, ſunk under the preſſure of unrelievable diſtreſſes, ſticking in the *miry clay*, refuſing comfort, and in appearance capable of none, it plucks it out of the clay, raiſes it out of the horrible pit, ſets its *feet upon a rock*, fills it with joy, yea makes it exceeding joyful, while even all outward preſſures and tribulation continue, yea are increaſed. It enters into the ſoul, lays hold on the reigning luſts, to which all formerly had ſubmitted, and that with delight; it tries and condemns thoſe powerful criminals, makes the ſoul throw off the yoke, and join in the execution of its ſentence againſt, and on them. Now where the caſe is thus ſtated, how can the ſoul, that feels this powerful word, that comes from the Lord moſt High, do otherwiſe than *fall down*, and own, *That God is in it of a truth*.

9. Whereas ſome may hereon object, " That many, who " have for a long time heard and peruſed this word, have not " perceived this light, nor felt this power, and, on this ſuppo- " ſition, ſeemed exempted from any obligation to believe the " word." I anſwer,

(1.) Many who have ſpent not a few years in prying into the works of God in the world, have not diſcerned to this day the beaming evidence, and clear declarations of his glory in them; yet none will hereon ſay, that they are excuſable, or that want of an evidence is chargeable on the works of God. And why ſhould not the caſe be allowed the ſame as to the word? May they not have this evidence, though men do not diſcern it? And may not men, even on account of this evidence be obliged to believe them?

No wonder many diſcern not this light, and are not affected with it, ſince all men have put out their own eyes, or impaired

by

by their own fault, that faith or power of difcerning the voice of God, fpeaking either by his word or works, which our natures originally had. In many this evil is increafed, and this power further weakened by their fhutting their eyes, and entertaining of prejudices, manifeftly unjuft, againft God's word and works. Others turn away their eyes, and will not look to, or attend to the word in that way wherein God ordains them to attend to it, that they may difcern its light, and feel its power. And God has hereon judicially given many up to the power of Satan, to be further blinded. And no wonder they, whofe eyes the *god of this world has blinded*, fhould not difcern the glory of the gofpel of Chrift, who is the *image of God, fhining into their minds.*

(3.) No wonder they fhould not difcern this; for God to this day has not given them *eyes to fee, ears to hear*, or *hearts to perceive*. It is an act of fovereign grace, which God owes to none, to open their eyes, which they have wilfully blinded: and where he fees not meet to do this, it is not ftrange, that they are not affected with the cleareft evidence.

(4.) Light, however clear, cannot of itfelf fupply the defect of the difcerning power. The fun, though it fhines, cannot make the blind to fee. The word has this light in it, though the blind fee it not; yea I may adventure to fay, that the word of God contained in the fcriptures, which he has magnified above all his name, has in it more, and no lefs difcernible evidences of the divine perfections, and confequently of its divine original and authority, than the works of creation, fome of which are fufficient to carry in fome conviction of God in it, even on the minds of thofe who are not favingly enlightened, if they attend but to it in the due exercife of their rational abilities, that is, in fuch a manner as they do, or may attend to it, without faving illumination, laying afide wilful prejudice; which though it will not be fufficient to draw fuch an affent, as will engage and enable them to receive the fcriptures, in a due manner, to the glory of God, and their own falvation, and comply with them, yet I conceive it will be fufficient to juftify againft them the word's claim to a divine original, and cut them off from any ufe of, or excufe from a plea of the want of fufficient evidence of the divine original of the word. I doubt not, but many of thefe, who upon conviction faid, *that Chrift fpake as never man fpake*, were ftrangers to faving illumination, and yet faw fomewhat of a ftamp and imprefs of divinity in what he faid, and the manner

manner of saying it, that drew this confession from them, that rendered them inexcusable, in not listening to him, and complying with his word. Yea I doubt not, that the case will be found the same as to many, with respect to the written word, and would be so to all, if they seriously, and without wilful prejudices, attended to it.

10. I further observe, That to engage to this assent, it is not requisite, that every one feel all these, or the like particular effects at all times, but that the word have this power, and put it forth, as occasion needs, and circumstances require it.

Having thus explained, we are now to prove our assertion, " That the ground whereon we are in duty bound to believe " and receive the word of God as his word, and not the word " of man, and whereon all who have received, and believed it " in a due manner, to the glory of God and their own salvation, " do receive it thus, is the authority and veracity of God speak- " ing in and by the word, and evidencing themselves by that " light and power, which is conveyed into the soul in and by " the scriptures, or the written word itself."

Many arguments offer themselves for proof of this important assertion, which hitherto we have explained; some of the most considerable of them I shall shortly propose, without insisting largely on the prosecution, designing only to hint the arguments that satisfied me, that I was not mistaken as to the grounds whereon, by the forementioned experience, I was brought to receive the scriptures as the word of God.

Arg. 1. God ordinarily in the scriptures offers his mind, requiring us to believe, obey and submit to it upon this and no other ground, viz. the evidence of his own testimony. The only reason commonly insisted on to warrant our faith, oblige us to believe and receive, is, *Thus saith the Lord.*

Arg. 2. When false prophets set up their pretended revelations in competition with his word, he remits them to the evidence his words gave by their own light and power, as that which was sufficient to distinguish and enable them to reject the false pretensions, and cleave to his word, Jer. xxiii. 26,—29. *How long shall this be in the heart of the prophets that prophesy lies? That are prophets of the deceit of their own hearts; which think to cause my people to forget my name by their dreams, which they tell every man to his neighbour, as their fathers have forgotten my name for Baal. The prophet that hath a dream, let him tell a dream, and he that hath my word, let him speak*

my

my word faithfully: What is the chaff to the wheat, saith the Lord? Is not my word like a fire, saith the Lord, and like a hammer that breaketh the mountains in pieces? In the latter days of that church, when the people were most eminently perplexed with false prophets, both as to their number and subtilty, yet God lays their eternal and temporal safety or ruin, on their discerning aright between his word, and that which was only pretended so to be. And that they might not complain of this imposition, he tenders them security of its easiness of performance: speaking of his own word comparatively as to every thing that is not so, he says, It is as *wheat to chaff*, which may infallibly, by being what it is, be discerned from it; and then absolutely that it hath such properties, as that it will discover itself, even light, heat, and power. A person divinely inspired was to be attended to for no other reason, but the evidence of the word of God, distinguishing itself from the pretended revelations, and satisfying the mind about it, by its light and power.

Arg. 3. When further evidence, as that of miracles, is demanded, as necessary to induce them that are unbelievers to receive and believe the word, it is refused, as what was not in the judgment of God needful, and would not be effectual; and unbelievers are remitted to the self-evidence of the word, as that which would satisfy them, if any thing would. This our Lord teaches clearly in the parable of Lazarus and the rich man, Luke xvi. 27. to the end. The rich man being disappointed as to any relief to himself, in the preceding verses, is desirous of preventing the ruin of his brethren, and for this end is concerned to have them induced to believe. To which purpose he proposes, ver. 27. the sending of Lazarus from the dead to certify them of the reality of eternal things: *I pray thee therefore Father,* says he to Abraham, *that wouldest send him to my father's house: for I have five brethren; that he may testify unto them, lest they also come to this place of torment. Abraham saith unto him, They have Moses and the prophets, let them hear them. And he said, Nay, father Abraham; but if one went unto them from the dead, they will repent. And he said unto him, If they hear not Moses and the prophets, neither will they be persuaded, though one rose from the dead.* Here the case is plain. The rich man desires a miracle to satisfy his brethren. This is refused, and they are remitted to Moses and the prophets, as what was sufficient. He insists, and thinks a miracle would be more satisfying. This is still refused, and it is plainly ly taught, That where the evidence of the word of God will not induce or perfuade to believe, the moſt uncommon miracles would not do it.

Arg. 4. When the queſtion is confidered particularly, 1 Cor. xiv. What gifts were moſt to the ufe of the church, the miraculous gifts of tongues, &c. or the ordinary gift of prophecy, or preaching of the word? this laſt is preferred, as what was not only more ufeful for the edification of believers, but for inducing unbelievers to receive the word, and fubmit to it; and the way wherein it does this, is mentioned, which is no other than by its evidencing itfelf upon its naked propoſal, in preaching, by its own light and power. Let the whole paſſage be confidered from ver. 22. but efpecially ver. 24, 25. *But if all prophefy, and there come in one that believeth not, or unlearned, he is convinced of all, he is judged of all: And thus are the fecrets of his heart made manifeſt, and fo falling down on his face, he will worſhip God, and report, that God is in you of a truth.*

Arg. 5. The conſtant practice of the apoſtles fully proves our aſſertion. The way they took to perfuade the unbelieving world to receive the gofpel, was not by propofing the arguments commonly infiſted upon now, for proving the truth of their doctrine, nor working, nor infiſting upon miracles wrought by them, for confirmation of the truth, but by a *bare propoſal* of the truth, and a fincere manifeſtation of it to confciences, in the name of God, they proceeded, and demanded acceptance of it, *as the word of God and not of man*; and by this means they converted the world. And when they did refufe it, thus propofed, they *ſhook off the duſt of their feet for a teſtimony againſt them*, and fo laid them open to that awful threatening of our Lord, of puniſhments more intolerable then thefe of Sodom and Gommorrah.

Arg. 5. The experience of thofe who do believe aright, confirms it fully. However they may be relieved againſt the objections, and capacitated to deal with adverfaries by other arguments and means, yet that whereon believers of all forts, learned and unlearned, lean, is the word of God evidencing itfelf unto their faith, by its own light and power. The unlearned are for moſt part capable of no other evidence, and yet upon this alone, in all ages, in life and death, in doing and fuffering, they have evidenced another fort of ſtability and firmneſs in cleaving to it, and fuffering cheerfully for it, on this account only, than the moſt learned, who were beſt furniſhed with arguments

ments of another nature, but wanted this: and indeed if this is not allowed to be the ground of faith, there can be no divine faith leaning upon a divine and infallible bottom; and the vulgar, who are uncapable of any other evidence, must rove in uncertainty, and *pin their faith upon the sleeves of their teachers:* but blessed be God, here is a ground sufficient to rest on, that will not fail. He speaks, and his sheep, notwithstanding that simplicity, which makes them contemptible in the eyes of the world, *know his voice, hear it,* and *follow him,* and *will not hear the voice of a stranger.*

PROP. XI. " Whereas it may be pretended, that on sup-
" position of what has been now asserted, the people of God, at
" times when they discern not this light, feel not this power,
" have no ground for their faith, with respect unto those passages
" or portions of scripture, which do not thus evidence them-
" selves to be from God, at the time of their perusal, or of their
" hearing of them, by affecting the believer's mind, with a
" sense of this divine light and power. In opposition to this
" objection, and for removing the ground of it, I offer the fol-
" lowing truth, which afterwards I shall clear, That there is no
" part of the scriptures, in so far as God speaks in them, but
" doth thus sufficiently evidence its authority in its season, unto
" persons capable of discerning it, and duly applying them-
" selves in the way of the Lord's appointment, in so far as they
" are at present concerned to receive, believe and obey it, in
" compliance with their present duty, and reach the meaning
" of the proposition in and by the use of the means of God's
" appointment."

This objection has sometimes had a very formidable aspect to me, and therefore I shall distinctly propose, so far as the brevity designed will permit, the grounds whereon I was satisfied about the truth proposed in opposition to it, in the following explicatory and confirming observations, referring for further clearing, as to the way wherein the Lord quieted me, and relieved me of objections, to the foregoing chapter.

1. We are to observe, that faith, or that power in man, whereby he assents to truth upon testimony, is corrupted, as well as his other powers, by his fall. And though in believers it is renewed, they receiving an understanding, whereby they know him that is true, and *know his voice from that of a stranger,* yet even in them it is imperfect, and habitually weak, they
being

being renewed but in part, and so knowing but in part, as it is with respect to his other powers, so it is as to this. And besides this habitual weakness, which engages them to cry to the Lord daily for carrying on the *work of faith with power,* and an increase of faith to believe and live to God in a due manner; besides, I say, this habitual weakness, it is liable to various extraordinary incidental disorders, arising from inward and outward occasions, while the believer is here in this valley of tears, subject unto the miseries occasioned by the remaining power of indwelling corruptions, which are in themselves restless, and raise many fogs, damps and mists to overcloud the soul: and by the violence of outward temptations, which Satan and the world throng in upon them, through the wise permission of God, for the exercise of their faith in this state of trial, the darkness is exceedingly increased, faith weakened, or at least straitened as to its exercise. And by this means this spiritual discerning is sometimes more, and sometimes less obstructed and darkened. Now if at such seasons, while the believer finds himself thus out of order, he cannot discern this evidence of the divine authority of the word, no not where it shines clearest, in so far as to quiet him, he has no reason to reject the word, or question it for want of evidence, but may be, and ordinarily believers are exercised in complaints of their own darkness, as the cause of their not discerning God in his word: *Vitium est in organo,* there is no fault in the word, but in the discerning power. The argument, if it be urged with respect to such a case as this, would prove that there is no light in the sun.

2. The Lord's people, through the power of corruption, and force of temptation, are often negligent and inadvertent, and do not apply their minds, nor incline their hearts unto the word, with the attention necessary to discern the evidence of God in the word; and as a punishment of this, God withdraws, and leaves their minds under the darkness they are hereby cast into, and then when God passes by before, or on the *right* or *left hand,* and worketh round about them, they cannot perceive him. If we turn our back to the light, shut our eyes, or will not be at pains to remove motes, or humours that obstruct our sight, no wonder we do not discern the light. When we have idols in our hearts and eyes, no wonder we see not God. If we lay not aside the filthiness of our hearts, we cannot *receive the ingrafted word, that is able to save our souls,* in a due manner.

3. Al-

3. Although the whole scriptures come from God, are his word, yet every propofition contained in them, as it is a propofition in itfelf, expreffive of fuch a particular purpofe or thought, is not his word: for God tells us men's words, and the devil's words. Now though God fpeaks them in fo far as to teach us that they are fuch perfon's words, yet the propofitions in themfelves are not to be received with faith; but we are only to aſſent to this upon the authority of God, that they faid fo and fo; not always that thefe are true; for oftentimes in themfelves they are falfe and pernicious. Now, evidence as to any more than the truth of God in the hiftorical narration of them, is not to be expected, nor are the fcriptures to be impeached for the want of it.

4. Although every divine truth which God fpeaks, has equal authority, and fufficient evidence, yet every fcripture truth has not a beaming evidence, equally great, clear and affecting. The fcripture is like the heaven, another piece of divine workmanfhip. It is full of ftars, every one of thefe has light fufficient to anfwer its own particular ufe for which it was defigned, and to fatisfy the difcerning and attentive beholder, that it is light; but yet every one gives not a light equally clear, great, glorious, affecting and powerful: *There is one glory of the fun, another of the moon, another of the ftars: and one ftar excelleth another in glory*; and fometimes the greateſt light, if it is at the greateſt diftance, like the fixed ftars, affect us lefs, and fhine lefs clear to us, than weaker lights, which, like the moon, are nearer. In the fcripture there are propofitions which tell us things, which though they are in their own place and proper circumſtances, ufeful to them, for whom they are particularly defigned, and to their proper fcope; yet they are comparatively of lefs importance to us, as acquainting us with things of lefs confiderable natures and ufe to us, and which lie not fo far out of our reach, being in fome meafure known, or knowable without divine revelation, though it was neceffary, that in order to their particular ufe to us in our walk with God, they fhould be better fecured, and offered us upon the faith of the divine teftimony. Again, there are other propofitions, which hold forth to us truths in their own nature of more importance, that lie further out of our reach, being neither known, nor indeed knowable by us, without divine revelation; and which in our prefent cafes and circumftances are more nearly fuited to our cafe, and wherein therefore our prefent concernment doth more directly appear to be

intereſted

interefted, and which therefore imprefs us with, and leave in us effects more lafting and difcernible. Now it muft be allowed, that the truths of this laft fort have an evidence more bright, great, affecting and fenfible, than thofe of the former fort. 5. Hereon fundry fubordinate obfervations offer themfelves, which are of the greateft importance for clearing the difficulty under confideration. 1. Truths in fcripture, or propofitions acquainting us with things, otherwife in fome refpect within our reach, and only vouched by God in order to the ftability of our faith in them, (in fo far as we are in practice obliged to lay weight on them) and to give us, not fo much fatisfaction as to their truth abfolutely, as fome additional fecurity about them; thefe cannot be fuppofed fo difcernibly to affect our minds, as truths of another nature, in as much as this additional evidence is more difficult to diftinguifh from the evidence we have otherwife for them. Befides that, God feeing that we are not fo hard to be induced to a belief of them, or fo liable to temptations that may fhake our faith, fees it not meet to ftamp fuch bright, lively and affecting impreffions of himfelf on them : for it is unworthy of him to do any thing in vain. 2. On the other hand, thefe propofitions which difclofe the fecret purpofes, or knowledge of God, and things hid in it, that lie within the reach of no mortal, or perhaps created underftanding, without revelation, muft make a more vivid and lively impreffion on the mind, as illuminating it with the knowledge of things, whereto it was, and by its own reach for ever muft remain a ftranger. 3. In like manner truths, wherein our eternal falvation, or prefent relief from incumbent trouble, is directly concerned, do more forcibly affect, and have a more powerful influence, than thofe which lie more remote from our prefent ufe, of how great advantage foever in their proper place they may be. The moon, which points out my way in the night, guides me, and faves me from lofing myfelf or way, at that time affects me more than the light of the fun, which I have formerly feen, but do not now behold; though the moon comparatively has no light, and borrows that which it hath from the fun. In like manner, truths in themfelves of lefs importance, and which derive all their glory from thofe that are more important, yet, when they fuit my prefent cafe, affects me more, and their evidence appears greater. *Every thing is beautiful in its feafon.* That there is fuch a city as Jerufalem, or that there was fuch a one, the fcripture tells

tells us. Of this we are otherwife informed, and are not likely to be tempted as to its truth: this however is told us in the word, and therefore we are to receive it on the teftimony of the word; but the faith of it is not fo difficult, on accounts mentioned; it is not told but with refpect to fome particular fcope, and we have only an additional fecurity about it. Hereon our minds are not fo illuminated, influenced, and affected with the difcovery, as when God tells us, he *was in Chrift reconciling the world to himfelf*. The difcovery of this fills us with a fenfe of *the glory of God*, hitherto unknown, and that lay far out of the reach of vulgar eyes, or any mortal to difcover, without divine revelation. And therefore the difcovery affects the more. Again, I am perplexed about through-bearing in fome particular ftrait; a promife of grace to help in it, though it is of lefs importance than the forementioned difcovery of reconciliation, and has no efficacy, light or glory, fave what it derives from the former, yet coming in the feafon wherein I am wholly exercifed about it, and the cafe whereto it relates, it affects me more. 4. Where the fame truth is at the fame time difcovered by different lights, it is not eafy for perfons, if not very difcerning and attentive, to underftand the diftinct and particular influence of the feveral lights; fuch as that of natural light, human teftimony, and revelation; and yet each of them have their own particular ufe, which upon its extinction would appear by the defect we would feel.

6. With refpect to truths of high importance, otherwife unknown, which affect our minds with the enriching light of things, by us formerly not known or knowable, and which by their fuitablenefs to prefent circumftances, or exercife, do more ftrongly affect with a fenfe of the divine authority, and illuminate the mind, there is no difficulty, fave in the cafes afterwards to be taken notice of, or the like.

7. As to thefe truths and fcripture propofitions which relate to things not fo remote from our apprehenfions, or are not fo fuitable to our circumftances, at prefent, or difcover things of lefs importance to us, it is owned, that even real Chriftians who have faith, or a fpiritual difcerning, for ordinary, are not, upon hearing or reading them, ftruck or affected with fo fenfible, clear and affecting evidence of God, as they are in other fcriptures of a different nature and relation, which arifes from the nature of the truths in themfelves, the manner and defign of God in the delivery, our prefent circumftances, the weaknefs

and

and imperfection of our faith, the incidental indifpofitions we are under, and other caufes which may be eafily collected from what has been formerly hinted in the preceding obfervations.

8. All this, notwithftanding the leaft confiderable of thefe truths, has a fufficient evidence of the divine authority, that is, fuch an evidence as anfwers the defign of God in them, and is able to determine the believer's affent, and oblige him to obey or fubmit, and is every way fuitable to the weight that is to be laid on them, with refpect to the fcope they are mentioned for, and importance of the matter; which though at all times it is not equally difcernible, for the reafons above-mentioned, or others of an alike nature; yet in its proper feafon it is obferved by judicious, obferving, and reflecting Chriftians. As for inftance, when any of thefe truths, of the leaft apparent importance, are queftioned by Satan or men, then the authority of God is felt to have that influence and awe upon the confciences of believers, as will not allow them to part with the *leaft hoof* or *fhred* of divine truth, and will make them maugre all oppofition, cleave to it, though it fhould coft them their life. Likewife when the Spirit of God is to apply thefe truths to the particular fcope at which he aimed in afferting them in the book of God, then not only have they fuch evidence as influences affent and adherence, but emboldens the foul to lay that ftrefs on them, which the cafe doth require.

9. Whereas neither our prefent imperfect ftate and capacities, the nature of the things, nor other circumftances, allow of an evidence equally clear and great as in other truths, the wifdom and goodnefs of God, in confideration of this, to prevent the fhaking, or at leaft failing of our faith, have as to thefe provided many ways for our fecurity: as, 1. Though in the particular paffages, fuch evidence fhines not in themfelves apart, yet there often appears a beaming light, when they are prefented in reference to the fcope intended by God. 2. Other paffages are joined with them, placed near them, and related to them, which have a further evidence of God, and though we cannot difcern them when they are looked at abftractly, yet when we look to them in relation to thefe, on which they hang, and to which they are connected, we are fatisfied. And I conceive there may be an eye to this, in dropping doctrinal paffages, and inferting them in fcripture hiftory. 3. This objection principally refpects the Old Teftament; as to the divine authority of which we are particularly fecured by plain and evident teftimonies in the New.

4. Some-

4. Sometimes with such truths there are direct assertions of the Lord's speaking of them joined; of which there are many instances in the books of Moses, wherein it is expresly declared, that what was then enjoined, was by the particular command of God. 5. Believers for ordinary, being, in the reading of the word of God, made sensible of his authority, will not be easily brought to admit of any suspicion, that a book wherein God shews himself so evidently concerned, and owns, as to the bulk, to be from him, is or can by him be allowed to be in other places filled up with propositions, or matters of a coarser alloy: And therefore they will rather question themselves, and their own ignornace, than impeach the divinity of the scriptures on this account.

10. Though no faulty obscurity is chargeable on the scriptures, (as much of them as in present circumstances is of absolute necessity to believers, in order to their acceptable walking with God, being clearly revealed) yet there are many truths not understood by all, nor perhaps by any, therein inserted, to leave room for the diligence, trial of the faith of Christians, their progress in knowledge, and other wise ends. Now, till in the use of appointed means, the Spirit of God open to us the meaning of these scriptures, we cannot perceive the light and power that is in them: but whenever he opens these scriptures, that same light that discovers the meaning, will not fail to affect, and make *our hearts burn within us*, with the sense of divine light, authority and power. Of this the experience of the people of God, as they grow in knowledge, furnishes them daily with new instances, and therefore they do not stumble at the want of the present sense of this light, but are quickened to diligence, excited to frequent cries for opening of their eyes, that they may understand the wonders, that by the knowledge of other parts of the word they are induced to believe couched in these parts, which yet they know not.

11. As has been before more than insinuated, there are, in scripture, truths designed for, and suited to different persons, in different circumstances; the book of God being designed for the use of the whole church, and all in it, in all stations, relations, cases, temptations and different circumstances, in which any are, have been in, or may be in. Now when God speaks to one, what he says cannot be so affecting to another, no wise in the same or like case; though yet he may know somewhat

what of the Lord's voice in it. And the fame is to be faid as to the fame perfon, with refpect to different cafes.

12. It muft be ftill minded, that though every part of fcripture has, in it proper place and degree, a fufficient evidence of the divine authority, yet the actual difcerning of it depends very much upon the prefent ftate of the difcerning power or faith of the Chriftian, which difcerns it or not, or difcerns it more or lefs clearly, as it is ftronger or weaker, more free from accidental indifpofitions, outward temptations, or more affected by them. And the fame is to be faid, as to its being more or lefs intently and orderly applied to the obfervation of the evidence of God in the word.

13. Yet whereas they, who are once renewed, do continue ftill *children of the light*, and have a fpiritual capacity of difcerning the *Lord's voice* from that of a *ftranger*, they do for ordinary, in the fcriptures, find the authority of God evidencing itfelf fuitably to the particular exigence of their particular cafes, where the truths that occur are not fuch wherein their prefent faith or practice is immediately affected; or where the truths are fuch as to which, in their own abftract nature, no more is required fave a bare affent, they being only inferted with refpect to fome other particular fcope, where the truths are not prefently affaulted, where they are not immediately called to hazard much upon them, or in other the like cafes, they are indeed lefs affected; but one way or other, from one thing or another, as much of God fhines in them as is fufficient to engage to a prefent adherence, and fome becoming reverence as to the oracles of God, which may in their feafon manifeft their ufefulnefs to us, and do at prefent manifeft it to others. And where truths are of a different nature and importance, and fuit prefent neceffities, and require more diftinct actings of faith or obedience, and we are called to lay more ftrefs on them; in that cafe the evidence of God fhines more brightly. And fcarce ever will a difcerning and attentive Chriftian, who is not grievoufly indifpofed by fome cafual difoder, read the fcriptures, or any confiderable part of them, but fome where or other, in the fcope or particular words, and propofitions, or their contexture, fome light will fhine in upon the foul, enforcing a conviction, *That God is in it of a truth*.

14. When the faith of the Lord's people is affaulted as to the truth of the word; when in difficult cafes and duties they are called to lay much ftrefs upon the word, and hazard as if were their all; when they are diftreffed with particular and violent

violent temptatations, and need comfort; when under spiritual decays, and God designs to restore them; when newly brought in, and need to be confirmed; when they are humble and diligent, and the Lord designs to reward them graciously, and encourage them to go on; when difficulted to find duty, and waiting on the Lord for light, in cases of more than usual importance; when the Lord has a mind to carry on any to peculiar degrees of holiness and grace, and employ them in special services; and, in a word, wherever any extraordinary exigence requires, then the Lord opens his people's ears, removes what intercepts the discoveries of his mind, fixes their ear to hear, and speaks the word distinctly, powerfully and sweetly to the soul, and gives them in and by it, such a taste of his goodness, wisdom, and power, and experience of his authority in the word, and his gracious design and hand in its application at present, as fills the soul with the *riches* and *full assurance of faith*, peace, joy, and stedfastness in *believing*.

PROP. XII. " Whereas there are different readings of par-
" ticular places in ancient copies, and places wrong translated,
" in our versions, it may be pretended, that we are, or may be
" imposed upon, and assent to truths, or rather to propositions,
" not of a divine original, casually crept into our copies of
" the original, or translation. In answer hereto, the forego-
" ing ground of faith lays a sufficient bottom for the satisfaction
" of Christians, in so far as their case and particular temptati-
" ons require."

To clear this a little, I shall offer the ensuing remarks:

1. Where the authority of God evidences itself in the way above explained, and confirmed to the mind, believers have a stable and sure foundation for their faith, whether they use *translations* or the *originals*; though it must be allowed, where persons are capable of it, the originals are most satisfying. And this is plainly the case, as all real Christians from certain experience know, as to all the truths of the greatest importance, and whereon our faith or obedience are more immediately or directly concerned: so that as to these there is no room left for this objection.

2. The wisdom of God has so carefully provided for the security and stability of our faith, as to particular truths of any considerable importance, against pretences of this, or an alike nature, that our faith rests not upon the evidence of one single
testimony

testimony, but such truths upon a variety of occasions are often repeated, and our faith leans upon them, not only as thus frequently repeated, but cleared and confirmed by their connexion to other truths which infer them, and to the whole analogy of faith, or current of the scriptures, with respect to that which is the principal design of God. So that we are in no hazard of being deprived of any one truth, of any considerable influence, in faith or practice, by pretended corruptions, or wrong translations. The famous Dr. Owen, who had considered the whole various readings, and well knew the failures of particular translations, observes, That were all the various readings, added to the worst and most faulty translation, the church of God would not sustain by it the loss of one important truth.

3. Where any person is particularly concerned to be satisfied which is the right reading of any particular passage, and how it ought to be translated, they may, by the help of the ministers of the gospel, such of them as are particularly fitted with skill in such matters, and by the endeavours of learned men, who have particularly considered every one of these passages, in a humble dependence on God for the blessing of these means, (which the wise God has multiplied, since difficulties of this sort begun to create any trouble to the faith of his people) by these means I say, joined with an eye to the Lord, they may come to be particularly satisfied. *If any man will do his will, he shall know the doctrine, whether it is of God.*

4. Where there is not access to these means, which will not readily happen to persons called to such exercise, (which rarely befalls the ordinary sort of Christians) yet the Lord can easily relieve the person thus exercised, by evidencing his authority to the conscience in a satisfying light, or by enabling him to wait for light until the solution comes, or by removing the temptation, when it becomes too strong, or by leading him to rest in the particular truth, as secured by other passages not questioned, or by some such like way.

5. The difficulty as to translations is really of less importance; and as to the other about pretended corruptions, ordinary Christians, whose consciences are daily affected with the evidence of God's authority in the word, and his owning it as his word, speaking by it to them, and conveying divine influences of light, life and comfort, will not fear or entertain any suspicion so unworthy of God, as that he could allow the word he thus owns, under a pretence of his authority, to impose on them assertions of human

man extract, and of any ill confequence to their faith or obedience.

6. I fhall only fubjoin this one obfervation, That enemies gain more by propofing thefe pretended corruptions *in cumulo**, and in fuch a bulky way, as to affright Chriftians who are capable of fuch objections, than by infifting upon any particular one, and attempts to prove them of equal authority with the reading retained in the approved originals. Their unfuccefsfulnefs in endeavours of this laft fort difcovers, that there is really nothing of weight in that fo much noifed objection about various readings; for if there were any fuch readings as could really make any confiderable alteration, and were fupported with any authority able to cope with the received readings, why do they not produce thefe? Others are of no confideration; thefe only are to be regarded: and of this fort there are but very few that the moft impudent dare pretend; and thefe few have been difproved and difallowed by perfons of equal capacity and learning. But to leave this, which is above the ordinary fort of Chriftians, the Lord's people, to whom he has evidenced his own authority, in the way above mentioned, will be moved with none of thefe things. They will not forego the word, but retain it as their life, and pay refpect to it as the word of God; and they have good reafon to do fo.

I fhall now obferve hence,

1. How juftly divine faith may be faid to be infallible, as ftanding on an infallible ground, the faithfulnefs and truth of God in the word. Through darknefs we may fometimes not difcern, through negligence not obferve, or through the force of temptations interpofing betwixt us and it, we may lofe fight of the evidence of this authority; and fo our faith may fhake or fail. But while it fixes on this, it cannot fail, though we may quit, or by violence be beat off; the ground is firm, and cannot fail, the fcriptures cannot be broken.

2. Hence it is, That the meaneft and weakeft believers, who know nothing of the props others have to fupport them, do cleave as firmly to the word, run with all courage, and as much cheerfulnefs, all hazards for it, to the lofs of whatever is dear to them, life not excepted, as the moft judicious divine, and oftentimes they are much more firm. This is upon no other grounds accountable. This *reafon of faith* is as much expofed to them as to the moft learned.

3. All

---

* " In bulk."

3. All objections arising against this *ground of faith*, will be easily solved, if we consider, 1. That the scriptures are a relief provided by sovereign grace, for those of the race of fallen man, to whom God designs mercy, and so God was not obliged to adjust it in all respects to the natural capacities of men in their present state, but it was meet that the word should be so writ, that room should be left for the discoveries of the sovereignty of grace, and the other means God designed to make use of in subserviency to the word. It was not meet nor necessary that all should be so proposed, as to lie open to men without the assistance of the Spirit, and without the ministry of the word. 2. The word was not designed alone to conduct us, but God has given the Spirit with the word, who teaches us in and by it, as he sees meet. 3. The word is designed to be a rule to all ages, and therefore it was not meet or necessary, that what concerns persons in one age should be equally exposed in its meaning unto other persons, who lived in a different time. It is sufficient, that in every age, what concerns that time lie so open, that in the use of the means of God's appointment, they may reach that wherein they are concerned. 4. The word was designed for persons of different stations, capacities and cases, who ought to rest satisfied in the obvious discoveries of what concerns them, in their own particular circumstances, and is required to be believed and obeyed, more particularly in a way of duty, of them, though they cannot see so clearly what belongs to others in different circumstances. 5. God has not systematically and separately discoursed all particular cases under distinct heads; but to leave room for the conduct of the Spirit, for exciting the diligence of Christians to study the whole scriptures, and for other reasons obvious to infinite wisdom, he has digested them in a method, more congruous to these wise ends. 6. The Lord designing the exercise of the faith of his own, and to humble them, and to drive them to a dependence on himself, and to punish the wicked, and give them who will stumble at the ways of God somewhat to break their neck on, he has digested them so, as that there may be occasions, though always without fault on God's part, for all those ends: *Wisdom will be justified of her children,* and to some *he speaks in parables, that seeing they may not see.*

F I N I S.

INDEX

OF THE

Authors and *Books* quoted in the preceding *Work*.

AIKENHEAD's Speech.
Alcoran.
Amyrauld de Religionibus.
Aristotle's Ethicks.
August. de Civitate Dei.

Bayle's great Hist. and Crit. Diction.
Baxter's Animad. on Herbert.
—— De Veritate.
—— Reason's for Christian Religion.
—— More Reasons for Christian Religion.
Becconsal on the Law of Nature.
Blount's Oracles of Reason.
—— Religio Laici.
Boyle's Excellency of Theology beyond Natural Philosophy.
Burnet on the Thirty-Nine Articles.

Cæsar de Bello Gallico.
Cicero's Tusculan Questions.
—— De Natura Deorum.
—— De Ligibus.
—— De Amicitia.
Clarkson's practical Divinity of the Papists.
Claudian.
Clementis Alexandrina Stromata.
Clerk's (Le) Parrhasiana.
—— Comput. Histor.
Collin's Discourses de Animabus Paganorum.

Dacier's Plato.
Deist's Manuel.
Discourse on Moral Virtue, and its Difference from Grace.
Dryden's Hind and Panther.

Epictetus.
Ferguson's Enquiry into Moral Virtue.

Gale's Court of the Gentiles.
Growth of Deism.

Heid. (Abrah.) de Origine Erroris.
Herbert de Veritate.
—— De Relig. Gent.
—— Religio Laici.
Hornbeck de Conversione Gentilium.
Hieroclis Carmina Aurea.
Hobb's Leviathan.
Howe's Living Temple.
Humphrey's Peaceable Disquisitions.

Jamblichus de Vita Pythag.
Jesuits Morals.

Laertius (Diog.) de Vitis Philosophorum.
Letter to the Deists.
Limburch's Conference with Orelius the Jew.
Locke on Human Understand.

Locke's Reasonableness of Christianity.

Maximus Tyrius.

Nicol's Conference with a Theist.
Nye (Stephen) on natural and revealed Religion.

Ovid. de Ponto.
—— Metamorph.
Owen on the Sabbath.
—— Theologum.
—— on the Hebrews.
—— De Justitia Vindicat.
Outramus de Sacrificiis.

Parker's (Sam.) Defence of Ecclesiastical Polity.
Prudentius (Aurelius).
Puffendorff's Introduction to the History of Europe.

Reflections on the Growth of Deism.
Remonstrant. Apologia.
Rivet on Hosea.
Rushworth's Histor. Collections.

Seneca's Epist.
———— De Ira.
———— De Providentia.
Simplicius in Epictetum.
Spinoza's Ethicks.
Stanley's Lives.
Stillingfleet's Origines Sacræ.

Tuckney's (Anth.) Sermons.
Turretine.

Wilson's Scripture Interpreter.
Wolseley's (Sir Charles) Scripture Belief.
Videllii Arcana Arminianismi.
  And his Rejoinder.
Videlius Rapsodus.

www.ingramcontent.com/pod-product-compliance
Lightning Source LLC
Chambersburg PA
CBHW022138300426
44115CB00006B/242